The Blacketts

A Northern Dynasty's Rise, Crisis and Redemption

Greg Finch

© Greg Finch

ISBN: 978-1-8382809-9-4

All rights reserved. No part of this book may be reproduced, stored or introduced into a retrieval system or transmitted in any way or by any means (electronic, mechanical, photocopying, recording or otherwise) without the prior permission of the publishers.

The opinions expressed in this book are those of the author.

First published in 2021 by:
Tyne Bridge Publishing
City of Newcastle Upon Tyne
Newcastle Libraries

This edition published by Tyne Bridge Publishing in 2022

Front cover illustrations: 'Grey Horse Inn, Quayside, Newcastle upon Tyne', c 1830-35, by George Balmer, collection of Laing Art Gallery, Newcastle, reproduced courtesy of Tyne and Wear Archives and Museums; excerpts from Plates 6 and 21 (for credits see Plates section overleaf). Back cover: from frontispiece to J.Brand, *History and Antiquities of Newcastle* (1789).
Design by Greg Finch and Derek Tree.

BAC Wadsworth Prize

Winner of 2022 Business Archives Council Wadsworth Prize for outstanding contribution to British business history

About the Author

Dr. Greg Finch worked in IT and business consulting for over 20 years. He has written widely on aspects of English history between the 16th and 20th centuries. In 2013 he edited *A Pack of Idle Sparks*, a collection of early 18th century letters on social history in the North of England

Contents

Preface and Acknowledgements
Notes on Terminology

1	Newcastle	Page 1
2	Hamsterley to Gateshead	Page 23
3	Troublesome Tymes	Page 37
4	Kirkleys and Commonwealth	Page 51
5	Merchant and Trader	Page 67
6	Underground Ventures	Page 81
7	The Plastic of its Age	Page 99
8	A Great Many Men	Page 115
9	A New Industrial Giant	Page 133
10	The Newcastle Grandee	Page 151
11	Strange Histories of their Coal Works	Page 167
12	Taking Stock of William Blackett	Page 179
13	Brothers	Page 197
14	Resurgence	Page 213
15	Popular in his Country	Page 235
16	Hobbled from Above	Page 249
17	A Fool or a Knave	Page 267
18	The Foundations of Redemption	Page 279
19	Blacketts, Newcastle and History	Page 301
	Appendices and Bibliography	Page 318
	Guide to Abbreviations used in Notes	Page 320
	Notes and References	Page 322
	Index	Page 355

Plates

1. Fleshmarket, Newcastle, c.1820 copyright John Moreels, reproduced by permission.

2. The Side, Henry Perlee Parker, c.1820. Newcastle City Library.

3. Tyne Bridge end, T.M.Richardson, 1763. Newcastle City Library.

4. Newcastle Quayside in 1820, after T.M.Richardson. Newcastle City Library.

5. Jacques Savary, *Le Parfait Negociant*, 1675, frontispiece.

6. 'Blasting', Northumberland lead mining scenes. Reproduced by permission of the Science and Society Picture Library, The Science Museum.

7. Dutch flyboat, Wenceslas Hollar, 1677. University of Toronto.

8. Smelting the Ore, David Allan, c.1780s. Scottish National Portrait Gallery, National Galleries of Scotland. Accepted by HM Government in lieu of inheritance tax and allocated to the National Galleries of Scotland, 2008.

9. Newcastle, The Sandhill, T. Allom, 1832/3.

10 . Newcastle Guildhall, from J.Brand, *History and Antiquities of Newcastle*, (1789).

11. Corbridge Bridge. © Russel Wills, Geograph.org.uk/ Creative Commons licence.

12. 'Pack horses', Northumberland lead mining scenes. Reproduced by permission of the Science and Society Picture Library, The Science Museum.

13. Detail from Weighing the lead, David Allan, c. 1780s. Scottish National Portrait Gallery, National Galleries of Scotland. Accepted by HM Government in lieu of inheritance tax and allocated to the National Galleries of Scotland, 2008.

14. Newhouse, Weardale. Reproduced by permission of Durham County Record Office, reference D/CL 27/277/903, copyright Miss N.Dawson, St.Johns Chapel WI.

15. Allenheads Inn, Greg Finch

16. Dukesfield Hall, reproduced by permission of Hilary Kristensen.

17. Fallowfield House. © Mike Quinn, Geograph.org.uk/ Creative Commons licence.

18. Greyfriars – Knyff and Kip, *Britannia Illustrata*, 1707. Newcastle City Library

19. Coal Waggon, Newcastle, drawn by William Beilby 1773. Esther M. Zimmer Lederberg Trust

20. Wallington Hall. © Stuart Shepherd, Geograph.org.uk/ Creative Commons licence

21. Probably William Blackett 1621-80, by John Riley and John Closterman, Wallington Hall. ©National Trust Images

22. Possibly Elizabeth Kirkley, 1617-74, Wallington Hall. ©National Trust Images

23. Possibly Margaret Rogers, 1631-1710, by John Riley and John Closterman, Wallington Hall. ©National Trust Images

24. Sir Edward Blackett, second baronet. Reproduced by permission of Sir Hugh Blackett

25. Probably William Blackett, 1657-1705, Wallington Hall. ©National Trust Images

26. Possibly William Blackett, 1690-1728, attributed to Enoch Seeman the younger (c.1694 – possibly London 1744), Wallington Hall. ©National Trust Images.

27. Walter Calverley/ Blackett, 1707-77. Bradford Museums and Galleries/ Bridgeman Images.

28. Probably Julia Conyers, Lady Blackett, Wallington Hall. ©National Trust Images.

Preface & Acknowledgements

This book has two points of departure: a conservation and heritage project centred on the remains of the old Dukesfield lead smelting mill in woodland next to the Devil's Water south of Hexham in Northumberland in the early 2010s, and a lecture given to the Society of Antiquaries of Newcastle-upon-Tyne in 2016. As the conservation, archaeology, and documentary research of the wonderful lottery funded Dukesfield Smelters and Carriers project progressed, hints emerged of the age, scale and spread of the industrial concern the mill belonged to, and of the audacity and ambition of its founder, William Blackett. The discovery and transcription by our project's enthusiastic 'Dukesfield Documents' team of many hundreds of letters from two of his sons, many of which had been buried deep in Cambridge University Library for centuries, opened up a whole new window into the mercantile north-east of England in the late seventeenth century. It was increasingly obvious that it would be rude not to look through that window and describe the scene. This point was made to me in very clear terms after that Newcastle lecture about the Blacketts and their business, when I was told to 'write the book'. Professor Roberts, here it is.

It has often felt like an arduous walk along sinuous and obstacle-strewn carriers' tracks over the moorland heights between lead mines, mills and quays, the map of which was unclear until the end. It has only been possible with the help, specialist knowledge, frank advice and cheerful encouragement of the many people encountered along the route. I am very grateful indeed to them all, including those whose anonymous work on building online catalogues and digital content has so greatly extended the access and reach of archival material for researchers in recent decades. The National Archives' Discovery catalogue, the North East Inheritance database, the Institute for Historical Research's 'British History Online', the Scotland, Scandinavia and Northern European Biographical Database (SSNE) hosted by St.Andrew's University, Open Archives Netherlands, the Sound Toll Registers Online, the History of Parliament Online, Google Books, FamilySearch, the Internet Archive and the catalogues of various county and university archive collections have been very useful. The same goes for the patient and thorough work of Victorian antiquaries such as Messrs Dendy, Longstaffe, and Welford in compiling records which ease the mining of high-grade ore to this day.

Today's archivists and librarians have also been very helpful, including past and present members of the Northumberland Archives team at Woodhorn Museum led by Sue Wood, and those at The National Archives, British Library, North Yorkshire County Record Office, West Yorkshire Archives Service, the John Rylands Library in Manchester, Newcastle University's Robinson and Cowen libraries, Newcastle City Library and Liz Bregazzi at Durham County Record Office. Michael Stansfield, Michael Harkness and Andrew Gray of Durham University Library Archives and Special Collections provided great assistance, as did Maria Nagle and Sarah-Jane Raymond at the Durham Cathedral Library. Jennifer Hillyard, Simon Brooks and Robert Forsythe of Newcastle's North of England Institute of Mining and Mechanical Engineers assisted me with its fine collection, and so too Paul Gailiunas at the tremendous library of the Literary and Philosophical Society in Newcastle. I also thank Mark Cordell, Rachel Gill and Zoe Walker at Tyne and Wear Archives, Lloyd Langley at Wallington Hall, Christopher Hunwick and Gemma McGuirk who oversee the Archives of the Duke of Northumberland at Alnwick Castle, Robin Darwall-Smith at University College, Oxford, and Sweden Riksarchivet's Jan Mispelaere for their help. Viscount Allendale and Sir Hugh Blackett generously allowed free access to photograph contents of their extensive archives at Woodhorn.

Extracting and telling the story from such a breadth of raw material has benefited enormously from the knowledge and thoughts of an equally wide range of people. In particular, Ian Forbes and Peter Scott gave freely of their time to read the entire manuscript and provide highly insightful and valuable feedback. Many others have been generous with their own researches, perspectives and thoughts. My thanks go to Max Adams, Jean Allen, Tim Barmby, Tony Barrow, Vanessa Beaumont, Jeremy Boulton, Alan Blackburn, Martin Blackett, Mark Blackett-Ord, Caitlin Blackwell, Alex Brown, Andy Burn, Roger Burt, Richard Carlton, Hugh Dixon, Susanne Ellingham, Ray Fairbairn, Roger Fern, Marie Gardiner, Tim Gates, Mike Gill, Martin Green, Dave Greenwood, Pat

Halcro, Ian Hancock, Chris Hartnell, Dave Heslop, Bill Heyes, Margaret Jackman, Pete Jackson, Marc Johnstone, Al Kirtley, Joost Jonker, Pete Lee, Stafford Linsley, David McCollum-Oldroyd, Tom McGovern, Tom McLean, Leos Muller, Richard Pears, the late Bill Purdue, Yvonne Purdy, Matt Ridley, Liz Sobell, Kate Sussams, Les Turnbull, Andy Wood, and my fellow contributors to Dukesfield Documents. The prodigious fruits of this team's labours are freely available online (see the 'Guide to abbreviations' section): upwards of 12,000 documents and counting. Many fine nuggets of material have been sent my way entirely unsolicited, and I feel much the wiser for valuable conversations throughout the time taken to write this book. Where I have failed to understand such contributions properly, and for any contrary conclusions I decided to draw, I am entirely responsible.

I am grateful to Alejandro Basterrechea of the National Galleries of Scotland, the Hon. Wentworth Beaumont, Sir Hugh Blackett, Hilary Kristensen, Charlotte McDurnan of the National Trust, Jasmine Rodgers of the Science Museum Group, and an anonymous portrait owner for generously granting permission to reproduce images of their artworks and photographs. Image reproduction permission granted by Bridgeman Images and the Durham County Record Office is also acknowledged. Derek Tree of Tyne Bridge Publishing quickly saw potential in the book and I am very grateful to him for his strong, heartening and patient support in seeing it through to publication. My thanks also to Vanessa Histon at Tyne Bridge for her thorough proof reading.

Finally, for putting up so politely and indulgently with Blacketts, lead and seventeenth-century Newcastle for so long and yet still be there to provide love, encouragement and support I am eternally grateful to Jenny, Rosie and most of all Julie.

Greg Finch
July 2021

Notes on Terminology and Values

In the interests of legibility, dates, weights and measures have been modernised. The legal year commenced on 25th March before 1752 but January to March dates are given here using the modern calendar instead. Weights of lead and coal are given in imperial tons rather than the then customary fothers, bings and chaldrons. The latter are explained in the relevant appendices but this jargon is avoided in the main text. Sterling currency has been decimalised.

Comparisons of contemporary financial values with today are often made based on changes in the price of common foodstuffs. The National Archives currency converter (https://www.nationalarchives. gov.uk/currency-converter) suggests that £1 of purchasing power in the seventeenth century was worth the around £110 today. Prices of the most widely consumed items were largely stable during this period, so there is no need for significant inflation adjustments within the century covered by this book. However an approach relying upon comparisons of staple goods prices feels unsatisfactory. It does not allow for the enormous improvement in living standards in the last three centuries, or changes in the nature of the economy and consumption patterns. The text which follows does not attempt to convert seventeenth century money to a modern equivalent. Emphasis is given instead to contemporary costs and earnings relative to each other. Nevertheless, a vague notion of perceptions of comparative value might be drawn from changes in relative annual incomes, ie. the standard of living rather than its cost. Household income of £25 per year (ten shillings per week) was probably getting on for double the level of bare subsistence income in the 1680s.[*] If for simplicity's sake this is VERY roughly equated to £25,000 today, the multiplier is an easy-to-use 1,000. £1,000 might therefore have been regarded in the seventeenth-century north of England broadly as we might regard £1 million today.

---

[*] R.C.Allen, *The British Industrial Revolution in Global Perspective*, (2009), p.50.

Figure 1.1 Newcastle upon Tyne

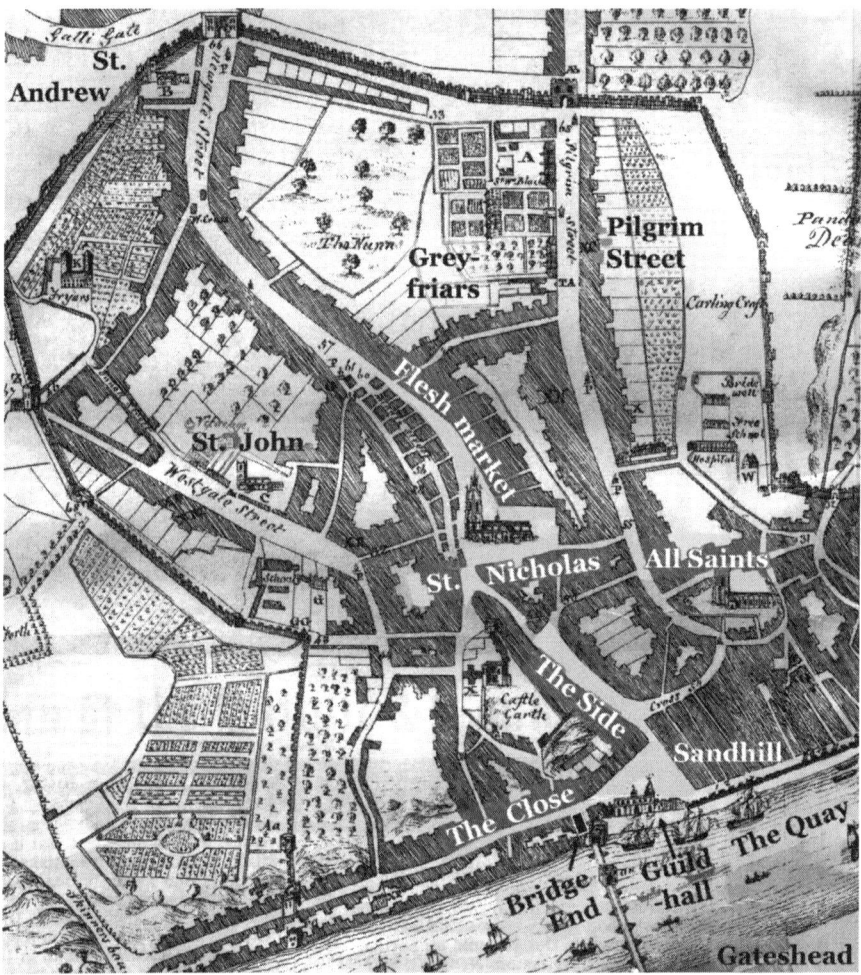

Based upon James Corbridge's map of 1723 (Newcastle City Library)

Chapter 1

Newcastle

A State Occasion

Late in the afternoon of Monday 7th October 1728, the long and sombre funeral procession of Sir William Blackett set out from the extensive grounds of Greyfriars. It was the grandest house in Newcastle upon Tyne, the thriving commercial hub of the north-east of England. Newcastle's size (the fourth largest town in England with about 17-18,000 people in 1700), sophisticated trading network reaching across Europe, economic power and civic splendour made it a city in all but name.[1] Greyfriars and its gardens on the high ground above the Tyne occupied nearly a quarter of the compact space contained within the town's medieval walls on the north bank of the river. It had been the Newcastle home for three generations of the Blackett family for over half a century, three Sir Williams in a row. To avoid tedious frequent repetitions of full names they are hereafter referred to as William I (1621-80), William II (1657-1705) and William III (1690-1728) where identification is in any doubt.

Greyfriars' magnificence is captured in an engraving by Knyff and Kip published in 1707 (see Plate 18). It shows an aerial view of the mansion, its formal gardens and grounds, something of the teeming streets that surround it and views to the hills above the Tyne valley to the west.* Greyfriars' domination of the physical civic landscape in the upper part of the town was matched by the Blacketts' status within the economy and society of Newcastle, and of its regional hinterland. The late William III was one of Newcastle's members of Parliament, a long-standing member of the governing Common Council, mayor in 1718, and governor of the Hostmen's Company, associated with the town's critically important coal trade for over a century. He had trading interests, owned

---

* The mansion was also known as Anderson Place, and Newe Place at different times, but it was Greyfriars in the will of William I, and that name is used here. J.Kip, *Britannia Illustrata* (1707).

coal and lead mines, landed estates in County Durham and Northumberland, and another impressive mansion at Wallington, 20 miles to the north-west.

Within days of his death on 25th September, funeral invitations were issued to the great and the good of the region. 'My Lady Barbara [his widow] and the executors of Sir Wm Blackett, intending to solemnise his funeral on Monday the 7th Direct me on this Melancholy Occation to Signify that your Company is Desired that day...' [2] The meticulous logistics of the event included the despatch of black mourning cloth around the region, carefully graded by social station. John Armstrong, manager of the Allenheads lead mine far away in the North Pennine hills, was sent broadcloth costing 10s 6d (52.5p) per yard for himself and six others at the mines and mills in Northumberland and in Weardale to the south. This was 'to be made up by themselves' into suitable dark outer cloaks. The cloth given to the senior agents, was of the 17s per yard variety, while 15 'close mourners' - relations and executors of the deceased - were sent 'superfine cloth' to be fitted 'by 3 women in the office ... at 2 a Clock [sic] when they came to the funeral'.

The logistical challenge extended to the careful ordering of the procession from the large throng that assembled at Greyfriars that autumn afternoon, and presumably also the discreet reduction of an inevitable murmur of conversation to silence as the cavalcade moved off. It was led by two beadles of the parish church of St Andrew's, followed by the master and 30 boys of its charity school, established by William II, all cloaked in black. Then came two beadles of St Nicholas', the principal church of Newcastle, final resting place of all its leading citizens, and therefore the afternoon's destination. They were followed by the 'mutes', silent and solemn servants dressed in black, setting the tone for those standing along the route. For respectable funerals there would usually be a pair of them, standing guard by the deceased's door. Blackett had 24. After all, there were many doors to guard at Greyfriars, and their number reminded all present of the importance of the deceased. Those left in any doubt surely got the point as the procession passed by. It was marked by the firing of a half-hour gun salute. [3] The *Newcastle Courant* provided a summary, reporting that the funeral was 'solemnized with great decency and order... After [the mutes] 12 of his stewards. Next the Clergy of the Corporation, followed by the vicar alone. Then the led horse, and after him the banners. Then the corpse, supported by 8 gentlemen. After them a number of clergy and gentry. Then came the Mayor and Aldermen in their robes, before whom the mace and sword were carried in deep mourning. After them followed the Common Council. Next upwards of 200 gentlemen to whom were given scarves and gloves. Then upwards of 2,000 freemen, who had gloves; and the stewards of the companies were presented with rings. The procession was brought up with a great number of coaches: the first of which was his own, in mourning, drawn by 6 horses, and on the forehead of each was his crest most curiously emblazoned'[4]

Its sheer scale was a reflection of the position occupied by the deceased amongst the elite institutions and society of Newcastle, Northumberland and Durham society. Here were the carefully ordered ranks of the county gentlemen, Newcastle's mayor and magistrates who led the corporation's Common Council, the management hierarchy of the Blackett business, the stewards, officers and members of the town's guilds and liveried companies, and gentlemen of the town. No women took part. Blackett's widow, the Lady Barbara, and other female relations presumably remained in their own deep mourning clothes, and with their own thoughts, inside the state room at Greyfriars, away from the spectacle making its stately progress through the streets beyond.[5]

Which streets? The shortest way along narrow and steep streets would have been highly unsuitable for such a grand parade. Besides, the meticulously detailed processional order of the mourners, and allowing for the freemen to march ten abreast, suggests it must have been a good third of a mile long. The beadles and charity boys would almost have been arriving at the church as the last of the freemen of the guilds were leaving the gates of Greyfriars. A longer route along wider roads can be walked today. At a slow and funereal pace amongst the throng of shoppers in the city centre, it takes about half an hour, but no matter how well the streets had been swept in advance of the funeral the going underfoot was probably harder then, even though the route was fairly level. So, allowing for the length of the procession, the whole solemn spectacle, a state occasion for the town, could have taken an hour or so to reach St Nicholas' for the funeral service in the late afternoon.[6]

William III was interred in the same place as his father and grandfather. A memorial slab used to lie in the Choir commemorating William I, his first wife and son Michael. The inscription given by Henry Bourne in his invaluable 1736 *History of Newcastle* makes no mention of his son or grandson William, but their final resting place was here somewhere, along with those of the other leading members of Newcastle society.[7] In 1728 William III had left directions that his funeral was to follow the pattern of his father's as exactly as possible. In the winter days of December 1705 this must have been an even greater logistical challenge, for William II had died in London while on Parliamentary business. His draped coffin was carried northwards in nine days accompanied by 12 horsemen with pennants and the English flag 'through all great towns', resting in state each night in a suitable room dressed in deep mourning and decorated with silver candlesticks for the wax lights. The principal rooms of Greyfriars were likewise draped in dark velvet and bays, a 'chayre of state & Footstoole' set in one chamber in which the widowed Lady Julia Blackett was to receive the queue of mourners. 88 yards of fine bay cloth were hung in St Nicholas' church.

Amidst all the detail of the preparations for William II's funeral, the agent accompanying the coffin from London advised his counterpart in Newcastle to find £1,500-2,000 to pay for it all (roughly the amount 60 to 75 semi-skilled workers might earn in a year).[8] The bills for his son's funeral in 1728 added up to around £1,400, without the elaborate winter journey from London.[9] No details have survived regarding the funeral of William I in 1680, but he set aside £1,000 for it in his will. It is therefore likely he too was seen off in similar style, accompanied from Greyfriars to St Nicholas' by the civic, mercantile and landed elite of the town and adjoining counties, with mourning cloth, gloves and scarves provided. Surely the son and grandson were deliberately following the public spectacle of sombre grandeur of the funeral of the founder of the family fortune. Order, scale, continuity. However, on closer inspection, all was not well by the time of William III's funeral.

It went beyond the inevitable minor niggles that accompany a great family and public occasion. William III's brother-in-law, Sir William Wentworth of Bretton Hall in Yorkshire, married to sister Diana, complained that 5½ yards of mourning cloth were not enough, only to be told politely but firmly by the office staff that this was strictly in accordance with the deceased's instructions.[10] Other details spoke of deeper problems. John Wilkinson, once an executor of William II and for many years chief agent to his son, did not attend the funeral and sent back his scarf. The grieving widow, Lady Barbara, married again with indecent haste, scarcely five months into the traditional year of mourning. There was no son, no fourth Sir William. The heir was Blackett's nephew, young Walter Calverley of Esholt Hall near Bradford, the son of the deceased's sister Julia. There were conditions to his inheritance: he was expected to marry Blackett's illegitimate 16 year-old daughter Elizabeth within a year and change his name to Blackett. It was probably a setback for brand continuity that he had not been christened William, but at least he would become a Blackett and 'Walter' would have to do. Still two months short of his 21st birthday as he walked alone directly behind his uncle's coffin that autumn day in 1728, the calculating eyes of the unfamiliar Newcastle merchants upon him, young Walter might have felt his to be a dubious inheritance. In addition to the burden of expectation that came with being the heir, the next embodiment of the Blackett brand, there was also a huge burden of debt. Yes, there were houses, estates, mines and the hope of a wedding within a year, but this hope was not shared by his intended wife, and the property was encumbered by loans and other liabilities of over £100,000, a potentially crushing sum.

This book charts the rise of the Blacketts in the mid-17th century to the position of regional splendour so carefully displayed in their funerals, and it then explores what brought them to such a perilous state by the 1720s. As an account of a trader who also developed a mining empire, it is centred on Newcastle, the heart of northern commercial life.

Seventeenth-century Newcastle

Newcastle's location meant it had long been strategically important to the English crown as a northern bulwark against Scotland. If the accession of Scotland's James VI to the English throne in 1603 gave the appearance of reducing the historic threat from the north, another strategic imperative had arisen to reinforce Newcastle's position – the growing dependence of London on Tyneside coal for fuel. Coal seams alongside the Tyne upstream of Newcastle might be over 300 miles from the capital, but they could be mined with relative ease in Tudor and early Stuart times, and their produce transported cheaply by river and sea. The location of Britain's coal deposits and the fuel's low ratio of value to weight meant that no other region could feasibly supply London in any volume. Annual shipments of coal from Newcastle were some 70,000 tons in 1570 but had reached 470,000 tons by 1633-4.[11] Its supremacy amongst harbours from the Scottish border to Hull was enshrined in its customs port status, the centre from which trade was monitored and taxed on behalf of the Exchequer, covering the 90 miles of coast from Amble to Whitby.

As an east coast port, with a sheltered harbour ten miles in from the sea, Newcastle also had long-standing trading ties with the ports of northern Europe, alongside those of Hull, Kings Lynn, Yarmouth and - of course - London. From the Atlantic coast of France to the low countries with the great entrepôt of Amsterdam, to Hamburg, Scandinavia and as far east in the Baltic as Danzig and the Russian port of Narva, merchants and ships from the British east coast could be found (see Figure 1.2). In his will of 1597, Newcastle merchant Henry Riddell wished to be buried at Elbing, on the Prussian coast east of Danzig. The probate inventory taken in 1621 of the goods of Michael Kirkley, Newcastle merchant, included sums 'remaining at Danzick in the hands of Robert Cooke 450 Polish guilders.' Alongside the 12 Lubeck marks were in the hands of Peter Clarke in Hamburg, Kirkley's inventory exemplifies the network of English partners spread overseas dealing in various currencies.[12] The cosmopolitan outlook of the English merchant community overseas in the 17th century is exemplified by the careers of William Maister and William Strang of Hull. They became subjects of the Danish crown and settled in Elsinore in order to avoid duties at the Sound Toll, which taxed shipping passing

Figure 1.2 Northern Europe

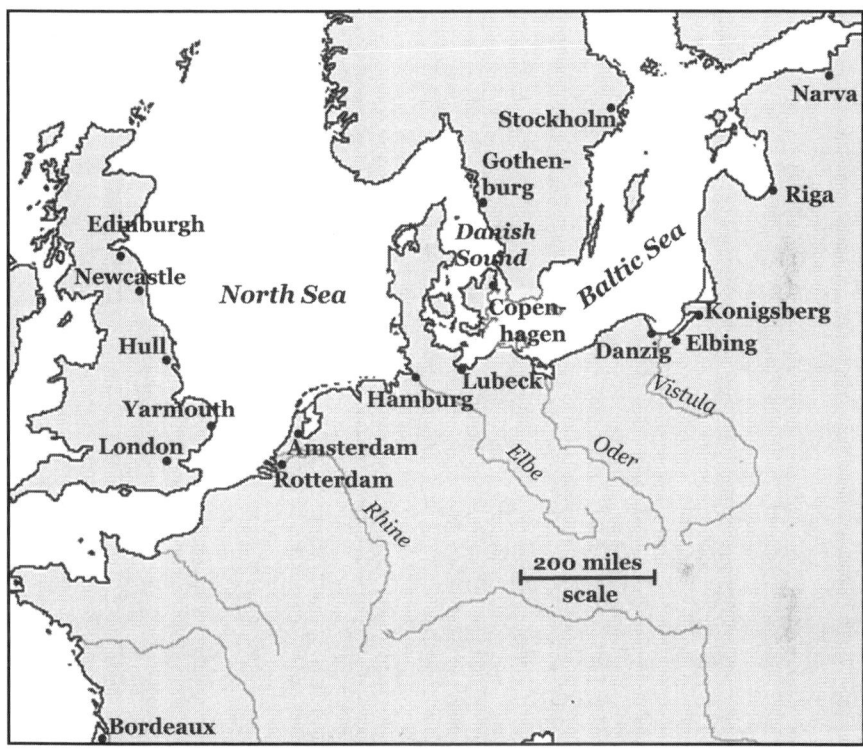

through the Copenhagen-Malmo bottleneck between the Baltic and North Seas. They traded goods between Stockholm, Riga, Narva and the Dutch Republic more than with England.[13]

Into Newcastle came iron from Sweden, timber and rye grain from Danzig and the other eastern Baltic ports, hemp and flax from Konigsberg for rope and sailmaking, increasingly shipped directly to England rather than via Amsterdam as the century wore on. Out went English woollen cloth - and some coal - in return. Accounts were balanced and cleared in sterling, Dutch guilders, Hamburg marks, and Swedish riksdollars. There were direct links between family members, partners and other trusted correspondents in the major ports, skilled in assessing market trends, providers of capital, and masters of weights, measures, currencies and exchange rates. The 73 foreigners buried in All Saints churchyard in the 1600s, mostly from the Netherlands and Baltic region, had presumably contributed just a small share of the overseas voices and language heard in and around the town's quays.[14.]

Intangible though they might be, such networks were clearly highly valued assets. How better to explain the attraction of Newcastle as a port from which to ship Bradford cloth to Europe in the 17th century as well as from the geographically far more convenient port of Hull?[15] Relatively little attention has been paid by historians to Newcastle's cloth trade during this period, presumably because it was overshadowed locally by the great rise of the coal industry, but the monetary value of kersey cloth shipped annually from the town in the mid-1610s is likely to have been around £40,000, which was hardly trivial compared to perhaps £60,000 of coal shipped both domestically and abroad.[16] It remained focused squarely on the market for old fashioned heavy coarse woollens at a time when attention was shifting to the growth of the lighter, finer 'new draperies'. Nevertheless a worthwhile, if declining, market remained for cheap heavy textiles in the colder climes of northern Europe. While the value of Newcastle's cloth shipments was probably down to a third of the coal trade's by the 1660s, the trade survived into the 18th century. It helped generations of merchants cut their teeth in the business of buying goods in one location, shipping them to another and selling them there at a sufficiently higher price to make a living.

The importance of Newcastle's network is illustrated by the number of sons of West Yorkshire clothiers apprenticed into the town's Company of Merchant Adventurers, the exclusive merchants' guild, in the first half of the century. There were 24 in the 1630s alone, or 20% of the total. Similar patterns can be seen amongst the cloth makers of Cumberland and Westmorland during the same period.[17] Edward Mann came from Hutton Roof near Kirby Lonsdale, 110 miles away across the North Pennine hills in 1615. As an established trader two decades later, plugged into Newcastle's overseas network, Mann in turn took on James Briggs from Grigg Hall, west of Kendal. Briggs repaid the compliment by taking John Mann of Hutton Roof as his own apprentice in 1647, surely a relation of his own earlier master. Mann was related to Newcastle merchant Edward Archer, originally of Kendal. Among his other bequests Archer left money to the church in Kendal and his will of 1647 was witnessed by James Briggs.[18] Thus were links maintained to the distant cloth-producing areas of Yorkshire, Cumberland and Westmorland, for there was little tradition of cloth making for export in the Newcastle area. The town's comparative advantage in the cloth trade lay in the commercial skills, capital and knowledge of its merchant traders and their web of connections inland and across the seas, rather than in a competitive local industry.

Newcastle's merchant community was therefore central to the town's economy, and dominated local society and politics through the institutional channel of the principal guilds of the town: the Company of Merchant Adventurers, (hereafter the merchants' company) and the Company of Hostmen of Newcastle, the 'lords of coal' (hereafter the hostmen). Guilds were characteristic of incorporated boroughs and cities with Royal charters, many proudly proclaiming their ancient medieval origins - and rights. These rights typically entailed control over each principal craft or trade undertaken within their town. Only those admitted as freemen of each guild or 'mystery' were permitted to work in the respective crafts. Sons of existing freemen could be admitted, by patrimony, but outsiders had to complete long apprenticeships. By the 17th century these restrictive practices were increasingly undermined. In Newcastle, however, the merchants' company remained influential and accommodated increasing trade within its own ranks. The hostmen rose in prominence alongside coal shipments and London's dependence upon them. Their company was spun out from the merchants' company as a separate incorporated body in 1601 as part of an arrangement which - in essence - saw a Crown grant of the monopoly of the Tyneside coal trade in return for a tax on the coal shipped. Henceforth only hostmen could deal in coal along the Tyne and for all practical purposes also came to dominate mining.[19]

A list of contributions from the merchants to a loan made in 1643 contains 119 names, in perhaps 80 different families.[20] It is less easy to determine the number of hostmen, but 56 were admitted on the company's founding date in 1601, at least 35 of whom were also merchant adventurers.[21] This was a group small enough for everyone to know each other, in many cases bound together by the ties of kinship, apprenticeship and business partnership. It was an urban elite. Ties with the gentry of surrounding counties were largely restricted to absorbing younger sons who also sought a commercial career, and if mercantile success led to the purchase of landed estates these were invariably sought for their coal reserves rather than for status alone.

Newcastle's merchants were also neighbours. Until later in the 17th century most lived near their warehouses and lofts which lined the river. Their tall houses lay along The Close upstream from the bridge, on Sandhill - the centre of civic life dominated by the Guildhall, Exchange and Merchants Court (Plates 9-10) - or on The Side, the steep narrow street which snaked up to St Nicholas', and beyond it to the Fleshmarket and Biggmarket in the upper town. Despite the huge changes to the physical fabric of Newcastle in the centuries since, glimpses of the 17th century merchant town can still be seen in the magnificent Guildhall court overlooking the Tyne, the Quayside pub, once a river-front warehouse, and the steep flights of steps connecting The Close to the upper town. The wood panelled parlour of the grand Bessie Surtees House on The Close is reached through a square stair-well which carries the stairs and oak bannisters up all five floors of the building. A similarly impressive staircase survives in Alderman Fenwick's house on Pilgrim Street, with a wind vane above the skylight, a reminder of the importance to its merchant owners of variations in wind direction and what this meant for ships entering and leaving the river.

These were the homes of the men who held power in Newcastle. Civic office was worth much more than the fine robes, rituals, banquets and processions, 'the whole glory of the town which for state is second only to London', important though these outward trappings must have been to many.[22] Newcastle's corporation owned and let a great deal of property in its own right and collected tolls from markets and shipping, earning around £7,500 annually by mid-century. Municipal property, income and control of the town's courts conferred great influence and powers of patronage upon Newcastle's civic leaders, influence that extended well beyond the confines of the town itself. Newcastle claimed the right to control the Tyne and its traffic all the way from the estuary at North and South Shields inland nearly as far as Wylam, 20 miles from the sea. It not only fought off various attempts to break this monopoly, but had managed to extend its influence from the late 16th century. This was mostly at the expense of the major power to the south, the Bishopric of Durham, from which Newcastle obtained beneficial leases of Gateshead's salt meadows, and - most importantly - the 'Grand Lease' of the rich coal seams at Whickham. In these affairs the corporation's careful management of its relationship with the Crown was critically important. Newcastle's civic and mercantile leaders counted for something in London.

Government of the town was in the hands of the mayor, the sheriff, the Common Council, comprising ten aldermen and 24 other councillors, and - notionally at least - the Guild, an assembly of all the freemen of the various tradesmens' 'mysteries' meeting three times a year. Aldermen were selected for life, but the rest of the Common Council, the Mayor and the Sheriff were elected annually by the freemen. If this sounds simple and enlightened, read on.

> 'Each of the twelve mysteries of the town name and present two men. These 24 delegates, called former electors, elect the old mayor and three aldermen. The four thus elected then elect and add to their own body seven aldermen, and one person, who either is or has been a sheriff of the town; or, if they cannot find seven aldermen, they have to elect eight persons who have been sheriffs; or, if they cannot find these, they have to elect eight burgesses. The old mayor and three aldermen, when joined to these eight, are called the twelve first electors. Each of the twelve mysteries next send one of their body, out of which the first electors choose six, who, joined to themselves, make eighteen electors. Each of the fifteen by-trades also choose one of their body, who again choose twelve freemen, out of which the eighteen electors before mentioned choose six, making in all the number of twenty-four electors; which twenty-four, or the greater part of them, elect the mayor, recorder, and other officers. ... [in] the puzzling intricacy ... will be found, on examination, a despicable mockery of independence.' [23]

By such byzantine procedures, loaded in favour of those on the inside, and with all its possibilities for deals in smoke-filled rooms, did the town's elite control the levers of power. All 28 different mayors of Newcastle between 1600 and 1640 were merchant adventurers, and all but two also hostmen. Only one of the 42 who served as sheriff during the same period was not a merchant adventurer, and he was a hostman, and all eight different members of Parliament were merchants' company members.[24] Newcastle's Parliamentary electorate of freemen was over 1,000 strong, which might have been difficult to control, and required successful candidates to have deep pockets and a measure of popularity. However, the corporation was evidently usually able to manage affairs by the presentation of two candidates for the two seats and thereby relieve the freemen of the bother of voting. Such was the small group of families comprising 'the Inner Ring' which controlled the levers of commercial and civic power.[25] How many dozing aldermen of a certain age woke up and needed a few moments to recall whether today they were in a meeting of the merchants' company, hostmen or Common Council?

At the risk of great simplification, the small merchant community sat atop a three-tiered pyramid of urban society. They were set apart by wealth and status from the families of the rest of the freemen in other guilds, the butchers, smiths, masons, carpenters, coopers and tanners and others to be found in all large towns, and those of the more specialised skilled trades of a great seaport: shipwrights, rope and sailmakers and mariners. Beyond these vigilant corporate guardians of their traditional rights, privileges and respectability were the numerous ranks of the labouring poor.

In 1600-5, of those Newcastle households for whom occupational information can be identified, around 17% were headed by merchants and professionals, 33% by manufacturers/craftsmen and 50% by those who survived by selling their labour. By 1700-5 these proportions had shifted decisively: 8% were merchants and professionals, 20% manufacturers, and 72%, nearly three quarters, were wage labourers.[26] The town's population had probably increased from around 10,000 to 17,000 during the intervening century so it seems reasonable to conclude that almost all the increase was accounted for by the growth of the labouring population. It was a workforce in which the keelmen loomed large, those who provided the brute force on the river to move coal from staith to ship, up and down the Tyne on each tide. The keelmen were regarded as a race apart by nervous contemporaries. Most lived hard by the river in the overcrowded and squalid streets and alleys of All Saints parish, downstream from the Tyne Bridge, and eastwards beyond the city wall in Sandgate. Many were said to have come from Scotland, part of the great flow of migrants attracted to Newcastle as a growing town offering casual work to the desperate and careers to the ambitious. The rhythm of their work was governed by the tides and the seasons, the latter exacerbating the precarious living to be made on the Tyne. But a collective awareness of their critical link in the coal trade, and the sheer demand for their services, meant the keelmen obtained some improvement in their income through occasional strikes as the 17th century wore on.[27]

The festering and densely packed Sandgate suburb wasn't far down the quayside from the Sandhill and The Close, the seat of civic power and home to many merchants. The wealthy would have been all too aware of the potential for unrest on their doorstep, and it was arguably an important consideration in the constant attention of the corporation to protecting its claims over the Tyne, hindering the development of quays closer to the sea, thus effectively requiring ships to load coal in the river from keels. The cultivation and protection of a 'vertical interest group' between hostmen and keelmen could help keep the civil peace on the Tyne, whatever other tensions such identity politics might create between Newcastle and those outside its sphere of municipal patronage.

However, it would be wrong to characterise the institutions at the heart of Newcastle's power as an entirely defensive, closed and self-perpetuating elite. Yes, the town was proud of its identity, strength, wealth and ancient corporate guilds and stately dignity, but its leaders understood that its fortunes rested heavily upon the outside world, and particularly on London, the growing capital city and vital outlet for Tyneside coal. The hostmen knew that the support of Crown and Parliament in London was the cornerstone of their coal trade monopoly. In dedicating a book in 1630, the puritan lecturer of Newcastle Robert Jenison deferred to the primacy of the 'Metropolis or Mother-Citie'.[28]

Likewise, for all the aggressive vigilance of the guilds and companies in protecting their claimed monopolies, Newcastle's traders were not mercantilists seeking the fallacious triumph of exports over imports. In March 1652 the merchants' company petitioned against provisions of the recent Navigation Act, which restricted shipping by foreign vessels and impeded imports. If shipping was restricted it would encourage the 'engrossing of all sortes of comodityes into particular men's hands, who will make their owne rates in a short tyme'. On the perceived threat of the Act to trade, the merchant petitioners pointed out that they were

> 'seated in a barren and pore country, which commonly requires great supply of corne and other necessaryes: that they are not endowed with great estates, yet through God's blessing a considerable number of them have from tyme to tyme obtained comfortable livelyhoods to themselves and familyes with a small trade in northeren cloth, and other native comodityes to Holland and other places adjacent, and have beene very serviceable to these 5 northeren countyes, in their great wants and penury, by supplying them with corne, and other usfull comodityes at reasonable rates and prices, which they were better able to do by reason of the advantage and opportunity they have above other places in the commodity of cole, by which they commonly make their voyages outwards and bring home their returnes for small freight'.*

A similar submission stressed that the existence of a 'return trade' in flax from Holland made cloth and coal exports worthwhile compared to receiving and exchanging money, especially as the flax sustained the poor in spinning linen yarn.[29] Even allowing for the florid exaggerations of petitions, these lines speak of a clear understanding by Newcastle's merchants of the basis of their prosperity, and the wider benefits of exchange. As William Gray put it in his homage to his home town in 1649, 'our most provident and glo-

---

*The '5 northeren countyes' were Northumberland, Durham, Yorkshire, Cumberland and Westmorland. MA Records-1, p.179. (See the 'Guide to abbreviations used in notes' for expansions of shortened references given here and on subsequent pages.)

rious Creator hath so furnished all countries with severall commodities, that amongst all nations there might be a sociable conversation and mutuall commerce, one people in need of another'.[30]

This was, of course, written from a town whose practitioners of 'mutuall commerce' still tried to keep it to themselves. And in common with most other guilds many members were admitted to the freedom of the merchants' company by patrimony, sons following fathers into the privileges and protections of the fellowship. However, while the Company might try to prevent outsiders from trading, its members were certainly open to recruiting capable newcomers through apprenticeship. Of those known to have been admitted to Company membership between 1635 and 1664, 156, or 63% of the total, had completed an apprenticeship, many more than the 87 sons of existing members.[31] Barriers to entry remained. It was certainly not a staircase of social mobility for the labouring poor. No apprentice merchant could expect to survive without the ability to read, write, count, calculate and draw accounts. In addition to the various registration fees due to the Company there was the significant cost of the master's binding fee or premium, effectively the tuition cost of a business education. There is little direct evidence of the going rate for merchant adventurer binding fees in Newcastle, though in 1620 Robert Bewick, already a leading alderman, ex-sheriff, merchant adventurer, hostman, coal and cloth exporter, took an apprentice for a binding fee of under £67. Thomas Bonner left his son £50 in 1660 to be bound as a Newcastle merchant apprentice at 17 and 20 nobles (£6.67) for clothing.[32] These were fees low enough to permit recruitment of young regional talent much more widely than from the small number of families already within the 'Inner Ring'. Christopher Brooks' study of apprenticeship and social mobility found evidence of a similarly open approach in other English cities between the late Tudor period and the eve of the Civil War.[33]

Perhaps the Company's outlook would have been more restrictive had trade been stagnant, but as Newcastle grew and prospered from the late 16th century, its ordinances mark a progressive expansion of its own ranks. Until 1575 the Company attempted to restrict apprentices to an absolute maximum total number at any one time, but from that year permitted each member to take one apprentice each, so that the total number of apprentices could thereafter increase with the number of freemen. From 1621 a master was allowed to have a second apprentice as long as the first was at least three years into their ten-year term, and a third as long as the first had at least eight years of service and the second five years.[34] This was a key mechanism in assisting what was seen in some quarters as the replacement, in the early 17th century, of an old Catholic oligarchy of coal owners by a new puritan nexus of merchants in the town.[35] There was certainly religious and political strife, as we shall see, but arguably there was not so much a single replacement of one faction of the town's elite by another as a constant refreshing of the ranks over time, alongside a shared view that Newcastle's prosperity and business mattered more than sectarian division. One of the features of successful and enduring organisations is the recruitment by current leaders of people more able than themselves. Bright, bold, sharp-witted and commercially-minded newcomers such as William Blackett could rise to the top from relatively modest origins and make their own contribution to the energy, creativity and commercial possibilities of 17th-century Newcastle life and trade.

The Blacketts

So who were the Blacketts? Their profile and legacy means the general story has been told before.[36] William I came in from County Durham to be apprenticed to a Newcastle merchant before the Civil War, became a great trader, coal and land owner, alderman, mayor, MP, and was knighted by King Charles II in 1673. In the words of a later descendant, Charles Trevelyan, he left a fortune great enough 'to make two elder sons' – his eldest son and heir Sir Edward Blackett, by then of Newby Hall in Yorkshire, and the younger William II, for whom a new baronetcy was created in 1685.[37] Sir William II, apparently as astute as his father, continued to develop the family coal and lead business and bought Wallington Hall and estate from Sir John Fenwick in 1689. He died in 1705 leaving William III as his heir, generally thought to be the typical third generation son. His alleged fondness for riotous living is said to have piled up the debt and sent him to an early grave, for he was just 38 at the time of that grand funeral in 1728.

    The spectacular rise of the William I, his influence in Newcastle and beyond, the even greater prominence of his son William II, and the flamboyant tragedy of grandson William III, cast long shadows over the town and its history during a tumultuous century. Historians over the years have found it hard to get out from those shadows, to see more than the silhouettes of myth. One of the most enduring of these myths concerns the origin of the first William I's wealth, often repeated since it first appeared in print in 1819:

> 'Sir William, soon after he commenced business, risked his little all, in a speculation in flax, and having freighted a large vessel with that article, received the unpleasant intelligence that the flax fleet had been dispersed in a storm, and most of the vessels either lost or afterwards captured by the enemy. He took his accustomed walk next morning, ruminating on his supposed loss, and unconscious how far he was going, when on a sudden, he was aroused by the noise of a ship in the river: he jumped upon an adjoining hedge, hailed the vessel, and found it to be his own, which had miraculously weathered the storm, and with difficulty had gained the port. He instantly returned, and hiring a horse, rode in a very short time to London, and hastening to the Exchange, found the merchants in great alarm about the loss of the flax fleet, and speaking of the consequent high price of flax. On informing them that he dealt in that article, and had a large quantity to dispose of, speculators soon flocked around him, and he sold his whole cargo at a most extravagant price, and the produce of that adventure laid the foundation for one of the largest fortunes acquired in Newcastle. This quick decision, in disposing of his cargo, proved to be correct, as several other vessels afterwards got into port, and the markets in a few days fell to the old price. Sir William (as also his children) is said to have regarded with a kind of veneration the hedge from whence he first perceived the vessel and made it the extent of his future morning walks. We are informed it is yet in existence.'[38]

The 1819 author, Newcastle's John Straker, says only that this 'interesting anecdote has been communicated to us from a source, which induces us to have not the least doubt of its authenticity', perhaps a family member, albeit three or four generations after the event. As a great story it's hardly surprising that it has been repeated, although with due caution more recently.[39] Perhaps it is rooted in truth, if embellished over time with hedges and hard riding to London. It would not be at all surprising to find that Blackett traded in Baltic flax, for it was a common staple of Newcastle's commerce, and the dates might work if mention of 'the enemy' placed the event in the first Anglo-Dutch War of 1652-4. Whether true or not it's one of those stories which must have sounded believable, given what was known or thought to be known of its subject, in this case the boldness, luck, trader's flair, fast reactions, and rapid rise to fortune of William I. But it remains a myth that cannot be verified from contemporary sources.

Ambiguity also surrounds the Blackett family portraits at Wallington Hall, now in the care of the National Trust. There are lots of them hung around the central gallery. Most have identifications in the corner of their canvas but these were added much later and it's not at all clear that they can all be trusted. The three Sir Williams are almost certainly there, their wives too, and most of the numerous daughters of William II, but who is really who? Are they hiding in plain sight? As with the 'ship that came home', the material is fairly well known but it's difficult to pin down the facts.[40]

This first full-length study of the 17th- and 18th-century Newcastle Blacketts does not, therefore, have to raise them from complete obscurity but there are myths to be dispelled and simplifications to be overcome. Only a limited amount of direct material has come down to us, including books of copied outbound letters from Edward, and from his younger brother Michael, a few letters to William I and some financial accounts. Instead, therefore, a great deal of indirect evidence has been pressed into service – letters between others, records of civic and guild business, parish registers, wills, lawsuits, property deeds and abstracts, tax, customs and other official records. Despite their fragmentary coverage, these isolated morsels can be pushed and sequenced together and set in the context of their contemporary geography, people and events. They are surprisingly illuminating, adding extra depth and colour to the picture. Inevitably, some of the many gaps between the stark facts have to be filled with inference and some with speculation, but these are, I hope, distinguished clearly. The result, in recovering additional detail of the lives of the Blacketts, has its own interest, but the mere accumulation of facts is not the purpose of this study. It is not just what this energetic family achieved and when that matters, but how and why, and the wider implications that follow.

At a regional level the family was of central importance to the rise of the North Pennines lead industry. The history of lead mining and processing in north-east England has hitherto focused on the well-documented North Pennines heyday in the 18th and 19th centuries. As early as 1705, however, the outward shipments of lead from Newcastle and Stockton, the principal regional ports, accounted for over a third of the English total.[41] The foundations were clearly laid earlier. An outline of the industry's dramatic development in the second half of the 17th century, and the crucial role of the Blacketts, can now be extracted from the breadth of surviving documentary material. The family also played an important role in coal mining, but Blackett involvement here has hitherto been glimpsed as occasional snapshots and asides. When considered as part of a single business from the mid-17th century onwards a different view opens up.

There is a wider point here. William Blackett's investment in coal took place alongside his emerging lead business after 15 years' experience as an overseas trader. His mining businesses placed quite different demands on management ability and capital. Taken together they offer insights into investment strategies and the mechanisms of development at work in 17th-century England. It was a time when the national pace of economic growth quickened and productivity and prosperity rose. This must have depended to a significant extent on increasing internal and external trade, associated with greater farming specialisation and closer regional integration. This in turn was the result of myriad individual decisions to buy, sell, ship, mine and make. Yet while the painstaking work of historians allows us to look back with hindsight and from a great height to discern the broad sweep of change, it is harder to imagine the viewpoint of those in business at the time, looking forward into their own future and deciding what to do. As markets widened and deepened, as industry grew, more people with commercial aptitude and resources must have come forward to connect the places in which an increasing range and number of goods were being made to those distant places where they were consumed.

Relatively little has been written on the lives of English business people before the industrial revolution, certainly little in comparison to accounts of the lives of heroic explorers, monarchs, aristocratic landowners, politicians or generals. Perhaps the growth of trading or industrial concerns has been thought to lack the drama and glamour of great statecraft and military battles. Then too, describing those who rose to public prominence from a commercial background as having simply become 'rich and successful merchants' might be excused by a lack of the records needed to support a more forensic examination. But where such material does survive, a biographical perspective can explore how 17th-century business talent might realise its potential, and contribute to wider economic change.

Interestingly, two of the few such studies from this period are also set in north east England. William Cotesworth was another driven man who rose from humble origins to commercial prominence on Tyneside, a generation later than William Blackett I. In the 1680s Ambrose Crowley, originally from Worcestershire, settled on the region as the location for his advanced ironworks.[42] What was it about an open and bustling seaport that gave men like this a start in business and the chance to thrive? How might they tap into the capital needed to flourish? How did they build, control and sustain their empires? It was an era in which businesses are seldom thought to have survived their creators, but the Blacketts created something more enduring, as did the Crowleys. Business longevity might allow an ever-larger scale of operations to develop and possibly a quest for monopoly. How intertwined was this with favours needed from local and national politics? William I's life in Newcastle during the turbulent decades before, during and after the civil war and commonwealth had a political dimension within the crucial relationship between Newcastle's elite, London and the English state. That relationship continued to evolve through the rest of the century and into the 1700s, frequently beset with crises, and Williams II and III were often directly involved in these moments of national political drama.

This is a multi-generational biography substantiated with numbers, a business history centred on people. It follows a narrative arc, with occasional pauses to set context, to analyse and to consider. After exploring the rise to wealth and influence of William I through the mid-17th century, the focus shifts to his sons Edward and, particularly, William II, and then on to the third William in the early 18th century. It questions the three-generation trajectory of rise and crisis and adds a coda which looks at the decade after the inheritance of young Walter Calverley in 1728. William I is the key to it all. Unfortunately, no matter how hard we sweat the surviving records, it is difficult to be sure of his personality and of the roots of his motivation, but an understanding of his family background and formative years can help. It is possible to piece together new clues to this. We need to start 30 miles south from Newcastle in the County Durham countryside.

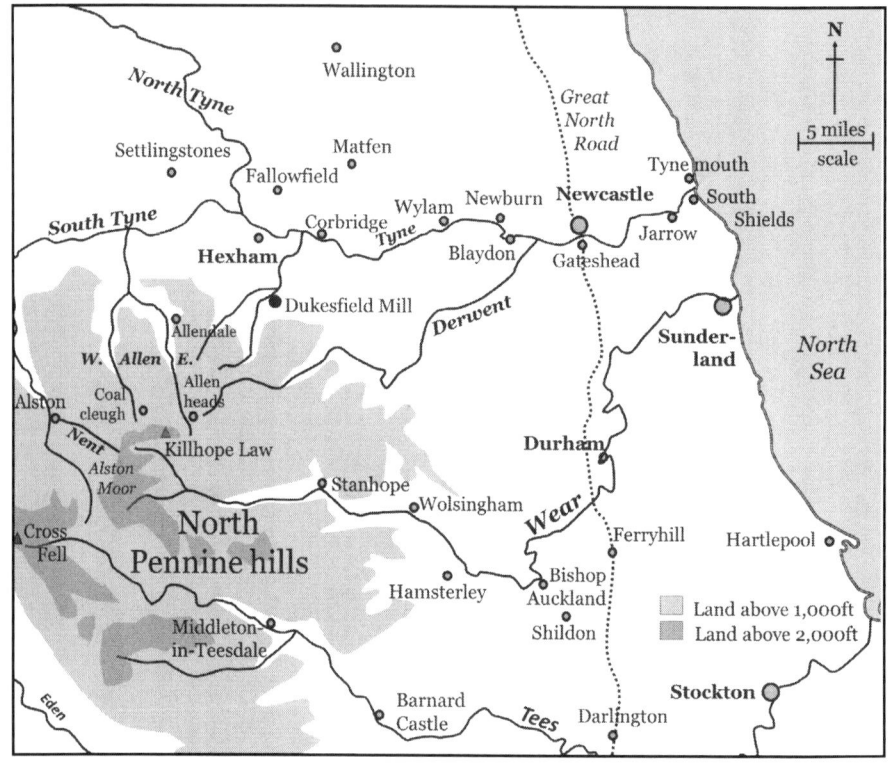
Figure 2.1 North East England

Chapter 2

Hamsterley to Gateshead

William I was born in 1621, the third child of yet another William Blackett, hereafter 'William Snr' where identification is unclear. His elder brothers were Christopher and Edward, born in 1613 and about 1615 respectively. Little is known of the life of William Snr. Previous accounts have concluded, reasonably, that he was a man of some means for he was able to marry Christopher off to Alice Fenwick, apparently the daughter and sole heir to an estate and manorial lordship in Wylam in the Tyne Valley west of Newcastle. For Christopher to inherit an estate from one of the many branches of the Northumberland Fenwicks he would have been expected to provide a suitable 'jointure' estate for his wife in the event of her being widowed. Apprenticeships for Edward and William I to masters in the prestigious Company of Merchant Adventurers of Newcastle also required means. William Snr might have left few traces behind but it's worth examining them as far as we can for clues to his ability to give his sons these good starts in life.

He was baptised in 1587 at the parish church of Hamsterley, the eldest son of Edward and Jane Blackett.[1] Hamsterley lies just to the west of the River Wear, a few miles above Bishop Auckland, and is 12 miles south-west of Durham. This is a country of quiet wooded hills between the better known Weardale and the North Pennine moors to the west and the old coalfield towns downstream to the east. Fast-flowing streams dissect the land beneath field and copse as they hurry towards the Wear. Narrow lanes climb through the hills, their bridges giving glimpses of the singing burns and the occasional dipper and kingfisher flashing through the sunlight. To the west, open moorland rises to 1,500 feet in altitude, some of it today colonised by the conifers of Hamsterley Forest. It was on the south-facing slopes outside the village that Edward Blackett and his brothers farmed their own smallholdings at Shipley in the late 16th century.[2] There is still a 'Blackett's Gill' down which a stream falls swiftly through the woods to the Wear at Low Shipley. The family were apparently originally from higher up Weardale, with an ancestral home at Woodcroft between Stanhope and Frosterley, where a senior branch of the family claimed the status of minor gentry with a coat of arms in the Tudor period. The Heralds sniffily remarked that the Blacketts' pedigree was testified by the mark rather than signature of Thomas Blackett of Woodcroft.[3]

Edward, however, was a working farmer, albeit a reasonably prosperous one. He could not sign his name, but he could certainly count. In 1617 he bought two fields at Wolsingham from John Eden and a year later he was able to buy the farmsteads of Hoppyland and three at Burnley Row, all adjacent to Shipley, from William 4th Baron Eure of nearby Witton Castle.[4] When he died in June 1628 he left his lands and £381 in bequests. The inventory taken of his effects for probate purposes shows a humbly furnished house, but nearly £200 of farming assets, overwhelmingly cattle and sheep.[5] A recent survey of rural County Durham covering this period has demonstrated the success and confidence of a rising class of yeoman farmers in exploiting rising demand for agricultural produce from the 16th century. Purchasing land from the Eures and selling beef, hides, mutton and wool, Edward Blackett exemplifies this trend.[6] Within little more than two years of his death, one of his grandsons married a Fenwick, and another commenced his merchant apprenticeship. It would be simple to conclude that this legacy provided his son and heir William, who could write, with the means to give his own young sons a good start in life, launching them serenely into the world from the stable family home of Hamsterley. It's a beguiling story: from small-scale tenant farming to manorial lordship in two generations. We don't have to dig very far, however, to find a different story.

A significant rift between father and son is revealed by Edward's will. Of that £381, William was bequeathed £24: £20 for himself and £1 each for his wife Isabel and three sons. And this came with the emphatic proviso that 'my said sonne William doth reste himself contented with my sade gifte of twenty pounds without troubling of my wife or other childering for any other demand in my goodes or estate, which if he make further truble, then my gifte of twenty poundes to be void.' This referred to Edward's second wife Ann Lilburne, whom he had married in 1602, and their offspring.

24 | *The Blacketts*

Figure 2.2 Blacketts of Hamsterley.

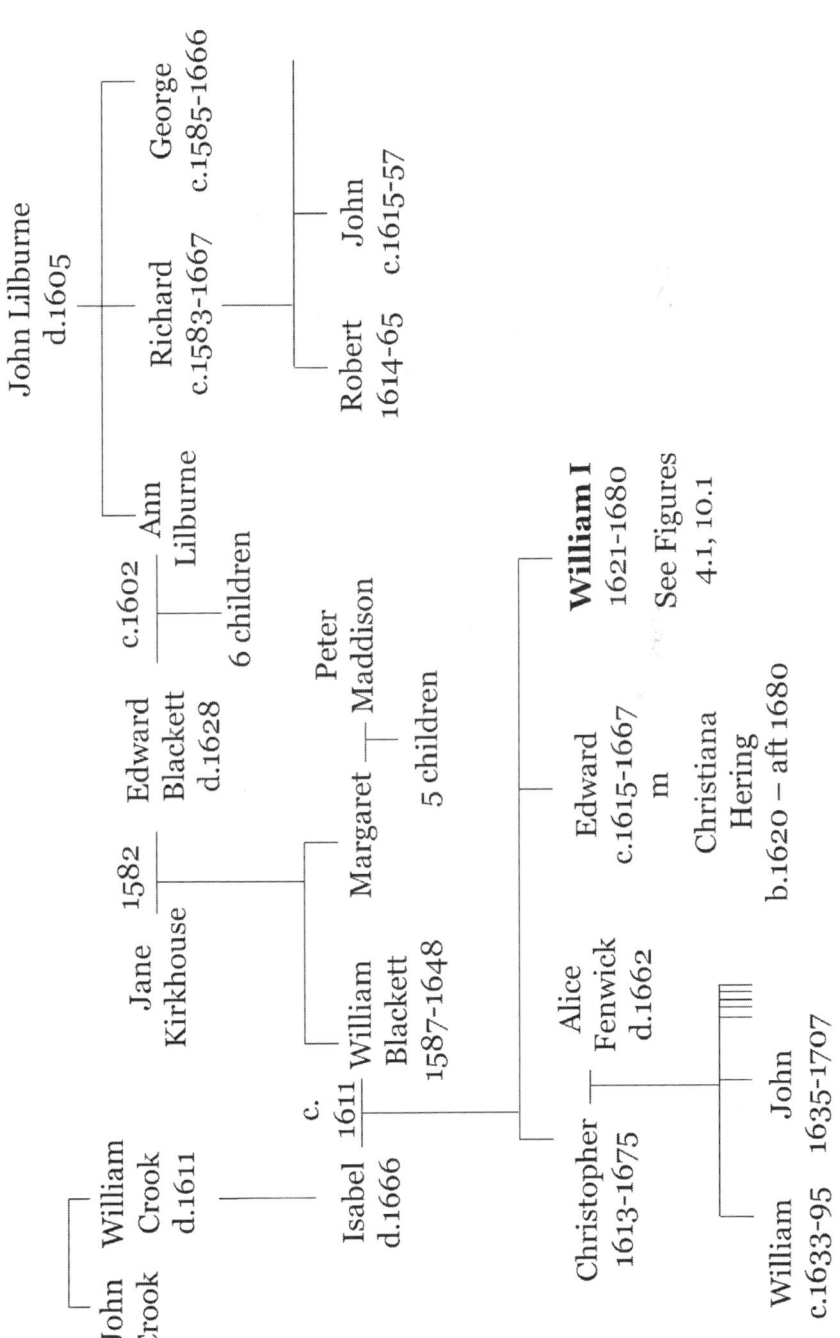

Further detail is provided in Appendix 6, Table A6.1.

Ann, or Agnes, was the daughter of John Lilburne, the owner of Thickley Punchardon, a small manor near Shildon, south of Bishop Auckland. With their own grant of arms from the heralds, they appear to have been a slightly grander family than the farming Blacketts, but probably no more prosperous. William was aged about 15, possibly not much younger than his step-mother, at the time of his father's second marriage. Edward Blackett and his new brother-in-law Richard Lilburne appear to have been rough and ready characters. In January 1610 they were accused of attacking Henry Gibson, deputy to the bailiff of Darlington ward, when they attempted to recover a horse of Lilburne's that had been impounded. The Lilburnes, however, had horizons wider than those few miles of quiet country alongside the River Wear. Unlike the Blacketts, the Lilburnes could sign their names when their pedigree was accepted by the heralds.[7]

Richard Lilburne was married a few years later to the daughter of a family in Greenwich with court connections and spent a few years living there with his in-laws and infant sons before returning north in 1620. Two of these sons were to become prominent opponents of the monarchy before and during the Civil War. Robert became an MP and major-general in Cromwell's army. He was for a short time military governor of Newcastle, and was one of those who voted for the execution of King Charles in 1649. John Lilburne was better known as 'Free-born John', a leading radical Leveller, thinker, campaigner and 'militant Christian', of whom it was said that 'if the world was emptied of all but John Lilburne, Lilburne would quarrel with John, and John with Lilburne'.[8] Their uncle, Richard's brother George Lilburne, was in Sunderland by the late 1610s, where he built a thriving mercantile career. He too would go on to become heavily involved in radical politics, and was imprisoned in Durham in 1642 for his opposition to the monarchy and the established church.[9] There is no evidence that the Hamsterley Blacketts shared or opposed the dangerous opinions of the Lilburnes, but they would have been difficult to ignore.

Edward Blackett's will favoured his second family. To them would go the Burnley Row tenements, £180 and various specific bequests. Sons Henry and John of his second marriage were to be his executors, not William. They were to be supervised by their uncles Richard and George Lilburne, Edward's 'beloved brethren', who were about the same age as William. What of Hoppyland, the purchase of which in 1618 was witnessed by William amongst others? Expectations William might have entertained of enjoying that large farm were undermined by it having been divided in two by his father in 1619, with only half going to William, which he kept until his death. The other half went to his full sister Margaret and her husband Peter Maddison. It would be another 56 years before the property was reunited by one of William's grandsons, and then through re-purchase.[10] If William was aggrieved, it's reasonably easy to see why.

We know next to nothing of William's character, although if - as seems likely - he was the William Blackett of Lynesack, just west of Hamsterley, indicted for hunting without permission throughout Weardale in 1609, he hardly showed an unswerving respect for authority.[11] Furthermore, while it is always possible that the implication in Edward's will that his eldest son was troublesome and greedy might have been unduly biased, there are similar hints in the will of William's father-in-law of August 1611. By that date William was married to Isabel Crooke, daughter of William Crooke, yeoman of Wolsingham. Here was another comfortable Weardale farmer who left a mixture of wheat, oats, barley and rye in his barns, cattle and sheep in the field, adding up to £110 of a total of £162 in assets. His will confirmed that Isabel had already received a marriage portion (of unstated value) and additionally bequeathed a bed, 20 sheep and 4 young cattle 'in full ... paiement of all suche summes of money and all other goods ... whatsoever the said Isabell or her husband William Blackett may ... att any tyme hereafter challenge or claime to be due.' [12] Perhaps this was just providing unambiguous cover to his sons in administering his estate, but equally could be an irritated reference to an unattractive side of his son-in-law. William possibly resented half of Hoppyland being given almost immediately to his brother-in-law instead of being preserved intact for himself as eldest son. And this might have come on top of other perceived slights, going all the way back to his father's Lilburne marriage when William was about 15 years old. What does seem clear is that Isabel's dowry did not set William up for a life of comfortable repose any more than his father's later bequests. He left Hamsterley in the 1610s, and moved his family several times over the next 30 years.

William and Isabel's first son, Christopher, was baptised at Hamsterley in January 1613. Edward was probably born around 1615/6, and William I in 1621 so there might have been other siblings who didn't live to be provided for in their grandfather Edward's will of 1628. All three boys later baptised a daughter 'Christian', a rare girl's name that does not appear in earlier Blackett generations. Perhaps they were named after a dearly loved and lost young sister. There is no sign of Edward's baptism in the apparently reasonably complete Hamsterley parish registers there - or anywhere else nearby. William's destination is unclear, but there are enough faint traces here and there in surviving records to show moves around the region. Thus his third son William I was baptised in Gateshead, just across the Tyne Bridge from Newcastle, in 1621.

The ecclesiastical parish of Gateshead was quite compact, so it is likely that this meant residence within the built-up area lying along the south bank of the Tyne or up the steep road which climbed from the bridge past St Mary's church to become the main road southwards through County Durham. It seems likely that he was the William Blackett appointed as a churchwarden in Gateshead at Easter in 1630, but in Edward's apprenticeship indenture in December that year William Snr was a yeoman of 'Reed Howse, in the Countie of Yorke'.[13] Reed Howse is impossible to locate with certainty but there are two candidates in the lower Tees valley. In 1631 there was a 'Red House' in Middleton St George parish east of Darlington but this was just in Durham.[14] Red Hall Farm is in Kirklevington parish, Yorkshire, just south of the Tees at Yarm. There is a tantalising hint of another Teesside connection in William I's will of 1680. He included the poor of the parish of Hartlepool alongside those of the four churches within Newcastle, and St Mary's in Gateshead, as recipients of £2 per year to be administered by each of their vicars. No evidence of any other business or family connection between William I and Hartlepool has yet come to light, so it leaves the possibility that he could have spent part of his childhood in the area, perhaps at a school.

According to William I's apprenticeship indenture of 1636, his father was of Jarrow by then, on the south bank of the Tyne.[15] A child of William Snr's eldest son Christopher was baptised at Jarrow just a year earlier. In 1640 William Snr helped with a probate inventory in Sunderland, not long before the Scottish army occupied the town. A year later he was back in Hamsterley, with son Christopher and young family, and William appears to have seen out his days there, presumably at his half of Hoppyland.[16] His burial was recorded there in 1648, 61 years after his baptism in the same church. His widow Isabel followed him into the same churchyard in 1666. Wills survive for neither of them.

In summary we can suggest that William and Isabel left Hamsterley shortly after 1613 for one or more unknown destinations, before moving again to Gateshead where they spent the 1620s. They might then have been somewhere near the Tees estuary for a while in the early 1630s, within the large parish of Jarrow in the mid-1630s, had a connection with Sunderland in 1640, before returning to Hamsterley shortly afterwards. What are we to make of these movements around County Durham? William Snr would have been far from alone in moving to Tyneside, and not the only one who moved more than once, an often overlooked feature of migration. Is there any discernible pattern which could help explain his ability to launch his three sons into their careers by the 1630s?

That 1640 Sunderland probate inventory which William helped take provides a possible clue. The deceased was William Thomson, a blacksmith at 'Sunderland Pans'. His probate accounts indicate that Blackett owed Thomson £5. Thomson had six anchors lying around amongst his effects and a small debt owing for an anchor, which could imply that William too owed money for an anchor, but keel or ship building seems an unlikely trade for someone without the right maritime background. Thomson's location at Sunderland Pans, alongside the Wear close to salt pans, suggests another possibility: that he made or repaired the flat iron beds suspended above coal fires on which salt was evaporated from brine. Was the £5 owed for work on a salt pan because William was engaged in the salt trade? This could explain his presence in Jarrow parish, which stretched from as far up the Tyne as Heworth, out to the estuary at South Shields, renowned for its extensive salt pans, and down the coast to Whitburn. Then there is that possibility of time spent around the Tees estuary, where salt was also made.[17]

On the Tyne estuary, North and South Shields were able to exploit the almost uniquely favourable economics of estuarine salt.

'Pan coal' unfit for shipping to London as domestic fuel, and cheap transport by river and sea fostered a profitable industry based on boiling seawater in iron pans from the late 16th century, an industry sustained for two centuries. It grew rapidly alongside rising coal production on Tyneside in the early decades of the 17th century.[18] However, it would surely have been difficult for an outsider with little capital to break into the trade, particularly as many of the pans were in the hands of established Newcastle coal owners and other merchants. William Blackett's name appears nowhere amongst any surviving salt pan leases or other records of the industry in the 1620s and 1630s, but this doesn't rule out his involvement as a steward or manager for one of the larger operators.[19]

One such merchant, in Sunderland from at least the 1610s, was William's radical puritan step-uncle George Lilburne, one of the 'beloved brethren' of Edward Blackett. By 1622 at the very latest, Lilburne was an established coal merchant. As a magistrate and later the mayor of Sunderland, Lilburne witnessed many wills in the 1620s and 1630s. In early 1641 Thomas Triplet, the rector of Whitburn, and no friend of Lilburne, said that 'his trades are infinite, chaundler, grocer, mercer, linen draper, freitore to ships, farmer of collieries, farmer of land, keelman, brewer etc'. In a flavour of the religious antagonism that would act as such an accelerant to the fires of conflict in the 1640s, Triplet castigated Lilburne's father-in-law in the 1630s for welcoming 'the Sunderland puritans like rats over the water … where all these pestilent nests of puritans hatched … where they swarm and breed like hornets in a dead horse's head'. Lilburne was also named amongst the local salt entrepreneurs.[20] Sunderland, Whitburn, Jarrow, South Shields and Gateshead were all fairly close together in the northeast corner of County Durham. Monkwearmouth parish, just north across the Wear from the town of Sunderland, is the only parish in the area for which no registers survive from before the 18th century.

Could it be, therefore, that this is where William Blackett moved in the 1610s, where his son Edward and possibly other siblings were born? William might have been given something useful to do by his step-uncle George Lilburne at the request of his father Edward back in Hamsterley, to get William's bickering out of his earshot, and at the same time help Lilburne manage his expanding business empire. William could then have moved on Gateshead by 1621 with his step-uncle's help and connections. There were salt-meadows just downstream on the south bank of the Tyne, which had been leased by the corporation of Newcastle from the Bishop of Durham since the mid-16th century, but it is not clear that salt-pans were being worked there in the 1620s. However, there is a possibility that William was involved in another riverside activity - managing ballast shores.

These were a consequence of the nature of the Tyneside coal trade and Newcastle's aggressive protection of the monopoly it claimed over the tidal range of the Tyne from the estuary almost as far upstream as Wylam, 20 miles away. The corporation insisted that ships navigate the river shallows in order to load and unload their cargoes on the quayside in Newcastle, ten miles in from the sea. Since incoming shipments rarely came close to the weight of coal taken away, many arrived with ballast, usually sand and gravel. This had to be discharged at various points below the town and ships were charged for the privilege by the corporation. Challenges to this monopoly usually ended in tears, the most well-known being that of North Shields brewer Ralph Gardiner because of the book he dared to publish on the subject.[21] Ballast was meant to be piled up at agreed 'shores' on the north and south banks between Newcastle and the estuary, special quays or staiths. If ships could tie up at a shore, ballast might be discharged directly, but it was also conveyed from mid-channel by keel. The accounts of the corporation's Chamberlain record receipts of payments from ship-masters for ballast taken to shores often leased out on generous terms to favoured Newcastle merchants, who were reimbursed for taking, moving and stabilising it and maintaining the quays to prevent the growing weight of sand collapsing into the river.[22]

Minutes of the Newcastle common council meetings indicate some kind of business relationship in the 1640s between William Snr and Anne Alvey, when he took a bond from the council in respect of debt owed to her connected with her ballast shore.[23] She was the daughter of Henry Chapman, a Newcastle merchant adventurer, and inherited his ballast shore in 1633. The shore, evidently somewhere near South Shields, was amongst a number nearby against which a complaint in 1633 was made for taking 'unfitting' ballast and failing to prevent it washing out into the river.

Christopher Blackett was named as the 'keeper' of the shore 'lately belonging to Mr Henry Chapman and now in the possession of Arthur Alvey, gent' (Anne's husband).[24] A co-incidence of names cannot be ruled out, but it seems highly likely that this Christopher was William Snr's eldest son, given the later association of William with Anne Alvey. We know Christopher was in the area in the early 1630s. Keeping a ballast shore was a difficult and unglamorous management job, taking care of the owner or leaseholder's responsibilities to convey ballast from incoming ships and have it safely disposed of on the shore, dealing with the keelmen and collecting payment from ships and the corporation. If, however, this was indeed the same Christopher Blackett, what was the young man, apparently now married into the Northumberland gentry, doing grubbing about on the Jarrow shore?

It turns out that Christopher's marriage at the age of 18 was not so lordly after all. A closer look at Alice Fenwick's family shows that her father Thomas was not lord of the manor of Wylam but a tenant farmer at West Matfen, eight miles to the north-west. His probate inventory of November 1631 described a modest and simply furnished farmhouse and valued his possessions at £264. It was mostly in livestock and recently harvested grain, and was a noticeably lower total than the effects of Edward Blackett of Hamsterley three years earlier. Half of Fenwick's modest estate had been promised to William Snr 'in full satisfaction of the filial portion of Alice' but only when William made good his 'late promise to convey ... all his lands in Durham unto Christopher and Alice as heirs'. Fenwick's other half was left to his two executors - his brothers-in-law - apparently to cover his outstanding debts. Whether we call it reasonable caution or mutual distrust, Fenwick wanted to guard against William Blackett not living up to his side of the bargain and, for his part, William had two of his own Hamsterley cousins go up to Matfen to be amongst the appraisers of Fenwick's inventory lest any of the assets be squirrelled away.[25] Even this modest inheritance was not immediately forthcoming. Christopher Blackett had to institute proceedings in 1637, six years later, to seek an account of the estate from Fenwick's executors. In 1649 Christopher was described as a yeoman rather than a gentleman.[26] Far, then, from being a marriage which propelled young Christopher Blackett into a comfortable life amongst the Northumberland gentry, it seems he would have been unable to derive any material benefit at all from his wife's modest inheritance for several years. His family were indeed settled at Wylam at a later date, but this was mostly due to purchases his second son John was able to make in the 1670s and 1680s.[27] For Christopher in 1630/1 perhaps the best his father could or would do was to get him a supervisory job amongst shipmasters, keelmen and labourers shovelling endless loads of sand and gravel on the cold tides at Jarrow and answering for the crumbling walls on the riverside.

We cannot know this for sure, however attractive or even plausible the imagined narrative. All we know about William Snr with any certainty before he returned to Hamsterley by 1641 is that he turned up at various places around the north-east coast after 1613. Whatever his itinerant work, salt making, ballast shore keeping or otherwise, he remained outside the great regional metropolis of Newcastle at a time when its civic and mercantile institutions threw their weight around up and down both sides of the Tyne. It seems unlikely that William had the capital to engage directly in business on any meaningful scale, and his name does not appear among any surviving lists or records of salaried municipal or other institutional officials. He was always described as a 'yeoman', that vague catch-all term for the middling sort of people: above the rank of labourer, below that of clerk, and less specific than any of the usual crafts. So perhaps he carved out enough of a reputation as a competent manager of the affairs of others, whether or not starting with his industrious and well-connected step-uncle George Lilburne, to get by. He certainly had such a position in the 1640s after his return to Hamsterley, for he was one of those appointed by the Weardale 'moormaster' to manage his lead mining rights there, probably with Lilburne's help.[28] It is unlikely to have made him rich. This might not have mattered as far as Christopher's marriage was concerned. The Fenwicks were of a similar social position and apparently required no more than a legally secure promise of the eventual transfer of William's half share of Hoppyland to his eldest son. Money was, however, still needed for his two younger sons' merchant apprenticeships, a career path which William Snr appears not to have considered Christopher capable of following.

Masters of merchant apprentices could be as young as their

mid-20s.²⁹ It seems reasonable to assume that young and new masters could not command binding fees as high as those with more experience but it is noticeable that William Snr bound his two younger sons to older and more experienced men, as we shall see in the next chapter. He might have taken advice from John Crooke, the uncle of William's wife Isabel, who was an established merchant and Company member in Newcastle by the time of William and Isabel's marriage in around 1610.³⁰ But whether or not he had any assistance from John Crooke, William Snr did not wish to set his sons up on the cheap.

How much money did he need? We saw earlier that the fee for merchant apprentices in Newcastle under even a quite senior master could be under £70 in the 17th century. If £5 per year is allowed for additional living costs for a decade, that would add up to around £250 over the 15 years between 1630, when Edward commenced his, and 1645, when William I ended his, or a crude average of £17/year. Let's allow £15/year for a modest standard of living for an adult couple.³¹ If William Snr and his wife could live on that, they would have needed a joint income of perhaps £32/year overall to pay for the two apprenticeships through the 1630s and early 1640s. This was within the range found by Grassby for 'general managers' and at the low end of the earnings for 'middling farmers'.³² These are all very rough guesses, but the point is that William Snr would not have needed to be rich to apprentice two sons as Newcastle merchants a few years apart.

William I therefore probably spent his childhood in Gateshead, within sight of the keels riding the tides laden with coals and the great ships coming in from London and Europe. From the age of nine he might have been somewhere on Teesside and educated in Hartlepool before moving back to the south bank of the Tyne close to the acrid smoke of the salt pans, and the shifting hills of ballast. Who knows what thoughts were drummed into the boy and his elder brothers by their apparently argumentative, restless, energetic and driven father and (to us) invisible mother? There was, however, respect enough from all three sons for them to give the names William and Isabel to their own children in due course. It seems likely that while William Snr remained outside Newcastle, a manager of others' concerns, he saw that the town was the place to be. Rather than complain about the injustice of its claims over

Tyneside the thing to do was to be on the inside. We can imagine the boys being told to follow their father's example to make their own future by working hard and being bold. Thanks, probably, to a great deal of parental sacrifice, Edward and William I had apprenticeships which gave them the opportunity to thrive. These were opportunities they both took and, in William I's case, took spectacularly.

Chapter 3

Troublesome Tymes

Newcastle Merchant Apprentices

For all the importance and prestige of Newcastle's merchants' company, and its vigorous defence of its ancient trade monopoly, it was not a closed body. This arguably followed from the nature of the company itself. It was an institutional umbrella for individuals and fluid partnerships pursuing their own self-advantage through overseas trade rather than a mature single business, protective and defensive in outlook. Consequently, when trade flourished, as it did from the late Tudor period, company members sought new talent – and found it from a relatively wide cross-section of society. By the 1620s and 1630s this was working on an impressive scale. Around a dozen boys were enrolled each year. Given the 10-year term, there would typically be over 100 Newcastle merchant apprentices at any one time. William Blackett's sons were at the right age at the right time.

Apprentices became part of their master's family, household and social circle. During his Newcastle merchant apprenticeship in the 1640s, Ambrose Barnes had to share a bed with a fellow un-named apprentice in the garret. According to Barnes' memorialist, his bedfellow 'kept such disorderly hours, Mr. Barnes never knew when he came to bed, and Mr. Barnes was so assiduous in his master's business, the other never knew when he got up'.[1] As we shall see, Barnes was not shy of pious self-justification, but the records of the merchants' company's courts also make frequent mention of the misdemeanours of errant apprentices. It would surely be odd if they did not, what with lots of young men being thrown together in a lively town. In addition to the merchant adventurers there were 11 other trade guilds with apprentices, so there would have been several hundred in the town at any one time. Student high jinks in Newcastle's 'night time economy' are hardly a new phenomenon. Complaints were made in the 17th century concerning drinking, music, gambling, dress codes and haircuts. In 1603 'greate disorder and abuses have been committed and practised by manie of the apprentices ... as well in their common and outward behaviour towards their superiors and betters, as also in excessive, extraordinarie, and costlie apparel' [2] and so on. Naturally these tiresome offences continued, leading to repeated strictures against disrespectful apprentices. There is no record of the Blackett boys being hauled up in front of the Governor and assistants of the company for contraventions of the apprenticeship code, but William I was doubtless meant to feel embarrassed when, in due course, one of his own apprentices, George Carter, ignored company warnings about his hair and dress. In December 1649 Carter was sent to the barber to have his hair cut short according to the regulations, but was imprisoned a month later for refusing to appear at the merchants court and was perhaps slightly more chastened, at least outwardly, when summoned for examination of his 'hayre and apparell' in May.[3]

Far less information has survived on the humdrum but central question of how Newcastle apprentices learned their trade. Although it is a single example and dates from a century later, the diary kept by Ralph Jackson, apprenticed to a hostman in 1749, is helpful. Jackson was sent out within his first few days alongside one of his master's older servants to take account of his keels and their equipment. Within a few weeks he was down at the river to check how repairs were progressing. There were menial errands to run, cash books to buy and coal stock ledgers to copy. He also attended horse races with his master and friends, which presumably helped develop the crucial network of contacts amongst the coal owners, ship masters and other hostmen who acted as the brokers or 'fitters' between mine and ship. Alongside all this, Jackson was taking classes from private tutors, particularly in maths.[4]

By Jackson's day there appear to have been a number of schools able to provide a suitable elementary education. The Grammar School's curriculum was not attuned to the practical needs of commerce. 17th-century provision is much more sparsely documented. In endowing a charity school in St. John's parish in 1705, the lawyer, mining rights owner and financier John Ord alluded to having attended a basic school in the parish, which was probably in the 1660s.[5] Several were established by puritans in the 1650s, and although the motivation might have been primarily religious zeal, it is perhaps unlikely that the Sunderland school was alone amongst them in being expected to instruct children to write and learn arithmetic 'to fit them for the sea or other necessary callings'. A Newcastle school was described in 1706 as teaching poor children to read, write, and – tellingly - cast accounts, and the same was available at the All Saints parish charity school established in 1709.[6] A clue as to the commercially-focused curriculum on offer in William Banson's 'free writing school', associated with the Grammar School, can be seen in the contents of his publications of the first decade of the new century.[7] The long catalogue of books sold by William London from his shop on the Tyne Bridge in 1658 included several on accounting, trade, commercial law and navigation. He was one of at least three or four booksellers on Tyneside in the 1650s.[8]

George Errington, the master of John Blackett, second son of William I's eldest brother Christopher, agreed in John's 1652 apprenticeship indenture to 'well and faithfully to teach ...the Art, Science and Mistery or Traid of a Merchant Adventurer after the best manner he can.' This has a formulaic ring to it, but it did also stipulate specifically that young John would be taught how to keep accounts 'after the manner of the Cittie of London', which lubricated the wheels of trade through common standards.[9] Contemporary educational handbooks convey more detail, as shown by the full and typically lengthy title of one such from later in the century. This was John Vernon's 1678 *The Compleat Countinghouse, or The Young Lad taken from the Writing-School, and fully Instructed, by Way of Dialogue, in all the Mysteries of a Merchant. From his First Understanding of Plain Arithmetick, to the Highest Pitch of Trade. Whereby the Master is saved much Labour, and the Lad is led by the Hand to all his Work and Business; which to Youth is accounted Troublesome, but will here seem Pleasant. A Work very Necessary for all that are concerned in keeping Accompts of what Quality soever.*[10]

Vernon's guide, set out as a conversation between a youth and a master, gives a flavour of the underlying procedures of transacting trade an apprentice merchant had to learn: collecting the post, weighing and measuring commodities, filling out a ship's bill of lading exactly, calculating interest and commission fees, creating the matching invoice, dealing with the customs house, handling bills of exchange, copying outgoing letters and keeping up the accounts. Numeracy, diligence, precision and briskness were emphasised. Merchants needed to be exact to protect their reputation. Tabulated 'ready-reckoners' were published to assist speed and accuracy of calculation – crucial aids in a sophisticated commercial world lacking calculators and spreadsheets, and in which the concept of logarithms was brand new and slide rules in their infancy. This all mattered. Rather than being relaxed about the 'trifling' difference between interest and discount over the course of a quarter or a year, 'when you pass for a Merchant, I assure you, you will find it a difficult matter so to do; for they see that ... you are weak in your Judgment and very lavish in your Purse; and will all say, You were never bred a Merchant.' Many pages of the book are taken up with explaining double entry book-keeping, the mainstay of trade accounting since the heyday of the medieval Italian merchant grandees: 'let us consider of coming to the booking of every thing, in such order, as that when ever I have a mind, I may presently see what I have in the World, and see what is due to me, and what I owe unto others ... you will find much pleasure and satisfaction in it'.[11]

This prospectus was typically accomplished between a desk in the master's office and down by the river around Sandhill, with its close conjunction of quay, storage cellars and lofts, customs house, weigh-house and Exchange, alive with the busy traffic of porters, merchants, shipmasters and messengers. Many, however, were sent to the European ports in which their masters did business, a positive attraction for some. The father of William Skepper was able to change his son's master in 1629 in order for him to learn the way of trade in Hamburg and a foreign language.[12]

Edward Blackett, indentured in December 1630, spent much of his apprenticeship in Amsterdam learning the role of a cloth merchant. His master was John Butler, a freeman of the company for nearly 30 years. Butler was trusted to investigate breaches of the company rules, and a company steward in 1618. Being abroad gave Edward Blackett logistical trouble obtaining his freedom because 'his constant residing [sic] being at Amsterdam, from whence he hath twice repayred hether to demaund his fredome, but did not receive it by reason of troublesome tymes, which then hindered this Fellowshipp from keeping courts'.[13] Edward remained in Amsterdam until 1652, acting as a local factor for several merchants' company members. The registers of the city's English Presbyterian church, of which Edward was a deacon, document the christening of seven sons and daughters there between 1644 and 1651, three of whom survived to be named in their uncle William I's will in 1680.[14] One of them might have been responsible for outgoing letters in Dutch from William I in 1670, although the latter would have seen the value of some personal foreign language skills.[15]

Capable apprentices were able to become proficient in far less than the prescribed 10-year term, earning the trust of their masters. The frequent repetition of company orders against apprentices trading within their term on their own account, or jointly with their masters, and the penalties levied on transgressors, shows that the able started making their own way with indecent haste. There was some limited recognition of this by the company in allowing apprentices to share in £20 of joint trading stock with their masters after five years, and £40 after eight. It wasn't enough to prevent 11 apprentices being hauled before the court in 1654 for trading contrary to the company's rules. Ambrose Barnes, seven years into his apprenticeship, was first on that list so there might have been a grain of truth behind the swaggering claim in his memoirs that

> 'his master entirely confided in him. The weight and burden of the trade which was very great, lay upon him. His opinion was a law to his master.... [who] treated him like a partner, permitting him to venture on his own bottoms [ie. ships], whereby he cleared seven or eight hundred pound to himself and this before the tearm of his apprenticeship was expired'.*

William Carr had set up his apprentice Robert Potter to run a shop for him in Penrith, six years into his term, and tried lamely to defend himself in 1645 by saying that the shop only handled deliveries sold by Carr himself in Newcastle. Randall Preston was five years into his merchant apprenticeship to John Lancaster in 1661

---

*Incidentally, despite these claims, his master, Samuel Rawling, made no mention of Barnes in his will of 1656: TNA PROB 11/258/436. Longstaffe, *Memoirs of the life of Ambrose Barnes*, SS 50, (1867), p.37.

when his master asked him to remain with his wife for at least six months to help gather in his debts, after which he would be given £123 6s8d towards fees to a new master.[16]

Newcastle's Turbulent Decade

The features of life as a Newcastle merchant apprentice described here might well have applied to William Blackett I, but the circumstances of his formative years in the town were far from normal. From almost the moment he arrived, Newcastle was beset by a series of severe crises that disrupted the growth in commerce of recent and more benign decades.

To start with, during the summer of 1636 a devastating outbreak of bubonic plague ravaged the town. With its maritime connections to London and the North Sea ports, Newcastle was no stranger to the plague but the epidemic of that hot summer of 1636 was one of the most severe, carrying off up to half of Newcastle's population before its fury was spent. Its impact and consequences have recently been studied in systematic, vivid and moving detail.[17] By the time William I's apprenticeship indenture was signed on June 1st the epidemic had taken a firm hold in the dirty, densely populated alleys of Sandgate so its fearsome presence therefore seems not to have prevented him moving in. Several previous epidemics had largely been confined to Sandgate and other densely populated parts of All Saints parish, but this time it swept like wildfire up through the town, and by August dozens of plague victims were being buried each week in the more well-to-do parishes of St Nicholas' and St John's. According to Ambrose Barnes' memoirs, during a later, minor, epidemic his master fled to Hamburg leaving Barnes 'shut up in an empty large house near the Exchange ... and in this hideous lonely manner he spent severall dayes and nights'.[18] In 1636 town life did not come to a complete stop. Wrightson notes that ships continued to arrive and leave, albeit in sharply reduced numbers, but it was inevitable that 'the normal rhythms and patterns of daily life must have been drastically disrupted and recast into a new routine of survival, marked by anxiety and watchfulness' in the disturbingly quiet streets.[19]

In the summer of 1638 coal shipments from the Tyne were

disrupted when shippers reacted with a boycott to another attempt by the hostmen's cartel to keep coal prices artificially high. A keelmen's petition from that year claimed, probably with a dose of exaggeration, that the 'stoppage of the coal trade by sea has thrown at least 3,000 men out of employ, and unless some course be taken to encourage the ship-masters to go to Newcastle again this winter, they will be in danger to assemble themselves and make an uproar in the town, as they did of late.'[20]

Meanwhile a more strategic political threat to the town and its trade was already emerging in the north. Scotland was in a religious ferment over what was widely seen as the arrogant imposition of a neo-papist prayer book by King Charles I in 1637. Tens of thousands signed a solemn 'national covenant' the following February, a totem of the country's fierce Presbyterians intent on purifying their kirk of all residual traces of Catholic ritual and royal interference. This is turn was taken as a rebellious insult by the brittle and tactless King. Before long, armies were being mustered with some enthusiasm by Scotland's Covenanters and, beyond the outraged confines of the royal court, with foot-dragging reluctance in England. In June 1639 the small English force led by Charles came through Newcastle *en route* to Scotland but near Kelso thought better of taking on their more numerous and determined opponents. An uneasy 'pacification' was agreed at Berwick and the King withdrew his troops to prepare for another attempt to quell his mutinous Scottish subjects the following year.[21]

Newcastle's strategic location was therefore once again in the national spotlight. Viewed from London it was simultaneously a vulnerable bulwark of loyal defenders of the King's high church and a dangerous harbour of outspoken puritan clerics linked to their Scottish Presbyterian brethren, not to mention the large number of Scottish migrants mining coal and keeling it down the Tyne. Local theological bickering took on a wider importance, and would effectively soon mutate into factions supporting King and Parliament in the English Civil War. Royal commissioners had come up from London early in 1639 to inspect the state of the town wall defences before moving on to check the border garrison at Berwick. They helped the royalist faction coalescing around Sir John Marley to prise out puritan speakers William Morton and Robert Jenison, the latter exiled to Danzig until 1645. But Marley did not have it all his own way in municipal politics and Jenison's half-brother Robert Bewick, merchant adventurer, hostman and puritan, was elected mayor in September 1639.[22]

In August 1640 the Scottish army swept into Northumberland, defeated an English force at Newburn, and entered Newcastle, knowing well the pressure that could be put upon the King by closing off London's coal supply. Despite the orders of the Scottish commander Leslie that his men should behave with discipline and buy their provisions, reports soon emerged of pillaging and 'intolerably insolent' soldiers 'voyolent in their actions and discourse'. Marley and other prominent members of the Corporation fled south, but Bewick entertained Leslie and his officers to dinner on the day they arrived.[23] His troops were to remain for a year. As for trade, there was inevitably some dislocation with the departure of several merchants and coal-owners, but it was hardly in Scotland's interest to halt the coal trade completely, seeking instead to export to northern Europe and keep the tax and duty raised. Nevertheless, the demands of feeding an occupying army through winter in an area that largely depended on imported grain for its own needs must have caused hardship both in Newcastle and within an increasing radius of the country as the garrison went out in search of supplies.[24]

While the Scots' departure in 1641 must have eased economic conditions, there was no return to any semblance of civic harmony.[25] Marley and his fellow royalists were back in town, and high church symbolism was soon re-imposed. The Common Council included supporters of both King and Parliament but Marley was elected mayor in October 1642 and retained it, highly unusually, through the next two annual elections. As King and Parliament descended into conflict that summer and autumn, the Earl of Newcastle had been sent as military governor to the town to secure it for the royalist cause. Parliament's response was to impose a blockade on the Tyne and the Wear from early 1643, leading to a disastrous reduction in the trade Newcastle depended upon so heavily.[26] Now it was the turn of the Puritans and supporters of Parliament to be purged by Marley as aldermen and councillors and it was a royalist garrison that had to be fed.

Conditions deteriorated in February 1644 as the Scottish army returned to the gates of Newcastle in support of the London

Parliament, this time laying it under siege until October. Newcastle's resolution in defending its walls does not necessarily imply widespread support for the crown as much, perhaps, as antipathy towards the Scottish army. Memories of the earlier occupation were still fresh. Even amongst merchants supporting the crown, however, let alone those trying to keep out of politics altogether, the capture of Sunderland by the Scots in March 1644 gave pause for thought. With the Wear now opened for coal shipments to London, would Newcastle's monopoly on the coal trade be permanently broken? The subsequent debates taking place within the besieged town can only be imagined, for few records of those dark days have survived. Doubts must have grown, but Marley held out for the King through the summer by placing the town under strict military control. When the final assault came in mid-October he refused to sue for peace and retreated to the castle with his diehard supporters. He was captured, imprisoned and was destined for the axe before escaping, or being quietly allowed to.[27] Newcastle was secured for Parliament. The puritans could return to pulpit and civic office, the royalists were removed and the Scottish army was back in town. This time they remained until February 1647, when they were paid off again.

William Blackett's Apprenticeship

During the whole term of William Blackett's apprenticeship Newcastle suffered economic and social upheaval and dislocation brought about by plague, military occupation, plunder, siege, attack, religious and political strife and blockade. Although we have no evidence of how this affected him personally, we can perhaps get a little closer to it by piecing together the background of his master, William Sherwood, merchant adventurer, hostman and alderman.

Sherwood was born into an established Newcastle merchant family in about 1570. Marriage to the daughter of Thomas Liddell of Farnacres and Ravensworth brought Sherwood into coal ownership for Liddell was one of the 'lords of coal' with a direct stake in the hugely lucrative Grand Lease of Whickham. Sherwood was admitted as a hostman in 1609 and became an alderman two years later. In 1614 he and his wife's uncle, Francis Liddell, were accused of undermining nearby workings, robbing their coal and then flooding the worked seam to cover their tracks. Sir Thomas Liddell accused Sherwood, his brother-in-law, of solving his own drainage problems by deliberately flooding Liddell's adjacent and lower seams in 1619, prompting Sherwood to respond insouciantly that Liddell should drain his own mines better.[28] Such was the buccaneering territory of Tyneside coal, particularly in the heavily worked Whickham fields, as the seams got deeper and wetter.

Exploiting its energy supply monopoly over a distant but captive market, the hostmen's company set and policed coal production quotas and attempted to keep prices high. The tactics will be recognised by those who recall the Persian Gulf oil embargoes and production quotas of the 1970s. In 1617 and 1622 Sherwood was allowed to mine around 6,300 tons per year. This relatively modest amount might have needed no more than 40 miners, but it is possible that he was still working in collaboration with one or other of his neighbouring Liddell in-laws at Whickham, who were allocated 19,000 tons of production between them.[29] Sherwood was assessed amongst the top 50 householders in Newcastle in 1621 when it came to paying the Lay Subsidy.[30] He was listed under the parish of St Nicholas', perhaps in one of the tall old merchant's houses in Fleshmarket, just up from St Nicholas' church where his daughter-in-law Joanna, widow of his eldest son and heir Thomas, was assessed on a large 10-hearth house in 1665 (see Plate 1).[31] It was no longer the most fashionable part of town, overtaken by Sandhill and The Close, and the wide street outside was home each Saturday to what Gray thought to be the greatest market in England for all sorts of flesh and poultry. It had 'such a concourse of people out of the country ... to sell all sorts of corne and flesh, buy all sorts of provision for house and family, receive money of maisters of cole for cole-work, that every saterdays Market is like a fair, for all sorts of wares provisions and manufactours.'[32]

We might safely imagine William Sherwood raising his family in the old medieval family home here, four or five tottering storeys rearing up above the market hubbub and filth. Thirteen sons and daughters of William and Elizabeth were baptised in St Nicholas' between 1600 and 1621, and many had Liddells and other 'gentleman' coal-owners for godparents. Sherwood's fortunes are harder to follow in later years. In 1627 his coal production quota had dropped to around 4,300 tons, but so had most others. Continuing involvement in the industry can be assumed for the apprentice he took on in 1628, Henry Pauston, was a hostman by 1641. Other than this, the scale of Sherwood's mining and trading business at the time he took on William Blackett in 1636 is quite unclear. He had been a force to reckon with in his prime, holding his own amidst his fellow scheming and sharp-elbowed coal-owners, but he was 66 when he took on young Blackett, his last apprentice. William Blackett senior might have hoped Sherwood could introduce his son into the booming coal trade, but the amount of practical hands-on experience Sherwood was able to offer was probably quite limited.

At least four of Sherwood's children were married by 1636, but some of the younger ones might still have been at home in the Fleshmarket house when William I moved in as the junior apprentice. The plague was taking hold of the town. No Sherwoods are listed among the St Nicholas' burials of that summer but they may have evaded the magistrates' lockdown and quarantine measures and fled during the worst months, perhaps to the Liddells' country seat at Ravensworth in the Team Valley. We just don't know whether the 15-year-old William remained in the midst of all this horror with his new master and family, or managed to get away back 'home' to Jarrow – largely free of the contagion that year - but at the very least his apprenticeship must have been disrupted until the cooler weather of late autumn brought some relief. The merchants' company, who usually held a monthly court, did not meet between March 1636 and January 1637.

The dislocation of the times was compounded for William I by the death of his master in April 1640. Sherwood's wife had died a year before.[33] Although William Sherwood left no will, we know from his oldest son Thomas's will that he inherited the Fleshmarket house and that Thomas already had his own apprentice. When he took a second, in December 1641, it was not William Blackett. It looks as though William was on his own in April 1640, not quite 19, less than four years into his turbulent Newcastle apprenticeship and with a Scottish military threat looming over the northern horizon.

The next we hear of him is an appearance at the Merchants

Court in January 1642 where 'great complaints were [laid] against him in regard of living with Michall Dawson, a stranger, not free of this Company.' It seems likely, however, that this was the Michael Dawson who had married Eleanor Sherwood, one of William's daughters, in 1629, in which case Blackett had not been turned out of his deceased master's extended family. Dawson not being a merchant adventurer was, of course, a problem and nearly two years had passed since William Sherwood's death, technically two lost apprenticeship years. Under company rules, if a master died an apprentice had 40 days to find a new one or risk being asked to start his entire term again. However, that court appearance in January 1642 wasn't a case of the 20-year-old Blackett being hauled before the company governor and wardens to account for his sins but rather by his own petition, seeking to be 'set over' to a new master after all that time. Though not recorded in the minutes, he doubtless made the point that no meetings of the Court had been held for the entire year of the Scottish occupation. He must have made a compelling case for the court 'did condiscend to his request, out of their special respect to the younge Mans Condition, not intending to make it a p[rec]ident, & he was accordingly sett over to ... Joane Carr to serve forth the residew of his terme'.[34] Whatever William had been doing during the preceding 21 months he did not have the time added to his term, still less have to wind the clock back nearly six years, and he had been granted his request to become Joan Carr's apprentice. Who was this lady who salvaged young William's apprenticeship?

Crucially, of course, she was a merchant adventurer, 'a sister of this Company'. According to the list of 120 company members assessed for the January 1643 'loan' to the royalist garrison, nine were women. As a proportion of the total membership they hardly challenged male domination of commercial life and its institutions and they were probably all widows of deceased freemen, but their presence corrects any notion that women were utterly excluded from trading on their own account. Elizabeth Kirkley had been a widow for over 20 years, and Joan Carr's husband Ralph had died in 1635 so these two at least had continued in business for several years without needing a male head of household.

Joan Morpeth had married merchant adventurer Ralph Carr at All Saints in Newcastle in 1617. They had two daughters, and lived at the foot of The Side, near Cale Cross at the opposite end of Sandhill from the Guildhall (see Plate 2). Carr's probate inventory taken in January 1635 contains a particularly detailed list of his business stock and debts showing that he dealt mainly in flax, tow and hemp, raw materials from the Low Countries and Baltic for marine sails and rope. He also traded oats, rye and barrels of salted herring and cod. Just under half of the debts owed to Carr were for small amounts from a large number of customers so he was evidently running a local retail business, as well as selling goods in larger quantities, including to overseas markets. The £100 owed to him from Amsterdam is likely to have been for cloth. His inventory does not reveal a comfortable state of affairs. 40% of the debts owed to him were declared to be 'desperate' by the appraisers of his inventory. Setting those to one side his shop stock and 'good' debts added up to £1,474 in total assets, against which his widow faced a liabilities of £1,832 owed to his suppliers at home and abroad, together with £55 to pay for his funeral. It is possible that he had goods purchased overseas waiting to be brought back to England, as yet unknown to his appraisers, but on the face of it the shortfall of £413 between liabilities and secure assets was not covered by the valuation of his personal household goods of £276.[35]

Joan had work to do, creditors to keep at bay, goods to sell, debts to collect. Both of her late husband's apprentices were 'set over' to her soon after his death, one of whom, Robert White, was already five years through his term. Still living on The Side in the 1640s and assessed for the 1643 'loan' in the middle rank of the merchants, Joan Carr clearly survived and the business recovered, weathering the storm of the trade blockade and Scottish siege of 1643-4. A dispute with fellow merchant John Emerson in 1648 over a consignment of imported rye also shows her to have been dealing in some at least of the same commodities as her husband 15 years earlier. She was probably also still concerned in overseas trade, for it seems her apprentice White had been in Rotterdam. She died in 1649 and left the house at the foot of The Side, and other property outside the town walls, to her married daughters.[36]

Taking on William Blackett in January 1642 must have suited her as much as it did him. Because of the hiatus in Merchant Adventurers' court meetings during the Scottish occupation, Robert White could only have taken his freedom towards the end of

1641, after which the free labour of an additional apprentice moving into the house near Cale Cross would presumably be welcome. This was part of the deal. Masters or mistresses received a binding fee (though it is unclear if a proportion was always passed on to a second master), and - hopefully - an increasingly capable yet cheap servant, effectively an intern, for the duration of his term. To some extent merchant apprenticeship was, of course, a cost of restrictive practices, a 'rent' to be paid to become an insider, but plenty of capable young men came forward with families willing to pay. In return apprentices were meant to obtain a 'hands-on' business education, experience, useful contacts for the future, and the ultimate prize of acceptance within the company's monopoly as a freeman, and a licence to trade.

There is no record of Blackett being hauled up for trading on his own account while still apprenticed to either of his masters, but it is not entirely surprising that he petitioned for his freedom in late June 1645, nearly a year early.[37] Since 1636 he had probably obtained experience of coal mining and fitting from William Sherwood, and the Dutch, Scandinavian and Baltic trades from Joan Carr, to add to whatever management basics he picked up in his father's house as a boy. But taking into account the extended gap following Sherwood's death, he was formally under a master for scarcely seven of the normal ten years. Some of that time was surely lost to the devastating plague of 1636. The households he was bound into also had to contend with two Scottish occupations, a trade blockade, political strife, civil war, blockade, siege and military assault. Blackett nevertheless had the self-confidence to find a new master in abnormal circumstances, and to obtain his freedom early. The court heard him out, took his £20 for appearing a year early and admitted the battle-hardened young man to the freedom of the merchants' company.

Chapter 4
Kirkleys and Commonwealth

Capital

A mere 20 days after being admitted to the Company, William Blackett married Elizabeth Kirkley, the daughter of a Newcastle merchant, in July 1645. William was 24, and Elizabeth nearly 28. The wedding must have been the immediate reason for the purchase of his early freedom for apprentices were not allowed to marry. We know nothing of his private thoughts, nothing of the extent of his affection for Elizabeth Kirkley and vice versa. They had nine children, the youngest, Christopher, born when Elizabeth was 41. Six of them survived into adulthood. Whatever the depth of their relationship, however, this must have seemed an advantageous match to the apparently talented but financially constrained young William Blackett. As we have seen in chapter two, it seems unlikely that William's father was able to do more for him and his elder brother Edward than to provide for their apprenticeships.

Having served his turbulent years under Sherwood and Carr, he surely knew the nuts and bolts of a trader's life, how to check, weigh and measure outbound and inbound commodities on the quay, prepare and handle all the paperwork needed for shipping, customs, payment and receipts, and maintain a set of trading accounts. Familiarity with the shipmasters, suppliers of export goods and correspondents in overseas ports used by his masters must have given young Blackett a start in building his own network of contacts. Those correspondents in turn might recognise his name and already have some regard for his ability. He would doubtless already have some useful product and market knowledge, a developing sense of what, where and when to buy and sell, the ability to negotiate deals accordingly and the basics of contract law. However, to set up on his own account, competence was not enough. He also needed capital.

This was not capital in the form of large and indivisible amounts of fixed investment often associated with the creation of tangible assets in mines, factories and machinery. The tangible assets required by a merchant might not extend further than a furnished office, warehouse and cellar and even these were much more likely to be rented than owned. Blackett's need was rather for short-term working capital to cover the mismatch in timing between initial outlays on goods to sell, shipping, customs and other costs and the eventual receipt of payment. Availability of credit eased the cashflow strain but could also complicate it. Merchants expected their suppliers to send them their goods for shipment first and take payment two or three months later. Conversely, the purchasers of the cloth in Hamburg, Koenigsberg or Danzig would expect a similar period of credit from the merchant. This might be largely cancelled out by credit extended, perhaps from the same overseas merchant, for timber, flax or other commodities purchased to bring back to England. On being sold in England the buyer would often expect to be given a further three months or so to settle the bill. Overall, taking into account journey times, it could be more than six months before the merchant actually saw his profit in cash terms. Cycles of credit overlapped as subsequent voyages embarked before the profits from the first journey were cleared, especially in compressed sailing seasons.

The significant problems this created for a new merchant can be illustrated by a hypothetical first voyage. Let's assume that in order to make a living and start accumulating some reserves, young Blackett needed to make a profit of £100 in his first year. The headline difference between the sale price of commodities and their original cost could look spectacular and was often excitedly proclaimed, but when the additional costs of transport, customs, port dues and exchange fees are taken into account net profitability was usually much more humdrum. Grassby quotes examples of 15 to 25% net profit. In 1660, by which time Blackett had been trading for 15 years, he expected no more than 15% profit on cloth sent to Stockholm.[1] In his detailed study of the huge mass of accounts and letters of the London-based Marescoe-David family in the 1660s and 1670s, Roseveare gives examples of net gains from Charles Marescoe's trade between London and European ports in the late 1660s of between 6.5% and 22%.[2] Let's assume that first voyage was successful, yielding a 20% return on turnover. The sale of £500 worth of imported goods would be needed to generate gross profit of £100.

Suppose our new trader started off by buying cloth from a Westmorland supplier for £250 in Newcastle, intending to sell it in Hamburg. As a new merchant without an established reputation, it is likely his supplier will have demanded immediate payment, so the young man will have needed to find that £250 from somewhere else. The goods might wait for a while for a ship from Newcastle and terms had to be agreed with the shipmaster. Again, a new merchant could surely expect to have to pay at least some proportion of the freight costs at this point together with the export customs dues. To keep things simple, let us further assume that once his bales of cloth reached their destination they were quickly sold in return for the purchase of deals or planks which were brought back in the same ship. In the 1670s ships clearing the Tyne for Hamburg typically arrived back after a round trip of five or six weeks. Actual sailing times would vary depending on the prevailing winds, but days or weeks could be spent waiting in ports for cargoes, official clearances and tides.[3] Eventually, however, the planks were landed and sold to shipwrights for £500. The buyers gave bills of exchange or promissory notes for payment after a further three months. If our new merchant bought his cloth in February, was able to ship it in March, received his return cargo by the end of April and sold it promptly, it could still be August before he received his £500 and could clear his prior outgoings of £400. If that £400 had been borrowed in the meantime, the interest owed would have been around £10, making a noticeable dent in that £100 profit.[4] These hypothetical figures accord reasonably well with Grassby's view that an initial investment of £500 was needed to enter foreign trade in the first half of the century.[5]

This assumes all went well on this first venture. Any one of a number of risks could cause serious financial problems. His cloth supplier might sell defective goods, although vigilance at the quayside should guard against this. Shipping remained hazardous in an era when small wooden vessels faced walls of cold grey water in North Sea storms. Piracy and maritime conflict compounded the danger in wartime. In January 1674, during the third Anglo-Dutch War, Ralph Grey lamented the loss, to the north of Tynemouth, of 'twenty Sayle of Shipps besides those that are foundered; pray God send us peace that shipps may not be forced a winter trade'.[6] Maritime insurance was developing to reduce the financial risk of complete loss at the cost of premium and excess. But the impact of delays and losing a good market, or the spoiling of goods while at sea could make the difference between profit and loss.

Price volatility between the decision to buy and the arrival of the goods in a distant market could bring unexpected windfalls or erase any prospect of a profit. If the latter, a decision had to be taken whether to take a loss and sell at the current price or to hold in the hope of better times and thereby incur the cost of storage and tying up working capital for longer. Unless he accompanied his goods, the merchant had to delegate judgement on these matters of timing to his agent in the destination port. Herein lay the possibility of the incautious merchant being defrauded, highlighting the importance of building a network of trusted overseas correspondents over time. And after all these hazards had been navigated there was always the possibility of default by the final buyer. Some or all of that hypothetical £400 laid out might never be recovered.

The description of risks necessarily paints a bleak picture. Probability of occurrence was manageably low overall. If it hadn't been, trade could not have flourished. For an individual merchant the important objective was to achieve a position of scale such that mishaps on any one voyage could be covered by successful outcomes on others. Higher turnover and more voyages increased the working capital burden, however, hence the need for the young merchant to earn enough profit to build up his reserves. As he established a reputation he would have able to buy on credit rather than for cash, effectively borrowing from his suppliers to reduce the capital strain imposed by the time spent by goods in ship's holds and warehouses and in waiting for payment from purchasers. But real money was needed to underpin this precarious structure. Reputation was everything. Should a merchant be unable to repay what he borrowed on credit from his supplier, be unable to honour his bill of exchange, his 'IOU', word would soon spread, and his ability to borrow again would be severely damaged. Thus, if let down through any of the hazards of trade described above, it was important that he had sufficient cash reserves to draw upon, his 'core stock', to honour his own obligations. As Defoe put it, 'a man that can pay his own debts, whether other people pay him or no, that man is out of the question; he is past danger, and cannot be hurt: But if he trusts beyond the extent of his stock and credit, even HE may be overthrown too'.[7]

How much stock was needed in proportion to turnover? Across the English economy as a whole, statistician Gregory King assumed in the 1680s that £1 million of capital financed £3 million of goods in circulation. A similar ratio can be observed in the accounts of the Marescoes, established merchants engaged in European trade, but others might be more cautious.[8] Thus, while the establishment of a reputation might enable the new merchant to exploit the market for credit, his underlying cash reserves needed to be built up as a cushion against the inevitable buffeting of fluctuating trading fortunes.

What of the sources of capital for the new merchant? Where was that first £400 to come from? Those with family wealth behind them were clearly in a strong position, able to go beyond the cost of providing their sons with an apprenticeship to the usually more substantial cost of setting up in business. For everyone else, this was often too formidable a barrier to overcome. Only 22% of apprentices within the Gateshead merchants' company in the 1680s went on to take on apprentices of their own in due course, probably a good indication of established mercantile careers.[9] Applying this approach to the Newcastle apprenticeship registers for the longer and earlier period between 1625 and 1664, the years within which Blackett started his career, reveals a broadly similar pattern (see Table 4.1).

485 young men commenced apprenticeships between those years, but little over half of them are known to have been granted their freedom as merchants. Only 27% of the 485 took on apprentices of their own in due course, or just over half of those who had been granted their company freedom. It was far from easy to set up as a merchant, even for those who completed their apprenticeship. However, breaking down the figures by family background shows that this cannot be completely explained as the rich pro-

Kirkleys and Commonwealth

Table 4.1. Newcastle Merchant Adventurers apprentices 1625-64.

	Total	Admitted as merchants, and as % of (1)		Took on apprentices, and as % of (1)		(4) as % of (2)
	(1)	(2)	(3)	(4)	(5)	(6)
Total	485	260	54%	132	27%	51%
Sons of						
Yeomen	107	58	54%	32	30%	55%
Craftsmen	74	47	64%	26	35%	55%
Professionals	29	13	45%	7	24%	54%
Gentlemen	234	118	50%	54	23%	46%
Merchant	26	16	62%	8	31%	50%
Not stated	15	8	53%	5	33%	63%
By patrimony		94		44		47%

Source: MA Records-2, pp. 244-292

gressing while the modest were starved of the capital needed. Instead, a more interesting pattern emerges.

A higher proportion of the sons of fathers giving their occupation as yeomen or craftsmen eventually took on apprentices of their own – 30% and 35% respectively - than the sons of those in the professions and gentlemen - 24% and 23%. Some care is needed here for 'yeomen' probably included some prosperous farmers in Newcastle's hinterland, and some of the craft occupations could reflect privileged membership of other town guilds rather than actual practice of the trade. Nevertheless, it is striking that even those of a mercantile background, whether starting as apprentices or admitted by patrimony, did not score more highly in comparison. The overall ratio was held down to 27% not by the inability of yeomen's sons to progress as merchants, but by the sons of lawyers and gentlemen. Of those admitted as merchants, a higher proportion from yeomen and craftsmen families later took on apprentices of their own (55%) than did those from a Newcastle merchant adventurer's own family (47%). Relatively speaking it suggests that gentlemen's sons, even merchants' sons, were prone to dabble with the idea of apprenticeship and a merchant's life, whereas more of the capable sons from humbler backgrounds seized their one opportunity for a better life and stuck at it. And they evidently surmounted the capital barrier.

Something interesting was going on in the commercial and institutional environment of Newcastle during the middle decades of the 17th century, whatever the scars inflicted by plague, civil war, invasion and blockade. Explaining it fully awaits a more comprehensive study of the paths taken by those 58 sons of yeomen and craftsmen who later took on their own Newcastle merchant apprentices. Some might have been able to take advantage of a few charitable bequests by deceased merchants of interest-free loans to young freemen, but these were for £100 or less, and security had to be provided, which was not always available to new traders.[10] More are likely to have been given their start by masters or employers evidently impressed by their ability and in need of additional talent to expand their own businesses. William Cotesworth, the capable son of a humble Teesdale farmer, was taken into partnership by the widow of his Gateshead master, having to find just £20 as his contribution to a partnership capital of £600. He married into the family nine years later.[11] William Blackett trod a similar path, but not through either of the families of his erstwhile masters.

The Kirkleys

The Kirkleys lived across the road from Joan Carr on Newcastle's steep and busy main thoroughfare, The Side. They gave Blackett his start in business, but not through the instant provision of a handsome capital dowry brought by his new wife. Elizabeth, the youngest of seven children, can hardly have remembered her father, for he had died in 1621 when she was three. Michael Kirkley was a merchant adventurer who prospered from the Baltic rye and flax trade to judge by his will and inventory.[12] He left each of his surviving six children £200 on either marriage or on reaching their full age, a respectable but not head-turning sum to a prospective

Figure 4.1 The Kirkleys of Newcastle

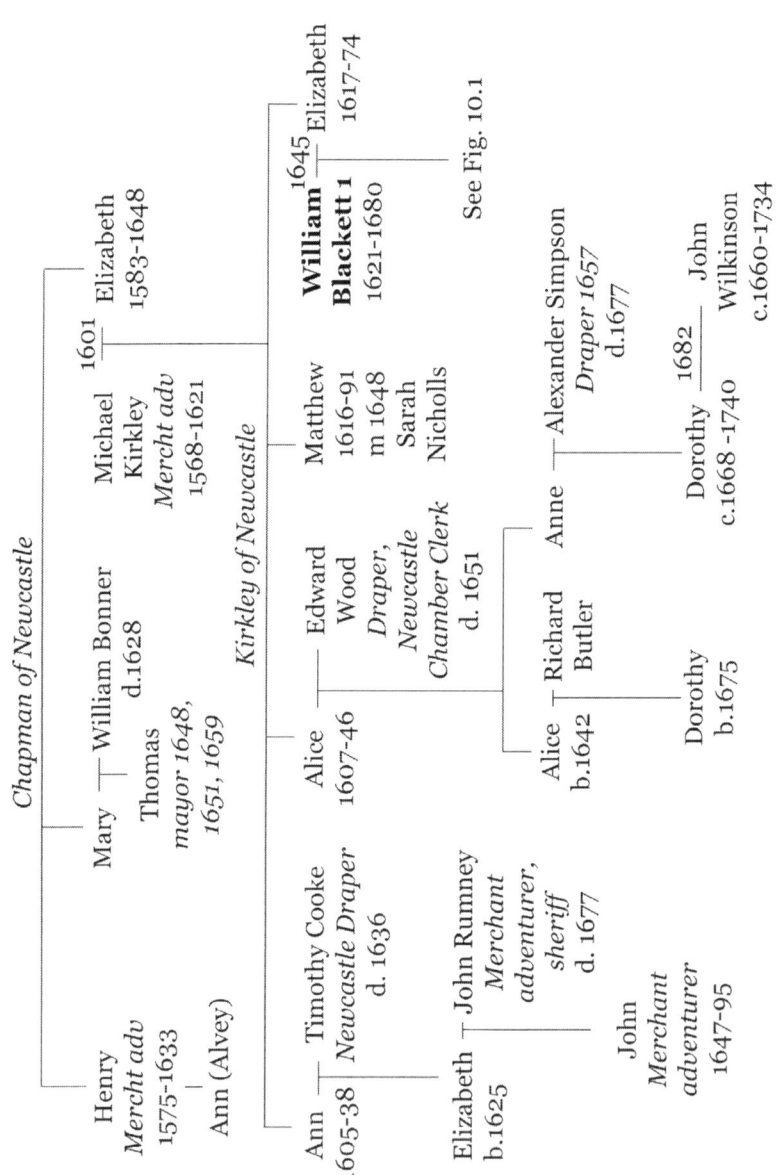

Further detail is provided in Appendix 6, Table A6.2

merchant husband. Michael's widow was the Elizabeth Kirkley mentioned in the last chapter who carried on the business for decades afterwards on her own account.

Widow Kirkley was also from a trading background, the daughter of merchant adventurer Matthew Chapman. Her rich uncle Henry was one of the Tudor coal-owning grand lessees and hostmen.[13] In the 1630s Elizabeth was dealing in raisins, almonds and indigo, commodities listed in court cases brought against her in London by metropolitan suppliers chasing her for payment for what she claimed were defective shipments. Despite being illiterate - her son Matthew read incoming letters to her - Elizabeth seems to have flourished as a trader. She was assessed at 8s in the 1621 Lay Subsidy, placing her in the middle ranks of the 82 Newcastle residents named.[14] In January 1643 her contribution to the merchants' company's 'loan' to the royalist garrison, assessed at £8, was more than twice the average levy, placing her in the top 12% of members.[15]

Domestic life was more harrowing. Three of Elizabeth's offspring had died as children. Her eldest daughter was Ann, whose husband Timothy Cooke, a draper, perished in the 1636 plague along with at least two of their children. Ann too died as a widow in 1638, leaving a further four young children to the care of her mother.[16] The searing family impact of that plague year might explain the otherwise curious location for Elizabeth's youngest daughter's marriage to William Blackett in the summer of 1645 – back in William's parents' parish of Hamsterley, rather than in Newcastle's All Saints church. Plague had once again spread rapidly up through the town from Sandgate since May and at the time no-one could have known that it would prove any less devastating than the 1636 epidemic.[17] The remote County Durham countryside must have been comparatively attractive that summer. William's apprenticeship thus both started and finished with bubonic plague on the loose in the narrow streets of Newcastle.

Just a year after William's marriage, his wife's only surviving sister also died. In 1631 Alice Kirkley had married Edward Wood, another draper, and she left him with at least five young children in 1646. Elizabeth the mother was, therefore, survived by just two of her seven children, the youngest: Matthew and Elizabeth. It seems she had increasingly depended on them to help run the business. Two apprentices had been set over to her in the 1620s, but the company registers do not show that any were taken on to replace them in the 1630s. Her unmarried son Matthew was admitted as a merchant adventurer by patrimony in February 1643 at the age of 27, and daughter Elizabeth also remained at home rather than leaving to get married with her father's £200 as soon as she was 'of age'. It looks as though her mother was calling the shots, waiting for an impressive enough commercially-minded man who could be persuaded to work for the Kirkley business. This much is revealed in her will of May 1648.[18] It also gives some insight into the force of her personality.

Although daughter Elizabeth had been entitled to her father's £200 either at marriage or when she came of full age, according to his will of 1621, it was bequeathed again by her mother in 1648, six years after the younger Elizabeth had reached 'full age' and three years after her marriage to William. Even then it was to be paid in two instalments six months and a year after her mother's death, but sweetened by an additional £100 to be paid a year after that. Young Elizabeth still lived in the family home on The Side, for her mother's 'mynde is that William Blackett my sonne in lawe shall remayne within my now dwelling house for ... twelve months next after my death in as large a manner as he hathe enjoyed the same.' The house itself was given to son Matthew but under its roof the young couple were bringing up their first two children, each left £5 by their grandmother. Any residual doubts that William Blackett was effectively his mother-in-law's live-in employee, or at best a very junior partner, are surely dispelled by the fact that Thomas Glover, formally Blackett's merchant apprentice since February 1647, was described by Elizabeth Kirkley as her servant.[19]

We can see the shape of a deal here. In 1645 Elizabeth Kirkley obtained the services of a young man whose commercial aptitude was surely already evident as an apprentice. He was taken on either as a paid employee or as a prospective partner bound through marriage to the family concern. He probably came to her attention as Joan Carr's apprentice across the road. Mrs Carr's views are unknown, but she too was by then fairly old. Her two daughters were already married to other merchants. One of Joan's son-in-laws, Samuel Rawling, exchanged apprentices with William Blackett in the summer of 1647, when William was almost certainly still acting as his mother-in-law's proxy.[20] This is unlikely to have happened had a rift opened up between Elizabeth and Joan over Joan's erstwhile apprentice being poached by her near neighbour. What about William Blackett's side of the arrangement? For a man of his limited means this was a pragmatic route into a merchant's career. It gave him access to an existing trading stock and credit arrangements, a wife familiar with mercantile life and a network of local and overseas contacts. His mother-in-law was 62 at the time of his marriage. In view of her age perhaps he calculated it was worth biting his tongue over that £200 his wife had long been owed, especially with the extra £100 being dangled in front of them after she died. As it turned out he had just three years to wait.

There remains the question of why he took his freedom early. William had a year of his apprenticeship to run in 1645. It looks as though his future wife wasn't going anywhere her mother didn't want her to. Why not wait until the following year and save the £20 fee to the merchants' company – enough for a young man to live on for a year? The most logical answer lies in the improvement in trading conditions. Civil war, siege and blockade had left their mark in the shipping movements in and out of the river. The number of ships clearing from Newcastle show that traffic more or less dried up between early 1643 and late 1644 (see Figure 4.2). No accounts were kept between July and November that year in the chaos of the final months of the siege but matters improved swiftly after the Royalist defeat. More ships cleared in December 1644 alone (121) than in the 18 months prior to the siege being lifted and the pace quickened rapidly in the spring of 1645. Here was a tide to be taken at the flood. Now was the time for Elizabeth Kirkley to reinvigorate her business with new blood and the opportunity for William Blackett to embark on the road to fortune. It was also a road that led to early civic responsibilities, an important facet of his career.

Figure 4.2. Newcastle trading activity 1642-5.

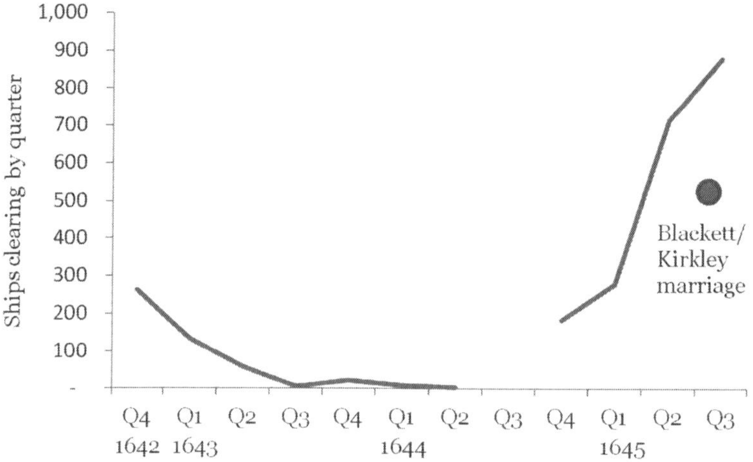

Sources: TWAM MD.NC/FN/1/1/14, Appendix 1.

Civic Life under the Commonwealth

Previous accounts of Blackett have concluded that he was a quiet royalist, mainly on the grounds that he flourished in business and political life during the years after the restoration of the monarchy in 1660. This new study takes a different view. There are indications that he was quite closely involved in the new Parliamentary and Presbyterian regime in Newcastle from the outset, probably under the influence of his Kirkley in-laws.

We saw in the last chapter that the lifting of the siege and the rout of the royalists saw the return of the supporters of Parliament. They began taking control of the town's principal offices in the winter following the ending of the siege in October 1644 and the re-opening of the coal trade. Legitimacy was conferred through a Parliamentary ordinance for the town's government the following May, this degree of national attention confirming Newcastle's continued strategic importance. Because of London's reliance on the need to re-establish a secure supply of Tyneside coal, Parliament had to moderate any temptation for local vengeance to overthrow the traditional coal owners completely. Consequently, Leonard Carr and Robert Shafto were retained from the royalist regime alongside the readmittance of older Parliamentary supporters such as Henry Warmouth, Robert Ellison and John Blakiston and new men including Henry Dawson and Thomas Bonner. Rather than replace the merchant and hostmen's companies, members of the new regime joined them.[21] The basic institutional structure of Newcastle's civic life continued, albeit in largely new hands, and with it the primacy of promoting the town's business and trade, but it was subject to closer external control. The Scottish army remained until paid off in February 1647 but was immediately replaced by a series of military governors of the town, appointed from London, well into the 1650s. As one of them, Sir Arthur Haselrig, put it in 1649, 'there is no part of the commonwealth that more concerns the state to keep from distemper than the north'.[22]

The close link between town's Parliament-supporting municipal leaders and the Presbyterian church is illustrated by the Common Council's deliberations over the appointment of suitably 'well affected' ministers to the four parish churches in 1646. With the abolition of the church diocesan hierarchy, Parliament issued instructions for the appointment of 'elders' and this was complied with at Newcastle that year.[23] The close relationship between civic power and Puritan ideals under the Commonwealth can still be seen at Sandhill. An illuminating survey of the decorative woodwork adorning the merchant houses across from the Guildhall, itself rebuilt by the confident puritan elite in the mid-1650s, identifies it as part of a co-ordinated plan of architectural work fired by religious zeal and the profits of commerce. The long runs of casemented windows mimicked Solomon's house in the Geneva Bible. From their upstairs bays the town's morals could be watched over in Newcastle's central public space. The 'rod and staff' detailing on the pilasters are redolent of puritan ideals.[24] Here still are echoes of civic pride and mercantile confidence taken to an austere spiritual plane transcending the commerce of street and quay. The stern observers of the 1650s would surely have been appalled by the late-night revelry on their ground floors and spilling out into the street today.

Stern indeed were the clerical and lay guardians of public morality under the new regime. The common council helped bring in a frenzy of witch-hunting in 1649, culminating in trials and executions in the following winter and spring. Blasphemy, drunken behaviour and 'idle living' were pursued with severity, and actors were whipped.²⁵ This was the time in the late 1640s and 1650s when many merchant apprentices were hauled before their guild's court for offences regarding 'hayre and apparell'. The need for commercial pragmatism might have required the inclusion of some experienced hands in the governance of the town, but it is as if any suspicions this raised in the more fundamentalist victors were deflected by allowing them a free hand against errant townsfolk who failed to meet their puritanical ideals.

In this climate a new merchant might have decided to lie low, focus on doing his mother-in-law's bidding and build his own trade and reputation. However, William Blackett was closely linked to members of the new regime. As we saw earlier, he lived for a while in the house of Michael Dawson, son-in-law of Blackett's late master William Sherwood. Dawson was quite possibly a brother of Henry Dawson, the Presbyterian mayor in 1646 and close ally of Thomas Bonner, mayor in 1648. Another Sherwood daughter married Puritan merchant William Johnson, whose own daughter's later marriage to Thomas Bonner's son cemented an alliance which saw Johnson be mayor of Newcastle for two years from 1653. Johnson and Blackett were part of a merchants' company delegation sent to London in 1657 to lobby for the company's rights.²⁶

The Dawson-Bonner clique dominated civic power throughout the interregnum, the years of Parliamentary/ 'commonwealth' control and Cromwell's 'protectorate', and profited personally. Bonner was the cousin of Blackett's wife Elizabeth (see Figure 4.1). Her brother-in-law Edward Wood had been appointed alongside Dawson and Bonner in December 1644 to the local sequestration committee, which dealt with estates confiscated from the defeated Royalists. Under the Parliamentary settlement for Newcastle's government in May 1645, Wood was made clerk of the town chamber, effectively the treasurer, and obtained a £40 increase in his annual salary 'over and above what former Clerks of the Chamber had and enjoyed, because at that Tyme the Towne was newly reduced, and his paynes extraordinary in settling the unsettled affaires of the Chamber occasioned by the storming of the Towne'.²⁷ Blackett therefore married into a family close to powerful and zealous men at the very time they were being installed in the town's leadership.

As far as religious leanings are concerned, there is no expressly devout phrasing in Elizabeth Kirkley's will of 1648 to mark her out as a puritan, but she, surely, selected the ardently religious Ambrose Barnes as her son-in-law Blackett's apprentice in 1646. Her son-in-law Wood was certainly a fervent puritan. His will of 1650 entrusted his soul to his saviour and redeemer in the expectation that he would enter the Lord's kingdom alongside 'all his elect children'.[28] Blackett's puritan step-uncle George Lilburne was master of all he surveyed in Sunderland. Lilburne's nephew Robert, a general in the Parliamentary army, was installed as military governor of Newcastle for the best part of a year between 1647 and 1648.

This might simply have been family circumstance. A young man in Blackett's position can hardly be blamed for taking the opportunity the Kirkleys offered to launch his business career, not to mention the potential value of their connections to the new powers in the town. There are no obvious clues to Blackett's own religious views, other than that, many decades later, an unobjectionably orthodox Anglican was asked to give the address at his funeral in 1680.[29] The puritan Barnes was quickly exchanged for George Carter, but it strains credibility to believe this was because of doctrinal differences between master and apprentice. In any case, with Elizabeth Kirkley still alive, Blackett was unlikely to have made that decision.

Nevertheless, there are signs of more active involvement by Blackett in Newcastle's new regime. According to Barnes' memorialist, 'when the Scots had surrendered the King upon articles, and Major General Skippon [of the English army] carried down the money in specie to the Scottish army, Mr. Barnes, being an apprentice, was ordered by his master to be one of the Tellers'.[30] Blackett was still Barnes' master when the Scots were paid off in February 1647. £200,000 in cash had to be counted in Newcastle, a 50% down-payment of the full sum promised by Parliament for the Scots to withdraw and hand over the King after nine months' captivity in some style in Greyfriars.[31] Newcastle's chamber clerk, Edward Wood, must have been central to the transaction so it seems he recruited his highly numerate young brother-in-law Blackett to help oversee proceedings, under the watchful scrutiny of the outgoing and incoming Scottish and English generals. Two months later William Blackett was elected a 'church officer', a term used by puritans, at his parish church of All Saints, making him an active participant in the new Presbyterian regime of church government.[32] Wood was a leading parishioner at All Saints.

In October 1648 Blackett was elected to the town's Common Council.[33] He was one of the 'Twenty-Four' ostensibly selected by the town's guilds but effectively appointed by the mayor, sheriff and aldermen, firmly under the control of the Dawsons and Bonners. Blackett must therefore have been seen as competent and 'well affected' by the new regime, a young man who could be relied upon. Cousin Thomas Bonner was the new mayor that autumn and Ralph Jenison, nephew of the puritan preacher, his sheriff. Bonner's accession was not universally welcomed. On the way home from his election, there was a minor riot, Bonner was attacked and stones were thrown at his Sandhill home.[34] Although much of the corporation's business was taken up with the mundane issuing of leases and granting of minor petitions, Blackett was joining an already strongly partisan body. He was surely among those present at a sumptuous dinner given to Oliver Cromwell by the new mayor in the Guildhall that October. He sat on the council alongside Alderman John Blakiston MP, one of the Parliamentarians who sentenced the King to death. He was present at the common council meeting in March 1649 that promised action against the witches.

However, we might still wonder how committed Blackett was to the cause. Although present at the relevant council meetings he was not amongst those who signed orders by the council to disenfranchise several freemen in April for alleged earlier military assistance to the Royal cause, or to reward Newcastle's military governor Sir Arthur Haselrig in September with honorary freedom.[35] He missed four council meetings between May and August and stood down in October 1649 after just one year, to be replaced by his brother-in-law Matthew Kirkley. Perhaps it was all too highly charged. The return of stable government, locally and nationally, was surely welcome after the traumas of the civil war, but there might have been just too much rejoicing for comfort around the council table at the execution of the King in January 1649. It could always be, however, that Blackett simply made a practical decision to stand back from active engagement in the highly-charged politics of the town for, as we shall see in the next chapter, he was busy in these years building his trading business.

Chapter 5

Merchant and Trader

Newcastle's Trade 1645-60

The start of William Blackett's business career co-incided with the dramatic recovery of Newcastle's trade in 1645 and his marriage into the Kirkley family. As we now examine William Blackett's rise as a merchant it's helpful to look beyond that initial recovery to seek a broader view of Newcastle's trading activity during the next 15 years. These were the years of the Presbyterian ascendancy in Newcastle politics, between the end of the siege and the restoration of the monarchy. Did William rise to material comfort in a benign period of commercial expansion or have to struggle against more of the disruption which marked his apprenticeship?

The surviving evidence is mixed. Newcastle was secured for Parliament but there were still distractions. The Scottish army occupied the town until early 1647. Royalists in Northumberland and County Durham plotted against Parliamentarian control of Newcastle, including unsuccessful revolts in 1648 at Tynemouth Castle and more widely in 1655.[1] There were further plague outbreaks in Newcastle in 1647 and 1651, although on a much smaller scale than in 1636. The first Anglo-Dutch war greatly increased the hazards to commercial shipping between July 1652 and April 1654. This was an entirely maritime conflict caused by disputes over trade and featured piracy between armed merchant ships as well as set-piece naval battles. Cromwell's general Monck summed it up bluntly and depressingly enough: 'The Dutch have too much trade, and the English are resolved to take it from them'.[2] English victory certainly removed a great deal of Dutch rivalry on the seas in the following years but there were two further wars in subsequent decades.

On the other hand, such information that can be gleaned on the level of shipping activity to and from Tyneside shows that the recovery seen in 1645 was sustained thereafter (see Figure 5.1). This all suggests that the recovery of trade in 1645 continued into the 1650s although there was a noticeable decline during the first Anglo-Dutch War which clearly affected the coal trade along the

English east coast as well as overseas shipping. New merchant apprentice numbers broadly follow these trends. From very low levels in 1642-4 there was a surge in new apprentices between 1645 and 1647 before falling back a little until 1651. Very few commenced apprenticeships in 1652 and 1653, but numbers recovered again thereafter.

Figure 5.1. Annual shipping movements Newcastle 1635-61

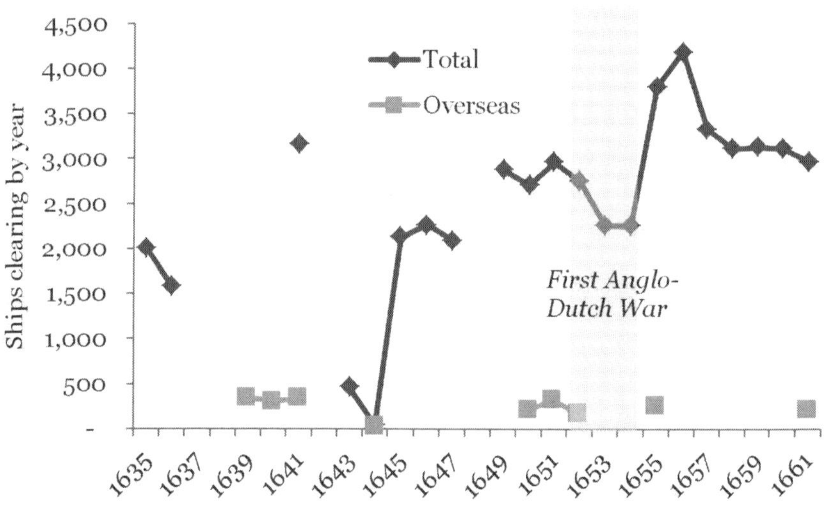

Sources and discussion: Appendix 1.4

For overseas shipping, there are few years in which traffic can be isolated from the coastal figures but it is clear that the volume of traffic was dominated by coastal vessels. In value terms, however, coal was bulky but cheap. It typically cost 15p/ton as it moved from keel to ship, but even if valued at the price fetched in London of approximately £1, a 180 ton cargo was worth £180 – but most of the average return cargo was worthless ballast. On the other hand, a typical consignment of 100 kersey cloths from Newcastle in the 1650s might, conservatively, sell for £500 and a return cargo of rye and flax could be worth over £1,000. So, while there were ten coastal journeys for each one to overseas destinations, it is likely that in value terms Newcastle's overseas trade was worth nearly as much as the coastal trade.[3]

The number of overseas voyages in and out of Newcastle does not appear to have grown during the Commonwealth period (see Figure 5.1). Where estimates can be made, they show around 200 sailings per year, with some higher and some lower totals (see Appendix 1.4). The number of Newcastle passages through the narrow bottleneck of the Sound between Copenhagen and Malmo also shows no growth in this period. Amsterdam and Hamburg probably remained the most important destinations from Newcastle, destinations that lay to the west of the Sound, for the Sound toll passages seem to have accounted for no more than between 10% and 20% of all overseas voyages from the Tyne. Ship capacity might have increased, as it appears to have done in the colliers, but there is no direct evidence of this in the overseas trade, nor for a change in the mix of commodities imported and exported.[4] The best we can say is that the number of overseas trade voyages from Newcastle remained roughly constant during the period as a whole. It might, however, be characterised as stability rather than stagnation. The town's leaders certainly had the confidence to rebuild their Guildhall, Exchange and council chamber overlooking the quayside in the later 1650s to create their own version of the civic magnificence greeting ships in Amsterdam and Hamburg (see Plate 10).[5]

Blackett the Trader

This is the context for the first 15 years of William Blackett's business career. Conditions were reasonably benign compared to the turbulent times of his apprenticeship, but stable rather than spectacular. That he prospered is in little doubt. As we shall see later, by 1660 Blackett was able to invest over £2,000 in mining and still have nearly £1,000 in working capital supporting his trading concern. He probably had a house on The Close, and was soon to have a second. Clearly well-regarded by his fellow Newcastle merchants, he had been to London in 1656 as part of a small delegation to lobby for the rights of the Newcastle Merchant Adventurers. His progress cannot, however, be tracked with any precision in terms of the exact export and import merchandise handled, the ports he dealt with, the extent of his involvement in the domestic coastal trade, or the volume of his trade and its profitability. We can however, draw useful inferences about his life in these years from a variety of other sources.

Domestically the young couple appear to have adhered to the provision in Elizabeth Kirkley's will for them to remain in her house in The Side for a year after her death. Their first three children, Elizabeth, William and Isabel, were baptised in All Saints church, the last named in August 1648. The christening of their fourth child, Edward, took place in St Nicholas' in October 1649, indicating a move before that date. It was a large parish. By the early 1660s Blackett owned two substantial houses within it on The Close. The larger of them was at the very end of the Tyne Bridge, on the western or upstream side. Oliver's detailed map of Newcastle shows it as separate properties by 1830, with river and street frontages. It was assessed on eight hearths in 1664. An inventory of its contents in 1683 at the death of its occupant Michael Blackett, William I's second son, shows five spacious chambers, some identified by their colours: red, green and yellow, and a hall with room for two dozen chairs and hung with pictures, maps and gilded red leather hangings. There was an equally large dining room, kitchen and other rooms. At least six storeys of storage lofts in the gable end can also be seen in an image of the new Tyne Bridge in the 1780s.[6] Here was the family home and the headquarters of the growing Blackett business until the mid-1670s, a few steps from the Exchange and Guildhall, with a view eastwards across the bridge approach onto the quayside and direct access for cargoes to be winched from keels and wherries into the riverside lofts (see Plate 3).

Blackett's other, smaller, house was further west along The Close and also faced the river. Since it was purchased between 1660 and 1665, by which time Blackett was already in Bridge End, it seems to have been bought afterwards - from William Bonner, Elizabeth Kirkley's nephew - for additional storage and office space.[7] Unlikely though it might be that Blackett moved straight to the large Bridge End house as early as 1649, we cannot rule this out and it is possibly relevant that by 1653 he was renting 'cellars and lofts' almost directly opposite, west of the Castle Stairs.[8] He probably needed a large enough house to accommodate not only a growing family and trade goods but also a rising number of apprentices. His brisk recruitment of them shows his ambition, rapid business development and his gaming of the system.

A master was allowed up to three apprentices at a time under merchants' company rules, as long as the second was taken on after the first had completed three years of his service. A third was allowed after the first had served eight years and the second at least five. In practice, the company allowed some masters to take extra apprentices more quickly and sometimes to exceed the maximum of three, on payment of a fee (dressed up as a fine).[9] Part of the growth in apprentice numbers from 1645 as markets opened up is accounted for by some long-established traders, such as Robert Ellison, Christopher Nicholson and Mark Milbank, taking on additional apprentices in this way. William Blackett, on the other hand, was a young newcomer.

The picture is complicated while his mother-in-law was alive. At least as far as Thomas Glover was concerned, Elizabeth Kirkley was calling the shots, even if it was Blackett's name in the company's enrolment register. Taking on Ambrose Barnes in 1646 might also have been her idea, so too the exchange of him for George Carter with Joan Carr's son-in-law in the summer of 1647. However, while Elizabeth's 'servant' Glover was set over by Blackett to his brother-in-law Matthew Kirkley a few months after Elizabeth's death, George Carter was unambiguously Blackett's apprentice from then on. In December 1648 he also took on Henry Hargrave, even though Carter would not complete his first three years as an apprentice until the following March. To get around this, or at least to try and delay the levying of a fine, it seems Blackett exploited the timing delay between when an indenture between master and apprentice's father was agreed and when the indenture was enrolled and thereafter visible in the company register. Length of service was calculated from the indenture date, not the enrolment date. Hargraves' indenture was not enrolled for nine months, in September 1649, by which time Carter was six months into his fourth year.[10]

By this time Blackett had also taken on a wholly irregular third apprentice, in June 1649. The new boy was his nephew, the eldest son of Blackett's brother Christopher, yet another William Blackett. Fancier footwork was needed this time. The new apprentice's indentures bound him not to William I but, improbably, to

Merchant and Trader | 71

William I's brother Edward, long-term resident of Amsterdam. It was June 1650, a year later, before William I sought to enrol his nephew's indenture, ostensibly on his absent brother's behalf. He would have known full well that the company regarded such non-residence of a master to be 'flatt against our acts'. The court decided, very generously, as a favour to Edward, that William I was 'suffered to take him'. How much Edward actually knew of the arrangement is anyone's guess. On the very same day as this charade, 21 June 1650, the company's court decided to reiterate the rules regarding the taking of multiple apprentices, concluding that 'whereas of late yeares some brethren who were great traders have prevailed with this Companey ... to take apprentices sooner than the tyme limited, it is therefore further ordered that hereafter noe brother be permitted to take any apprentice ... contrary to this acte.' It's clear who they had in mind.[11]

Perhaps it was this incident that lay behind an outburst against Blackett on the quayside in the summer of 1649, when he had those two new unenrolled apprentices on his books in addition to George Carter. John Emerson, according to at least two witnesses, told Blackett that he was 'an interloupeing and giddy headed fellow, sayeing 3 or 4 tymes he lyed in his throate, and that he would not give a jackinapse a reason for what hee did, with many other villifyinge tearmes.' Emerson was 20 years older than Blackett, an established merchant and hostman who had been sheriff in 1639. Yet far from being chastened and cowed, the young independent trader Blackett complained to the company court, petitioning 'for repayre for the abuse he suffered by uncivill and disgracefull tearmes'. The company decided this was 'fineable in high measure', and sent for Emerson, who refused to attend.[12]

Blackett was at it again in the summer of 1655, taking on a fourth apprentice, George Thursby, but not quite getting around to enrolling the indenture until the following March. This was, conveniently, three months after George Carter had been admitted as a freeman, but still slightly short of the eight years Hargrave was meant to have served by then to make Thursby a legitimate third apprentice. Furthermore, Thomas Glover, formally set over to Matthew Kirkley in 1648, might still have been under Blackett's direction. It was Blackett's name that appeared as Glover's master when he was sent to Hamburg in 1656 to obtain his freedom.[13] John

Strother was then set over to Blackett in December 1656 so, including Glover, Blackett effectively had five apprentices in early 1657: Glover, Hargrave, Thursby, Strother and nephew William, now overseas.

Board and lodging had to be provided but, with binding fees coming in, it must have been more cost-effective than paying wages to clerks. More to the point, the numbers show that Blackett rose briskly to a large enough scale of operations to keep three of them busy by the summer of 1649 (four, depending on who was really directing Glover). This was just a year after his mother-in-law's death. The apprentices mostly had similar backgrounds to their master, and perhaps this was deliberate. George Carter's father was a yeoman from Lambton Staithes on the Wear upstream from Sunderland. Henry Hargrave's father was a 'yeoman' of Barrowford in Lancashire when Henry's older brother James was apprenticed in 1646 but a 'clothier' in Henry's indentures of 1648. This might have been mutually advantageous to Blackett and Hargrave senior – the former obtaining a supply of cloth to export on reasonable terms, the latter a secure outlet for his product. Nephew William's capabilities must already have been familiar. Only Glover's background was slightly different, his father's occupation given as clerk, ie. minister, of Startforth just south of the Tees near Barnard Castle. Glover might well have been selected by Elizabeth Kirkley - another Presbyterian perhaps, like Barnes, also from Startforth.

It's doubtful that Blackett ran a business school to improve social mobility as a benevolent act, but his apprentices did later progress to their own successful commercial careers. If there was exploitation there was also opportunity. Carter and Hargrave were amongst other apprentices reported to the Merchants' court in October 1654 for improper trading. Since it is hard to imagine Blackett tolerating much freelancing from his busy servants it seems far more likely that they were exercising commercial judgement on Blackett's behalf with his blessing.[14] Of them all it was only nephew William who never took his freedom as a Newcastle merchant. By the time this would have been permitted, in the summer of 1659, he was active as a merchant in Stockholm. He had been there for at least three years. The timing and destination suggest his uncle was at the forefront of a significant change in the structure of northern European trade.

Sweden was an important source of iron, but until the 1650s very little had been shipped directly to England. Until then the trade was mainly controlled from Amsterdam. However, Dutch losses from the 1652-4 war opened the way for a direct trade of Swedish iron to England. From 750 tons of bar iron in 1652 the Stockholm export trade direct to England reached 3,440 tons in 1659 and approximately 5,700 tons in 1661.[15] By 1656-7 nephew William was a substantial buyer of bar iron from the Momma-Reenstierna company, one of the largest producers in Sweden, surely for his uncle to ship back to England in exchange for cloth. Newcastle master mariner Henry Kirkhouse (a shipmaster close to William I) passed through the Sound en route to Stockholm in May 1657 with a cargo of cloth, woollen stockings and lead, returning in early July with iron and tar. Blackett senior had at least one such voyage under way in 1658, when his cargo of cloth was seized by the Danish King, then at war with Sweden.[16] His nephew William is said to have married Maria, the daughter of Andrew Boij or Boig, a long-standing Scottish resident in Stockholm, wealthy iron maker and deputy mayor of Stockholm in the 1660s. It is a match uncle William might well have encouraged. The younger William Blackett was still in Stockholm in April 1669.[17] From the mid-1660s he had been joined there by John Strother, his erstwhile fellow apprentice, and Strother was to remain there as an independent merchant well into the 1680s.[18] Blackett senior was said in later years to have managed Newcastle's iron trade, probably assisted by his protégés placed in Sweden.[19]

Little is known of Blackett's other trading destinations in the 1640s and 1650s. For what it's worth, Brother Edward was in Amsterdam until the outbreak of the Anglo-Dutch War in 1652, while Glover was sent to Hamburg in 1656. The earliest year for which the extent and range of Blackett's overseas trade can be reconstructed is as late as 1661, however (see Table 5.1 below). The Newcastle overseas port book which survives for that year illustrates the geographic range and type of commodities he dealt in during that one year, but it possibly records the minimum level of his trade. Its coverage is restricted to voyages between Newcastle and overseas destinations only.[20] If Blackett bought and sold goods between Newcastle and London, whether through direct bilateral voyages or as part of triangular routes involving, say, Amsterdam or Hamburg they are hidden from us. He had joined the hostmen's company in 1652. This would have allowed him to act as a 'fitter', arranging the shipping and sale of coal on behalf of a coal owner on a commission or for a flat annual fee, or through buying and selling coal on his own account.

Table 5.1. William Blackett's overseas trade through Newcastle, 1661.

Goods	quantity	Approx. value	
Exports		**£3,300**	*Destination*
Cloth	1,200 pieces	£2,400	Amsterdam, Hamburg, Emden, Stockholm, Bordeaux
Lead	44 tons	£620	Amsterdam, Stockholm, Bordeaux
Butter	112 firkins	£95	Holland, Bordeaux
Coal	48 tons	£75	Stockholm, Holland
Stockings	1,400 pairs	£90	Emden, Stockholm
Imports		**£3,600**	*Source*
Wine	74 tuns	£2,250	Bordeaux
Rye	30 tons	£600	Hamburg and Emden
Iron	36 tons	£500	Stockholm
Miscell.	Prunes, tar, deals, whale fins	£240	Bordeaux, Norway, Greenland

Sources: Appendix 1.7. Values rounded

Of the trade we can see in 1661, Blackett's exports were dominated by cloth. This was still the staple of Newcastle's export trade, mainly in the form of cheap northern cottons (actually coarse woollens from the Kendal area), with a smaller number of higher quality northern kerseys and dozens. He also had a share in the rising outwards trade in knitted stockings and, most importantly for the future, lead. Overall, he had cargoes in nine outward overseas voyages from Newcastle that year and nine inwards, but this apparent symmetry does not mean they were straightforward return journeys on the same ship. In fact he had cargo in only one such journey, sending out Kendal cottons, butter and lead to Bordeaux on the *Barbara and Anne* in late August and unloading wine and prunes when it arrived back in early November. All of the others were either on separate outwards or return legs.

Approximate values are given to these transactions in Table 5.1, but these cannot be pushed any further than indicating rough orders of magnitude. Very little price information is available at all, let alone on the difference between English and overseas commodity prices in 1661. Nevertheless, it does seem clear that Blackett's trade balances were lop-sided between different markets, with probable export surpluses to northern European destinations and a net import deficit with Bordeaux. However, even if there were financial imbalances to cover between ports, European credit markets were sophisticated enough to cope. As long as the merchant's credit remained sound, bills of exchange drawn on London, Amsterdam or Hamburg would be accepted by Bordeaux's wine exporters. Edward Blackett, William's older brother, also appears to have engaged in lop-sided overseas traffic from Newcastle. He consigned cargoes of stockings and kersey cloths on seven outwards journeys to Amsterdam, his old home, to the value of around £1,700, but there is no sign of any imports in return. Edward and William's trading activities appear complementary. William had no commodity dealings with Amsterdam apart from a single sailing there in late November, two months after Edward's last shipment, and Edward traded to none of William's other ports. This suggests some co-ordination, if not direct collaboration or partnership.

What, then can we conclude about the position William Blackett had reached as a merchant trader just after the Restoration of Charles II? Without pressing the evidence of a single year's recorded overseas trade to and from Newcastle too far, it is clear that he was engaged in transactions as far afield as Bordeaux and Stockholm. The export of cloth and import of wine were important activities. In 1661 iron imports were not, apparently. The 36 tons he is recorded as having brought into Newcastle were a small fraction of the 800 tons passing westwards through the Sound in Newcastle-registered ships in that year. As far as his income is concerned, the sales value of his imports to England are assumed to represent his final revenue, his export earnings having been used to purchase those imports overseas. If the 15% gross return on trading revenue discussed in chapter 4 is applied to a sales estimate of £3,600, he will have cleared over £500 on that year's overseas ventures alone, plus whatever was earned from coastal shipments.

As a trader with more than 15 years' experience he might well also have taken commission business on behalf of others. Between 1664 and 1667 the London merchant Charles Marescoe's commission income from handling exports and, especially, imports contributed over a quarter of his overall earnings from trade.[21] A man with Blackett's reputation, product and market knowledge could earn over 2.5% of the value of imports sold in England for overseas merchants, more perhaps if he bought the commodity himself from his distant client and then sold it on for a profit in a rising local market. Furthermore, as a hostman from 1652, a reasonable amount of commission income might have been earned from 'fitting' coal, but this too remains unquantifiable.

It does not seem fanciful, therefore, to estimate that Blackett's trading business earned him well over £500 in 1661, more than enough to live on in some style. His family had grown to seven children by this time, aged between two and fifteen. As we shall see, he was also by then engaged in other business concerns and so might well have recently reduced the level of his overseas trading to free up capital to be employed elsewhere. The scale of his trade probably placed him in the middle ranks of Newcastle's merchant community rather than at the forefront. He had been given a start through the existing Kirkley business but, if the evidence of rapid apprentice recruitment is anything to go by, much of the growth took place on Blackett's watch from 1648. It was recognised in Newcastle that he had reached a position of some prosperity in a trading climate that was more steady than spectacular. By 1660 he was a respected member of the town's business and civic elite.

A Return to Municipal Politics

As we saw earlier, Blackett was involved with Newcastle's Parliamentary and Presbyterian regime in the late 1640s, possibly under the influence of his Kirkley in-laws. He returned to the common council in October 1656 at the same time as the prim young puritan Ambrose Barnes. The Dawsons and Bonners were still very much in charge. Their notoriety had achieved greater visibility the year before, with the publication of Ralph Gardiner's *England's Grievance*. Although Gardiner railed against the monopolistic abuses and 'tyrannical power' of the Newcastle corporation in general, he specifically criticised the corruption of Bonner and the Dawsons.[22] Alongside them the military governor Sir Arthur Haselrig had shamelessly acquired lands confiscated from royalists and clerics, not least land and the lead-rich mining rights of Weardale since the abolition of the Bishopric of Durham. Even if, therefore, Blackett's first foray into public life had been heavily influenced by his in-laws in the 1640s, a decade later he was an established merchant in his mid-30s. To return to the council must have been his own decision and made in full awareness of how the town was being run and for whose benefit. Whether or not it was bound up in some way with his lobbying work for the Newcastle merchants' company in London that year is impossible to tell, but his fellow delegate was the puritan William Johnson, who had recently completed two years as mayor.

An illuminating case came before the common council in 1657. Charges were brought against Leonard Carr, by then over 80 years old, an elder statesman of the town who had been an alderman since 1642 and governor of both the hostmen and merchants' company at various times. In Carr's view, as he informed his fellow councillors, Mr. Dawson and Mr. Bonner 'had chosen mayors as they pleased, against the mind of the burgesses'.[23] Despite his great age and infirmity, Carr remained dangerously independent of the Dawson-Bonner clique and so had to go. As if by co-incidence, the Council of State in London promptly accused Carr of collusion with the royalists during the time of their ascendancy in the early 1640s, charges which no-one had felt it necessary to bring against him at any time in the previous 12 years. In January 1658 Carr was dutifully removed as an alderman by the Newcastle corporation and the far more reliable Ambrose Barnes was elected in his place.[24] This was an unusually rapid ascent. Barnes had completed his apprenticeship only three years earlier. Barnes' memoirs coyly say only that 'though there was no objection against his person, yet slight objections were made against his being so young'. He claimed to have attempted modestly to excuse himself, but was chosen 'unanimously'. The whole business was, however, too much for councillor George Blakiston, who resigned in protest at Barnes' election.²⁵ What of Blackett's role in this unsavoury affair? After all, this was the Leonard Carr who, as governor of the merchants' company in 1642, had 'out of their special respect for the younge man's condition' indulged Blackett's request to be set over to Joan Carr (no relation) despite the very long time that had elapsed since the death of his old master William Sherwood. Sixteen years later Blackett was amongst those who signed the order to have Carr removed, and did not follow Blakiston in resigning over Barnes' dubious election as alderman.²⁶

While Blackett does not appear to have been at the forefront of the Newcastle regime during the interregnum, his periodic engagement was clearly not that of a quiet royalist keeping his head down while hoping for happier times. Not that he suffered for it at the Restoration of Charles II. The flexible allegiance glimpsed in Blackett's disturbing indifference to the fate of Leonard Carr was on display much more clearly as commonwealth gave way to monarchy and amply demonstrated by several others too. The Dawson-Bonner clique did, however, lose its hold on the levers of local power and wealth. Bonner gave up the stewardship of the manor of Gateshead and Whickham in September 1659, with its lucrative influence over coal mining, although he did manage one last year as mayor from that autumn, a year that encompassed the return of Charles II. With the eclipse of his patrons, Barnes resigned his controversial aldermancy.²⁷

The limited survival of the municipal calendar and orders between late 1659 and 1661 means that the exact course of Newcastle's Restoration transition is unclear, but it appears to have been managed smoothly enough. It was epitomised by Mark Milbank, a merchant of humble origins who married into the prominent royalist family of Ralph Cocke before the civil war, was sheriff in 1638, but remained on the common council throughout the Interregnum. He was an alderman from 1646 and mayor in 1658. Despite his close association with the Bonner/Dawson regime Milbank allegedly also supplied funds to the exiled king Charles II and was offered a baronetcy in return.²⁸ Milbank would doubtless have rebuffed any charges of being a turncoat by stressing the importance of supporting Newcastle's interest in a stable business environment and a competent continuity of civic order. Ralph Jenison, Robert Ellison, Robert Shaftoe and John Emerson were also visible in the affairs of the town in both the 1650s and the 1660s. In late 1659, when the opposing generals Monck (by now for the King) and Lambert (considering a rearguard action to defend the commonwealth) were on the move, both, pragmatically, were entertained on their way through Newcastle.[29]

Blackett was another who navigated the transition with apparent ease. He declined the role of Bonner's sheriff in October 1659 and left the Common Council, but accepted that role under John Emerson's mayoralty a year later, opting to serve with the man who had accused him of lying in his throat 11 years earlier. It was mistakenly reported to royal officials in London that Blackett had been elected mayor and he was described in the same report as 'a loyal man, much beloved, and fit for the office.' His swift move to join the celebrations of Charles II's coronation in 1660 by giving a £22 tun of wine to run through one of the town's fountains doubtless helped visibly to demonstrate said loyalty. It also happened to promote his French imports.[30] Scarcely a year later, with typical self-confidence, Blackett petitioned the King over that consignment of cloth which had been seized in Denmark in 1658. The King responded by 'earnestly desiring that Mr. Blackett's losses might be fully repaired'.[31] They never were, and the King was hardly committing himself to action, but he could easily have dismissed the petition as coming from a supporter of the now discredited regime. As for the Danish debt itself, Blackett's business was by then set on a different and ultimately far more profitable course.

Chapter 6

Underground Ventures

William Blackett branched out into new ventures in 1659-60 despite much national political uncertainty. Although the civil war had been fought partly to remove the hereditary power of monarchs, Oliver Cromwell was succeeded as Lord Protector by his son Richard in September 1658. Amidst rising tensions between the army and a restored civilian-dominated Parliament, Richard was effectively deposed by Parliament in May 1659. During the summer and autumn the army then prevented Parliament from sitting. Doubtless it was prudent of Newcastle's municipal leaders to entertain the opposing generals Monck and Lambert as they passed through the town the following winter. Monck's arrival in London in January 1660 effectively tilted the country toward the restoration of the monarchy, but it was another three months before the future direction was clear when a newly elected 'Convention Parliament' agreed terms for the King's return in May.

The new ventures Blackett launched during these unstable times were as follows. Firstly, in May 1659 he took a bond from William and George Pearson, who leased lead mining rights in Allendale, underwriting 'certain indentures' of the same date (now missing). Given the context of subsequent transactions it looks as though these indentures gave Blackett a year's sub-lease of part of their lead mining territory. He was evidently pleased with what he found during this exploratory year for in November and December 1660 he paid £1,400 to buy out the remaining nine years of parts of Pearson's mining lease in the Allenheads area of East Allendale.[1]

Secondly, in June 1659 Blackett was granted a 21-year lease of ground at Ouseburn, a small tributary flowing into the Tyne just to the east of Newcastle beyond Sandgate 'with liberty to build a house & other conveniences for lodging his materials and boiling his adventures from Greenland'. This probably concerned the highly noxious processing of whale oil into soap using cheap local coal, the oil either landed from the Arctic in Newcastle, or imported from Holland.[2] Soap was used extensively in the cloth industry and would therefore have been a logical commodity to send back on the packhorses which brought cloth to Newcastle's quayside. There is no other mention of Blackett's Ouseburn works and it is pointless to speculate on them further. What matters here is that it was another new venture and embarked upon at the same time as his quite separate foray into lead mining.

Lastly, he joined with fellow Newcastle merchants Ralph Jenison and William Carr in February 1660 to share in a quarter of Sir Richard Tempest's coal mine known as the Stella Grand Lease, held under a lease from the Bishop of Durham.[3] Stella was on the south bank of the Tyne, two to three miles west of the Whickham mines with which Blackett must have had some familiarity from his days as William Sherwood's apprentice. As far as we know, this stake in Stella was Blackett's first direct involvement in coal mining, despite having been a hostman since 1652.

These are the dates of the legal agreements, the culmination of decisions made and planning undertaken over previous months. They record a hyperactive burst of investment in three different businesses as the Commonwealth period was moving towards an uncertain end in 1659 and must have taken place alongside his existing trading concerns. With the possible exception of the whale oil works on the Ouseburn, this was not mere dabbling. The exploratory lead mining lease in Allendale must have required serious attention underground, at an unknown cost, and led to the commitment of £1,400 before the end of 1660. Few figures survive for the Stella transaction but, as detailed later, Blackett's initial commitment was probably at least £700, possibly more. There is no information on how much it took him to set up his Ouseburn works and fund it for the first year of operation but an allowance of £100-200 is probably reasonable. It would mean that he probably committed somewhere upwards of £2,000 of capital to his new ventures. Since no evidence has survived amongst the various schedules of Blackett deeds to indicate that any mortgages were taken out in these years, it seems that they were funded from retained profits freed up by reducing his trading activity. It is interesting to note that he had also just lost at least £1,600 worth of cloth, seized by the King of Denmark in 1658.[4] Despite this, if his overseas trading revenue was at least £3,600 in 1661, as estimated in the last chapter, then the crude 3:1 ratio of revenue to capital stock also discussed there indicates he probably still had at least £1,200 in underlying working capital to support his overseas ventures, plus an unknown amount for any coastal trade. It is quite possible, therefore, that by the end of 1660 Blackett had twice as much capital invested outside trade than in it, a change made in less than two years. This was decisive and achieved at speed.

As usual with William Blackett, we can observe what was happening but not why. Had he wound up his trading business and directed all his capital into land, a small estate might have produced £200 per year. Quiet country comfort is, however, unlikely to have appealed to the William Blackett who emerges from the account of his career so far and he was still under the age of 40. Aside from it being almost certainly lower than his current annual income, where would be the action, the adventure, the power, the outlet for his energetic self-confidence and ambition? It is equally difficult to imagine him settling for the purchase of a state office, a boring sinecure bringing a regular income taxed from the value created by others.

I believe we can assume that getting rich was part of his motivation. In a rare surviving later letter he observed that a father could take great comfort to 'see that his Endeavours were Seconded with a Blessing from God So far as to leave his children in possession of a Considerable and well acquired Inheritance'.[5] We cannot know what target he had in mind, if any, but the outward trappings of life as a respected merchant and civic leader did not come cheap even in provincial Newcastle. He had four sons and three daughters by 1659, for whom those considerable inheritances would be required one day. The £20,000 which, towards the end of the century, Sir Josiah Child felt was an estate adequate to support a merchant in comfort and status provides one yardstick of success.[6] Blackett was scarcely a sixth of the way to that level at the Restoration.

This is probably the context for his reallocation of capital but how much was it the result of careful investment appraisal and how much sheer opportunism? He committed to lead mining only after a year's trial exploration and his coal investment at Stella was probably also carefully considered. We can say no more about his Ouseburn works but in financial terms it was a minor commitment compared to his mining interests. So whether or not the whale oil venture was opportunistic, there is reason to think the rest was part of a much more deliberate strategy.

It can be dangerous to look back and rationalise decisions based on later results, or to ascribe modern analytical concepts to 17th-century business thinking. However, coalowners already recognised that the intensive mining of productive seams could reduce the capital cost per ton through economies of scale. As Hugh Bird of Newburn pointed out to the Earl of Northumberland in 1616, the 'water charge [ie. drainage cost] is constant, and so will be reduced the more pits that are working'. Daniel Hechstetter, who had Newcastle links, made similar observations regarding his copper mines near Keswick.[7] Newcastle merchant Edward Mann's evidence to an enquiry in the 1650s into the town's monopoly of trade on the Tyne showed a sound grasp of capital investment and depreciation. In complaining about losses suffered at the Winlaton colliery due to the war with Holland in 1653, the lessees had calculated the impact at a unit cost level.[8] Charles Montague took a thorough and analytical approach in the 1690s to deciding on his Gibside colliery investment, waggonway route, staith location and the scale needed for profitability.[9] So while sufficient data rarely survives to allow us to reconstruct the return on capital achieved in 17th-century enterprises it seems clear that at least some of Newcastle's shrewd merchants were calculating it and weighing opportunity against risk in seeking to do better.

Blackett was surely among them. A study of what he did and, just as importantly, didn't do with his capital arguably reveals a pattern with three key features. Expressed here as hypothetical selection criteria, a case can be made that they guided his strategic decision-making for years, starting with that initial burst of activity in 1659-60. I believe Blackett sought to invest where he felt he could:

1. deploy a substantial sum of capital, a significant share of which took the form of fixed assets rather than working capital alone,

2. benefit from profitable market growth or at the very least increase his share of the market and then to

3. lock in the gains to sustain good returns over a period of time.

Combining criteria 1 and 2 generated economies of scale from more intensive use of those fixed assets, and thereby higher returns on investment. Criterion 3 protected the financial benefits which scale could provide. It is worth examining this because Blackett wasn't the only merchant to redeploy profits accumulated from trade into industrial investment. Although we cannot generalise from speculations on the strategy of one individual, they might provide theories to be tested elsewhere. Let's start by considering what he did not do.

Manufacturing Industry and Trade

Aside from that obscure and minor whale oil venture there is no evidence that Blackett took an active role in any of the industries with which he was undoubtedly familiar as a trader. Woollen cloth, knitted stockings, salt and glass featured prominently in outwards shipments from Tyneside. Shipbuilding was a growing activity downstream from Newcastle and relied heavily upon imports of timber, flax, linen and iron. But none of them gave obvious opportunities for scale economies and locking in any gains.

Blackett had been intimately involved in the cloth trade since his apprentice days. That very familiarity, however, must also have made clear the lack of opportunity for a Newcastle merchant to add value to the production process. It was a mature craft-based industry with hand spinning and weaving dispersed across the north. The limited amount of capital needed to replace looms and maintain fulling mills to thicken the cloth was provided by established clothiers in Kendal and elsewhere, whose sons provided connections with Newcastle as apprentice merchants. The market for the heavy coarse woollens produced in the region might have remained quite large in the mid-17th century but it was in long-term decline. This contrasts with the booming markets for west-country serge and perpetuana cloth, in which Exeter merchants took up the strain on working capital created by growth in production in their hinterland. Such supply chain finance often led to the direct employment of once independent craftsmen rather than buying their end product.[10] In Newcastle's hinterland there was limited need for fixed capital (criterion 1, c1), little prospect of growth or control (c2), and therefore no prospect of economies of scale or gains worth locking in, even if that was possible.

Knitted woollen stockings constituted the one growing part of the Newcastle clothing trade in the Restoration years. In 1661 91,000 pairs were shipped out, growing to 200,000 pairs in 1676, by which year they were probably worth more than twice as much as cloth exports. Edward and William Blackett accounted for around a third of Newcastle's 1661 exported stockings.[11] Surprisingly little is presently known of the industry. Although a knitting machine had been invented in Nottinghamshire in the late 16th century its use was apparently mostly confined to the East Midlands until the 18th century, and to the use of silk rather than wool. Some of the hand-knitted stockings despatched from Newcastle probably came from far afield, for there was a growing focus on woollen stocking knitting in the Kendal area and Ralph Grey alluded to his father-in-law buying stockings in Wensleydale in 1676.[12] But it was not an exclusively rural occupation, for Gateshead was said in 1669 to be renowned for the quality of its worsted stockings.[13] So there might have been growth (c2), and this could have drawn in some working capital to finance increasing yarn supplies to domestic workers, but this far-flung and labour-intensive craft is unlikely to have needed much fixed capital (c1).

Salt and glass production, on the other hand, was comparatively hungry for capital for pans and furnaces (c1), and largely concentrated at the mouth of the Tyne and on the Ouseburn. Salt production might reasonably be expected to grow, but as we saw earlier ownership of the pans was already fairly concentrated, so competition from dominant established suppliers might not have been attractive to a new investor (c2). Glass making had been protected by a monopoly during its early development on Tyneside prior to the civil war. Despite being more open thereafter, it appears that the Ouseburn glasshouse lessees, mostly Londoners, were unable to make a success of them in the 1640s and 1650s, so market growth prospects were evidently dubious.[14] In any case, although these industries were more capital intensive than textile-making, increases in production required the addition of more pans and furnaces. The technical innovations and mechanisation that would create opportunities to exploit assets more intensively in manufacturing still lay a century in the future. Until then more output always required more input and more labour, whether or not there was great competition between suppliers.

Ship and keel building and refitting was a rising trade after the first Anglo-Dutch war, employment in which increased both in absolute numbers and as a share of the total alongside the Tyne during the century as a whole.[15] Growth was potentially healthy (c2) and the trade needed capital, but in the form of the working capital required to cover the long period of construction between paying for supplies and labourers and receipts from sales of finished vessels. It too remained a traditional craft-based trade in the hands of individual master shipbuilders, whose raw materials and half-finished hulls lay along the high-tide line downstream from the town's quay. Nails, however, those humdrum essentials of wooden shipbuilding consumed in huge quantities, are worth considering. Flinn felt that before the end of the 17th century they accounted for between a third and a half of the entire output of the iron industry.[16] Unlike, say, sail and ropemaking, nailmaking was partly mechanised from the early 17th century with the introduction of slitting mills which cut bar iron into rods for hand-nailers to finish. But it took until the 1680s for slitting mills to be introduced to the North East, and then by Ambrose Crowley from Stourbridge in Worcestershire, rather than local entrepreneurs. Crowley eventually prospered, especially after moving his works to Winlaton from his initial regional bridgehead in Sunderland, but initially he struggled to find suitably skilled nailers. Familiar as Blackett was with the iron trade it's possible that he missed an opportunity here, but there were still drawbacks. Although capital could be employed in slitting mills and high production could generate attractive scale economies, they depended heavily on maintaining a supply of high-quality bar iron. Furthermore, Crowley might have built a large and profitable manufacturing business but much of his capital was always tied up in materials, work-in-progress, finished goods and unpaid sales.[17]

If industrial processing did not offer the prospect of creating additional value to a merchant with capital, why not simply remain a merchant bringing in those raw materials and exporting the end product? Do the three criteria give any clues as to why he decided to move away? After all Blackett had evidently made great progress as a merchant since 1645, and trade could reasonably be expected to grow further (c2).

There were broadly two ways for a merchant to earn serious money: to bet on consistently high returns from each voyage, or more modest returns on very high volumes. The canniest merchants looked to use their product knowledge, market intelligence and judgement to buy cheap in one place and sell dear in another, even to the extent of exploiting exchange rate variations along the way whenever possible. Ralph Grey wrote from Newcastle to his son in France in 1675 asking 'what advance your exch[ange] produceth profitt between here & London, if exch be high it is more profit to order moneys to London'.[18] Price differences between markets could open up new routes and foster greater specialisation. Yet while many attempts were made to lock in the difference through monopolistic trading companies they were eventually competed away as trade volumes increased (c3). And the most astute merchants surely understood that windfall gains from particularly beneficial voyages could not be repeated each time. Past success was not a guide to future returns. There was always the chance of a complete loss such as the seizure of Blackett's 1658 cloth shipment, a loss which perhaps had some bearing on his move away from trade the following year. The law of averages also meant that a trader eventually suffered from the other common risks described earlier, especially in an age of small ships in capricious weather. A neurotic thread runs through mercantile correspondence. As Ambrose Barnes' memorialist put it, 'a merchant is a client of the sea'.[19]

A sustained high rate of profit could not therefore be reasonably expected over a long period of time, but an alternative path to fortune could lie through growing a business to such a high level of trade that a large absolute income might be gained, albeit at lower margins – the strategy of 'quick returns and small gains'.[20] There was also more safety as the scale of operations increased, with risk spread across many voyages. The annual trading profits of London merchants the Marescoes normally ranged between £500 and £2,500 between the early 1660s and 1680, with occasionally more lucrative years that brought in over £4,000. In 1668 a profit of £5,140 was made. However, the balance sheet reconstructed by Roseveare shows that £33,500 of working capital was employed by the business in 1668.[21] This illustrates a key problem.

Low margins meant that to earn a high income from trade a high turnover was required, which in turn had to be supported by a capital base large enough to withstand shocks and protect the merchant's most critical assets: reputation and credit rating. Trade might not have required high initial investment, but as turnover increased, capital had to rise with it. There was little scope for economies of scale that could raise income at a faster rate than the capital needed to underpin it. For Blackett to enjoy an annual trading income to match the Marescoes of his world, his capital would have needed to grow tenfold, which would take many years of profit reinvestment and material self-denial. Instead, he moved in the opposite direction. He exported nearly 1,200 cloths in 1661, but under 700 five years later. Blackett had stakes in 18 overseas voyages from Newcastle in 1661 and just ten in 1666.[22]

As Blackett withdrew capital from trade, he directed it overwhelmingly into mining. Coal and lead extraction was no more mechanised than manufacturing. Indeed, it would remain based on hard physical labour until the 20th century, but it needed capital and in ways that were different to the needs of craft-based manufacturing. Blackett's investment in coal mining at Stella was far from being the most important of his interests, but because it provides an excellent illustration of these distinct capital needs and their likely appeal, it is considered in some detail in the rest of this chapter.

Coal and the Stella Grand Lease

Simplistically, the investment attractions of coal mining can be summarised against Blackett's three hypothetical investment criteria as follows.

    1. Mining was certainly capital-intensive. Several decades of coal extraction on the easiest seams close to the surface upstream from Newcastle meant shafts had to go ever deeper. Aside from the cost of sinking new and deeper shafts to reach the coal seams, drainage was also a problem. Practical minds had to focus on how to lift water from shafts fast enough to enable mining to continue. The region saw a variety of experiments with buckets on chains or rag pumps driven by 'engines' turned by horses or water wheels. Hatcher estimated that the fixed capital of the larger coal mines was effectively replaced completely in cash terms every three to five years and in even less time in most smaller mines. Each ton of output in the 17th century, worth 15-20p, was backed by around 10-15p of fixed capital stock, of which a fifth to a third had to be replenished each year.[23] With about half a million tons of coal each year being produced on Tyneside in the late 1650s, a crude extrapolation using Hatcher's estimate means annual investment of more than £30,000 was needed. Coal mining could absorb a great deal of capital.

2. It had grown rapidly over the previous eight decades and fortunes had been made. A body of practical geological knowledge developed on Tyneside and was passed on between inquisitive miners, overmen and agents, the forerunners of later generations of world-class geologists and engineers. While the industry's rise could not necessarily be extrapolated into the future, London's population continued to grow so demand was likely to continue rising. Production was dominated by the 'lords of coal', but the disruptions of the Interregnum might create opportunities for new entrants such as Blackett. He might hope to share in the industry's growth. As long as seams remained productive of good quality coal, drainage manageable, markets open and prices stable, surviving accounts show that mines could make profits of between 15% and 30% on each ton.[24] Once the fixed assets of shafts and pumps were in place, economies of scale could be exploited to reducing the cost per ton, as Bird had observed at Newburn in the 1610s.

3. A successful mine held a local natural monopoly for the duration of ownership or the lease term. As we have seen, the Newcastle hostmen often tried to manipulate the market as a whole, but even on those occasions when they had to settle for the disagreeable reality of taking prices from the market, those with access to good coal that could be mined and shipped at low cost enjoyed an advantage over neighbours who did not. Ultimately, of course, the economically recoverable reserves would dwindle. Extraction is exhaustive. But while the seams remained accessible and productive, which could be for decades, this local geographic and geological advantage could not be competed away.

Before getting carried away by this giddy prospectus, although many were, the risks must also be considered.

By 1660, decades of intensive mining meant that the easy pickings close to the surface and close to the river had long since been taken. Seams might prove poor or unreliable but only found to be so after the expenditure of thousands of pounds. Even if the coal was good, draining might be either impossible or too costly. Those attractive returns mentioned above can be estimated only for mines that made it into production. Coalmining could certainly absorb capital but it frequently dissolved it altogether. Local writer William Gray understood the perilous nature of mining. In his *Chorographia* of 1649 he said that 'yet for all his labour, care, and cost, [a coal owner] can scarce live of his trade; nay, many of them hath consumed and spent great estates and dyed beggars'.[25] There was barely-concealed pleasure at the failure of naively optimistic outsiders such as Huntingdon Beaumont from Nottinghamshire. Here was a man in the first decade of the 17th century of 'great ingenuity and rare parts' who tried to develop mines to the north of Tyneside near Blyth. According to Gray, he brought with him innovations such as the ability to 'boore with iron rodds to try the deepnesse and thicknesse of the coale', an evident attempt to reduce prospecting risk ahead of sinking shafts. Yet 'within a few yeares he consumed all his money and rode home upon his light horse'.[26]

Trading might be risky but we have already seen that, if undertaken on a large scale, the risk could be spread over many voyages, products and destinations. An equivalent sum of money could easily be lost in a single mine. In such a hazardous enterprise, were William Blackett's more experienced partners taking him for a ride in persuading him to take a minor share in the Stella Grand Lease? Ralph Jenison and William Carr were near contemporaries, puritans, first cousins from old Newcastle trading families and about ten years older than Blackett. Jenison appeared to be the lead partner, signing on their joint behalf in minutes of the Stella lessees.[27] The lease was not a new venture. The Catholic Tempests had joined with the Presbyterian Maddisons in the 1610s to take a mining lease in the Bishop of Durham's manor of Ryton, renewed in the 1630s.[28] Ryton was just to the west of the Tempests' small Stella freehold estate which, crucially, included the river frontage and was not far short of the highest navigable point on the Tyne.

The underlying geology was attractive, for the sedimentary 'Low Main' coal seam tilted upwards towards the west and south from where it outcrops at the foot of hillslopes towards Ryton manor's western boundary. Drainage and mining levels could therefore be driven straight into the coal. Gravity did the work of removing minewater, offering an enormous advantage over mines where vertical drainage shafts were required. Until the 1630s, however, the reserves in Ryton were relatively untouched compared to the heavily exploited seams to the east in Whickham and Gateshead because of their greater distance from the river.[29] Carriage of coal over little more than a mile of land by horse-drawn cart or wain could double the cost of coal, because of its low value compared to its bulk and weight.

From the 1610s or 1620s, this problem was tackled with waggonways: wooden railways upon which waggons with flanged wheels could run at about one third of the cost of a wain on the rutted and muddy roads, and operate for longer periods of the year.[30] Thus, mines could be sunk three times as far from the Tyne if served by a waggonway than before. Even if the cost of wayleave across someone else's land could be avoided, however, a waggonway was another expensive fixed capital investment, possibly around £750 per mile.[31] Once installed, it relied upon the mine it served remaining productive, loading the risk with additional expense.

On the other hand, and this is a key point in my view, if, despite favourable geology, that mine was previously unexploited because of its isolation, the capital needed might be just as great as in mature locations, but more of it would be deployed above ground (on transport infrastructure) than below (shallower shafts and cheaper drainage). This would represent an attractive shift away from the relatively risky unseen depths to surveying and constructing upon more predictable surface terrain. Mining on Tyneside could only be sustained by moving further away from the Tyne through the 17th century, but as those new waggonways snaked away further inland from the riverside staiths they probably marked some subtle reduction in risk even as they demanded more capital. As far as the Stella Grand Lease is concerned, a waggonway was probably laid in the 1630s, more than 20 years before Blackett and partners became involved. Despite all this, the lease still offered enormous potential in 1660. Annual output could have been in the region of 25,000 tons in the 1630s, falling by a half or more under the cloud of the first Anglo-Dutch War, before recovering to perhaps 30,000 tons by the early 1660s. By 1679 90,000 tons were being produced.[32]

Jenison, Carr and Blackett bought their quarter share early in this boom, and might have obtained a good deal in early 1660. The King's return seemed likely, but the political outlook remained unclear. The status of the bishop's estates was equally uncertain. Haselrig, who had so visibly 'enjoyed' them during Cromwell's time, had gone, leaving something of an ownership vacuum. Sir Richard Tempest had fled abroad in 1644 and, as with many returning royalists, was probably in need of cash on his return, perhaps seeing that the mines and waggonway needed investment he could not afford. The Newcastle merchants were probably in a position to drive a hard bargain for half of Tempest's lease share and the associated waggons, keels and staiths. Suppose production was back to 30,000 tons by 1659. Even taking the upper bound of Hatcher's rough guide of 15p of fixed capital per ton of output, Blackett's 1/12 share would have cost under £400. It is likely that the new partners would have been well aware of the need for further investment in short order and probably had to provide working capital to fund their share of production in the coming year ahead of their first sales, but Blackett might have gained his foothold as a coal owner for a commitment of £700 to £1,000. He was certainly happy to support negotiations for new lease terms in 1663 and renewed his twelfth share the following year. Far from being taken for a ride by Jenison, Blackett was happy to use his partner as a trustee in later transactions elsewhere.[33]

Blackett may well have seen the prospect of further growth, prosperity and coal consumption in London under a more settled political environment. Perhaps he saw the potential of the Grand Lease territory that was subsequently realised by a threefold increase in production within two decades (c2). Becoming the governor of the hostmen's company in 1662 and 1663 speaks of his confidence and commitment to the trade as much as it does of his fellow coalowners' confidence in him.[34]

Stella was arguably ripe for renewal and extension in 1660, and a shrewd, ambitious and optimistic investor such as Blackett was certainly capable of doing the right sums. Good potential for expansion also meant the prospect of reaping the rewards of capital economies of scale. The waggonway illustrates this well. Using the estimate given above, a three-mile double-track stretch running down to the Stella staiths will probably have cost in the region of £2,200 to survey, level and lay. It must have been the colliery's largest single capital asset. Making it pay probably required annual output of at least 22-25,000 tons per year to be carried down it to the staiths.[35]

A break-even level of production of around 25,000 tons was, however, surely far below the physical capacity of the line. The waggons would have been about half a mile apart. Although wear and tear would undoubtedly increase with increased use, the line's physical capacity could surely bear a tripling of the quantity of coal carried or more. At 90,000 tons, the volume of production reached by 1679, the capital cost per ton of the waggonway itself would have been reduced by around two thirds compared to the cost at 25,000 tons, even if additional maintenance and replacement decreased the life before replacement from five years to four. The capital cost of any drainage levels, shafts, engines and pumps will have been shared across higher production in the same way. So too was the rent payable to the Bishop, which did not vary with output.

Figure 6.1 illustrates the potential impact of output on the venture. The direct cost of mining the coal, usually referred to in the accounts as 'working' or 'winning', and transport by waggon and keel is assumed to vary in direct proportion to the amount of coal produced. With capital costs spread across much higher production, overall costs rose more slowly than production and revenue. The benefits can be observed clearly in Sir George Vane's accounts for his interests in both Stella and the older, more problematic Whickham in 1674/5. The unit cost per ton of mining and transport to the staiths at Whickham was 15p per ton, but only 10.5p at Stella, about a third lower.[36] Profits were consequently much higher at Stella, so too the returns on capital employed. Such were the fruits of economies of scale obtained from more intensive exploitation of fixed assets. For as long as the seams remained productive and easy to mine, the Stella lessees could also benefit from a natural local monopoly to keep costs down (c3).

Figure 6.1 Illustrative economies of scale in 1670s coal mining

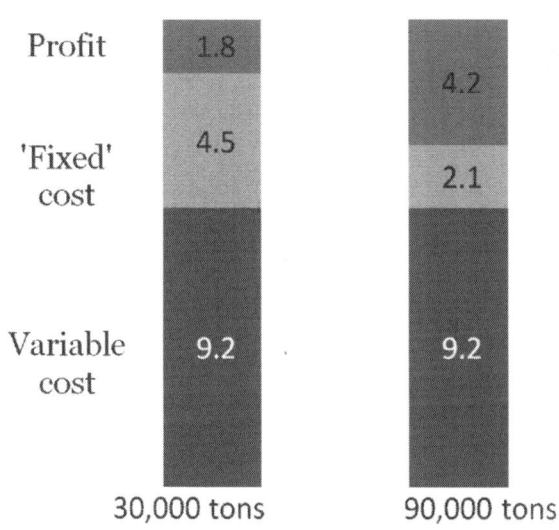

Source: Appendix 2.5, Table A2.10

So, both trade and mining could absorb substantial amounts of capital productively and offered a reasonable prospect of profitable growth (c1 and c2), in contrast to manufacturing industry during this period. What mining offered above trade was the need for fixed capital, the potential to exploit it to enjoy economies of scale and to lock in cost advantages that were more easily competed away in trade (c3). We don't know for certain how explicitly this was understood at the time, but the combined evidence of contemporary observation, analytical ability and decisions taken feels compelling. Capital was available from trade and in the North East much of it moved into mining. This was not new. As mentioned earlier, Newcastle merchant capital stood behind the acquisition of the important Whickham and Gateshead coal leases in the late 16th century.

In his study of 17th-century Stockholm merchants Leos Müller felt they 'actively sought ways of avoiding, diminishing or dispersing entrepreneurial risks. Consequently they shifted their activities from trade to other, more secure sectors.'[37] In Blackett's case, as for others on Tyneside, the most attractive new sector was not necessarily more secure, and nor was there an aversion to risky ventures. If there was further overall security it came from diversification. As we saw earlier, Blackett reduced his level of overseas trade but did not abandon it. By the end of 1660 he had capital deployed in trade, coal mining and lead mining as well as that enigmatic minor whale processing venture.

However, whether this represented a conscious fourth criterion, to spread risk by investing in a diversified portfolio, remains as hypothetical as the others. No record of Blackett's actual thinking and decision-making survives. But a logical pattern can be discerned from his actions which is consistent with evidence of a contemporary awareness of how spreading fixed costs over more units of production could increase profits disproportionately. Blackett was not amongst the Newcastle merchants in early 1663 who took up the offer of 18-year leases in what was left of the elderly Whickham Grand Lease, where such scope for scale economies was probably limited. The comparatively high unit production cost at Whickham compared to Stella 11 years later amply shows the wisdom of that judgement.[38]

One final point before we leave the Stella Grand Lease. Based on production levels and Sir George Vane's highly respectable 29% return on revenue in 1674, 1676 and 1679, which mixes good and bad years, Blackett's equivalent share of the annual profit was £290. This meets investment criterion 2 regarding profitable growth, but only up to a point. A twelfth part of the Stella Grand Lease was not going to generate enough cash to retire on in style. Perhaps he'd have taken a larger stake if it was available. William Carr died just two months after the lease share was taken in 1660 between him, Jenison and Blackett, but the beneficiaries of Carr's will held onto his share.[39] The Blackett stake never increased.

Furthermore, although each partner was responsible for his own individual sales, the mines and waggonway were worked in common. This made sense in the light of experience of the constant and expensive lawsuits between the independent coalowners at work in Whickham. The orderly management process between all the Stella partners described in 1679 had presumably been established many years earlier.[40] However, a minority share meant limited influence. Blackett was probably used to some form of collaboration in his trading ventures but had largely been his own master since his mother-in-law died in 1648. It might well have chafed to have limits to his input to monthly partners' meetings, or to suffer the meetings at all, and then only be able to vote his small share on decisions. And profitable though Stella was, it cannot have accounted for more than 6% of Tyneside's coal output in the early 1660s.[41] While the capital structure of mining offered an attractive formula for success, the realities and constraints of the mature coal industry on Tyneside meant that William Blackett would need to look elsewhere if he was to exert decisive influence and achieve scale. He found it with lead.

Chapter 7

The Plastic of its Age

Lead Mining and Smelting

The wind-blown summit of Killhope Law in the North Pennines stands 2,208ft (673 metres) above sea level. It is a mile to the east along the ridge of rough grass, heather and peat hags from Killhope Head where the three counties of Northumberland, Durham and Cumbria meet. The summit looks down to the headwaters of the River Wear to the south, and the West Allen to the north. The East Allen rises slightly further east and the Nent to the west. A bracing morning's ridge-walk southwards from Killhope Head has the youthful South Tyne river down to the right and the Tees ahead in the middle distance. This high land therefore lies at the watershed between the north-east's major rivers, which radiate in all directions before they eventually turn eastwards to reach the North Sea. On very clear days the sea might be glimpsed shining in the far distance, 37 miles away as the crow flies.

The upper reaches of the valleys below Killhope Law are the heartland of the North Pennines lead mines (see Figure 7.1). The extraction of lead from this remote and inhospitable landscape in the medieval and early modern period contrasts sharply with the economics of coal mining, clinging so closely to navigable water near the coast. Coal and lead are commodities extracted from the ground, usually by underground mining. They shared several techniques and became increasingly capital intensive, but they had little else in common. Coal was hewn in large quantities from reasonably predictable horizontal seams cheaply enough to be used up in its raw state as a fuel —as long it did not have bear the burden of land transport over any distance.

Veins of lead ore were typically more difficult to 'read' and follow underground. Simplistically, the North Pennines' lead-bearing ores are the residue of mineral-rich waters forced upwards around 300 million years ago by the geological heat engine of the 'Weardale granite' deep beneath the hills. The granite lies under repeated sedimentary layers of hard sandstone and limestone and softer shales. These beds were themselves forced upwards through time, fracturing in the process.

Figure 7.1 North Pennines lead in the mid-17th century.

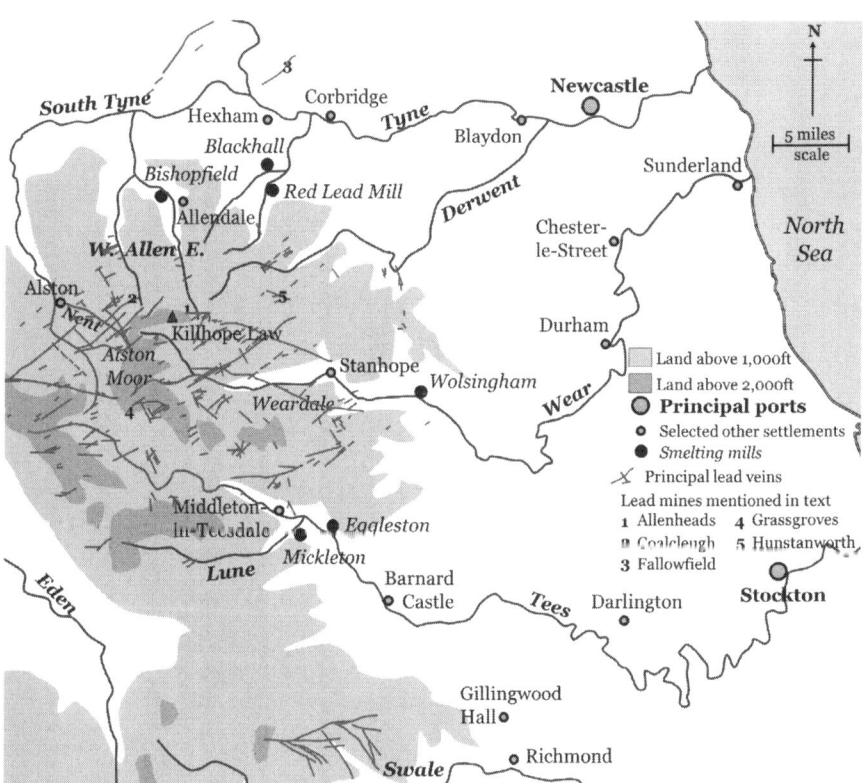

This made it easier for the warm mineral-rich water to find its way upwards and sideways through the cracks, particularly through the joints within the limestone beds. As the water cooled the precipitate left deposits of lead ore and other, economically worthless, minerals, another significant difference between the veins and coal seams. The sheets of vertical intrusions are the veins and the lateral extensions are known as flats.[1] Surface erosion by river and glacier has exposed the alternating sequence of sedimentary rocks on valley sides, the sandstone and limestone standing out as steep terrace edges between the softer slopes of the shales. The orefield lies in the high Pennine dales between Middleton-in-Teesdale in the south and Allendale in the north, between the heights west of Alston on the South Tyne and Wolsingham in Weardale to the east. Similar lead orefields lie to the south under the Pennines in the Yorkshire Dales and Derbyshire's Peak District.

Neither veins nor flats were reliable or consistent. Superficially promising orebodies could quickly disappear when explored further, making any commitment to pursue them far underground both costly and highly risky. It was said of the Peak District miners in the 1660s that

> 'sometimes after great expense and trouble, they miss the rake or vein, which if they chance to light on, it doth prove to be of little or no value, having but a small body of lead ore. These mines likewise are very casual, and many an ingenious man often undone by the venturing his certainty, for the uncertainty of the same'.[2]

Where a productive vein or flat could be worked, far more effort was needed to extract ore compared to mining coal. The hewn lumps of rock hauled to the surface then had to be crushed and sifted by hand to obtain the small pieces of metallic ore. Although the techniques and tools used in 'washing' the lead ready for smelting became gradually more specialised through the 18th century, it remained highly manual hard work. A collection of watercolour images from the early 19th century vividly portrays the rudimentary technology, physical labour, and sweat involved in lead mining and ore washing and something of the spirit of the hardy people it depended upon.[3] While it was possible, throughout the early modern period, for coal miners to produce 200 tons or more of coal each per year, more than five to nine tons of lead ore per miner ready for smelting was exceptional.[4]

Ore was converted into lead metal by being smelted at high temperature. This usually reduced the weight of material by up to a half or even more, which should have been encouragement enough to undertake smelting next to the mines. However the other vital ingredient in this process was fuel, wood fuel in the 17th century, and most mines were in uplands denuded of trees, not least as a result of mining in medieval times.[5] It was less practical to carry bulky wood than sacks of compact lead ore, and woodland was typically found downhill in the direction of navigable water, so smelting generally took place away from the mines, often several

The Plastic of its Age

miles away on poor roads across difficult terrain. Ore was therefore transported in sacks by trains of pack horses down to the smelting mills. Water power was harnessed to drive bellows to generate a controllable air blast into the 'ore hearth'. Blown air and fuel combined to generate the heat needed for successful smelting (see Plate 8). Ore hearth lead smelting mills originated in the Mendip hills in Somerset in the 1550s and spread rapidly in Derbyshire in the 1570s and 1580s.[6] Successful operation relied heavily on the skill and experience of generally well-paid smelters. They blended ore and fuel at the right time and, crucially, at the right temperature, working the hot fire in front of them and suffering the long-term consequences of inhaling toxic fumes.

The pieces of lead then had to be transported away from the mills to the markets and ports near the coast. Since the Pennine mines and smelting mills lay well inland around the 'backbone of England', further expensive overland carriage by further pony trains was unavoidable.

However, the high cost of remote and difficult upland mining, smelting mills and equipment, fuel supplies, skilled smelters, overland transport and logistical management was covered by the price of the dull grey metal produced at the end of it. While the volume of English lead production was tiny compared to coal, at around 13,000 tons in the 1630s, compared to some 500,000 tons or more of coal, the difference was much smaller in value terms.[7] Coal was sold in London, its principal domestic market, for around 90p per ton, but lead fetched £12-14.[8] Lead was in many respects the plastic of its age. It was malleable and resistant to corrosion, making it highly suitable for the building industry, for rooves, flashing, guttering, glazing bars, cisterns and pipes. 'Plumbing' after all derives from the Latin for lead. Lead is unusual among metals in that its compounds could be as useful as the metal itself. It was combined in small proportions with tin to make pewter, in common use as English domestic tableware from the Tudor period. Lead was further refined to produce litharge and small quantities of silver. Litharge was 'reduced' in another furnace to produce red lead used in glass making. White lead, derived from lead pieces in a long process involving vinegar and dung, was used in paint and cosmetics. Finally, given human nature, there was always a market for lead shot as ammunition.

The Demand for English Lead

As a non-corrosive metal, lead was often recycled, restricting new demand to a small addition to the existing stock each year. The amount of lead stripped from the rooves of monastic buildings during the dissolution of the 1530s and 1540s brought about a price crash which devastated mining for new supplies.[9] However, there are reasons to believe that demand increased during the 17th century. Burt makes an intriguing case for greater consumption of lead for military use driven by improvements in hand-held firearms. Guns could fire more shot and there were more guns. There was certainly no shortage of warfare. He speculated that European and colonial military and civilian use of unrecoverable lead could have approached 5,000 tons per annum in the late 17th century.[10] If so, English production would account for a significant proportion of the total through exports and its own 'consumption'.

Exports probably accounted for half or more of English production in the mid-17th century, perhaps up to 8,000 tons per year.[11] In the normal run of trade, Amsterdam and Hamburg appear to have been the key entrepots for lead exported from England, supplied mainly from London and Hull in the early 17th century. English supplies competed there with lead from further east in Europe. New analysis of the Sound Toll shipping records show that the great Baltic port of Danzig was shipping some 400 tons of lead per year westwards through the Sound before the mid-1640s, brought down the Vistula river from mines in central Europe. However, as Figure 7.2 shows, there was a dramatic change in the middle of the century.

Firstly, Danzig's own exports collapsed in the mid-1640s. All other things being equal, that 400 tons would have to be supplied from elsewhere. England was the likeliest alternative. Then, from the 1650s, lead traffic through the Sound picked up again, but this time the commodity was heading east, not west, and it came predominantly from Newcastle and Hull. By the 1680s English exports into the Baltic added up to around 600 tons per year. It might be too simple to add the displaced west-bound exports from Danzig before 1650 to the new east-bound exports from the 1660s, but even if the net swing was not quite as high as 1,000 tons per year it was worthy of contemporary notice. Newcastle lead merchant

Figure 7.2. Lead shipments through the Sound 1635-89 by port of origin.

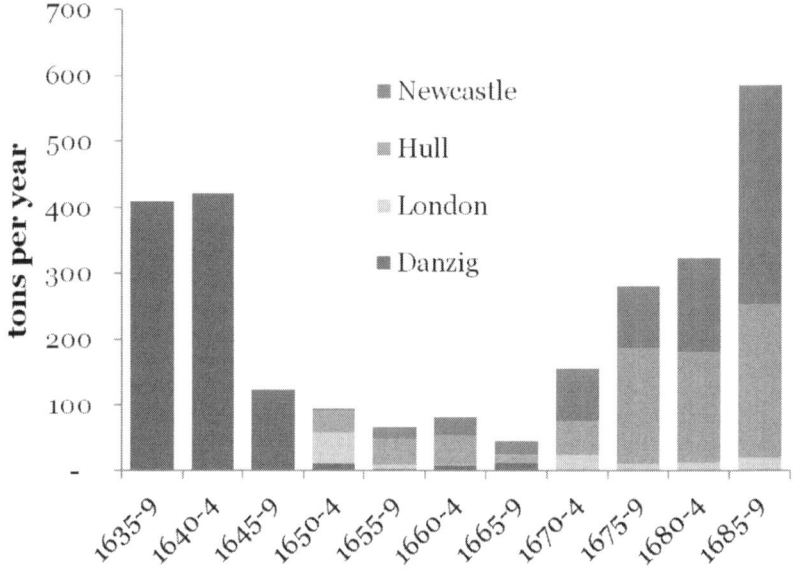

Source: Appendix 3.2.2, Table A3.2.

Ralph Grey wrote in March 1674 that 'I have not heard of such a Quantytye shipd to Danske. Great Quantytys of Lead use to Come downe out of Poaland to that poart, to sarve holland'.[12] This was a substantial structural increase in export demand and it came alongside long-term growth in markets in Southern Europe and in European tropical colonies and despite export tariffs of 8-10%.[13]

The domestic market was surely also buoyant. While lead could be recycled from previous uses, the increase in the quantity and quality of new building from the later 16th century, long described as the 'great rebuilding' of rural England, fed through to higher demand for building lead. Urban demand would surely have risen much faster, given the rapid expansion of London and other towns and cities. Public buildings, churches and the grander domestic residences would need much more lead for rooves, flashing, guttering, glazing bars, cisterns and pipes.

Then, after 1666, came what must have been an unprecedented domestic boost to lead production: the rebuilding of London following the great fire. 13,000 buildings were destroyed in the fire that raged on a dry east wind in September. The diarist John Evelyn described 'the Lead mealting down the streetes in a streame, & the very pavements of them glowing with a fiery rednesse, so as nor horse nor man was able to tread on them' thereby putting a great deal of the capital's stock of lead beyond any practical hope of being re-used.[14] A remarkable burst of regeneration saw the construction of 9,000 new houses along with many public buildings in the years that followed.[15] Builders were expected to adhere to high standards through a set of regulations which included the stipulation that 'In front of all houses erected in high streets ... water falling from the top of the said houses [shall] be conveyed into channels by pipes on the sides and fronts of houses'.[16] Lead was needed in great quantity for those channels, gutters and pipes, not to mention for the roofing of the more substantial buildings. The protection and decoration of woodwork in the grander buildings would have required paint using white lead as an input. Builders in the capital might well have required around 2,000 tons or more per year from 1669.[17] In the 1630s annual English consumption was probably some 5-6,000 tons. Even allowing for growth in the subsequent three decades, London's needs in the years after 1666 must still have placed a sudden and noticeable demand on the market. Indeed, the London merchant Charles Marescoe heard from one of his lead buyers in Hull in December 1668 that the word amongst local merchants was that 'if there is so little lead left at London and soe much weekely expended on the Citty buildings as is said, in all probability they'll strive to keep [the price] up and sell dear what they soe buy'.[18]

Nor did demand fall back to pre-1666 levels after the early 1670s. The rebuilding of St. Paul's Cathedral and 51 London churches was authorised in 1670, and extended over the next two or three decades. London continued to grow vigorously, expanding westwards from the City with high-status terraces and squares.[19] This surely also came against a background of generally rising demand for exports and to meet the domestic building needs of a relatively prosperous nation recovering in the 1650s onwards from the strife, and lead shot consumption, of civil war. How were these demands met?

The Supply of Lead

In the 1630s minor shares of English lead were said to have come from Yorkshire (500 tons), most of which came from mines in the central Pennine dales and carried mainly to York, and from Wales (1,000 tons) probably largely from North Wales, within reach of Chester and the Dee estuary. A more substantial 3,500 tons came from the Mendip Hills in Somerset, served by Bristol. By far the largest amount was ascribed to Derbyshire: around 8,200 tons, or 63% of the total.[20]

Lead mined in the Peak District had dominated the English industry since the later 16th century. Many smallholders and others staked claims as 'free miners' to extract lead on their own account. As the easy reserves were scratched away from the surface and from just below it, the usual problems of sinking, lining and draining deeper workings arose. While this made capital demands beyond the resources of free miners and drew in those with deeper pockets, the free miners continued to dominate the area in the second half of the 17th century.[21] Ore was sold and carried eastwards to smelting mill owners and operators established south of Sheffield, many of whom were also working on a modest scale.[22] From there lead was carried miles overland to navigable stretches of the river Trent from whence it was ferried to Hull, the principal outlet for Derbyshire lead. Hull's location on the east coast made it particularly important to markets in London and northern Europe compared to Bristol and Chester. Another of Marescoe's agents recognised this in the spring of 1669 by claiming that his district on the west coast of France was effectively insulated from upwards pressure on prices caused by the rebuilding of London because La Rochelle and Bordeaux had ample supplies from Chester and Liverpool instead.[23]

The pressure of demand from the growth of London, let alone the burst of rebuilding after 1666, and continental shifts such as the collapse of exports from Danzig must therefore have weighed heavily on the Derbyshire industry. Unfortunately there are no clear production figures available for the later 17th century to compare to the 8,200 tons said to have passed through the internal transhipment point at Bawtry in the 1630s. However, even if the 6,800 tons shipped out from Hull in 1705 understates the total amount of lead produced in its hinterland it does suggest dynamic growth in the intervening decades.[24] This is not surprising. Mines had been worked intensively for decades, requiring ever-deeper shafts and drainage investment. The industry's structure remained fragmented between mining, smelting and trading. More lead was produced in Derbyshire than anywhere else in England well into the 18th century but the industry there appeared increasingly unable to compete at the margin from the 1650s onwards. Herein lay opportunity in the North Pennines for the likes of William Blackett.

North Pennines lead had been exploited for centuries and made a significant contribution to national exports in the Tudor period.[25] Most of the veins had been discovered. However, lead mining had evidently fallen back in the early 17th century. The North East was notably absent from the 1630s survey of English lead producers. In his description of Newcastle published in 1649, Gray, the proud promoter of his native town, made no mention of lead amongst the other produce traded through the port. Lead was not even locally significant.[26] However, by 1705 nearly 5,800 tons was shipped out from Newcastle and Stockton, closing in on the total of 6,800 tons leaving Hull.[27]

The problems underlying these figures mean they can have only illustrative value. An unknown proportion of Stockton's 3,200 tons of lead came from Swaledale in Yorkshire as well as from Teesdale, which might have contributed to the 500 tons ascribed to Yorkshire in the 1630s. And such counts are only snapshots of single years in a volatile trade. It is nevertheless a striking illustration of change. From being overlooked in the 1630s, around a third of English coastal and overseas shipments of lead came from north-eastern ports by 1705. Analysis of the Newcastle, Sunderland and Stockton port books shows that this change occurred at speed from the 1650s.

There are limitations in the use of the port book records that chart this change, not least their patchy survival, especially for the years before 1660. The amount of lead consumed locally and therefore not visible in the shipping data, is unknown. However this was probably only a minor share of total production for even Newcastle was surely a small market for building lead compared to London and the major cities of Europe. Appendix 3.2 examines

Figure 7.3 Lead shipments from the North East 1639-1705.

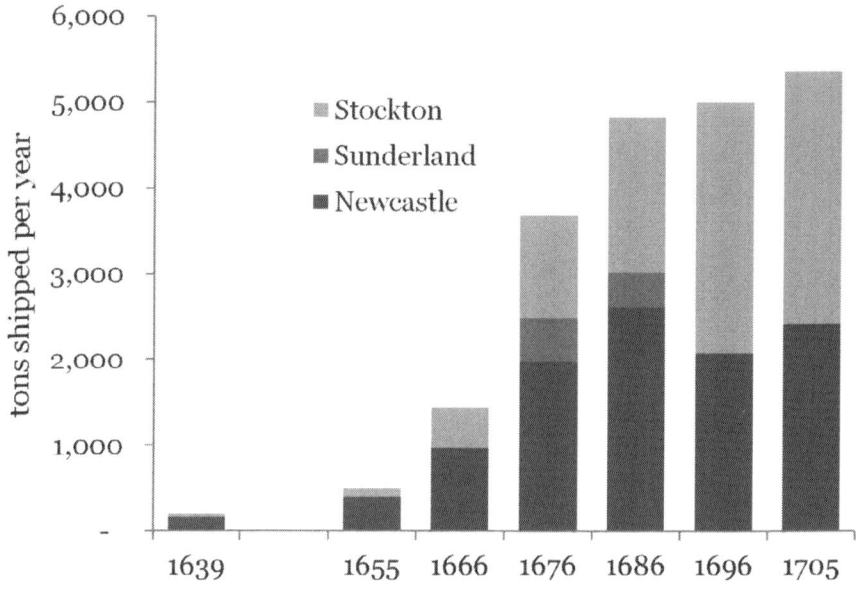

Source: Appendix 3.2.4

these limitations in further detail, alongside evidence that can reassure us on some points and how to mitigate them in others. Figure 7.3 summarises the results of this analysis for years in which both coastal and overseas shipments were recorded. Fortunately they fall at roughly ten-year intervals.

Despite the inclusion of guesstimates to cover gaps in the available figures for 1639 and 1655, totals in the region of 200 tons and 500 tons respectively, in each case mostly from Newcastle, are probably not too far off the mark. Given Gray's account of the town in 1649, which makes no mention of lead, and that only 20 tons was exported in 1640, it feels unlikely that the 1639 figure understated the true position. What is certainly clear is that there was a rapid increase in production in the quarter century after 1660. Total shipments from the three north-eastern ports reached 5,000 tons of lead in 1686, a remarkable ten-fold increase in 30 years.

The lead ore deposits in the hills of the North Pennines had not been worked as extensively as those in the hitherto vastly more productive Peak District.[28] They lay in the upper reaches of the dales, up to 40 miles of difficult country away from the coastal ports, but this did not make them any more remote from water transport than those of Derbyshire. In the early 17th century most mining was undertaken on a relatively small scale by local prospectors, often by pursuing surface veins through shallow pits or a continuous trench. 17th-century Weardale mining leases often described such trenches as slits. Worked at long enough they could become quite deep, aided in many cases by damming water on the hill crest above and then releasing it to wash away debris into the rivers below and possibly expose more of the vein. Today we know the deep scars that remain on the fellsides as 'hushes', a technique still heavily practised in the 18th century.

As in Derbyshire, the industry was fragmented between mining, ore dealing and smelting in the first half of the 17th century. Smallholders William Little and Cuthbert Dawson of Allendale testified to having worked as carriers for country lead ore dealers over several seasons in the 1620s. They travelled between Teesdale mines and Allendale and Hexhamshire, easily more than 15 miles apart along the high windswept watersheds between the Tees, Wear, East Allen and Devil's Water valleys.[29] The smelting sites to which they were carrying ore might well have been primitive compared to the mills in use in more technically advanced regions. At a time when some 50 smelting mills were at work in Derbyshire, there is secure evidence for only three in the North Pennines before 1640 and two of those had been constructed within the previous ten years.[30] There are hints elsewhere that some lead was still being smelted on inefficient and unpredictable bail hills, little more than bonfires set on western facing hilltops and relying upon the wind to achieve high enough temperatures to extract lead from ore.[31]

However, even before the Civil War there were signs of quickening development. The North Pennines enjoyed an important institutional advantage over Derbyshire. Unlike in the Peak District, where the lowly could stake claims to mine, most rights in the North Pennines were in the hands of a smaller number of landowners with extensive estates. They mostly had little direct interest in exploiting their mineral resources but preferred to lease them out. The Bishop of Durham owned the rights throughout Weardale and let the larger part of them from the 1560s onwards to a 'moormaster' in return for an initial fee and a tenth of all ore raised. A further tenth was due to the Rector of Stanhope as his ecclesiastical tithe.* The Bowes family were prominent in Teesdale. The Fenwicks of Wallington Hall controlled the rights in Allendale as lords of the manor of Hexham. From the 1630s Alston Moor mining was in the hands of the Radcliffe family, later the earls of Derwentwater. Traditionally, leases or 'tacks' were given to local miners, but this mechanism also offered a route into the industry for venturers from outside the hills.

In Weardale, Thomas Wharton Esq. of Gillingwood in Swaledale, another lead mining area, became moormaster in 1632. With the confiscation of the bishopric's estates after the civil war, Wolsingham manor and the dale's mining rights were purchased from the state for £6,764 in 1650 by Sir Arthur Haselrig, whom we met earlier as the Parliamentary military governor of Newcastle. Assuming a 6% rate of interest, Haselrig needed the estate to generate an annual income in excess of £400 to justify the price. When Bishop John Cosin carried out his own survey in 1662 after the restoration of the bishopric, he ruefully claimed that Haselrig had made 'at least £2,000 per ann cleare profit' as the *de facto* moormaster.[32] This is almost certainly an exaggerated figure but at even half that level Haselrig would have easily covered his purchase cost from lead proceeds alone within the eight to ten years of his ownership. No doubt he drove the mines hard while he could. A 1647 Parliamentary survey estimated the bishop's duty income to be £15/year. In March 1661 the moormastership was re-let to Wharton's son Humphrey for £60/year in lieu of the bishop's duty ore.[33] Both figures are likely to have greatly underestimated the true value of those rights, given the difficulty of verifying production throughout Weardale, but the fourfold increase must surely reflect a noticeable rise in ore production during Haselrig's rapacious years in control.

Newcastle's merchant community also took an interest in lead mining. In 1629, John Butler leased Fallowfield lead mines,

---

* In Weardale the moormaster was responsible for the payments to Bishop and Rector. He was effectively 'paid' by the miners by their having to sell all the ore raised at a discount to the going market price, estimated at about 25% in the 1660s: A.Blackburn, 'Mining Without Laws: Origins and Practices of the Weardale Moormasters', *Bulletin of the Peak District Mines Historical Society*, 12.3, (1994), pp.70-1.

north of the Tyne, and built a lead smelting mill at Blackhall in Hexhamshire. Butler was amongst the buyers of lead from Teesdale in the 1620s. He had interests in Hunstanworth by the 1650s.[34] When Butler's developing lead interests are placed on the map, a clear pattern emerges. The mill was roughly equidistant between his mining leases to the north and south and close to an established carriage route from Hexhamshire to the navigable reaches of the Tyne at Blaydon. Few port book records survive for this period but his name is shown against an overseas shipment of 10.5 tons in May 1639.[35] After the civil war Butler's son Gregory obtained 'certain lead mines, ore etc' on Alston Moor from the royalist Radcliffe family.[36] The Butlers were bringing lead mining, modern smelting, carriage and sale into a single vertically integrated business.

At some point between 1653 and 1657 Newcastle merchants Ralph Grey and James Briggs commenced a partnership mining lead at Grassgroves in Upper Teesdale, near the Tees-Wear watershed.[37] A key member of the partnership was George Bacon, originally from Clay Linn in Derbyshire, in lead smelting country south of Chesterfield. In the mid-1650s the partnership was linked with Red Lead Mill in Hexhamshire. The mill was still in Grey's hands in the 1670s, when he was also an active Tyneside lead trader.[38] Here was another integrated lead mining and smelting concern in operation by the mid-1650s funded by Newcastle merchant capital. In this case, the partners were also refining lead to obtain red lead, presumably sold to the Ouseburn glassworks.[39]

Change was underway in the North Pennine's lead industry by the 1650s, no longer a quiet backwater. Outside capital, not least from Newcastle, was now beginning to spread modern smelting technology, investing in mines and starting to connect previously fragmented small ventures into larger integrated concerns. Blackett himself was toying with direct involvement in the mid-1650s, as we shall see.

This was surely a market-driven response to an increase in demand at a time when the Derbyshire industry was struggling with the cost problems inherent in ever deeper workings. Its fragmented structure of ownership and production might also have hindered its responsiveness. Ideally we would see this reflected in the course of lead prices, but there is no continuous series in which we can be confident. Nevertheless, the data drawn from different

The Plastic of its Age | 111

sources in Figure 7.4 prompt some important observations. Crudely, the price of lead in London can be regarded as a measure of consumer prices, while the Derbyshire ore and Newcastle lead series give some idea of the cost of production.

Figure 7.4. Lead prices 1600-69.

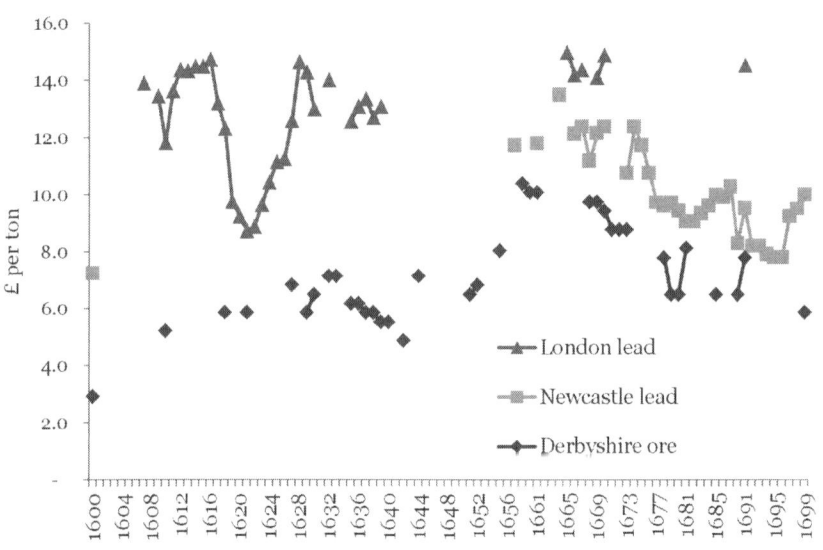

Sources: see Appendix 3.3

London prices, based on building supply accounts, show a marked reduction in the years around 1620 but otherwise appear to have varied between £12 and £14 per ton up to 1639. We do not have any reliable data for prices in London for the next 30 years or so, but they do not appear to have risen noticeably above this upper bound in the late 1660s when we can be confident that demand for rebuilding the city was suddenly much higher. While London's short-term needs might have been met by redirecting exports to domestic consumption, letters to London merchant Charles Marescoe from his buying agents in the north in 1668-9 indicate that overseas demand also remained strong.[40] It is surely reasonable to infer that the surge in production by then underway from the North Pennines avoided a crisis which might have driven prices far higher. Many of those fine Wren churches in the city of London must have been roofed with North Pennines lead.

The paradox here is that stable prices for consumers might dampen incentives for producers to make the commitments needed to increase supplies. Consider, however, relative prices between Derbyshire and Newcastle. For the years 1668-73 Derbyshire lead probably cost around £11.60/ton.[41] This was the same as the average price of lead sold in Newcastle over the same period. The former is cost alone, and possibly errs on the low side. The latter includes the producer's profit. A small number of prices communicated to Marescoe by his agents in Hull and the northeast support this inferred disparity. The crude average of prices sought between 1668 and 1670 by suppliers in Hull was £13.30 per ton, but only £11.90 in Newcastle.

Lead supplies from the North East held down London prices and in all probability squeezed the profitability of Derbyshire mining and smelting. The slower and later pace of mining development in Newcastle's hinterland makes it perfectly logical that lead could be produced more cheaply in the North Pennines than in the industry's traditional heartland to the south. This was not lost on the North East's merchants. The dealers in Stockton and Newcastle, told Maresco's buying agent in 1668 that they had 'had advise that seaverall lead mines were drowned in Derbyshire'.[42] George Bacon's successful move to Allendale from the smelt mills south of Chesterfield symbolises this shift in the centre of industrial gravity and he wasn't the only one to move north from Derbyshire.[43] William Blackett must have been well aware of all this as he pondered what to do with his capital in the late 1650s.

Chapter 8

A Great Many Men

Turning, then, to consider William Blackett's move into the lead industry, he was surely able to see that in the North Pennines the industry was in much the same position as Tyneside's coal mining had been 90 years earlier. Demand was healthy in London and there were large markets overseas. Limited earlier development meant lead could be mined relatively cheaply. Although some of his fellow merchants had already commenced work in the distant Pennine dales and others were joining them, production was not yet monopolised by a few established operators.

Blackett's father had spent some time as a deputy moormaster in Weardale in the 1640s and William I also had some knowledge of the lead trade before his 1659 investment in Allendale. A consignment of 12 tons was shipped to London in his name in February 1655, and a few months later he took a third share of a mining lease north of Haydon Bridge where a small scale trial was underway, probably led by Ralph Grey. It didn't amount to much. Blackett apparently mined less than six tons of ore there in 1657.[1] His brother Edward took an eighth share of Hunstanworth mine in 1658 from John Butler, son of Edward's merchants' company master of the same name.[2] Butler senior had built the Blackhall smelt mill in the year Edward started his apprenticeship to him. Edward Blackett's long residence in Amsterdam would have given him a keen appreciation of the continental lead trade transacted in the city. It is easy to visualise William sitting and considering it all from his vantage point overlooking the quayside and the Tyne. Lead mining needed fixed capital and growth prospects were good, so there was potential to achieve economies of scale. Gains could be locked in with the right lease terms. The industry matched the investment criteria hypothesised for him earlier. In the absence of any long-standing attachment to lead mining in the family, and little more than a passing familiarity with it, Blackett's decisive move into lead smacks of systematic and analytical logic instead.

His was a long-term strategy. That much is clear from

Blackett's periodic commitment of large amounts of fixed capital that would require several years to recover. It implies an ambition for scale, which in turn implies a confident view of underlying market trends (rather than short-term trading opportunities), and sound judgement of mines that could be productive for years. Deep pockets were needed, so too a great deal of courage, and a high tolerance of risk. This chapter examines the growth of his business and the scale it reached. The following chapter examines how efficiently it operated, and what this meant for the region as a whole.

Growth

Blackett's first significant direct involvement with lead appears to have taken the form of an exploratory year at Allenheads from May 1659.[3] Perhaps the word was out that the mine was already doing very well and looked far more attractive than his earlier minor trial had showed Hawdonfield to be. He doubtless hired an experienced local miner to assess the ground and existing workings. Blackett then made the large capital commitment of £1,400 late in 1660 to buy out some of William Pearson's mining lease high up in the East Allen valley. This was an ambitious, risky, and emphatic entrance into the industry.

Pearson was an Allendale man. His family were among the manorial tenants who enjoyed secure copyhold tenure of their land. Their land was at Bishopfield, near Catton, north from Allendale town alongside the East Allen river (see Figure 8.1). In December 1648 Sir John Fenwick granted a 21-year mining lease of all the lead mines in East and West Allendale to Pearson for an initial £100 entry fine and a duty rate of approximately a fifth of the ore raised. Remains of a smelting mill sit next to the river below Bishopfield so it seems likely that Pearson built it to smelt his own lead after taking the lease.[4] He was probably around 50 when he came to his arrangement with Blackett, so not necessarily looking to sell as a result of greatly advanced years.[5] Some of the sum advanced by Blackett in 1660 was doubtless an inducement to Pearson to come to terms in a rising market, but the rest must have reflected the residual value of Pearson's own investment in shafts and levels at the Allenheads mine. It was surely therefore already well-developed. 'Pearson's level', a possible example of his mine's extent, is shown on a 1790 map running for about 500 yards underground towards the prominent 'Old Vein' at the Allenheads West End.[6]

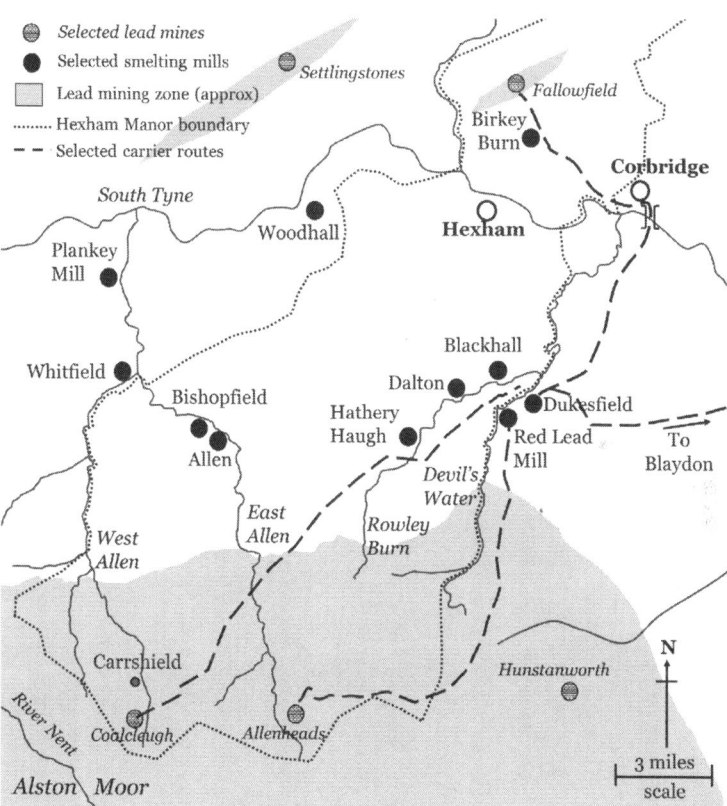

Figure 8.1 Allendale and Hexhamshire mines and smelting mills.

Yet the lease had only nine years left to run. In December 1669 the rights, and all accompanying underground workings, would revert to the owner, Sir William Fenwick, to be let again on new terms. Since Blackett had no guarantee of occupation beyond that date he did not have long to recover that large capital outlay and earn a reasonable profit on it. Given the highly unpredictable nature of lead veins, there was a risk he could lose it all. Not only did the reserves of lead ore have to remain productive in Allenheads, but the market prospects for the commodity had to remain strong. His confidence has to be admired. A rough idea of the annual ore production he must have needed can be guessed at from

A Great Many Men | 117

the £1,400 outlay, nine-year residual term, the prevailing price of lead in Newcastle and an educated guess at mining, carriage and smelting costs. With a long-term strategy in mind, he might have accepted a low return on his capital - 10%, say - in these first years. This translates into mining an annual average minimum quantity of 430 tons of ore per year, smelting down to 220-230 tons of lead.[7] We do not know how this compares to what Pearson had managed but it was presumably higher, for Pearson would otherwise have had little incentive to sell his rights to Blackett at the agreed price.

Blackett must have been content with the way this worked out, for in May 1665 he bought out the rest of Pearson's mining lease in East and West Allendale (mostly at Coalcleugh) for £420, now with little more than four years of the term to run. Applying the same logic as before to this extension of Blackett's interest, he will have needed to mine an extra 100 tons of ore each year to recover his initial outlay. Adding this to the first tranche above implies a target of mining at least 620 tons of ore in Allendale each year in the mid-1660s. The assumptions used here border on the heroic and the conclusions must be correspondingly cautious, but it gives some measure of what can be squeezed from a few dry entries in an abstract of leases. He certainly wasn't struggling, for he was prepared to lengthen payment terms to a buyer of his wine in 1664, lending an extra £30 on top of the £120 owed. In the summer of 1666 he spent perhaps around £200 to indulge in buying at least three ships captured during the second Anglo-Dutch war. These were not the actions of someone scrabbling for the cash needed to expand a new mining business.[8]

Mining more lead meant employing more miners. Population was sparse in the remote heads of the East and West Allen valleys but mining had probably always given some by-employment to the copyholding tenant farmers in the district. A survey of 1608 counted 37 of them in 'Allendale Forest', which covered the upper East Allan, and their households might have provided sufficient labour to meet Pearson's needs in the 1650s.[9] Blackett almost certainly needed more miners than could be found locally. Facing a similar problem five miles away at Boltshope Park in Hunstanworth, the Butlers were paying their lead miners a good daily rate of pay in 1663-4. They were paying it in cash at least quarterly and sometimes monthly.[10] This was a small affair, with no more than ten men named in the few detailed accounts which survive, whereas Blackett's ambition must have required a much larger labour force.

We have nothing on his lead mining pay policy earlier than his son Michael's letters from 1675 onwards, but they show that he was then employing a large direct mining labour force paid monthly at daily rates. Simply moving the payroll cash out to the hills was doubtless as much a headache as in later periods when heavily armed agents had to carry it from Newcastle.[11] Unfortunately we have little with which to compare Blackett's pay policy, but it was clearly a departure from the traditional patterns of small partnerships of self-employed miners taking leases in return for a share of the ore as duty. A variant on this was pursued in Weardale, where the moormaster Wharton remunerated miners by buying their ore at a rate which tracked the price of lead in Newcastle.[12] Weardale miners therefore took the market and mining risk, and probably had to wait for three months or longer for payment. By contrast, in the mid-1670s, Blackett assumed the risk, paid his miners a daily wage and paid it promptly. This policy was surely crucial to building up his workforce from the few dozen probably needed in the early 1660s. Judging from the amounts paid out monthly in 1675, he employed around 180 in Allenheads and Coalcleugh by then. In October 1675 he wanted to ensure he had enough money for the next monthly pay. He evidently took issue with Michael's musings in an earlier letter on the drawbacks of paying the same fixed daily rates to 'lusty able men' and 'lubbards' and in hacking through difficult and easy rock.[13] With the regional lead industry still growing and highly profitable, Blackett senior evidently wanted no debate about his simple pay policy aimed at attracting and retaining skilled workers.

It is unclear where he was smelting his ore during his early years in Allenheads, but it must have been through renting capacity at an existing mill owned by others. There were three obvious candidates: Pearson's own mill at Bishopfield, Blackhall Mill and Red Lead Mill in Hexhamshire. Pearson might well have had spare room at Bishopfield once he sold a share of his mining rights in 1660 and certainly after 1665 when he parted with the rest of them. However, when considering the need to get lead to Newcastle, it was less favourably located than the two mills in Hexhamshire. Red

Lead Mill was used by the Grey, Briggs and Bacon consortium, with whom Blackett was almost certainly involved at Hawdonfield, and Blackhall by Butler, and probably Blackett's brother Edward.

Capacity is likely to have been an issue. Most contemporary lead smelting mills were little more than sheds containing two hearths, their bellows powered by a single water wheel. There will have been very little room to handle ore from multiple sources at the same time. Owners surely gave priority to their own ore, particularly as their own operations expanded. George Bacon's agreement with Sir Francis Radcliffe to take all the lead duty ore from Alston Moor in July 1664 for three years must have increased pressure on smelting capacity at Red Lead Mill.[14] This compounded a significant logistical risk. Carriage of ore and lead was easiest in the summer. The moorland tracks from the mines climbing up over the barren watersheds and down to the mills and then the lowland ways onwards to the lower Tyne were difficult to use in the winter. If Blackett's ore could not be moved from Allenheads and Coalcleugh to, say, Blackhall Mill until April or May and then had to wait weeks until there was space at the hearth after other lead had been smelted and carried away, the prime sailing season could be over by the time his lead reached Newcastle. It is no surprise that in 1665 he built his own smelting mill to handle increased supplies of Allendale ore. The site was at Dukesfield, alongside the Devil's Water, a mile downstream from Red Lead Mill and close to Blackhall.

Dukesfield was well placed for transport to Newcastle from mines in Allendale and the 400 acre estate was available to buy in the autumn of 1665. Blackett's interest must have lain in its river frontage, location in relation to his mines, and established carriers' tracks to the Tyne. We can be reasonably confident that he built his mill in time for the 1666 summer lead carriage season.[15] Being close to two other mills might also have increased his chances of poaching experienced smelters. The initial configuration is unknown, but a standard two-hearth mill would probably have given him enough capacity to smelt the annual 350 tons of lead suggested earlier. His actual production in these years cannot be measured, but Blackett was probably an equal member of a group of Tyneside merchants taking a serious interest in lead by the middle of the decade. This was to change dramatically after the catastrophic fire that destroyed so much of the city of London in September 1666. Let us imagine Blackett sitting as governor amongst the hostmen in February 1667 as they grumbled about the imposition by Parliament of a new tax on coal imported into London to pay for rebuilding, a tax therefore levied primarily on Newcastle. Perhaps Blackett's eye was caught by the building regulations enacted and what they implied about demand for lead. This was surely an enticing prospect early in 1667, especially as the second Anglo-Dutch war was yet to conclude. Sharp minds in Newcastle must have seen in this a way for the London coal tax to be recycled back into the region. Blackett certainly moved quickly over the following year.

Most importantly, he brought forward the renewal of his Allendale mining lease. It was due to expire in December 1669, but he signed a new, and broader, arrangement with Sir William Fenwick of Wallington two years early. Blackett clearly had the measure of the spendthrift Fenwick. The Wallington baronet's son and heir John had married Lady Mary Howard in 1663. She brought a £5,000 dowry which Sir William promptly embezzled and spent.[16] The £3,000 that Blackett gave for the new lease would have been far too tempting to refuse. For this sum Blackett obtained a renewal of his Allendale lease, free of any annual duty payments (which had amounted to 19% under the previous lease), for a term of 23 years.

The new lease also included a vitally important geographic extension, giving Blackett the mineral rights north of the Tyne. Here the great prize was the Fallowfield lead vein. This had been worked intermittently earlier in the century, including by John Butler in the 1630s, so it might be that Blackett's brother Edward could give some indication of its great potential. More recently it had been in the hands of the royalist Erringtons, who actually owned the surrounding land but not the mineral rights, which remained with Fenwick. Blackett's new mining lease literally undercut the Erringtons. It is therefore not surprising to find that they were persuaded to sell the Fallowfield estate to Blackett just six months later.[17] The Fallowfield lead vein was rich, and because it ran across and then alongside a deep ravine, it offered the prospect of free drainage from short levels running from the ravine into the ore lode.[18] Nevertheless, as in 1660, Blackett was taking a huge risk that the veins there and at Allenheads would remain productive.

A Great Many Men | 121

As we shall see, however, Fallowfield was to become vital to the Blackett lead business, but there were two further obstacles to be overcome first.

Unlike in Allendale, Blackett agreed to an annual duty payment for ore raised from Fallowfield. This would be levied at the rate of 1/7 for the first 12 years of the new lease, and 1/6 thereafter. To be free of this obligation he paid Fenwick a further £1,050 in May 1669. Blackett could do his sums. His mercantile training equipped him to use an interest rate to discount a stream of future annual duty ore payments back to a present value, or 'ready money' in contemporary terminology. Valuing lead ore at –say- £4.40/ton in 1669, that £1,050 payment represented, at the 6% going rate of interest, the present value of mining 135 tons of ore each year over the 23-year term. The chances are that Blackett was initially mining less than this, which would make his offer to Fenwick seem more attractive. Whether Fenwick understood any of this is quite another matter. If Fenwick had a competent and questioning land agent, Blackett would doubtless have treated him to a catalogue of woes regarding the difficulty of getting the mines going again, poor drainage and transport problems. More likely Fenwick was one of those genteel landowners the writers of handbooks for agents had in mind when exhorting them, in their own interests, to master analysis and valuation rules. One such in 1730 lamented that 'the seeming Perplexities with which such a Computation is involv'd ... remains a Task insuperable to the Generality of People whom they concern'.[19] However, the certainty of £1,050 today instead of the possibility of £75 per year from 100-120 tons of lead ore was presumably the kind of arithmetic Fenwick could grasp.

If Fenwick enjoyed the short-term pleasure of obtaining £4,050 from Blackett in the space of just 18 months, good for him. The deal was excellent for Blackett. For just over double the money he had paid Pearson between 1660 and 1665 he obtained mining rights over a much wider geographic area and free of all duty payments to the landowner. Furthermore, instead of a nine-year lease he now had not far short of a quarter century in which he could make the most of a natural monopoly of high quality lead veins. It hardly needs be said that at Fallowfield Blackett was soon producing far more than 120 or 130 tons implied in the duty ore agreement. In 1675 800 tons of ore came out of Fallowfield. Had it still been subject to the duty payments Fenwick would have earned over £400 in that year alone.

The deal thus encapsulates the unequal contest between shrewd, numerate and ambitious merchants armed with capital, and unwary members of the landed gentry living beyond their means. And the Blacketts hadn't finished with the Fenwicks yet. When he lent Sir William Fenwick a further £2,000 in 1674, secured against the manor of Hexham, Blackett probably never expected Fenwick to be able to repay, therefore eventually having to forfeit the estate instead.[20] This we shall come to later, but for now the vision appears of a sleek and merciless predator on the savannah picking out its prey and setting off on a long and patient chase to bring it down.

The other obstacle to be overcome before the full potential of Fallowfield could be realised was a more practical one: the River Tyne. The mine was just eight miles north of Dukesfield but on the wrong side of the river, and there was no bridge. A petition to Parliament in late 1667 claimed that 'when the waters are high ... persons are either stop'd in their journeys or forced to ferry over the Tyne or foard it to the great hazard of looseing themselves and their goods above three score persons being att one time drowned in ferrying over att Hexham, besides many others yearly lost'.[21]

This petition from 'the citizens of Newcastle' was intended to prevent the Northumberland Justices of the Peace absolving themselves of responsibility for maintaining the decayed medieval bridge at Corbridge at the county's expense. It was claimed to be vital to moving goods to and from Tyneside from as far as Cumberland. Quite how vital the bridge was to this predominantly east-west traffic is less clear, however, than its obvious importance to north-south traffic between the two banks of the Tyne such as between the Fallowfield lead mine and Dukesfield smelt mill.[22] Blackett was of course a citizen of Newcastle and his signature is amongst those of the great merchants of the town, placed discreetly towards the foot of the list. The petition was granted, Northumberland's financial responsibility was confirmed and the bridge was rebuilt in 1674.[23] There it stands today, another visible legacy of the region's lead industry heritage to set beside the remains of the Dukesfield smelt mill and a subtle illustration of William Blackett's political skill and influence (Plate 11).

A Great Many Men | 123

Scale and Integration

A series of letters from Michael Blackett to his father between 1675 and 1678 following monthly visits to the mines allow us to reconstruct the extent of the family lead business after 15 years of investment and expansion. The 23-year-old Michael shared the monthly inspection duties with his even younger brother William II so their coverage is intermittent, but a very useful 15 reports have survived.[24] They portray an impressively large vertically integrated business connecting the mines in the high North Pennine dales down to the Newcastle quayside and onwards to various European destinations.

Extrapolating the monthly activity reported in October and November 1675 and February 1676 to an 11-month year (to allow for maintenance time) gives a total of 2,900 tons of ore mined and 1,600 tons of lead smelted. This ties in, reassuringly, to the 1,520 tons of lead of Blackett exports recorded in the 1676 Newcastle port book, to which might be added a share of the 43 tons shipped coastally that year.[25] Michael reported to his father in November 1675 that some 2,400 tons of ore had been stockpiled for smelting before the winter curtailed transport. It was a business at least ten times larger than in the early 1660s, a breathtaking rate of growth. This feverish intensification was reflected in talk of starting a night shift at Fallowfield.[26]

Figure 8.2 demonstrates the reach of Blackett's lead business across the North Pennines. Nearly three quarters of his lead ore was mined at Allenheads and Fallowfield. A further 14% came from Greengill and Redgroves on Alston Moor. He successfully prospected for lead at Greengill before taking a 21 year lease there in 1671 from the Catholic Radcliffes.[27] As before, religious differences did not get in the way of business. Here too Blackett increased production dramatically from an apparently standing start, for he extracted the huge amount of 650 tons of lead ore from Greengill in just six months in 1675, 167 tons in August alone.[28] His West Allen mines at Coalcleugh, Wellhope and Bates Hill were much smaller, delivering just under a tenth of his ore between 1675 and 1678. Ore also came in small quantities from Jeffrey's Grove in Hunstanworth and Rookhope in Weardale, almost certainly bought in rather than mined. Small parcels came from as far away as Dufton, overlooking the Eden Valley, and Lunehead, carried an extravagant 25 miles or more along the high ridges before losing nearly half their weight when smelted.

Figure 8.2. Estimated annual distribution of Blackett lead mining and smelting 1675-6

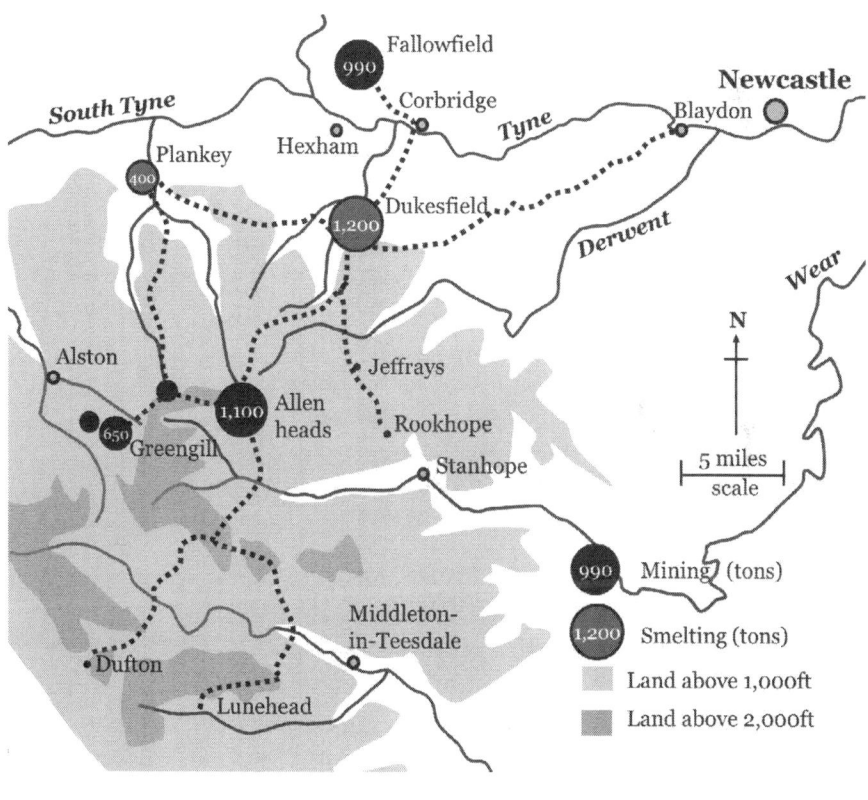

Source: MBL

The scale of Blackett's industrial ambition is also clear from Michael's accounts of the smelting operation. Rather than the usual two-hearth sheds of most mills, Dukesfield had six hearths at work in the autumn of 1675: five ore hearths and a slag hearth, at which the residue from the ore hearths could be recycled to extract more lead. By the following February, it was planned to add two more hearths. The growth of the business to such a size clearly pushed against the availability of skilled smelters. At Dukesfield 'is there nothing a wantinge butt Smelters, for most you have are either butt indiffrent workmen or Sicke.' They knew their own worth. A year later the smelters wanted advances against their wages while waiting for supplies of ore to arrive at the mill and Blackett was under pressure to do it for 'unlesse itt were done you would loose them all'.[29]

Dukesfield was probably developed in stages, a second building added to the initial two-hearth mill to provide extra capacity after the new mining lease was sealed at the end of 1667. The impressive civil engineering remains of a 600-yard long mill leat running from a weir on the Devils Water to the mill can be seen to this day and is likely to have been added in the late 1660s to improve the water supply.[30] Dukesfield was quite possibly unsurpassed in size by any other lead smelting mill in Britain for the next century. It could manage unprecedented throughput and handle the simultaneous smelting of varying ore quality from different mines and veins in separate hearths. However, Blackett needed yet more capacity and had therefore constructed a second mill, of two hearths, at Plankey on the lower River Allen, probably in 1673.[31]

There is, however, no mention of refining lead or of silver or litharge in Michael's letters. Had such further processing been carried out it would probably have been captured by a distinction in the port books between common and refined lead, the softer and more valuable lead resulting from a reduction process after the more brittle silver had been extracted, but it is all just 'lead' valued and charged at a single rate. The Tyneside glass industry presumably made use of red lead, derived from litharge, which we know was produced at Red Lead Mill in the 1650s. That might have been a short-lived experiment, for no mention of silver or red lead appears in the surviving 1670s accounts from Red Lead Mill and supplies to the glassworks were presumably imported.[32] This could all reflect nervousness amongst Blackett and other North Pennines miners over residual legislation claiming mines of precious metals for the Crown following the Restoration, legislation not repealed until 1688/93.[33] Furthermore, North Pennines lead veins typically contained little silver.

Blackett's business was impressive enough without refining for litharge and silver. Vast quantities of lead smelted at Dukesfield and Plankey were carried down to Blaydon by pony trains and cart.

Translating the physical logistics of this activity into a snapshot of daily activity brings the scale of Blackett's lead business to life. He probably directly employed around 430 miners, smelters, general labourers and agents. The level of production reported in Michael's letters means that on an average summer's day in the mid-1670s there was work for perhaps 30-50 contract ore and lead carriers. Some 100 horses brought two bags of ore each into Dukesfield from over the fells or across the Tyne at Corbridge, and a further 50 would make their way down the steep sides of Plankey's valley. 50 to 60 horseloads of chopwood fuel per day were lugged into Dukesfield from Hexhamshire's woodlands. Around 50 horses carrying two pigs of lead each set off from Dukesfield eastwards along the ridge to Blaydon, joined *en route* by another 20 or so from Plankey Mill. Some of the eastbound lead carriers were Dukesfield tenants, covering their rent with carriage earnings, thereby reducing the amount of cash that had to change hands.[34] By 1674 Blackett had his own dedicated staiths at Blaydon on which the pieces of lead could be piled, an important piece of infrastructure. From these tidal reaches of the Tyne, lead was keeled downstream to Blackett's storage cellars on The Close ready to be shipped out.

It is possible that he was also involved in some way with his nephew and ex-apprentice William in Scottish lead mines for they corresponded between Newcastle and Edinburgh at this time. Young William was an iron dealer in Sweden in the 1660s. By the summer of 1674 he was mining lead far up in Glen Lyon in the Scottish highlands, 40 miles northwest of Perth, such was the industry's dizzy mania.[35]

Weardale

Blackett clearly also coveted Weardale. The upper reaches of the valley to the west of Stanhope were crossed by a number of lead veins and Blackett cannot have failed to notice how Haselrig had enriched himself during the 1650s. However, from March 1661 this was Humphrey Wharton's own natural mining monopoly. The Swaledale gentleman and London barrister, slightly younger than Blackett, was appointed moormaster in Weardale by Bishop John Cosin for £60 per year, in lieu of the bishop's duty ore or lott, for the duration of Cosin's term as bishop.[36] Nevertheless, Blackett's name or influence appears periodically in the confusing jumble of leases, agreements, court cases, letters and an Act of Parliament that survive from the 1660s and 1670s in a wide range of archives. However, when ordered into chronological sequence, and when considering the interests of four key protagonists, Wharton, Blackett, Cosin and the rector of Stanhope, Isaac Basire, a plausible narrative of largely unedifying motives, actions and results can be teased out.

Basire matters because, in addition to the Bishop's claim to a tenth of Weardale's lead ore as his lott, the rector of Stanhope had rights to a further tenth as his tithe. The parish covers the entire upper part of Weardale, although the extent of the rector's tithe coverage was ill-defined at the Restoration in 1660. Like his fellow royalist churchman Cosin, Basire had spent the Interregnum years overseas, returning to Stanhope only in 1661. That August he leased his tithe rights to Wharton for a year at a rate that valued all the ore raised at £4.25/ton. Presumably because of the opportunities this gave for under-reporting, the following year this was replaced with a fixed sum of £200.[37] This was in stark contrast to Cosin's £60 per year. While the Bishop had agreed a payment representing annual output of around 140 tons of ore per year, not much more than a year later Wharton tacitly accepted, in his arrangement with Basire, that he was producing some 450 tons per year or more.[38] Furthermore, the annual tithe payment subsequently varied with the level of production (or as much of it as Basire could count). Cosin, who later grumbled that he had been 'surprised' into the 1661 arrangement prematurely, could only watch as Wharton's payment to Basire increased to £210 in 1663 and to £260 in 1665.[39]

However, an opportunity arose in 1666 for the terms of Cosin's moormastership lease to be reopened. Cosin was 72 and not in good health.[40] When he died, Wharton's lease would terminate. At a time when increasing demand for North Pennines lead created an incentive to invest in drainage levels in Weardale as mining intensified, the uncertain term of Wharton's lease made this risky. Wharton and the bishop had a shared interest in extending the lease term. A private Act of Parliament was brought forward in November to allow the bishop to grant a longer and more secure lease to the moormaster for three named lives rather than one.[41] Today we can admire a rational institutional change which encouraged mining investment. It was indeed swiftly followed by Wharton's construction of a new smelting mill on the Derwent river, en route from Weardale to the coast.[42] At the time, however, the process opened the door to tactical opportunism.

Basire saw an opportunity to enshrine in law the extent of his tithing rights in Weardale. This is where Blackett came in. In 1666 Basire granted a three-year lease of his lead ore tithes to Blackett for £300 per annum. Basire and Blackett then launched an Exchequer Court case against Wharton early in 1667 claiming underpayment of tithes, and won.[43] The Rector separately secured a clause in the private bill going through Parliament that all lead ore dug in Stanhope and Wolsingham parishes would be subject to tithe and this duly formed part of the Act which passed into law at the end of 1667. Blackett also took opportunities to cultivate a relationship with the Bishop at around this time. Writing in December 1666 as mayor of Newcastle in reply to a request from the bishop for charitable funds, Blackett said he 'intends shortly to waite upon your Lordshipp'. We can be pretty sure that other topics were on Blackett's agenda.[44]

What was Blackett up to? He might genuinely have believed that he could prise the moormastership away from Wharton. After all, he had obtained Pearson's evidently lucrative rights in Allenheads just six years earlier, having been prepared to pay handsomely enough. Before the end of 1667 he was able to lay out £3,000 to renew and extend the Allendale lease. He might have tried to dangle some of that largesse in front of Cosin in the winter of 1666/7. As it turned out, of course, Wharton was not dislodged and with the passing of the Act at the end of 1667 he was even more secure. With this timing in mind, it's possible that Blackett's renewal of the rights in Allendale and extension to Fallowfield was actually his 'Plan B', albeit a highly lucrative one as it turned out. In Weardale Blackett did have the Stanhope tithe ore lease and ratcheting up their annual value to the rector made it more likely that the bishop would seek a higher annual rent from Wharton. This duly came to pass. The new rent and lott ore payment agreed in January 1668 was £210 per year. Although low compared to the tithe rights, it was a marked increase on the previous £60 per year.

Blackett had helped drive up the mining costs of his principal competitor from that date onwards, although it cannot have added more than pennies to Wharton's costs for each ton of lead ore mined.[45]

Furthermore, it was dearly bought. Recovering the £300/year Blackett paid to Basire required the hard work of finding, collecting and carrying away his 10% of the ore from up and down Weardale. The volume of ore was not going to add much to his production in Allendale. However, it did give him the legal right to visit and inspect all the Weardale mines and gain useful mining intelligence. Furthermore, since the miners were obliged to sell their hard-won ore to Wharton at a substantial discount to the going rate, more than a few might have been tempted to sell some of it illicitly to Blackett's agents for a higher price. At the very least his presence must have been an irritant to Wharton, but there was also the prospect that as production rose, Blackett might hope to carry off more ore to Dukesfield for his fixed £300/year.[46]

It must have ensured constant wariness on Wharton's part thereafter. In the aftermath of Cosin's death in January 1672, the bishop's revenues reverted to the Crown until a new bishop was appointed. The moormaster was in no rush to confirm his lease and did not petition for its renewal until 10th December 1673.[47] This was just a week after Blackett became one of Newcastle's two MPs, with all the opportunities Wharton might foresee this would afford his rival in currying favour in London. Wharton's rivalry with Blackett must surely explain the otherwise incongruous appearance of Sunderland as a significant port for lead in the 1670s and 1680s, before and after which time it was of no consequence. In 1673 418 tons of lead was shipped coastally from Sunderland, 503 tons to coastal and overseas destinations in 1676, 515 tons in 1679 and 398 in 1686. Wharton's new smelting mill on the Derwent after 1668 was ideally placed between Weardale and Sunderland. One of his carriers said he carried lead to Lambton, near Chester-le-Street, from where lead could be ferried down the Wear.[48] Wharton might have had good reason to feel that Blackett's influence in Newcastle might hinder his trade there, making Sunderland a safer option. After Wharton's death in the 1690s no further lead left from Sunderland.

The Newcastle merchant had certainly continued to snap at

Wharton's heels. In 1676 Blackett bought the freehold estate of Woodcroft east of Stanhope.[49] It has been suggested that this was a purely sentimental indulgence. Woodcroft was the ancestral Blackett family home and was bought from a deeply indebted namesake, but it meant Blackett now owned a substantial estate in the valley, albeit one to the west of the worked lead veins.

Much more directly, he obtained a lease from the bishop in 1678 of the mining rights in the inclosed lands and parks in Stanhope and Wolsingham parishes through a third party. Importantly, this lease, which granted mining rights in the narrow band of cultivated enclosed farmland in the valley bottom close to the riverside, lay outside the jurisdiction of the moormaster. He couldn't challenge Wharton head-on any more, but he might be able to go around him. Just six months later Blackett purchased the copyholds of mining grounds at Killhope, Wellhope and Sparkshield near the head of the valley for £1,600.[50] Within weeks of this later acquisition Blackett was complaining to Parliament that Wharton's men had 'entered upon his possession'.[51] The timing suggests this meant the Wellhope and Sparkshield area, crossed by a lead vein, but an Exchequer court case launched by Wharton the following year mentions other upland farmsteads further east down the valley. Hillside common pastures such as Westgate Heights, Black Dean and Billing might have outer walls to separate them from the open waste still higher up the fell, but it was not at all clear that these lead-bearing areas of rough upland grazing were truly 'inclosed' under the meaning of Blackett's new lease deep in Wharton's territory.[52] Such vague definitions made the moorland heights profitable for lawyers as well as for miners. Either way, Blackett's ambition to continue expanding his lead interests clearly remained undimmed in the late 1670s. Wharton's Exchequer bill named Richard and John Mowbray and Christopher Copperthwaite, all of whom worked for Blackett in the 1670s, so it looks as though Blackett was serious about exploiting the hillside common pastures in Weardale from the outset.

They were an expensive addition to his lead interests and, as we shall see later, his son had to retreat in the 1680s. Given Wharton's secure control of Weardale, an objective observer might conclude that Blackett's manoeuvres were an obsessive distraction, a poor use of his time and capital bordering on a personal feud.

However, his track record of deal-making and the growth of his lead business made it a logical attempt at further expansion. Access to the multiple lead veins in Weardale could also have spread the risk inherent in his heavy dependence on Allenheads and Fallowfield remaining productive. Most importantly, this extra mining didn't increase output just for the sake of it, for Blackett had built a highly effective and profitable business, not just a large one, as we shall now see.

Chapter 9

A New Industrial Giant

Blackett's lead business was unprecedented in size within the North Pennines and it had built up rapidly in well under two decades. How did he control and manage it across 40 miles of difficult country? Simply keeping it going must have been a challenge, but there is also evidence of innovation and improvement and it appeared to be a highly profitable operation. Its scale and performance had a wider impact on the industry as a whole and the development of the regional economy in the years after the Restoration of the monarchy. This chapter addresses each point in turn.

Management

The integration between mining, smelting and the carriage of lead down to Newcastle was described in the last chapter. This was enough of a management challenge but it didn't stop there. Lead took Blackett back into overseas trade as a major exporter by the mid-1670s. Vertical integration extended outwards from Newcastle into domestic and European markets. In some respects this is surprising for it seems that there was distinctly more profit to be made in producing lead than on trading it beyond Newcastle.[1] Yet the trade was clearly attractive enough to tempt Blackett back to sea in addition to his domestic industrial interests. We saw earlier that he had export cargo in 18 overseas voyages in 1661 and just ten in 1666. Yet according to fellow Newcastle merchant Ralph Grey, Blackett had '30 sayle' in 1673, and the port book records show 27 separate cargoes of lead alone in 1675 and 35 in 1676.[2]

Most of it was destined for Amsterdam and Rotterdam, much more so than for Newcastle's other lead merchants.[3] He brought very little back from those ports by way of return cargoes. These were cash sales, taking advantage of important developments in Dutch trade and finance. Amsterdam's great building boom was over so there was probably limited local consumption of lead, but the city's sophisticated merchants continued to seek commodity imports to trade across Europe on commission. Aided by low domestic interest rates, perhaps between 3-4%, distinctly lower than England's official 6% rate, they attracted trade by offering generous payment terms.[4] There were merchants in Amsterdam and Rotterdam perfectly willing to remit bills to Blackett for immediate encashment on delivery of his lead at a low discount rather than make him wait the traditional three months. We see this in the gratitude of his son Michael to his Rotterdam correspondent who 'constantly remitted mee money before you were In Cash' and from whom he had also extracted a lower commission rate.[5] Ralph Grey was another Newcastle merchant asking his correspondent to return cash rather than goods.[6]

    This financial facility must have been a helpful boost to cashflow. Control of every stage of production and sale from mining up in the distant hills, contracting seasonal transport capacity, smelting en route to Newcastle, warehousing the lead, exporting it to Europe and collecting payment sounds very impressive and doubtless looked it too. But such 'vertical integration' put a strain on working capital, especially in a fast-growing business such as Blackett's. Many months could elapse between mining the ore and collecting overseas payment for lead sales, perhaps getting on for a year once winter closed the moorland ways and increased the perils at sea. Thousands of pounds could be tied up in stockpiles of ore and lead out in the country or in the Newcastle cellar by the mid-1670s. Paying miners and smelters promptly put further pressure on the time between outgoings and receipts. So being able to obtain prompt payment for lead sold thanks to cheap finance in Amsterdam eased the working capital burden for little in the way of lost revenue. He was seeking cash sales in Scotland too in 1676 and angrily berated his nephew William for delays in remitting payments to Newcastle.[7] Access to cheap credit outside England might well explain why Blackett was tempted back to trading, rather than let other merchants have the cashflow benefit. He was even trying to buy all the lead Ralph Grey had to hand late in 1673 to export it himself.[8] This was evidently all worth it. Operating a large and growing vertically integrated business avoided constant niggling battles and transaction costs between separate mining and smelting concerns as each sought to gain advantage over the other.* Managing his own sales and shipments also avoided being at the mercy of a ring of merchants at the quay who might try to drive down the prices at which they would buy lead, as happened at Stockton by the mid-1670s.[9] Vertical integration captured the profit available at each stage of the operation. It secured the benefits of the natural monopoly hypothesised for Blackett as a strategic goal in chapter six.

Blackett was not the first to connect together an integrated lead business in Newcastle's hinterland. John Butler did so in the 1630s. Grey and Briggs were running just such a business from the 1650s, and Pearson was probably smelting his own lead at the same time, but none approached the scale Blackett achieved in the 1670s. By then Butler had disappeared, Pearson bought out, and Grey was selling much of his lead through other merchants. Grey was in any case producing only around 200 tons of lead per year.[10] Wharton's Weardale lead business must have been significantly larger than the Grey consortium's, but it was even less vertically integrated.[11] The miners were effectively Wharton's sub-contractors or lessees, paid according to the market price for the ore they raised irrespective of how hard it was to win. Then, from 1670 he sub-let many of his mines throughout Weardale to fellow Yorkshireman Charles Paulet, soon to succeed his father as the Marquess of Winchester.[12] Wharton's lead was sold by merchants. The core of his direct business was lead smelting, at mills in Wolsingham, Derwent and just outside Stanhope. His son Robert managed Wharton's affairs in Weardale and was, logically, based in Wolsingham.[13]

For Blackett to achieve such rapid industrial expansion and then to sustain it on a large and integrated scale must have relied as much upon disciplined management as it did on entrepreneurial flair. Mining, ore carriage logistics, fuel delivery to the mills, smelting and lead carriage to the ports needed to be co-ordinated over 40 miles of hard country and then sales and payment managed between much more distant locations. Michael Blackett's letters and

---

*Carriage was the exception. Negotiating annual contracts with carriers could be tiresome but was evidently preferable to owning and employing large numbers of horses and carriers, with all that implied for land, forage, breeding, and stabling all year long. But as the largest operator, Blackett could presumably command cheap rates for the promise of volume of work, including for return journeys carrying supplies to the mines.

other evidence show that the foundations of the elaborate management structure through which the 18th-century business was run were laid by the mid-1670s. A central figure was John Mowbray, the smelting mill agent based at Dukesfield for whom the fine 17th-century farmhouse, still there today, was presumably built. He had children baptised at Wolsingham until 1665, was at Steel, near Dukesfield by 1668, and wrote to Blackett as his agent from Dukesfield in 1674 when setting on the lead carriage.[14] Mowbray was barely literate but clearly competent, and was surely recruited from Weardale to oversee the construction and management of the mill and the annual ore and lead carriage contracts.*

Mowbray's brother Richard was in charge of the Allen valley mines from 1668, just after the conclusion of the new mining lease from Fenwick.[15] Blackett's nephew John, younger brother of ex-apprentice William of Stockholm and Scotland, was installed in a similar position at Fallowfield. The present Allenheads Inn, surely the agent's house, and Fallowfield House also appear to date from around the same time. Although later changed and extended, we should recognise them and Dukesfield Hall as part of the 17th-century lead industry's visible legacy and its management infrastructure (see Plates 15-17). A fourth such house stood at Blaydon until the early 20th century, once the home of Michael Robinson, staithman, whom Blackett wished in 1680 to continue in that role for life 'if he carry himself honestly in the discharge of the same'.[16]

Owners at a distance from far-flung works were alert to the possibility of managers straying from the 'honest discharge' of their duties. Blackett put in place a regime of monthly inspections, sometimes carried out personally but by the mid-1670s usually delegated to Michael and his capable younger brother William II. The presentation of Michael's monthly reports shows that his father insisted on a standard pattern. They were designed to report key measures consistently: the amounts of ore raised at the mines and corresponding cost, the outlook for future production based on the state of the workings, fuel and ore delivered and stockpiled at the mines, mills, lead produced and the associated costs and amount

---

*Two other Mowbray brothers, Robert and Thomas, were at Dukesfield in the late 1660s, both of whom died there. It is tempting to see them as smelters, and that all four brothers were poached from Wharton's principal mill at Wolsingham: DPR1/1670/M15, 1672/M11.

of lead delivered to Blaydon. Their sharp-eyed recipient therefore had a regular view of operations, enabling him to query logistical bottlenecks or calculate variances in key production ratios that might indicate 'irregularities'. And query he did. Michael's reports to his father are sometimes followed within a fortnight by answers to questions such as why Richard Mowbray had been given more cash than strictly needed for the Allenheads pay.[17]

A Lean and Profitable Business

Keeping remote control of the business was one thing. Driving it on to greater efficiency was the real prize, reducing costs and increasing profits. Night shifts were one aspect of this, generating additional production for the same fixed infrastructure and drainage capital cost. The hilly terrain in which Blackett's mines were located lent itself to the fixed capital infrastructure of drainage levels being installed to reduce or remove the ongoing recurring cost of running engines and pumps. Work was underway for at least two years in the late 1670s to drive a level possibly up to a mile long to drain the Fallowfield mines at great depth.[18] Always assuming the veins remained productive, the capital cost could be spread over a rising quantity of ore mined. Most of the cost of lead lay in the mining stage of the operation.

Summing Michael's mining reports for various dates between 1675 and 1678, the direct costs reported for the mining and dressing of 2,340 tons of ore in Allendale, Nentdale and Fallowfield amounted to £2.26/ton.[19] Ore was being bought on the open market locally at around £4. Many would have been content to try no harder but Blackett clearly wished to push on. By the later 1670s this was probably just as well for the Newcastle lead price was falling. At the start of the decade it had been above £12 per ton but lead was selling at around £10.80 in 1675 and 1676, £9.60 a year later, and for £9.40 in 1680.

This might have had a direct bearing on the 'new order of pay' introduced at Blackett's 'positive order' in 1677. All the indications are that this entailed a move to paying the miners variable piece rates. Certainly this regime was in place in Fallowfield by 1680, when at least six different rates can be observed in the surviving accounts for mining at three different shafts over the course of six months. The rates went down as well as up, presumably reflecting changes in the ease with which ore could be mined as the veins were pursued from the shafts, as well as the price of lead.[20] Although this approach has many of the features of the later system of bargains struck between miners and agents, there is no evidence that the rates were negotiated at this stage, rather than being imposed on the miners. With the lead price falling in 1677 and some of the heat taken out of the market, it looks as though Blackett gambled that he could now make this change, in contrast to the stance he had taken with Michael over pay little more than a year earlier.

Because it transferred risk to miners hitherto paid a daily wage irrespective of underground conditions and productivity, resistance was doubtless anticipated. Michael's letters imply that this came from the agents as well as the miners. The new system meant extra work for them too, of course, having to assess the state of the vein at the various shafts frequently in order to inform their decisions on pay rates. To outflank a combined front of opposition and drive the change through, Blackett recruited Christopher Copperthwaite from Swaledale, whose arrival, predictably, did not go down well with any of the existing agents.[21] The grumbled complaints of Allenheads' Richard Mowbray and Fallowfield's John Blackett were, Michael reported to his father, 'not worth yo[u]r hearinge being all babbles' and the miners were eventually prevailed upon to comply with the new system. Copperthwaite was still at Fallowfield in the early 1680s and John Blackett had gone.[22] Perhaps the Swaledale man was used to a similar system in Yorkshire. It was more sophisticated than Wharton's apparent regime of paying Weardale miners based solely on the price of lead. The Fallowfield accounts suggest that rates took into account changes in underground conditions, and doubtless a key part of Copperthwaite's job was to sell the opportunities this presented to experienced and hard-working miners in deciding whether to take the contract at the rates on offer. This was clearly a more attractive regime for the mine owner given the capricious nature of both markets and lead veins, but here too were incentives for Michael's 'lusty able men', who could now hope to be rewarded for their skill and hard work and not be held back to a uniform level with the 'lubbards'. The lubbards presumably had to shape up or lose out.

Skilled and able men could get on. The Mowbray brothers appear to have had been of modest means in Wolsingham. John was surely originally a smelter, and quite possibly his three brothers were too, all drawn away from Wharton's principal mill. The memorial inscription on John's tomb in the privileged position of the choir of Hexham church in 1687 accorded him the title 'gent', and he left bequests of over £800 in his will.[23] By the time Richard died in 1693 he was carefully styled 'Mr Richard Mowbray, Steward to Sir William Blackett, of East Allenheads' in the burial register, in which position he was succeeded by his nephew George, 'Gent', by 1706.[24] John Snow was another Wolsingham yeoman who was in Fallowfield by the 1670s. His son Cuthbert was taken on as a hostman apprentice by Blackett in 1675, echoing his own route into a merchant's life decades earlier, and was evidently seen as reliable enough just five years later to be appointed a trustee of Blackett's will while still in his early 20s.[25] Edward Stoute, of an Allendale family, had taught himself to become the drainage engine expert at Allenheads by 1677 when he was asking Blackett via Michael whether he was needed in this capacity at Fallowfield.[26] Another of those who enjoyed the respect of their masters and whose name has come down to us was Joseph Bittlestone, a lead smelter with links to the Dukesfield/Red Lead Mill area.[27] By 1676 Joseph was Blackett's chief smelter at Plankey Mill, in which year he also married Margaret Swinburne, of a smelting family at Blackhall Mill, and in Durham cathedral of all places. In the early 1680s he was recruited to supervise the building of Sir Francis Radcliffe's smelting mill at Woodhall and subsequently to manage it. Men like Bittlestone were skilled and inquisitive tinkerers and improvers tackling local problems. Astute mine owners encouraged, respected and rewarded them.

This was certainly true of those who smelted the lead. Smelters were the aristocrats of lead industry labour, rewarded well for their skill and willingness to endure the life-stunting danger of sweating in the toxic fumes of an ore hearth. Few of them were needed compared to the dozens of miners working underground. Smelting typically accounted for less than a tenth of the cost of a piece of lead delivered to Newcastle's quayside. However, smelting efficiency had a disproportionate influence on overall

A New Industrial Giant | 139

costs and it was crucially dependent on the skill and experience of the smelters. Poor work and temperature control at the hearth could ruin a batch of ore. Conversely, the more lead that could be produced per ton of ore, the lower the cost of mining and ore transport embodied in the lead delivered to the quayside. This is the reason why, in the 18th century, there were agitated letters from agents to the smelting mills when the yield of lead from ore fell below 60%. However, the few ratios that can be calculated for the 17th-century North Pennines smelting appear to show that 50% might be a better benchmark in this earlier period. Trials in 1680 at Plankey Mill yielded lead at the rate of between 33% and 53% of the weight of ore consumed at the ore hearth. Detailed production accounts for the Birkey Burn mill near Fallowfield between 1680-6 show a yield of 50%. In 1706, a cost-benefit analysis comparing the Whitfield and Ryton smelting mill sites assumed a yield of 52.5%.[28]

If Blackett's contemporaries were complacent about costs during the great regional lead boom, there are signs that he at least sought a better return. His demand to know, each month, the amount of ore delivered to the mills and the amount of lead produced indicate an interest in smelting yield as well as production throughput and logistics. He must have picked key people for Dukesfield, masters of their craft, starting with John Mowbray. The mill's proximity to Blackhall and Red Lead Mill surely helped him poach experts from there too with the promise of higher wages, paid regularly. Yet the sheer rate of growth in his business must also have required a commitment to training bright, able young men to become expert smelters. All of this is hidden from us, but we know from elsewhere that Blackett took on capable youngsters as his Newcastle apprentices. Good smelters were worth indulging. In 1678 Robert Foster had 'a great quantity of Leed Lyeing ready att his harth' but told Mowbray or Michael that he was presently busy with his 'country employment', probably at a smallholding. In the time-honoured words of scarce skilled tradesmen through the ages, he said he would get back to smelting 'as soon as he can'.[29]

There is another aspect of lead smelting to consider here. Most smelting mills were handicapped by the lack of a slag hearth at which the residue of the first smelting could be reprocessed to wring out further saleable lead from the same initial quantity of ore. If Woodhall Mill near Haydon Bridge had a slag hearth at all, it was inefficient enough for a smelter to be eager in the 1730s to buy the slag still lying there for reprocessing.[30] Dukesfield already had a slag hearth by 1675 and one was added at Plankey between then and 1680.[31] One of only two others documented in the region before the 18th century was installed at Blackett's eldest son Edward's mill near Fallowfield by 1691.

With the introduction of a slag hearth the cost of smelting rose for an additional, and expensive, step was added to the process. Analysis of Edward's detailed mill accounts in the 1690s shows that slag processing added nearly 30% to the operating cost of ore-hearth smelting. However, it increased the amount of lead for sale by 16%.[32] Applying this to a smelting mill already achieving a decent yield gives the results shown in the illustrative calculations of Figure 9.1. Although the cost of smelting increased, this added just 23p/ton, for it was a small part of the total cost. However, because less ore was needed for each ton of lead sold, the cost of mining it, any duty owed to mineral rights owners and ore carriage reduced by far more, increasing profit accordingly. No wonder Blackett wanted to track these ratios. At this distance in time and with only partial survival of his monthly reports it is dangerous to come to any conclusion regarding what his mills actually achieved, but there are indications that his smelters might have extracted a yield of around 61% in 1678.[33] The economics of the lead industry pivoted on smelting efficiency, like a short powerful tail wagging a lumbering dog.

Blackett's agents, miners and smelters surely devoted attention to other aspects of the production process, wringing out incremental improvements under their master's demanding eye. This much can be surmised from the evidence of one such change distilled from the port book records. Pieces or pigs of lead produced at the ore hearth originally weighed around 8 stones (50 kg). For customs purposes the overseas port books usually recorded both the weight and number of pieces of lead in each consignment, allowing the average weight to be calculated. Lead pieces shipped abroad from both Newcastle and Stockton in the 1650s and 1660s all averaged around 8 stones each. This increased at both ports over the rest of the century. A detailed examination of the 1675 record shows clearly that this was led by Blackett (see Figure 9.2).

A New Industrial Giant | 141

Figure 9.1 Smelting yield and the unit cost of lead

£ per ton of lead	52.5% yield	61% yield
Revenue	11.20	11.20
Cost	8.52	7.92
Ore	5.18	4.45
Ore carriage	0.76	0.66
Smelting	0.80	1.03
Lead carriage	0.76	0.76
Overhead	1.02	1.02
Profit	2.67	3.28
As % of revenue	24%	29%

Source: see Appendix 3.4, Table A3.15. (£ profit rounded.)

The average weight of lead pieces in almost all his 28 separate overseas shipments was above 9.5 stones, whereas just 13 of the 51 shipments by other merchants were that heavy. Some variation was inevitable. Moulds could not be made to the same exact size, nor could they always be filled precisely to the brim with molten lead ladled from the hearth. But each piece of lead cast at Dukesfield and Plankey Mill was nearly 10% heavier on average than those from elsewhere. Blackett had surely increased the size of his lead moulds and the supposition is that this brought a slight reduction in lead carriage and manual handling charges for each journey. A horse that could carry two nine-stone pieces might manage two of ten, and the carriers expected to accept this without any increase in the charge. Given the quantities Blackett was producing, this may even have reduced any problems in physically finding enough horses for the summer lead carriage.

This can be pushed no further than to illustrate the fruits of an attention to detail which will be recognised by today's manufacturing process efficiency experts. When applied to large volumes of production the accumulation of such incremental improvements could make a substantial contribution to profitability. Alongside a carefully designed pay policy for a large industrial workforce, logistical control of throughput, unit-cost analysis, and a focus on high efficiency at the key smelting stage of production, Blackett was using an array of advanced management techniques across his vertically integrated business quite different from those he trained in as a trader. They also date from earlier than other examples hitherto brought to our attention.[34]

Figure 9.2. Average Newcastle lead piece size, 1675.

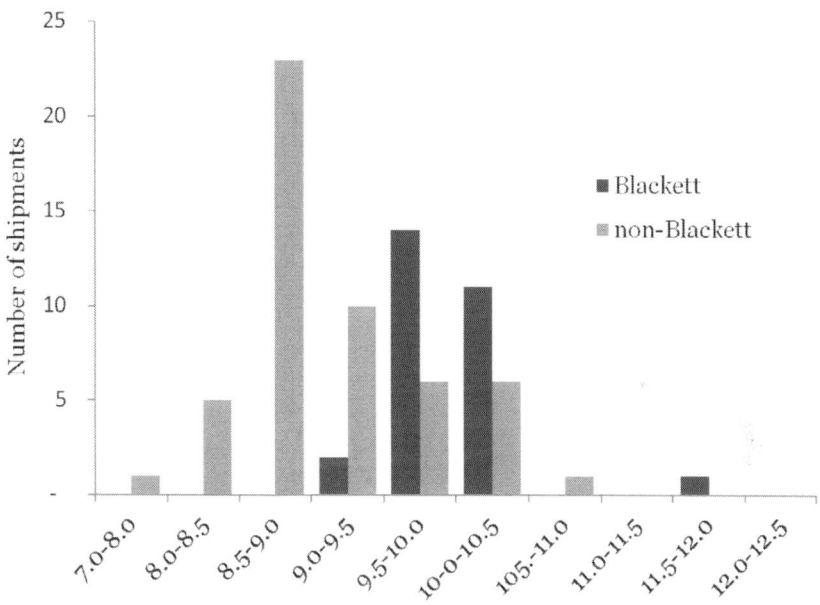

Source: TNA E 190/196/2 Newcastle overseas

It certainly paid off for him. Michael's reports on his father's business in the mid-1670s can be used alongside price data to estimate profitability at that date. His 1,500 tons of lead would have realised around £16,800 in revenue if sold in Newcastle. As we have seen, he actually shipped most of his stock to be sold in Amsterdam instead, but to err on the side of caution any additional revenue, freight cost and profit margin this might have generated is ignored. Michael's reports, cross-checked where possible against cost rates identified from other accounts have been used to compute his costs at around £11,900.[35] This possibly overstates his actual expenditure, so the calculated profit of £4,900 might underestimate the true performance of the business. At nearly 30%

it was still, however, a highly impressive gross margin on sales. Blackett's judgement, confidence, and willingness to embrace the monumental risk of lead vein failure at Allenheads and Fallowfield in the 1660s had paid off.

The dimly viewed snapshot of 1675-6 is unlikely to have captured a single good year. If anything the cost of mining surely rose rather than fell through time, whether through the need for deeper shafts, longer levels, more drainage or simply increased miners' pay in a booming market. Projecting backwards to the 1660s, during which decade the lead price appears to have been generally above £11-12 per ton, this suggests profit rates at least as healthy, albeit on lower levels of production. It is conceivable that the additional investment in mines, in the Dukesfield estate and mill, Plankey and even the sums successfully dangled in front of Fenwick for the lease renewal had all been generated from profits ploughed back into the business to help it grow.

The amount of capital Blackett had tied up in his lead business is difficult to estimate. We know about the £4,050 he paid Fenwick for mining rights on top of the earlier £1,820 paid to Pearson, but the shafts, levels, drainage engines, surface plant and buildings, land, smelting mills, leats, staiths and agents' houses also have to be allowed for, and renewed as they wore out. These demands were probably lighter than those of collieries. Although lead required smelting mills, these were typically not expensive. The lower physical quantity of material mined probably extended the life of underground infrastructure beyond that of coal and there were no waggonways to construct. Working capital was, of course, needed to pay the miners and smelters promptly while waiting many months for revenue to materialise, even if this was mitigated by the availability of cheap Dutch finance. Appendix 3.5 tentatively values Blackett's lead assets at £14,700, around 60% of which was fixed capital. A profit of £4,900 or more therefore gave him a return of about 33% on his capital in the mid-1670s.

Blackett's lead profits in the mid-1670s probably matched or surpassed those generated annually by the Marescoes' overseas trading business noted in chapter six. Even if we are unsure of the amount of capital Blackett had invested to earn these returns, it was surely nowhere near the £33,500 employed by the Marescoes in their trading concern.[36] He had therefore resoundingly broken free of the linear relationship between capital and earnings in mercantile trade by establishing a successful large and integrated industrial business employing hundreds of people. Disciplined operation across a high level of production yielded economies of scale and a very high return on his capital. The natural geological monopoly that supported it all was safe for another 15 years. He might not have been the first to seek vertical integration, but the scale and extent of his business was unique within the North Pennines and quite possibly within England as a whole. It was a hugely impressive achievement personally and one that transformed the industry in the region.

Blackett and the Northeast Lead Industry

So dramatic was the rise of Blackett's lead business that it drove the whole Newcastle market and achieved for him a central position in the regional industry. In 1661 he exported just 39 tons of lead. This gave him a tenth share of the total exported from Newcastle in that year. His 1,200 tons in 1675 and 1,520 tons in 1676, on the other hand, represented 77% and 80% of the total respectively. Put another way, William Blackett was responsible for nearly all of the rapid growth in lead exports from Newcastle between 1661 and 1676, and in so doing he came to dominate the market. No single other name is shown against more than 68 tons of lead exported from Newcastle in either 1675 or 1676. Even if Blackett had no hand in any other lead shipments from the region in 1676, (merchants are not identified in the coastal trade records), his Newcastle exports alone still accounted for 62% of 2,460 tons of lead shipped from there and Sunderland.[37] Was he deliberately seeking monopoly control?

If lead from the North Pennines had become vital to the demands of London and northern Europe by the mid-1670s then Blackett might well have fancied that his domination of the Newcastle trade could bring him some control over pricing. Perhaps this was what drove him to seek inroads into Weardale because Wharton must have been the next most important producer in the region. There is a hint of the pricing power that a monopoly could bestow in a letter from Ralph Grey in 1675 saying that no-one in

Newcastle sold lead at under £13 and Blackett for no less than £13 5s.[38] This is, however, a slender mark-up on the going rate and no similar complaints survive in the historical record. In any case, he could have forseen that if Newcastle lead prices rose too high Derbyshire lead would once again be able to compete in London and overseas markets. His business model was surely better served by stimulating demand, expanding his interests and reducing his unit costs.

Fostering a new cohort of management ability through his lead business was one of the contributions Blackett made to the wider regional economy which went beyond his own material success. There were other contributions, not least the rapid changes wrought in his mining districts and along the lead roads down to Tyneside. A very rough estimate of the population in Allendale derived from the Hearth Tax assessments of 1663-5 and 1673 suggest an increase of around 50% between these two dates across the whole parish, which encompassed both the East and West Allen valleys and Allendale town. All of the additional households were enumerated amongst those too poor to pay the tax, rising from 57 in 1663-5 to 149 in 1673, with particularly large increases in the district that included the expanding mining settlements of Allenheads and Coalcleugh.[39] Half of the names given in 1673 do not appear in the equivalent return of eight years earlier. Some came from as far as Derbyshire, but quite how they were recruited so quickly remains unclear. Mining leases typically provided for wood to be taken for 'houses, hovels and lodges', conjuring up an image of the rumbustious mining shanty towns of the American 'wild west' or, closer to hand, the rapid development of a proletarian mining village at Whickham several decades earlier.[40] Springing up very rapidly around the mine shafts at Allenheads in the late 1660s, and at Fallowfield too, were the forerunners of the later squalid mining hostels. They were occupied by young men attracted to a hard life in these barren valleys by the prospect of a decent cash wage.

The rapid rise of the North East's lead industry must have been shockingly vivid to the older residents of the remote, cold valley heads of the North Pennines, used to quiet continuity. Its economic impact was also felt more widely across the region, illustrated by the appearance of smelting mills between 1650 and 1690 (see Figure 9.3).

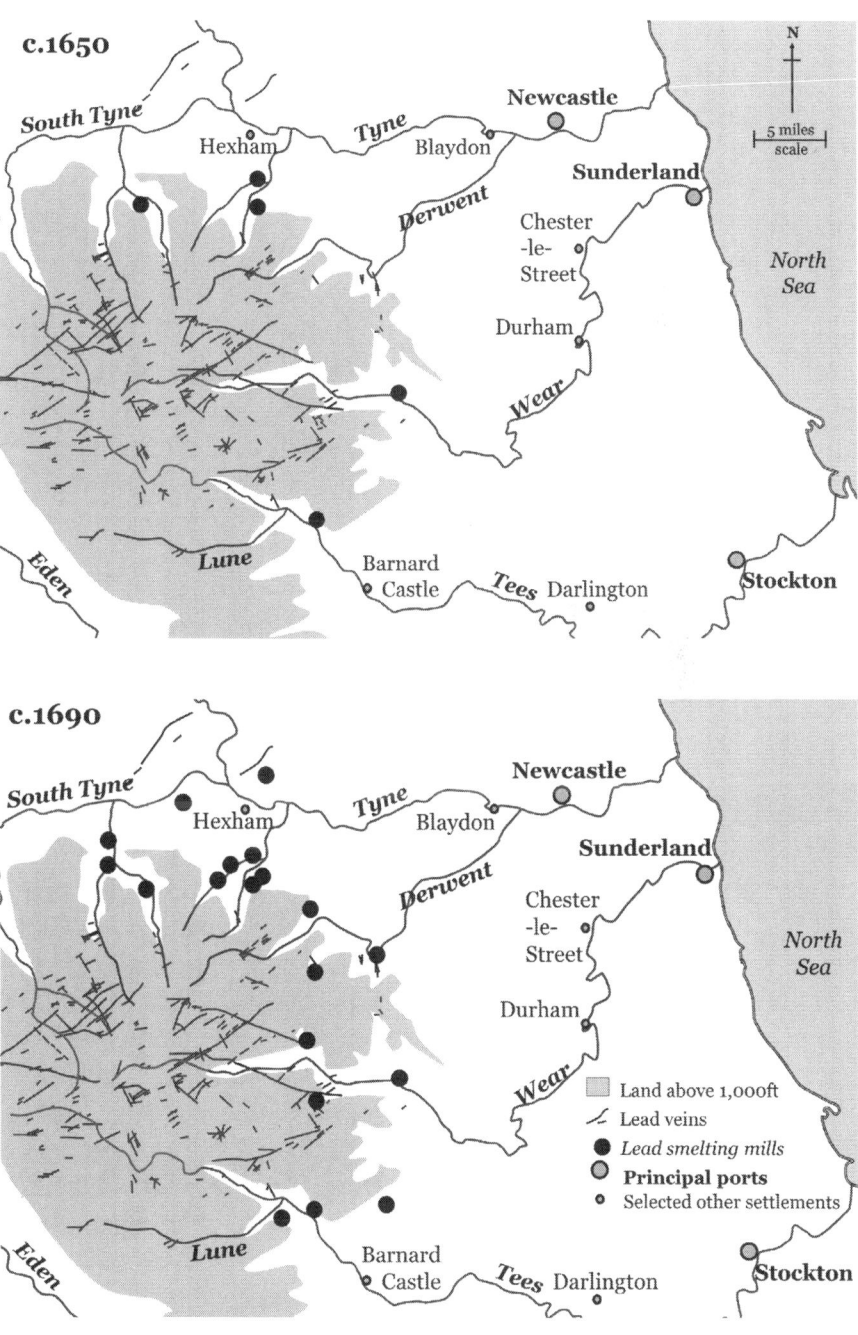

Figure 9.3. North Pennines lead smelting mills c.1650-1690

Source: see Appendix 3.7

In Hexhamshire alone, in addition to the large Dukesfield mill four others were at work nearby, between them creating, in fairly short order, a dense, dirty, noisy and busy industrial cluster where today are quiet paths beside shining clear streams. Getting on for 1,000 people must have been engaged in mining and dressing lead ore north of the Tees/Wear watershed by the 1680s, with a further 200 or so carrying freight between mines, mills and quays, and in smelting lead. These numbers had increased briskly over the previous three decades. Teesdale and Swaledale, supplying Stockton, must also have seen dramatic change. The population of the mining and smelting districts north of the Wear-Tees watershed was probably around 5-6,000 in the mid-17th century.[41] Within 30 years the lead industry probably added 25-40% to gainful employment, and in relatively well-paid work. It brought a dramatic burst of change and prosperity, affecting the very appearance of the land and settlements, the density of traffic and the accents heard amidst the noise, smoke, drinking and fights of new industrial communities.

The value of lead shipped from Newcastle and Sunderland must have been around £30,000 in the early 1680s. From a trading standpoint this probably displaced declining cloth exports. However, a great deal of the cloth shipped from Newcastle had been manufactured far to the west, whereas much more of the income generated by lead sales was retained and spent within the region. Consider the supply chain. Mining tools and smelting mill hearthstones called for regular high-quality ironwork, much of it undertaken on the Derwent below Shotley Bridge. Such was the reputation of the Allensford forge there that iron hearthstones were even carried overland to equip a smelting mill at Wanlockhead in the Scottish Southern Uplands in 1680, well over 100 miles away.[42] Large numbers of sacks had to be cut (from surplus Newcastle sailcloth or canvas?) and stitched to carry ore, many more horses had to be bred and fed, and vast quantities of wood needed to be chopped, seasoned and dried for shaft lining, props, baskets and smelting fuel. This is not to claim that lead alone transformed the regional economy, but it must have made a noticeable contribution to growth both directly and through its ancillary support trades.

The pace and scale of development drove further brisk specialisation and geographic reconfiguration in the use of labour and land. The upland dales had probably never been self-sufficient. Narrow ribbons of cultivated land hugging the riversides might raise poor crops of oats and hay but were mostly given over to rearing sheep and cattle. They certainly couldn't feed hundreds of miners. Fell wasteland was enclosed in a piecemeal fashion, but this was needed to pasture the rising numbers of horses engaged in industrial transport.[43] Yet every horse carrying ore away from the mines had to make the return journey, which provided a great deal of new transport capacity to bring food and other supplies up to the mines. Michael Blackett was buying corn for the 'greate many men' his father employed in his lead mines from an importer in December 1675.[44] The region as a whole, with its relatively large industrial workforce, was usually a net importer of grain. Nervy comments regarding food security are notable for their absence in the letters of Michael Blackett and Ralph Grey, suggesting a faith in trade and exchange quite unlike that communicated to Grey from northern France late in 1674, where 'they would rather kil shipp mastr and marinners then to suffer them to load any corne'.[45]

Standing back to take in the full picture in the Restoration period, rising demand for lead was one of the facets of increasing English urbanisation, building standards and prosperity. In response, the sinews of trade penetrated deeper into remote North Pennines country to open up additional competitive sources of supply. But this disembodies the process of economic change. The conscious agents were those who recognised the evolving pattern of demand, the potential of meeting it from new sources and then took the risk of constructing the means of linking them together. William Blackett wasn't the first to see it, but his ambition, confidence and decisive action in the 1660s and early 1670s took it to a scale that counted nationally, and placed him at the forefront of the regional industry. His lead business certainly met the investment criteria hypothesised for him in chapter six. He reaped spectacular personal rewards and arguably created wider regional value. This great lead enterprise would be enough to consume all the energies of most people, but William Blackett was, astonishingly, also busy on several other fronts during this same short period of time.

Chapter 10

The Newcastle Grandee

Civic and National Politics

A rising industrial magnate in the regional lead industry from the early 1660s, William Blackett's stature and influence also increased within Newcastle's civic establishment. He became much more centrally involved than in the short spells he served on the Common Council during the Interregnum. In October 1659 he had declined the position of sheriff to Thomas Bonner, paying £33 to the council to avoid the time-consuming responsibility it brought to preside over civil court cases and property deed enrolments within the town.[1] It was the very same time he was engaged in exploratory trials at the Allenheads lead mine, and presumably did not need the distraction in Newcastle. Agreeing to delay taking the post for a year, he became sheriff in October 1660 under John Emerson's mayoralty, with the transition to the Restoration regime in Newcastle largely complete.

Deeper involvement in the affairs of the town and its chartered companies began in January 1662 when Blackett became governor of the coal-owning and trading hostmen's company, a post he held for a second year commencing in 1663. He also took part in delegations to represent the merchants' company in London during these two years. In February 1663 Blackett and Samuel Cocke were in London meeting the Eastland Company, which was trying to reassert its monopoly over English trade to the Baltic. The Newcastle men were not there to champion the cause of free trade, but rather to preserve Newcastle's own restrictive practices by seeking agreement that they would police Baltic trade from the North East themselves as Eastland merchants resident in Newcastle.[2] Blackett was also back in London twice in 1664 on a similar mission, spending at least three months there with Robert Ellison negotiating on behalf of the merchants' company in its long-running dispute with the London merchants over their rights in Hamburg. Remaining persistent in the face of prevarication and obstruction by the London company they appear ultimately to have achieved a grudging acceptance of the Newcastle company's effective independence. Blackett followed this up by going to York on Newcastle's behalf in September to underwrite a joint arrangement with the Hull, Leeds and York merchants.[3] It all speaks of an impressive commitment to Newcastle's trading interests at a time when his personal concerns were moving much more strongly into mining, especially as the Allenheads mine was still at an early stage of rapid development.

Blackett was an alderman by April 1665. Within another 18 months he was elected as Newcastle's mayor, carried in state in the Corporation regalia from the carefully choreographed 'election' ceremony held at the 'Spital' at the bottom of Westgate Road down to the Guildhall. He was now firmly at the heart of the civic establishment: a leading merchant adventurer, alderman, mayor and, from January 1667, governor of the hostmen's company once again for another two years. For all the spectacle, these were far from ceremonial positions and these were no ordinary times. The second Anglo-Dutch war was raging, affecting Newcastle's coastal and overseas trading routes. In London the reputation of Tyneside's coalowners was at a low ebb following a mining embargo they imposed for a year from 1665 in a dispute over prices. Large swathes of the capital were also laid waste in the aftermath of the great fire. In turning to Blackett in the autumn and winter of 1666, Newcastle's merchant elite signalled their confidence in his ability to defend the town's interests in the wake of these crises.

His political judgement was on display that December in defusing a looming insurrection by the Sandgate keelmen, already suffering from the earlier year-long coal stoppage. Now they were refusing to pay the hearth tax. The tax collectors had been driven from the festering suburb twice already when Blackett accompanied them into Sandgate on December 7th and given short shrift. However, he was back in the afternoon 'and talked in a friendly way to the multitude, explaining that the tax was small, and promising that it should be taken from those only who were able to pay it … the tumult was appeased'.[4] The likelihood is that the vast majority of Sandgate's residents were exempt anyway due to poverty and Blackett must have calculated, pragmatically, that the yield from the other miserable single-hearth houses was not worth a full-scale riot, which would be difficult to contain.

Blackett's equally decisive role in dealing with another 'tumultuous assembling' of keelmen over their wages, in June 1671, was of a very different colour. The government was alarmed and the king instructed the Lord Lieutenant of Northumberland and Newcastle, the Earl of Ogle, to mobilise the magistrates and local militia to deal with the 'mutineers' with 'the utmost force and vigour'.[5] Blackett was a magistrate, deputy lieutenant and captain of a militia company. He carefully preserved two later letters from a very grateful Ogle. 'I have named you twice in my letters to Winsor [ie. to the king] as one of the best servants his Majestie hath at Newcastle ... perticulerly named you as most active in the reduceing these disorderly Keelemen ... I am very glad all is quiet there now'.[6] There is no direct connection between these two incidents, four and a half years apart, but it is plausible that in the wake of his tactical retreat over the hearth tax Blackett took determined steps to ensure that the outcome of the any future confrontation with the keelmen would be quite different and that he would be there to punch with an iron fist.

It certainly did his personal advancement no harm. Two days before he was returned as one of Newcastle's members of Parliament in December 1673 he was given a hereditary knighthood, a baronetcy, by the King.[7] It was a conventional honour for the town's MPs, but in a surprising departure from the usual 17th-century royal practice of expecting cash in return for such favours, the standard £1,095 fee was waived by the King, 'in consideration of [Blackett's] good services'.[8] This might be supposed to have referred to his suppression of the keelmen two years earlier, but such acts of gratitude by Charles II were rare. It is more likely to have been a tactic designed to keep a rising influential man 'onside' during stormy political times and likewise the strategically important city he represented.

Blackett was unopposed in replacing the old royalist MP Sir John Marley, who had died in October 1673 and represented Newcastle alongside Sir Francis Anderson. From the town's point of view, as well as being a formidable and capable champion of Newcastle, Blackett was a reliable supporter of Anglican order at a time of rising suspicion of Catholic influence at Court, of royal power, of profligacy and war-mongering. England had, once again, been at war with the Dutch since 1672, with the usual consequences for

The Newcastle Grandee

overseas and east-coast trade. Like-minded supporters of a fiscally responsible crown, the supremacy of Parliament and peace were beginning to organise themselves loosely as a 'country party' at Westminster, and Blackett was one of them, knighthood or not. He remained one of Newcastle's MPs until his death in 1680 and was active in Westminster on the town's behalf. He served on 32 Parliamentary committees, including on subjects of interest to Newcastle, such as coal export duty.[9]

A fine example of Blackett's industry and tactics as a political operator on Newcastle's behalf survives in a sheaf of papers he left behind dealing with a tax levied in 1677.[10] The relevant Act was passed by Parliament in the spring of 1677, declaring assessments and appointing commissioners for each county who were to work out the local details. A single monthly assessment was levied on the three 'counties' of Northumberland, Newcastle and Berwick, to be divided between them by their commissioners, of which 38 were named for each of Northumberland and Newcastle and 28 for Berwick. We can be sure that Blackett was active in the Commons ensuring Newcastle's ranks were as numerous as those for Northumberland, and his name is also to be found amongst the commissioners for both bodies.[11] He then proceeded to compare relative land valuations using a county book of rates drawn up in 1663, concluding that Northumberland was worth upwards of £100,000 per year, while the annual value of real and personal estate in Newcastle came to a much more precise £9,472 14s 6d. When allowance was made for Berwick, Blackett contended that Newcastle should account for no more than a twelfth part of the total levied on the three counties. He then reviewed the relative share of taxes paid by Newcastle under various Acts between 1660-72, finding that they ranged between a sixth and a quarter of the comparable total, the town having thus been 'greviously wronged' thereby. This was to be his principal ammunition in the debate to come.

The unsuspecting Northumberland commissioners arranged a meeting between all three parties in Morpeth in May to agree the allocations. Only ten of their 38 commissioners showed up, one of whom was Blackett, and another his son-in-law Robert Mitford, alongside six from Berwick, and they were duly ambushed by 19 mobilised to travel up from Newcastle. The assembled throng was taken through Blackett's bewildering array of numbers proving the justice of Newcastle's case and then treated to the magnanimous offer that the town would agree to pay a tenth of the overall assessment rather than a twelfth. Berwick had evidently been squared away beforehand and granted a mere fortieth of the total, leaving the large remainder to Northumberland. Unsurprisingly this was voted through by a majority of those present on the day, 23 of the 35 attendees, and Blackett's signature on the 'agreement' is the first and most prominent. He set off for London the very next day.[12] Newcastle's common council then took care to start paying their allocation immediately, preserving the Treasury's receipts, which effectively gave official endorsement of the town's correct share. Consequently, by the time Northumberland's commissioners realised what had happened and protested to London it was a *fait accompli*. Blackett was in Westminster during the autumn to fend off their belated complaints.

The vision, sound judgement, deal-making, ruthless tactical action, diligence and energy which underpinned Blackett's flourishing mining empire is therefore also seen in his political life. But was this just an indulgent distraction for a merchant who ought to have been more focused on his business than on the status, trappings and rewards of an increasingly public career? Blackett certainly made much of his elevation into the baronetcy. In April 1674 he submitted his family tree to the College of Arms in London, along with a donation to its rebuilding fund, presumably to speed the process whereby his right to the Blackett arms might be confirmed. He inflated his father's status to gentleman on the pedigree he prepared, not a label known to have been attached to William Snr during his lifetime. A silver tankard from around 1670 was decorated with the arms of the Blacketts of Woodcroft in Weardale.[13] No doubt the arms were also emblazoned on his carriage and the saddlery of his horses mentioned in his will. The portrait at Wallington of the proud new baronet, (see Plate 21) clad in knightly armour, was commissioned from John Riley, one of the country's leading painters. It surely hung prominently in Newcastle's huge Greyfriars mansion, the purchase of which in 1675 or 1676 crowned Blackett's position at the summit of civic society in one of England's most important cities. Letters from John Rushworth in London in 1676 mention the cost and quality of a 'cap of maintenance' Blackett was having made up. Although it was not unknown for such affectations to be carried and worn by knights, it was traditionally an emblem of monarchy and high aristocratic rank. According to Rushworth, Blackett's cap, complete with furring and tassels, compared well with that of the Lord Mayor of London.[14]

Such streaks of vanity might suggest he pursued political elevation for its own sake. However, the time Blackett dedicated to the merchants' and hostmen's companies, Newcastle corporation and Parliament helped promote his business interests - and the town's. As we saw earlier, he used his position as mayor, for instance, to gain access to the Bishop of Durham in late 1666 at an important time for decisions over the future of the Weardale moor-mastership. Newcastle paid its MPs a salary and the merchants' company reimbursed its representatives for their lobbying work in London. This gave ample paid opportunity for Blackett to develop relationships in the capital of value to his own private business. We also saw earlier that Humphrey Wharton was nervous about Blackett's potential influence on being elected to Parliament. Few were the successful merchants who could afford not to engage in political lobbying or to seek direct influence. The larger the business, the more this mattered at national rather than just local level. It also opened up new opportunities for personal enrichment.

Blackett was involved in at least two tax farms, the prevailing means by which the state contracted or 'farmed' out Parliamentary tax collection in the days before the rise of a large directly-employed civil service.[15] For short-lived specific levies this might be undertaken on a commission basis. As well as orchestrating Newcastle's raid on Northumberland in 1677 over its share of the 'seventeen month tax', Blackett offered to collect the share due from north-eastern counties for 1.5% of the proceeds, according to another bidder for the same commission.[16] Longer-term tax farms were usually sold for flat fees, giving shrewd, energetic, diligent and thick-skinned purchasers the opportunity to earn both profits and the enmity of tax-payers. This was the kind of fixed commitment that appealed to Blackett, so it is no surprise to find him involved in the farm of a salt tax in the early 1670s, and that from 1668 he was one of four men who bought the farm of the tax on exported coal from the then 'owner', Lord Townsend.[17]

Here we are deep amongst the rent-seeking holders of public offices purchased on generous terms through influence and patronage. Townsend, who had helped engineer the Restoration of Charles II, had been rewarded with the coal tax farm in 1664. Payment was set by the King at £1,000/year from 1667 for a tax which had hitherto been yielding the previous farmers many thousands of pounds per year. Townsend promptly sold it on for £3,200/year to Blackett and his partners. Their consortium petitioned the Treasury in 1677 to obtain compensation in respect of some coal having been exported custom-free, by which time Blackett's position in Parliament on the relevant committee gave him some influence. The absence of any official complaints in the previous decade suggests they must have been quietly enjoying profits from the arrangement, albeit on a fairly modest scale.[18] Taking Hatcher's data on coal exports during this period, their tax yield might have been around £5,000/year. Making an allowance for the costs of collection, each man probably gained about £300 per year.[19]

Michael Blackett's letters give a revealing insight into the grubby process. In 1678 the post of controller of customs in Newcastle was for sale and he sought his father's advice on whether to bid for it. The office was apparently in the gift of Customs commissioner Lord O'Brien, whose family were cronies of the King.[20] According to Michael, it was 'valewed att £1200. I suppose £1000 may doe the businesse. Mr Braband [Newcastle merchant and mayor] and others say that though I give £1200 itt will be as Cheape as fish, the place really being [worth] above £300 nigh £1100 p[er] annum.' Brabant apparently told Michael that he was not of a mind to let anyone know the real value of it, presumably lest O'Brien's asking price go up. This seems to have been enough to raise Michael's suspicions, especially when, despite having been led to believe it was his for the taking, he heard it was also being offered for sale elsewhere.[21] Such was the shadowy market in lucrative official posts and the opportunities open to those whose public roles brought them varying rights of patronage. Blackett's involvement in the farm of duty on exported coal demonstrates that, for all his wealth-creating ambition and ability, he was not above joining in with those who lobbied and paid for the right to skim off some of the wealth created by others. In the context of the times it is harsh to hold this against him. That was how the system worked. It is unlikely that many in a position to take advantage would have

The Newcastle Grandee | 157

been so high-minded as to pass on by. Also in keeping with the times, given the importance of kinship to civic and business connections, he was active in harnessing his family to his business interests as he sought to provide for their own futures.

The Blackett Family of Newcastle

William and Elizabeth Blackett had three daughters and four sons at home with them in Newcastle at the time of the Restoration (see Figure 10.1). As he developed his business interests and his civic and political career through the 1660s he also had to think about his children's futures and how they might enhance his own. The details of their education are unknown. Sadly, we also know nothing of the views, personalities and interests of his daughters so it is impossible to know how much say they had in choosing their husbands, but all three son-in-laws offered potential advantages to their father's business.

The first to wed, in January 1664 at St. Nicholas' in Newcastle, was the oldest girl, Elizabeth. She was just 17. Her husband, all of 21, was Timothy Davison, second son of Blackett's fellow merchant Thomas Davison with houses and warehouses on Sandhill, The Side and The Close. Timothy also flourished as a merchant and by the mid-1680s was the most prominent importer from the Baltic to Newcastle.[22] Davison's memorial tablet in St. Nicholas' notes his role as Alderman, mayor, governor of the merchants' company and that of his wife Elizabeth, who bore him 16 children, and saw six of them die young. She died at just 48 years old, just two years after her last infant was born and died. When Blackett was mayor of Newcastle in 1666, Timothy Davison was his sheriff and then mayor himself in 1673 at the time when Blackett was selected as one of the town's MPs. Timothy's brother Benjamin was one of the trustees of William Blackett's will. Elizabeth's dowry was probably £1,000, to judge by that given to his 18-year-old daughter Christian in 1669, when she married Robert Mitford. Here was another useful alliance, with a coal owning family based at Seghill to the north-east of Newcastle and with coal-bearing lands at nearby Heaton.[23] Isabella Blackett married Shem Bridges, a London merchant and lawyer, in 1672 when she was 24, giving her father a connection with the capital's legal establishment, with which he had many dealings.

Figure 10.1 The Blacketts of Newcastle.

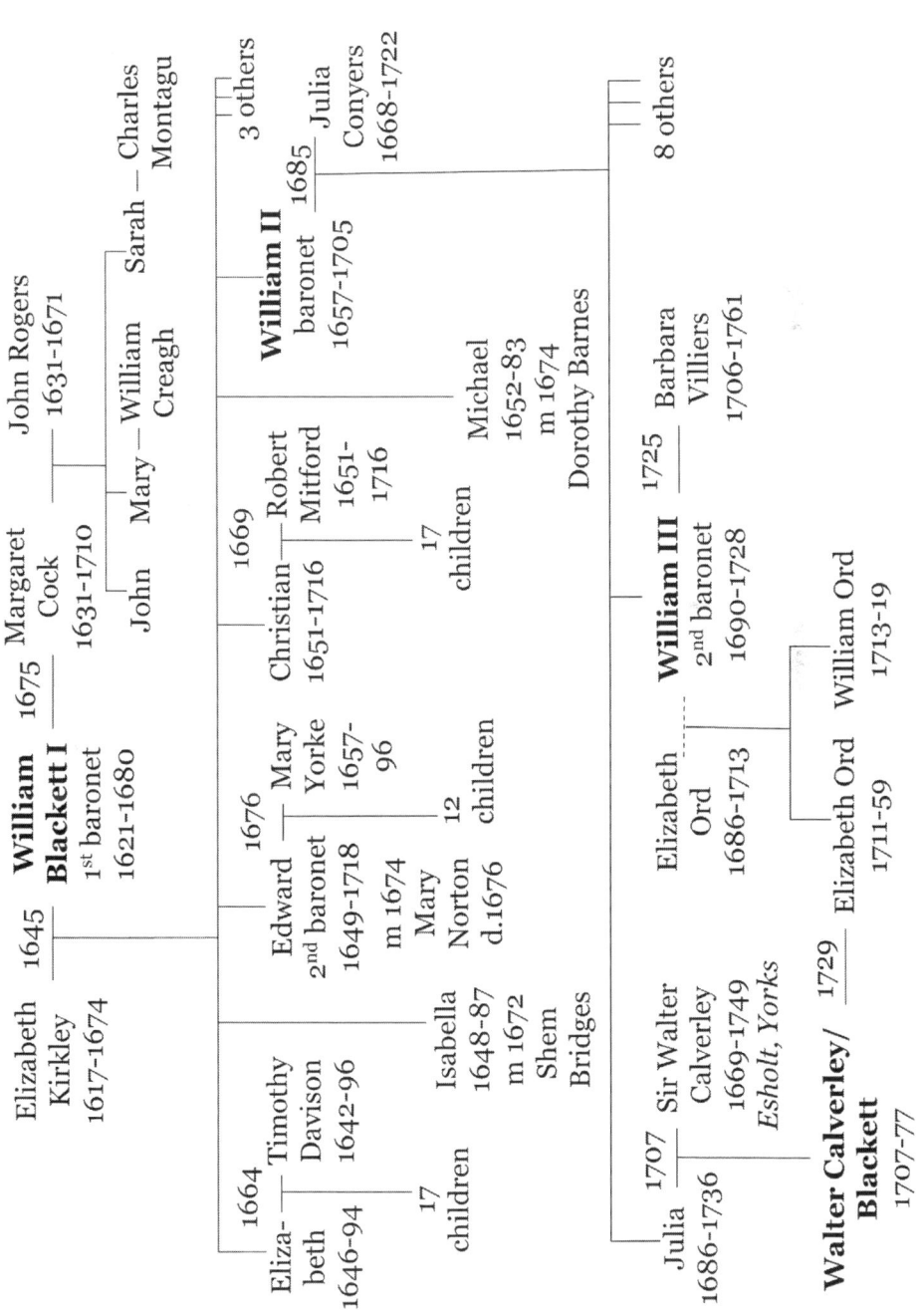

Further detail is provided in Appendix 6, Table A6.3.

Blackett's three elder sons were all involved in the family business. The youngest boy, Christopher, was destined to join them too for he accompanied Michael on at least one of his lead mine visits when aged 17. He was admitted to the merchants' company by patrimony in 1677-8, but died in July 1678, aged 19.[24] No registers survive from the 17th century for the town's Royal Grammar School so, despite its close connection with the Newcastle corporation it is not possible to say the boys were educated there. It might be that Blackett felt that the practical bent of the 'writing school' set up by the corporation was more suitable.[25] None of his sons went off to be distracted from the path of business by the Universities or the Inns of Court. We do, however, know far more about the sons than the daughters, as usual, greatly helped in the case of the Blackett family by the survival of letters from the older two, Edward and Michael.

When his older brother William died in 1654 Edward, aged five, became his father's heir. He was 22 when admitted to the merchants' company by patrimony in 1672. The inference of passing remarks in Michael's letters is that his elder brother was engaged in trade in the 1670s. Edward's own, much later, letters suggest steady business judgement, a fussy attention to detail and a close eye on his purse, all also evident in the meticulous Fallowfield accounts he kept from 1680.[26] There are signs of a certain indulgence from his normally hard-driving father in the 1670s. As the heir to a great man Edward (see Plate 24) might have been expected to make an impressive marriage alliance and William I invested over £7,500 in land west of Hexham in the two years from March 1672 to build up an estate in readiness to settle on him. However, Edward's first wife, Mary Norton, was the heiress to only a minor estate outside Bedale in North Yorkshire. Her father claimed that the property she brought to the marriage in May 1674 was worth some £4,000, but it turned out to be significantly lower.[27] Their short-lived son William was born in early 1675 and died within the year, prompting a touching letter of commiseration from William I to his eldest son the day after 'dear Willy's' burial at Bedale.[28] Mary did not long survive her only son, but even as she was ailing in May 1676 William I was, surprisingly, advancing her scarcely literate father Thomas a £200 loan. It was perhaps more in character for him also to have sought a medical report on his daughter-in-law's bleak outlook from a physician in York and to start some ruthlessly brisk contingency planning ahead of her death shortly afterwards.[29] Within two months the word on Newcastle's Exchange was that Edward was to be married again, this time to the daughter of a family with Yorkshire lead mining interests.[30]

Lady Mary Yorke of Richmond in Yorkshire, a widow of 13 years, was actually a cousin of Thomas Norton, but of much better circumstances. A marriage between Edward Blackett and her daughter and heiress Mary was doubtless attractive to William I, not least because of that lead.[31] Edward kept the Norton inheritance, of course, and brought the same Northumberland estate to the new marriage. Lady Yorke was no pushover and a degree of mutual respect can be seen between her and William Blackett in the negotiations over the terms of the marriage settlement. It culminated in Edward's second wife bringing an agreeable - and real- £4,000 dowry.[32] She was 18 and he 27 when they married in December, just six months after he had buried his first wife. Yet this was not merely a business transaction arranged by Edward's father. Just after the wedding, Lady Yorke said 'nowe none is more hapey then thus cupel Thinkes them selves to be.' Michael had tellingly written to his older brother during the negotiations in October that 'if yor affections bee settled I dare Sweare my Father will never bee aganist itt butt rather promote itt'.[33] The keenest observer of parental indulgence was always a sibling. It is not fanciful to detect a slight edge of sarcasm in Michael's remarks for there is scant evidence that any such indulgence was extended by his father in his own direction.

Michael, the second son, had also been groomed to help with the business from an early age and was admitted to the merchants' company by patrimony at the same time as Edward in 1672. At the age of just 24 Michael served as Newcastle's sheriff for the year from October 1676, and remained on the Common Council thereafter. He had married Dorothy Barnes, the daughter and heiress of a Darlington gentleman with mercantile connections, in September 1674.[34] There is no record of the value of the estate brought to Michael through his marriage, but he could have no complaints over the £6,000 settled on him by his father as part of the arrangement.[35] Michael's two surviving letterbooks deal only with business correspondence. They make no mention of the birth of his only child, Elizabeth, nor her death as an infant, unless this was one of the 'severall unlucky businesses' mentioned in passing to a correspondent in Hamburg scarcely a week after her burial.[36]

Nevertheless some glimpses of Michael's character can be seen in their pages. He could be witty and gregarious and tried to act as an honest broker in resolving disputes between others. He seems also to have been, for a while at least, an energetic and active trader, seeking deals far and wide around European shores. At other times he was sharp and bombastic, as if trying to cover for what he evidently felt to be his shortcomings amongst the calculating merchants surrounding him. 'I am a young trader, and have potent enemyes' he wrote to one of his father's ex-apprentices. It is odd that, in a bristling retort to a correspondent over a poor trade, he should choose to complain that he was laughed at in London coffee houses as Michael Blockhead instead of Blackett. He went on to express outrage that his account for the transaction should be questioned but then confessed to having indeed made an error, and deducted a tenth of the original amount charged.[37] The rough lash of his father's tongue can be imagined preceding some of Michael's hounded explanations, but he probably didn't help himself by admitting, for example, that he couldn't tell his father how much lead ore was stockpiled at Plankey Mill in one of his reports because 'to tell you the truth I forgot to aske'.[38] Poor Michael always signed off his letters earnestly craving his father's blessing, but we are left with the distinct impression that it was never forthcoming. He remained in the old family house at Newcastle's Bridge End and outlived his father by just three years, sad, childless and unfulfilled.

Although there is no direct correspondence to support it, William I appeared to place much greater trust in his third son, William II, of which Michael was doubtless also acutely aware. William II was already sharing reporting duties on the lead business with Michael by the autumn of 1675, when he was still just 18, with some additional responsibility for cashflow management. He was clearly at the centre of his father's business in April 1679 when he authorised the release of the £1,600 required to conclude the purchase of Killhope.[39] At the age of 23 in 1680 he was made the executor of his father's will and directed to administer the coal mining business in order to produce an income for Michael, rather than it being left directly in Michael's own care. While Michael and his wife remained at Bridge End house, the property was given to William II, and so too the grand mansion of Greyfriars. Although Michael died early, it was probably always William I's intention that the subsequent development of the Blackett enterprise would primarily lie in William II's hands.

Their mother did not live to see this. Elizabeth Blackett, the capable merchant's daughter who had assisted her mother's trade for many years, brought up her large family on Newcastle's quayside. She saw her dynamic husband prosper in business and rise in civic stature, her three daughters married and she had eight grandchildren nearby. It is possibly her looking watchful and weary in one of a pair of portraits at Wallington (Plate 22) alongside her husband which might have commemorated his becoming an alderman in 1665.[40] However, she enjoyed the later position of being Lady Blackett for just four months before she died in April 1674. She was 56. If a much later letter from her somewhat hypochondriac eldest son Edward can be relied upon, she had been ill for some time. Edward reported that he 'had a great Dizziness in my head & a trembling and shakeing all over my body. I beleive my mother was so some time before she died for her Distemper lay much in her head'.[41] Edward's own first marriage took place just a month after his mother's death. It might also just be an accident of timing over lawyers exchanging contracts, but her husband William I bought a small farm in Northumberland on 8th April, the day after her death and two days before her funeral.[42] Life went on, if with unseemly haste.

Blackett was a widower for about a year and then remarried. The new Lady Blackett was Margaret Rogers, a widow of nearly four years. William was 54, she a decade younger. Her late husband was John Rogers, recorded at various times as 'Mr', 'Captain' and 'Lieutenant Colonel'. He was apparently from Blaby in Leicestershire but was certainly in Newcastle by 1655, when he married Margaret, the daughter of Newcastle merchant Henry Cock, if not before.[43] Blackett will have known them all for many years. The wedding was in March 1675 and Blackett's purchase of Greyfriars from Sir Francis Anderson came soon afterwards.[44] Its acquisition marked the triumphal and highly visible ascent of Blackett to the summit of Newcastle's mercantile society. Did it also mark the successful end of a quest he set himself as an apprentice? Suitable enough as a King's gilded prison in the 1640s, it might just have been visible from Blackett's draughty garret window at the top of William Sherwood's house on Fleshmarket. Leaving this whimsical speculation aside, Blackett might well have considered that the heads of many rich widows would have been turned by the prospect of presiding over Greyfriars as 'Lady Blackett'. The counterpart to Riley's portrait of Blackett as a knight is probably Margaret, looking very pleased with herself, and they still hang next to each other in Wallington (Plate 23).

However, the language and provisions of Blackett's will of 1680 show that this second marriage was no love match. His bequests to his 'dear' wife Margaret 'were in full satisfaction of what my s[ai]d wife may claim out of my personal estate by the custom of the province of Yorke or otherwise but if my sd wife should not consent & accept of what I have here demised ... then my express will & pleasure is that all these legacies ... shall be utterly void'.* It is worth noting that Blackett had engaged in a flurry of estate buying and bequests in the short period of time between the death of his first wife Elizabeth and his second marriage, bequests that placed these assets beyond the reach of Margaret. In the six months alone before his second marriage Blackett made loans and family gifts to the value of over £9,000. This included Michael's £6,000, an additional dowry to Christian of £400 and a loan of £2,500 to her husband Robert Mitford. For all we know, his daughters Elizabeth and Isabella were similarly rewarded, but this large sum still excludes the £9,000 or more settled on Edward earlier in 1674.[45] Furthermore, the port book records of Blackett's lead exports in 1675-6 show them being shipped under a succession of different family names: Michael '& Co' until September 1675, then separately as 'Michael' and 'William and Christopher' (his two youngest sons, aged 18 and 16 respectively at the time), and only as 'Sir William Blackett' from April 1676. Michael started trading on his own account from September 1675, 'occationed by my Fathers marrying againe'.[46] It all seems carefully designed to keep the proceeds of sales made after the marriage but from lead mined, stockpiled, smelted and cellared before the marriage beyond the reach of any

---

*Blackett was buried next to his first wife Elizabeth in the choir of St. Nicholas'.

estate his new wife might one day claim.

What of Greyfriars? Margaret was required to move out on her husband's death in favour of his youngest son William II. Under the provisions of the will it seemed that William I intended to have her packed off to the small property at Haddrick's Mill, two miles north of Newcastle, where she would have the 'use & occupation of such furniture & household stuff as shall remain [there] at time of my decease'. Property and an annuity worth £450 per year were presumably thought enough to keep her quietly out of the way. Whatever the second Lady Blackett's opinion of the delights of Haddrick's Mill (near the present Millstone pub in South Gosforth), she was living in London when she died in 1710, never having remarried.[47]

What was it, then, about Margaret Rogers, the second merchant's daughter he had married, that could have so attracted Sir William Blackett that he took such care to isolate much of his wealth from her grasp? The obvious answer is coal. Chapter 6 examined Blackett's small share in the Stella Grand Lease, a minor coal investment soon overshadowed by his large and spectacularly successful lead business. Through Margaret, however, Blackett also obtained full control of productive and promising coal mining leases on the north bank of the Tyne. He was far from finished with any further involvement in coal, to which we now return, alongside his other investments in the 1660s and 1670s.

The Newcastle Grandee | 165

Chapter 11

Strange Histories of their Coal Works

Margaret Rogers' late husband John had operated coal mines north of the Tyne under three separate leases since the 1660s or earlier: Whorlton Moor, Newbiggin Hall and Brunton. He had been a Parliamentary army officer in the Newcastle garrison under Haselrig in the 1650s, obtained Tyneside coal interests and membership of the hostmen's company and was amongst those who flourished in Newcastle both before and after the Restoration.[1] They ran roughly in a line from south-west to north-east along an outcrop of the High Main seam, renowned for the quality of its coal. It was presumably therefore reasonably cheap to mine, being found at or near the surface. His widow inherited a third of his mining leases in the area, which came into Blackett's hands following their marriage in 1675. Since the other two thirds were left to Rogers' son and two daughters, all of whom were minors in 1675, they therefore also came under Blackett's control. Neither daughter married in Blackett's lifetime. John Rogers junior was apprenticed to a Davison until 1678, in Blackett's son-in-law's family.[2]

The important Whorlton mine is the only one for which any detail survives and Rogers had half of it (see Figure 11.1). Interestingly, the other half of the Whorlton Moor lease was already in Blackett hands, those of Sir William's elder brother Christopher. In fact the whole 21-year lease from the Earl of Northumberland had been Christopher's when taken out in 1665. Here's a surprise. Christopher, probably on Jarrow's ballast shores in the 1630s and a yeoman when his eldest son was apprenticed to William I in 1649, is not known to have had any other commercial venture to his name and was never a hostman. He had lived nearby, in Newburn, in the 1650s and early 1660s so knew the area, but at the time the lease was taken, early in 1665, he was back in Hamsterley. It is possible that his 30-year-old son John, later the agent to his uncle William I at Fallowfield, was involved, for he was admitted a hostman in 1664. There must be a suspicion that the whole venture was orchestrated by the enterprising William I. In any event, the timing was disastrous, for the Tyneside coalowners' production embargo started just two months later in response to attempts by the London authorities to impose a maximum coal price. It effectively brought the trade to a halt for the best part of a year. Even when mining began again in 1666, far less than 10,000 tons were wrought at Whorlton that year and the next. The venture was salvaged by bringing in a partner, John Rogers, in 1668, presumably accompanied by the additional capital needed to boost the mine. Output reached around 25,000 tons in 1669.[3]

Figure 11.1 Blackett coal interests 1660s-1710s.

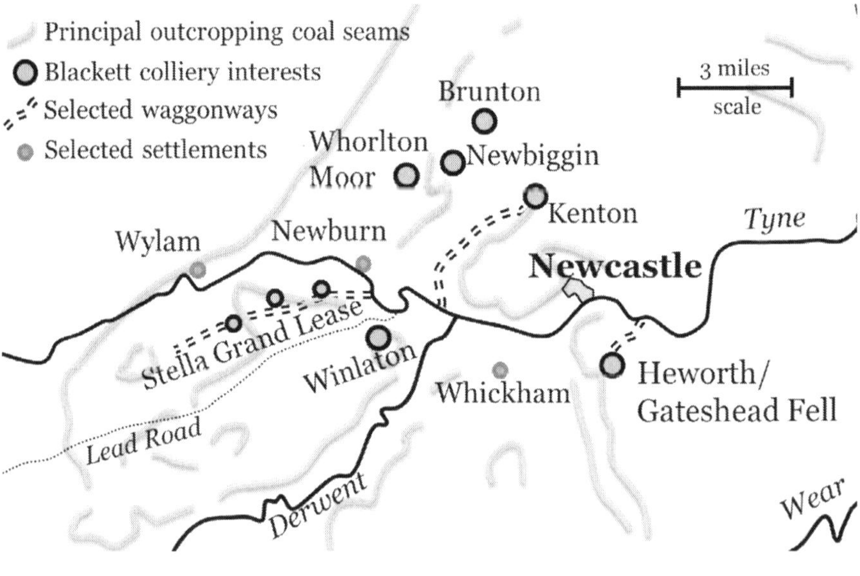

See Appendix 2.2.

Production at Whorlton remained at around this level until the Blackett-Rogers marriage, after which, under Blackett's direct control, output more than doubled to around 50,000 tons in the year to September 1677. The quantity of coal mined at Newbiggin and Brunton, the two other leases inherited from Rogers, is unknown. Coal from the High Main seam might have been easy to work and was renowned for its quality but the mines were over two miles from the north bank of the Tyne, and there was no waggonway, so this large increase in production could not have been at low cost once transport is taken into account. Nevertheless, Blackett was clearly keen to extend his coal interests north of the Tyne in the 1670s, and quite possibly had been doing so, via his brother or nephew, from 1665. It certainly wasn't his only decisive move into coal in the mid-1660s.

In the space of ten months from October 1668 Blackett took three separate leases of land and coal mining rights at Winlaton, which added up to seven eighths of the manor. The largest portion of this came from the ailing and indebted Selby family. Sir George Selby, the young head of the family, died in September 1668. Perhaps this drove Blackett's timing. However, it is unlikely he was exploiting Selby's vulnerable heirs by obtaining Winlaton's colliery on the cheap, for he committed to pay rent of over £750 per year for seven years. The other two leases were taken in April and August 1669 from the guardian of the daughters of the deceased William Hodgson, who owned three eighths of the manor. In total, Blackett's annual rental commitment was over £1,000.[4] Use of the staiths at Blaydon which this gave him was of course also valuable for his booming lead carriage, but even with this, income from the Winlaton farming tenants and a bullish outlook on both coal prices and estimated production costs, he must have realised that he needed to mine around 32,000 tons of coal per year to make it pay.[5] Although this appears to fit the by now familiar pattern of Blackett making a fixed financial commitment which only made sense if economies of scale could be obtained, this was particularly challenging at Winlaton.

Winlaton is on the south bank of the Tyne in County Durham, sandwiched between Whickham to the east and Stella to the west. The village sits on the hilltop between these valleys, with Blaydon's river frontage on the Tyne to the north. The manor runs south-westwards on hilly ground between the River Derwent and Blaydon Burn. Lying between two other important 17th-century coal estates, Winlaton had already been mined extensively for decades before Blackett invested there. As usual, the principal developments were undertaken by Newcastle merchants from the Tudor period onwards, from whose descendants Blackett took his leases. The riverside seams had long been worked out and mining had migrated further from the river, served by a waggonway alongside the Blaydon Burn, which was probably in place by 1633.[6] Supported by several drainage engines and levels driven in from the banks of the Derwent, production might have been around 33,000 tons of coal per year in the 1630s.[7] As a mature coalfield which presumably required heavy levels of continuing investment, Blackett's motivation is unclear, especially as the major expansion of his lead concern in Allendale and Fallowfield was underway at precisely the same time.

The state of Tyneside's coal trade in the mid-1660s makes it even harder to discern his logic. Blackett suffered his own losses as a Stella Grand Lease partner during the 1665-6 coal embargo. He endorsed the decision of his fellow coalowners with the comment that 'having at this present more coals than, in all probability, I can possibly vend this eighteen months, am therefore resolved to lay in my colliery for five month ensuing'.[8] The second Anglo-Dutch war didn't help either. While trade had recovered by the time Blackett took on the Winlaton mines in 1668, assisted by the London rebuilding programme, it was a recent painful reminder of the industry's volatility, one that affected him directly as a partner in the Stella Grand Lease. The affair also increased civic and Parliamentary vigilance in London over any hints of attempts by Newcastle's hostmen to form cartels. It was also only a few years since Blackett had declined to take any of the available mining leases at Whickham, also mature and costly, so what made Winlaton more attractive? The likeliest answer is control. Whickham had always been fragmented between multiple operators and lawsuits were probably as costly a hazard as flooding. The Stella Grand Lease was worked as a single entity, perhaps to avoid Whickham's interminable law-suits, but Blackett never had more than a 1/12 share. By the summer of 1669, however, he controlled all but an eighth of the Winlaton coalfield. His operational magic was yielding great results in lead mining. Would he have been entirely naïve to believe that a similar approach could rejuvenate Winlaton's mines?

Drainage tended to be the biggest problem of a mature coal mine, particularly as deeper seams were pursued. There is evidence that at some point Blackett put his faith in driving a long and expensive level to solve the problem, as with his lead mines. A high court judge visiting Newcastle for the Assizes in 1676 wrote of being entertained by the town's grandees and mentioned that:

> 'Some of the Aldermen related strange Histories of their Coal Works: And one was by Sir William Blackett who cut into a Hill in order to drain the Water, and conquered all Difficulties of Stone, and the like, 'till he came to Clay, and that was too hard for him; for no Means of Timber, or Walls, would resist, but all was crouded together; and this was by the Weight of the Hill bearing upon a Clay that yielded. In this Work he lost £20,000'.[9]

There is a studied nonchalance about Blackett's remarks as reported here, presumably intended to impress the well-connected visitor from London with the perils and costs that justified the price of coal and perhaps also to communicate a financial ability to shrug it off as a passing irritant. The amount is almost certainly exaggerated, and the true figure might have bundled in all his capital works or even operating costs at Winlaton over five or six years. Winlaton it must have been, however, and shows he was engaged in driving a level. Blackett was an enthusiastic driver of levels in his lead mines, recognising the potential value of such capital assets in reducing the ongoing drainage costs which could otherwise bear heavily on the profitability of his mines. In Winlaton though, it appears he was unsuccessful.

This was not Blackett's only problem at Winlaton. Later deeds make clear that his business there was badly affected by the third Anglo-Dutch war. Colliery operations were suspended at the outbreak of the war in April 1672, and were probably not restarted until nearly a year later. Blackett had taken care to include the usual lease clauses to reduce the rent in the event of 'wars or Superfluity of water' drowning out the mine but, inevitably, there were still disputes. The pragmatic outcome, agreed before the end of 1673, was for him to pay the 1672 rent but be allowed up to an extra five years after the end of the Selby lease in 1675 to make good his missed coal production rent free.[10] Whether this could have fully compensated Blackett for the hiatus caused by the war, let alone the difficulties with his drainage level, is impossible to say. However, as we have seen earlier, profit margins from mature coal mines could be quite slender. Blackett's son Edward made 19% profit on coal at Winlaton a decade later, in 1684 and 1685 and the whole mine was probably producing just under 30,000 tons by then.[11] The 1674 coal price was slightly higher than in 1684-5 but at the same unit cost and volume of production his father would have cleared £1,000 in annual operating profit. This might have been perfectly respectable but is hardly spectacular when measured against the outstanding performance of his lead business in the mid-1670s. Salvaging what he could from the tail-end of his Winlaton leases would surely have been the logical thing to do, put it all down to experience, move on and focus even more on lead. Instead, he bought the Selby half of Winlaton in December 1674 for £9,860, to be paid in instalments.

This was Blackett's largest land purchase to date. On conventional valuations it would be expected to produce over £500 gross rental income per year. By 1682, however, the land was probably yielding around £300 net. Even if there was strategic value in the Blaydon staiths from which Blackett's lead was sent downstream to Newcastle, the purchase price must have reflected his belief in a future for coal in 1674.[12] Less than a year later Margaret Rogers brought him the north of Tyne coal leases.

On the assumption that Blackett influenced or even controlled his brother's share of Whorlton, the addition of the Rogers inheritance, along with the Winlaton colliery, helped elevate him into the front rank of Tyneside's coalowners, as shown in the estimates summarised in Table 11.1. His involvement in Winlaton from 1668 accounts for the large increase in total production between 1660 and 1670, as his small share in the lucrative Stella Grand Lease probably never surpassed 7,000 tons of coal per year. The mines inherited from Margaret Rogers to the north of the Tyne were of increasing overall importance, especially as production at Winlaton was probably declining gradually. Blackett must therefore have accounted for more than a tenth of the coal mined on Tyneside by the end of his life. Only the Liddells, Vanes, Claverings and Carrs were owners on a similar or larger scale.[13]

Here again then we can see a rapid expansion of Blackett's business in short order in the 1660s and 1670s – and driven on at a time when the lead business was also growing quickly much further to the west. Coal logistics were simpler than with lead and the pits were much closer to Newcastle, but there was still much to do, not least hundreds of miners to mobilise, direct, monitor, pay and dismiss. In Tyneside coal mines this was generally the responsibility of overmen: gangmasters or contractors. They needed prior underground experience to assess a mine, assemble and direct the various types of labourer needed to hew, move and lift coal to the surface, agree rates of payment for production quotas and underwrite this by giving bonds. John Gillery was employed by Blackett as his overman at Blaydon in 1670 and his bond for his 'true delivery of all coals wrought from the pits' was for £100.[14] Michael Robinson, the Blaydon staithman mentioned in chapter 8, was surely managing the transfer of coal to keels there, as well as for lead. But it is unclear who was arranging terms and bonds and supervising the 'true delivery' of coals by the likes of Gillery and Robinson. Amongst Blackett's sons only Edward, 18 in the autumn of 1667, was old enough to have been directly involved at Winlaton, but was surely too inexperienced to deal effectively with the coalfield's hardened foremen.

Table 11.1 Estimated Blackett coal production 1660-80

	1660	1670	1675-6	1679-80
Production (tons)	2,500	47,000	55,000	66,500
Revenue	£380	£6,200	£8,700	£11,000
Profit	£90	-£310	£1,100	£1,600
Profit (%)	24%	-5%	13%	15%
Tyneside sales total	470,000	510,000	515,000	575,000
Blackett % of total	0.5%	9.2%	10.5%	11.5%

Source: see Appendix 2, Tables A2.2, A2.6

Brother-in-law Matthew Kirkley, merchant and coal-owner, was still nearby and was later left £20 per year for life under Blackett's will. Timothy Davison was a son-in-law from early 1664, master of the young John Rogers after 1677 and possibly also had a role to play. Michael Blackett's utter lack of involvement in the Winlaton and north of Tyne coal mines leaves a further gap in our knowledge when it comes to the 1670s. A letter from nephew John Blackett in 1676 does, however, indicate John's involvement in the mines north of the Tyne at an early stage of his uncle's ownership

Strange Histories of their Coal Works

and it was his name on the Blackett share of the Whorlton lease after his father Christopher died.[15] We saw earlier how quickly Blackett built up his roster of merchant apprentices in the late 1640s to manage his expanding trading concern. A similar pattern can be seen in the 1660s (see Figure 11.2) alongside the diversification and growth of his additional business interests. In particular the recruitment of hostman apprentices grew in line with his renewed involvement in coal from the mid-1660s.

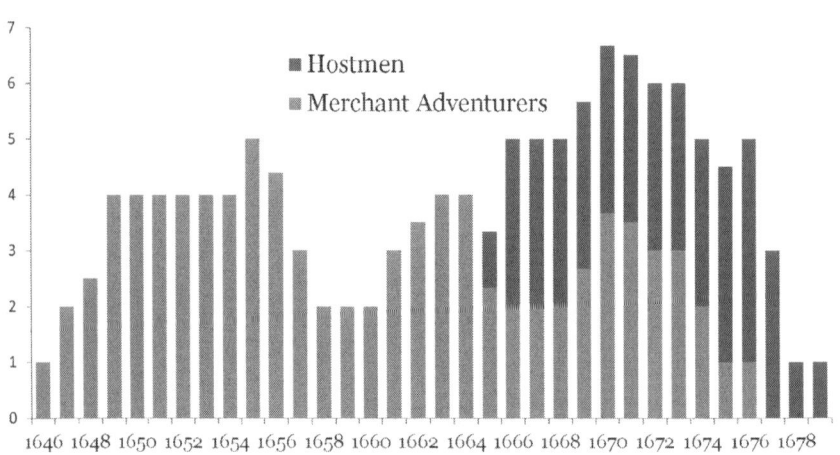

Figure 11.2 Blackett apprentices 1646-78.

Source: derived from MA Records-2, pp.263-96; Hostmen, p.287.

Blackett soon had three such apprentices at a time when only one was allowed, but as governor of the company, the necessary arrangements could presumably be made. As before, he selected boys from modest backgrounds. Cuthbert Snow of Fallowfield was mentioned earlier. George Headlam's father was a Weardale tailor and Peter Bell's a Newcastle carpenter. In the 1670s, reduced apprentice numbers probably indicate the increasing responsibilities taken by his sons. The appointment of William II to assist in the management of Winlaton after his father's death suggests a level of competent familiarity with the coal business there by the late 1670s. Whoever oversaw this great increase in the scale of Blackett's coal business at Stella, Winlaton and on the Tyne's north bank, it seems clear that his master was determined to be amongst the largest regional operators. However, the business could not have achieved the level of profitability being reaped from lead. The loss shown in Figure 11.1 for 1670 illustrates the impact price volatility could have in a lean year on a business already working on tight margins. Estimating how much capital he had tied up in coal is hazardous but using the ratios estimated by Hatcher for the industry as a whole in combination with what is known of the geology, location, infrastructure and age of his collieries suggest a figure in the region of £10,000 by the late 1670s. This implied a 15-20% return on capital in good years, but could often be lower.[16] Given what we know of the financial performance of his lead operation it seems a puzzle that he would choose to go into a lower margin business, even though the cachet of being a major coalowner within Tyneside's business community was presumably attractive. He was not mining more coal in order to trade it all directly. The 1679 port book records indicate that Blackett shipped around 10,000 tons of coal from the Tyne, probably only about a seventh of his output. He was evidently content to let other hostmen act as fitters for the majority of his production.

On the other hand, even though a return of less than 20% from coal was precarious it looks anaemic only in comparison with the outstanding returns of Blackett's lead business. It would have been comparable to the potential earnings from trade, which also fluctuated from year to year. Land or secure loans would generate no more than 6%. But he also had plenty invested there by the later 1670s. Always assuming that he was able to calculate all this at the time, at face value it sits oddly with the picture drawn so far of the ambitious entrepreneur.

Other Investments

In fact, Blackett probably had more capital invested outside his lead and coal businesses in his last years than inside them. Firstly, he had money out on loans secured against property. We saw earlier that William Fenwick had been lent £2,000 in 1674. In the same year he advanced £2,500 to his son-in-law Robert Mitford and in 1676-7 a further £2,500 was lent to Robert Brandling of Felling near Gateshead.[17] Yet even the 6% annually he earned here was higher than the net earnings that could be expected from landed property.

By the time of his death he had some £19,000 invested in land and other property (see Appendix 4.1). At this time land was valued at between '16-18 years purchase', ie. 16-18 times the gross rental value. Inverting this sum gives an annual yield of around 6%. Allowances for repairs, maintenance, land taxes, county rates and uncollectable arrears typically reduced net yields to 4-5%. Nevertheless, the purchase of land did not necessarily indicate a retreat from industry into country gentility. In the absence of more productive outlets for accumulated capital, land was a secure place to bank it, effectively taking the rent in lieu of interest, until such time as new opportunities arose. In 1690 the economist and financier Nicholas Barbon said land could bear a lower yield than the prevailing interest rate on money or stocks because 'land is more certain'.[18] It need not even be sold to fund new investments for loans could always be arranged on mortgages secured against the 'banked' estate. William Cotesworth adopted this strategy in the 1710s and 1720s.[19] Land thus 'encumbered' by mortgages is often taken as a sign of ailing fortunes and rightly so if the funds raised were used to settle gambling debts or high living, but it could equally provide cheap finance for a sound new business.

On a much smaller scale, but in common with other merchants, Blackett also had shares in ships. Many are the inventories of his 17th-century contemporaries which list eighths or sixteenths of Newcastle vessels as part of a diversified capital portfolio. Shipping shares generated some income from freight charges after master and crew had been paid and possibly gave preferential access when cargo space was tight. In the absence of an inventory there is no snapshot of Blackett's shipping assets at his death, but he was an active investor at various times. In 1666 he bought a 'great Scotch prize, laden with coffee ... and another coming laden with timber', quite possibly privateers taken in the course of the Anglo-Dutch war and sold on to interested merchants quickly enough by the Admiralty. Another prize, a Dutch one, was 'delivered to Alderman Blackett' that summer.[20] They might need some repair work, which could be done on the Tyne, but were probably bought cheaply as the Admiralty was always in need of funds. It is unlikely to have cost him more than £200-300. In 1675 he bought up a French ship 'shattered, weatherbeaten and eaten with worms' and sold it on after renovations. He had part shares in at least two other cargo vessels used in the European trade in the 1670s.[21]

The overall picture is of a diversified portfolio, rational and secure. A very rough guess of the spread of Blackett's capital by the time of his death in 1680 is that a third was in lead, a fifth in coal, a third in land and the balance of about 15% in secured loans.[22] This distribution of assets, around half of which was invested in the safe low yields of land and secured loans, superficially suggests that the restless and imaginative merchant was finally slowing down, even putting his feet up. It is hard to imagine. Perhaps instead Blackett was constrained by a lack of the management capacity which would be needed to widen his mining and industrial interests still further. Yet with one or two highly capable sons, trusted associates in Newcastle and a track record of developing talented youngsters, this too seems unlikely. In any case, the purchase of the Weardale mining rights within the inclosed lands and the Killhope/ Wellhope estate in 1678/9 signals a continued appetite for growing the lead business.

Looking again at that landed property portfolio we can see that most of it was linked directly to his core mining interests. Dukesfield was bought in 1665, primarily as a location for what was soon England's largest lead smelting mill. Its farming tenants earned their rent through lead carriage. Killhope and Wellhope only make sense in terms of lead mining potential. The most expensive of them all was Winlaton and here Blackett could reasonably expect to increase rents so that the purchase cost of his coal mining rights was better covered. Cash received from farming and house rents in such locations was also geographically convenient when it came to paying miners and smelters.[23] Only Greyfriars, the Tyne Bridge End house and, possibly, Woodcroft in Weardale did not have any such direct mining links, and together they probably accounted for less than a third of his landed estate in 1680.

What of the secured loans? There are hints of a longer game in each case. Blackett's motives in lending to Brandling appear similar to those I suggest he had in mind with the Fenwick loan of 1674: to obtain the property it was secured against when the debt could not be repaid. Brandling needed the money to pay off an old family debt, so it hardly amounted to a sound underlying new business proposition. The debt was secured on coal bearing estates on Nuns Moor and Jesmond on the outskirts of Newcastle as well as at Felling, but Brandling had inherited part of Winlaton manor through his marriage to a daughter of William Hodgson, which might well have also attracted Blackett's interest.[24] The loan to his Mitford son-in-law was also secured on various Northumberland estates with known coal reserves.

None of this suggests disengagement and retirement from the world of mining, but beyond a sensible level of diversification neither does it fully explain the shift of assets away from the high yielding growth and excitement of the previous two decades. A plausible answer is that the lucrative opportunities Blackett most cherished were closed off, particularly in Weardale thanks to Wharton's long lease from the Bishopric. Geographically, lead veins in the higher reaches of the dale would have fitted well with his existing interests in Allendale and Alston Moor, and their established supply lines into Dukesfield's mill. Ultimately though, just as he enjoyed the benefits of his own natural geological lead monopoly within Allendale, he was denied the chance to intrude on those held by others. Wholly owned assets and secure leases were only vulnerable to hostile takeover if overstretched owners incautiously took unrepayable loans against them. Blackett might have pursued this strategy against Fenwick and others but he had no such hold over Wharton. So, arguably, he invested in coal as the next best alternative use of his funds and where there was also a realistic prospect of scale economies. His move into Winlaton came a year after Wharton secured his new three life moormaster lease from Bishop Cosin, thereby closing off Weardale. Most of Blackett's property investments and secured loans can be associated with his mining interests.

Whatever the logic or circumstances behind his portfolio, it is clear that Blackett's business strategy was not constrained by a lack of capital. Even if he was particularly successful amongst his regional peers, the wider possibility here is that Tyneside's mercantile community had little difficulty in finding the capital needed to underpin the years of economic expansion after the restoration of the crown in 1660. Blackett remained at the heart of it until the end of his life.

Chapter 12

Taking Stock of William Blackett

The Business

As we take stock of William Blackett's final years, what did it all add up to? This chapter considers his business as a whole, how it was managed and developed, what he left behind and what we can say about the later years of the man who created it all. Annual revenue from lead and coal was probably £25,000 or more, generating profits of around £6,000. To this can be added rental income from his lands, perhaps over £700 per year net, and unknown additional income from his tax farms and his 'pay' from Newcastle Corporation as an MP. He was responsible for a workforce of 750 or so people including dozens of seasonal transport contractors.[1]

This was truly impressive in the context of the times, although before searching for other enterprises of comparable size remember that these figures are aggregated from separate businesses, rather than a single operation. The lead business was not integrated with the coal mines and the collieries were a few miles apart on different banks of the Tyne. This is not to reduce the scale of Blackett's achievement, nor to belittle the overall management of cashflow and capital allocation his conglomerate required, but it was not as if he ran a single huge factory. Nevertheless, even at 'just' 430 workers, the integrated lead business must have been among the largest concerns in a region that probably already stood out nationally because of its large coal mines.* Nef speculated that there were ten collieries on Tyneside employing more than 100 miners at the time of the Civil War and 12 to 15 by 1700.[2] The Stella Grand Lease must have been the largest in the late 1670s, producing 90,000 tons of coal in 1679. It probably employed between 450

---

* In the 17th century the only other large-scale enterprises were probably the Navy shipyards. In the 1650s around 2,000 men were employed in five yards. By 1688 Chatham employed 800 alone. While undoubtedly a great management challenge, the yards were not private enterprises competing for markets: J.Ehrman, *The Navy In The War Of William-III*, (1953), p.637.

and 600 miners in its various pits, co-ordinated under single management. It had grown from perhaps 30,000 tons in 1660 and around 175-230 miners. As a partner there, Blackett was well placed to observe the evolution of its orderly management process as he built his own lead concern in parallel.[3]

The sheer range of Blackett's business, civic and political activity in the 1660s and 1670s highlights the span of management control and organisation required to keep it all going profitably. Expansion often came in short bursts and on a broad front. In early 1664, for example, having just completed two years as governor of the hostmen, he made two separate journeys to London, one of three months' duration, to negotiate on behalf of the merchants' company. Meanwhile his Allendale lead mines were still being developed, his ore smelted in someone else's mill and the season's carriage contract had to be agreed and arranged. His share of the Stella Grand Lease coal business was also being renegotiated in 1664.

The two years from late 1666 were astonishing. Blackett became Newcastle's mayor in September and was soon at work defusing the hearth tax disturbance. At the same time his Dukesfield smelting mill was in the first year of operation and he was making forays into Weardale via the Stanhope lead tithes as Wharton's moormaster lease came into play. From January 1667 he was the hostmen's governor again as well as mayor and had to address the poor state of relations with London after the recent coal embargo. Alongside this, sensing the market opportunity for lead as the capital was rebuilt after the great fire, he brought forward negotiations with Fenwick to renew and expand the Allendale mining lease. He then had to mobilise mining at Fallowfield in 1668 and orchestrate opposition to the attempt by Northumberland's magistrates to give up their responsibility to the vital bridge across the Tyne at Corbridge. Dukesfield Mill was probably enlarged that year. If this wasn't enough, he might have introduced Rogers and his capital to expand coal mining at Whorlton Moor early in 1668 and then took on the extensive Winlaton coal mines later that same year.

In the 1670s he spent increasing amounts of time in London after his election as an MP in December 1673. Parliamentary sessions were usually of just a few weeks' duration but Blackett was also involved in Parliamentary committee work that kept him in

London. On one occasion he complained that it had 'put him so behindhand with his business that it would take him a month or six weeks to bring his books up to date.' Even if that is hard to imagine, for he was known to call his book-keeper to London, he certainly needed an effective management system back in Newcastle.[4] We must also remember that lead production continued to rise greatly in the mid-1670s, that the coal mines north of the Tyne inherited from Margaret Rogers were taken on at the same time and their production doubled within a couple of years.

Structure and order were vital given the growing scale and geographic range of Blackett's lead and coal business. Although on a smaller scale than in the 1650s, Blackett also continued to trade overseas, still bringing in cargoes of wine from Bordeaux and timber and iron from Sweden in 1676.[5] Some of the local agents, managers and apprentices were identified earlier, but it is unclear who Blackett relied upon most in the 1660s in his head office. There was stock to count, check, secure and move between various locations, payments to authorise and make, orders to fill, invoices to raise, receipts to chase, cashflow to manage and credit to arrange. In addition to supervising existing operations, Blackett must also have had assistance with developing and expanding the business when he was away lobbying on behalf of Newcastle and its merchants' companies. From the 1670s his sons, though still young, were able to help. Edward and Michael were admitted to the freedom of the merchants' company early in 1672. In October 1675 22-year-old Michael was already looking back on a time when he had 'men to command'.[6]

Other names not among the apprentices appear from time to time. In a lively but remorseful letter to Blackett in 1676, ex-employee Francis Draycott declared he was 'stark madd with my self in parting with Newcastle but at that tyme I had such a parcel of Love and Maggotts in my head that devowered all my braines'.[7] The terms in which the steadier Robert Pease is mentioned in Michael's letters indicate that he worked for his father in some office capacity in the mid-1670s. Slightly older than his employer, Pease's name appears on some of Blackett's Chancery bills or answers and he was a trustee of his will. He was a yeoman's son from near Darlington, and apprenticed to a Newcastle merchant in 1633. It looks very much as though Pease was a senior member of the office staff in Newcastle, closely involved in much of the perennial stream of the legal work affecting the business or generated by it. The well-connected London lawyer and politician John Rushworth, long retained by the town to lobby for its interests, also helped manage Blackett's legal affairs in the capital.[8]

Regular mine visits were an important part of the control system but faced the inevitable tensions between head office and operating units. As far as the lead business was concerned, the experienced and independent-minded Mowbray brothers clearly resented the regular intrusions of the young Michael Blackett in 1675. Richard was reluctant to tell Michael who was mining ore at Lunehead beyond Teesdale. Michael passed on to his father the truculent words of John Mowbray at Dukesfield, who claimed:

> 'he owes you Little [money] for he tould me plainly he is very much wronged in the acct so that he wonders you should be so strickt with him always saying to me if you will wrong him God forgive you but he hopes better things from you & you will allow of all his objections w[hi]ch is nothing but right.'[9]

Mowbray's defiance over what appear to be accusations of fraud exudes self-confidence in his position as a skilled and knowledgeable manager critical to a rapidly growing and highly profitable business. Blackett must privately have shared the views of other proprietors in a similar position. Charles Montague felt sure he was being defrauded by the manager of his Benwell colliery in 1697 but was reluctant to replace him for fear of not finding a capable replacement.[10] If petty theft was going on there was a limit to what could be proved in practice, even with the lodging of bonds by colliery overmen such as John Gillery. In accommodating themselves to this reality the likes of Blackett might have asked themselves whether it was actually much different to an occasional vagueness on their own part regarding their customs declarations or the informal perquisites of public office. Michael, meanwhile, must have dreaded his monthly excursions into the hills, propelled there by his father like a raw management trainee onto a factory floor ruled by grizzled foremen.

The detailed 'Law Book' created by Ambrose Crowley to govern every last operational detail of his Winlaton ironworks had the risk of fraud in mind at the turn of the century, but was more generally intended to ensure he could run it efficiently from London.[11] The absence today of any Blackett business records from before the 1720s means it is impossible to tell how systematic and codified his own management regime was, but clues remain. He had designed a set of regular reporting measures to allow him to check on the throughput, stock, cost and outlook for the lead business and presumably monitored his coal mines in similar fashion, especially as profit margins were much thinner. Edward's very detailed management accounts of his own lead business in the 1680s and 1690s hint at controls between each process stage learned from his father. And a century later Sir Walter Blackett's chief agent referred to 'all the abstracts I have of writings and all the Books of Acco[un]ts of the Family since the year 1670', an indication of the orderly record-keeping we might expect of the first Sir William.[12]

The rest can be imagined well enough. Around the office looking out from The Close to the Tyne, clamouring with seabirds and keelmen in the midday sun, are the shelves of contracts, partnership terms, wayleave agreements, land deeds and mine leases. Against a side wall are the invoices, bills of lading, receipts, bonds, open bills of exchange and sheafs of closed accounts. Great ledger volumes of accounts and stock inventories lie close to hand, next to the well-thumbed financial summaries for years past. An apprentice comes up from the lead cellar with his clutch of tallies from the wherrymen and reaches for the Blaydon staiths ledger and paybook. Neatly ordered files of inbound letters from London, Edinburgh, Amsterdam, Hamburg, Dukesfield, Allenheads, Stanhope, Blaydon, Newburn and Stella stand up just above the bound and dated volumes of copy outbound letters. One lies open on a desk, a clerk furiously copying a letter in time for the original to be rushed along The Close to catch a ship casting off on that afternoon's tide for Gothenburg. Everyone is on their toes for the great master is present, cloistered with Mr. Pease and young Mr. William next door reviewing the cashflow needs of the coming month. A lead pay is imminent in the hills and the balance of the Winlaton overman's dues are to find before receipts come in from the London coal dealers, so how many Dutch bills are on hand that can be sold for cash on the Exchange?

Beyond day-to-day management of the various divisions of the business lay decisions on future development. The hyperactivity of 1668, with the simultaneous opening up of Fallowfield, deciding what to offer Fenwick to buy out his duty ore rights and negotiating the leases to secure Winlaton's coal mines shows that Blackett was comfortable dealing with complexity or, at the very least, not afraid to seize opportunities on multiple fronts at the same time. All of this required analytical skills that went beyond those needed by merchants. The fixed and long-term capital commitments in mining brought different kinds of risks to those inherent in trading transactions and could not be assessed through the mechanics of a double-entry accounting ledger. It was not capital alone which merchants allocated from trading to industry, but the energetic ability to appraise quite different risks and opportunities and to master the demands of production and large-scale employment. How soon will that drainage level reach the coal shafts at Winlaton? What will it contribute to lowering the unit cost of coal at a higher level of production? Meanwhile, how quickly can I reach the level of lead production needed to recover the large initial lease costs? How many miners does this mean I need to recruit in Allenheads this year? Can I add smelting capacity, where should it be and can the masters train up and oversee enough able youngsters to use it properly? How much profit must I set aside to cover the sinking of new pits and building repairs?

We can be fairly sure that Blackett had the analytical tools needed to inform these and other decisions, even though no more than bare hints survive. They can be inferred as a precursor to his decision to add slag hearths to his lead smelting mills to improve efficiency and reduce the overall cost of delivering each ton of lead. Within a year of his father's death the well-trained eldest son Edward was calculating the unit cost of lead to help decide what to do with Plankey Mill. Such calculations added a level of more sophisticated management accounting to an underlying foundation of book-keeping and reporting now lost to us. In the 1690s the obsessive Edward agonised over how to allocate some quite trivial overhead cost elements between lead mines and mill, the better to analyse the profitability of each process stage.[13] It reveals a concern with accounting clarity and precision directed towards underlying business profitability thought to be largely absent until a very much later stage of British industrial development.[14]

In summary, the shreds of evidence which survive give confidence that Blackett established a management structure and system he could rely upon enough to run his large and diversified business. Capable agents and overmen at the mines, the mills and the staiths reported either to him or to his sons. Regular reports on production, throughput, carriage, the disposition of stocks, and operating costs were fed into Newcastle or London and clear instructions, Blackett's 'positive orders' according to son Michael, were relayed back. They kept coming until close to the end.

The Man

Blackett suffered from scurvy and jaundice during the last year of his life, to judge from a letter from physician Dr George Neale. Cataloguing Blackett's 'dejected appetite, Asthma ... shortness of breath, looseness of teeth, wasting of the gums ... high colord veine' and so on, Neale gave scant consolation to his important patient in going on to say that it was 'epidemical' in the northern counties, rather than some personal failing. The good doctor was being obliquely critical of local fare, for healthier diets were being followed elsewhere at the time. As a Leeds-based promoter of Knaresborough Spa, Neale naturally recommended taking the waters but also prescribed a vitamin C rich concoction of syrup of oranges, mulberries, wood sorrel, cowslips, lemons, pomegranates, cherries and barberries.[15] The 'great lassitude, weariness, drowsiness and sleepiness' from which Blackett apparently also suffered did not, however, appear to slow him down much. He had been in London in the autumn of 1678 while Parliament sat, was back in Newcastle between that Christmas and March 1679, during which time he was re-elected, or re-selected, as MP. He went again to London in March for the new Parliamentary session, returning by June, when his signature appeared on one of Newcastle's council orders in his usual strong hand.[16] Perhaps it was only after all this that fatigue caught up with him, bringing on the doctor's advice to rest, but he was off to London again in October. Killhope had also been bought in the spring of that year, so there were mines to open up or bring under control and extensions to the ore carriage to Dukesfield to be contracted.

Blackett was clearly restless and active, possibly to the despair of those beseeching him to slow down. He might have retorted that he had work to do, not least because of the political crisis arising from Parliamentary attempts to exclude the openly Catholic James, Duke of York, younger brother of the King, from the throne. Anti-Catholic feeling had been running high for years. It was stirred to feverish levels by the alleged 'Popish Plot' to poison the King revealed in the autumn of 1678. No matter how lacking in substance, it was exactly the populist conspiracy needed by the 'country party' in Parliament to fight against what it saw as the risk of tyranny and French influence under a future Catholic king. And when the King dissolved Parliament in May 1679 rather than see the Exclusion Bill passed, nervous onlookers could be forgiven for feeling that the disastrous descent into civil war in 1640 was being repeated. The 'country party', increasingly labelled as Whigs, won an overwhelming majority over the 'court party', or Tories, in the second election of 1679, held in September.[17] As usual, Newcastle hedged its bets. Its MPs, the past and present owners of Greyfriars, covered both bases. Sir Francis Anderson was the Tory court opponent of the exclusion of James, while Blackett was marked as a worthy supporter by the Whigs' leader, the Earl of Shaftesbury. Anderson died that July and was replaced by his equally Tory son-in-law Sir Ralph Carr.[18] Blackett was needed to retain the balance and to take his experience and guile back to Westminster to defend Newcastle's interests in critical times. Meanwhile, in Newcastle Michael became an alderman and young William II joined the Common Council that October.[19]

As it happened, Charles II did not allow Parliament to assemble for a further year and ultimately defused the exclusion crisis with a degree of political skill which his father had wholly lacked in the 1640s. And Blackett might not even have made it to Westminster. By the end of November he had been taken 'extraordinary ill' in York and Michael was probably not the only family member who rushed there in short order.* Whether or not thanks to further infusions of

---

* Michael might not have thanked his apprentice, John Wilkinson, for being so candid about his father's illness in letters to London correspondents on 2nd December. It was the sort of news that could move markets. On his own return to Newcastle by 23rd December Michael referred only to having been absent due to 'some extraordinary business in the country'.

vitamin C, Blackett was able to return to Newcastle before the end of the year to put his name to a deed for a small piece of property to the west of Hexham.[20] His last will was drawn up in March in which he was having none of the 'weak in body' nonsense often encountered in such documents. He was very firmly of 'perfect minde and memory'. Each of the 14 pages of the original document carries his unwavering signature. A month later he was still up to the task of giving a deposition in Newcastle in a Chancery case which featured the Brandling mortgage of 1676.[21] Within weeks, though, he was dead, having just passed his 59th birthday.

The £1,000 set aside in his will for his funeral was a huge sum. In his survey of a sample of the estates of London merchants between 1660 and 1730 Peter Earle came across nothing greater than £728 and everything was more expensive in the capital.[22] It is likely, therefore, that Blackett's funeral laid the pattern of a stately procession from Greyfriars to St. Nicholas' by the civic, mercantile and landed elite of the town and adjoining counties which was later followed by his son and grandson. He died on Sunday 16th May 1680. That the funeral could take place just four days later suggests that he had been sinking fast in the weeks beforehand. While the money set aside for his funeral suggests a grand occasion, an opportunity for the town to display the full extent of its civic glory, his memorial was a modest slab placed at the front of the choir in St. Nicholas'. It was nothing in comparison to the ostentatiously pious 1630s Maddison memorial nearby.

> 'Here lieth the body of Sir William Blackett, bart, alderman and sometime mayor of this town, and burgess in parliament for the corporation, and dame Elizabeth his wife, by whom he had issue 9 children, of which survived him 3 sons and 3 daughters, viz. Edward, Michael, William, Elizabeth, Isabel and Christian; she departed this life the 7th April 1674; and he the 16 of May 1680'[23]

The funeral address was given by St. Nicholas' lecturer, John Rawlet. No doubt it was suitably decorous. The words given by Straker in 1819 cannot have been from any reliable oral testimony but capture the flavour of the usual public homilies. Blackett was said to have been 'possessed of excellent talents for business, and unwearied in their application, though engaged in a great variety and extent of affairs; and being successful without pride, and rich without ostentation, he lived generally esteemed, and died universally lamented'.[24] This broadly accords with the career charted in these pages. He was certainly engaged in a great variety of affairs and was highly successful in applying his undoubtedly excellent business talents and capacity for hard work. His civic duties extended over decades in many different roles in Newcastle and London, often undertaking more than one at the same time. Blackett's achievements and ability might indeed have been 'generally esteemed', but such respect was given grudgingly and warily from some quarters and there are indications that it did not always extend to his conduct and character.

    A number of Chancery court cases brought against Blackett in the 1660s and 1670s alleged unfair and vigorous legal pursuit of often quite small debts.[25] Ambrose Barnes, the sanctimonious dissenter, Newcastle trader and Blackett's apprentice for six months in 1646, could not resist slipping in some oblique yet damning opinions into his memoirs. He recounted a 1667 letter from an unnamed 'dear good man' which casually castigated the impudence and villainy of 'W.B.' in a debt case, seeing him as worldly and carnal. Elsewhere, Barnes praised Sir Francis Anderson in contrast to 'two other gentlemen of his former acquaintance, who had made as strict pretences to reformed religion as he, [but] gave way to the times, and as a reward of their apostasy, were made knights,' a clear swipe at Blackett and Mark Milbank for their political flexibility either side of the Restoration and revealing his indignation that they had got away with it.[26] The royalist Anderson had suffered imprisonment and the sequestration of his estates after the Civil War. Although restored to public life in Newcastle and Westminster after 1660, he never recovered his solvency, despite pleas to the crown and its agents.[27] To see the upstart turncoat Blackett rewarded in the way described by Barnes, and to become his fellow Newcastle MP, must have stuck in the throat. The only share of Winlaton manor that was not leased to Blackett in 1668-9, the final eighth, was Anderson's. Having to sell him Greyfriars was presumably the ultimate humiliation.

    Blackett was almost certainly not 'universally lamented' by

the Northumberland gentry either. There were those such as the Fenwicks of Wallington who would come to resent being the personal casualties of Blackett's apparent largesse through business deals they probably didn't understand. Broader ranks of gentlemen were outwitted by him over incidents such as the rebuilding of the Tyne Bridge at Corbridge and the apportionment of the 17-month tax in 1677. And as for the one-time lowly apprentice boy being without pride and ostentation, the knightly display of arms, cap of maintenance, coach and horses and triumphal portraits in Newcastle's ultimate trophy mansion suggest otherwise.

This isn't entirely fair. Most of those with trade and business interests greatly valued stability, restraints on arbitrary rule and continuity of order whatever the government of the day. Newcastle was not the only commercial city whose rulers put its own rights and interests first, to the purist ideological distaste affected by the likes of Barnes. Likewise, sharp merchants could legitimately argue that they were not responsible for any lack of arithmetical skills or attention to contract detail on the part of the entitled gentlemen of ancient families they dealt with, or for the reluctance of their debtors to pay up. And austere indeed would be the rich self-made man who did not allow himself some personal and public indulgence, eventually, to mark his success. Indeed, bearing in mind Newcastle's traditional displays of civic pride and influence, it was expected that its leading merchant princes would wrap their personal achievements in suitably ornate outward trappings, the better to project the town's magnificence to the world. These considerations need to accompany Barnes' muffled asides in any overall assessment of Blackett's character.

In the absence of anything from his own hand and with few direct observations of others, we know very little of his personal traits and habits. But while we don't know what he thought, we do know how he acted and the circumstances in which he did so. Much can be discerned from critical decisions such as the huge sums expended to buy the Allenheads mining rights in 1660 and on the 1667 renewal and extension. The overriding impression left is of grand business ambition, determination and flair, accompanied by careful planning and judgement, both of opportunities and of people. This tempered his risky and audacious commitments and avoided sheer recklessness. They demonstrate remarkable courage and self-confidence, traits on show as far back as his time as a young merchant apprentice amidst the disease-ridden military, political and commercial storms of Newcastle in the 1630s and 1640s. Allied with shrewd tactical awareness, swift - often ruthless - action and a capacity for a great deal of hard work on multiple fronts, he was clearly a formidable and highly effective operator. He was a deal maker and a disciplined manager as well as a visionary, three quite different skills rarely found in a single individual, and particularly formidable when harnessed to great ambition and motivation. The motto which translates as 'We will labour in hope' was added to the family coat of arms at around this time, but there was much more to Blackett's endeavours than hard work and crossed fingers.[*] He gazes out confidently from his Riley portrait at Wallington, weighing us up with an air of calm calculation and determination (see Plate 21).

He might not have minded if he was regarded more with respect than affection. The few reflected glimpses that have come down to us speak of a sharp impatience with underlings evidently unable to keep up with his pace and high standards. Did Edward decide in the 1670s to establish his estate two days' ride away in North Yorkshire to escape being constantly hectored closer to home? Had Blackett's own letters and a greater range of contemporary comment survived, a character as wilful and abrasive as William Cotesworth and Ambrose Crowley might be visible to us. However, Barnes's limited, veiled and oblique criticisms suggest otherwise. More than a generation later even Barnes wished not to confront Blackett's reputation too directly. The roughest edges of the cocky young chancer from Gateshead who had to scrabble his way up in hard times might have been sanded off by the elders of the Newcastle Exchange in the 1640s – and by a shrewd mother-in-law wishing to ensure, for the sake of her daughter and business, that his clear potential did not go to waste.

And Blackett was not unremittingly flinty, short-tempered or calculating. A sequence of letters in March 1676 indicate a swift generosity in giving advice on the standing and credit-worthiness

---

[1] 'Nous travaillerons dans esperance'. It was not present on the silver tankard of c.1670 (see p.155) but accompanies the arms on the Kip portrayals of sons Edward and William's mansions of Newby and Greyfriars respectively in c.1700.

of one of the Ravensworth Liddells to someone he scarcely knew in London and of no direct business importance to him.[28] This might just be an example of sensible courtesy to someone who could be of reciprocal use in the future. The same applies to the letter from his maggot-brained ex-employee Francis Draycott, agent for the influential Sir Robert Clayton. More sentimental was his preservation of four prattling juvenile letters from his stepdaughter Mary Rogers later that year, each of which he had taken the time to answer affectionately, to her great joy.[29] This is all we have, but it shows that the hyper-active and sharp businessman and politician, could, at least later in life, relax and devote some gentle attention closer to home. The stipulations in his will around the (actually relatively modest) £12 annual charity money bequeathed to the poor are interesting. A grand public statement of family splendour and munificence would have seen the six parish representatives troop into the grounds of Greyfriars each December to receive their allocations. Instead they were to be paid by son William II at the old family home of Bridge End, the narrow tall building next to the smells and tumult of the bridge and river within view of William I's Gateshead birthplace. For all the European and metropolitan sweep of his commercial, industrial and political activity it is as if he wished to be remembered each year for his roots amongst traders, porters, rivermen, warehouses and commodities, a Newcastle merchant to the end.

The Legacy

It is possible to venture a rough estimate of the wealth William Blackett I had amassed by the time of his death. The sources, assumptions, details and summary estimates are tabulated and described in Appendix 4.1. He left assets to the value of around £69,000. At the prevailing level of profitability and stock in hand the lead and coal businesses were probably worth, conservatively, around £32,000 and £11,000. Land and property were worth about £19,000, which included his half of Winlaton manor, Dukesfield, Killhope, Wellhope, Woodcroft and Greyfriars house and grounds. We know of £7,000 in secured loans but there could have been others now lost to us because they never led to lawsuits. Nothing is allowed here for capital employed by his residual trading business, yet he shipped 10,000 tons of coal in 1679. Nor is there any provision for the value of any ship shares he held or of his personal effects – the household stuff, plate, jewels, coach and horses mentioned in his will.

Specific lump-sum bequests to family and others in the will came to around £6,000 and ongoing annuities another £2,000/year, including a £500/year 'estate of inheritance' to Edward. Around £47,000 of overall capital was needed to support these provisions. This left a remainder of £22,000 from the estimated £69,000 of assets: land, the lead assets (other than Fallowfield), coal leases and personal estate, which became William II's inheritance as the residual legatee and executor. The better William II could drive the business thenceforth, the higher his personal return would be.

Cautious as this £69,000 asset valuation in 1680 might be, it still does not capture the full extent of the wealth generated by Blackett during his working life. He had distributed around £18-19,000 to his children during the 1660s and 1670s. Whether still in his hands at his death or already passed on to his family, therefore Blackett was probably worth £87-88,000 or thereabouts by the time he died at the age of 59. Grassby's categories of the wealth of 17th-century Londoners defined the 'very rich' as being worth between £30,000 and £100,000. Above them were the 'unimaginably rich'. There were probably no more than 40 London businessmen with more than £30,000 in assets in the second half of the century.[30] In Newcastle Blackett surely stood apart and ahead of his contemporaries and whether he was 'unimaginably' or merely 'very' rich is an academic point. He had built up this estate quickly. Chapter 6 speculated that in 1660 the asset value he had tied up in trade and committed to new ventures was around £3,000, even after the loss of £1,600 in the cloth seized by the King of Denmark. Even if his net worth is inflated to £5,000 in 1660, the astonishing growth over the subsequent two decades is clear.

These estimates suggest he added £80,000 or so to his net worth in 20 years, or an average of £4,000 per year. Attention has hitherto generally dwelt on Blackett's role as a coal owner and merchant, but it is now clear that he owed it principally to lead. Blackett's annual lead profits were estimated earlier at nearly £5,000 in

Old houses in the Fleshmarket, Newcastle, c.1820, home of apprentice William Blackett I's master William Sherwood.

Above, The Side, c.1820. Joan Carr and Elizabeth Kirkley, under whom Blackett completed his apprenticeship and commenced his trading career respectively, lived on opposite sides of Newcastle's main thoroughfare.

Left, Tyne Bridge end looking south towards Gateshead, 1763. Blackett's house is seen on the right.

Newcastle Quayside, 1825.

Above left: Merchants in a port striking a deal.
Above right: Lead ore miners at work in Allendale, early nineteenth century
Left: Seventeenth century Dutch flyboat, the mainstay of northern European trade.

Two lead ore smelters working at a hearth, late eighteenth century. Working the hearth and ladling the molten lead into a mould to cool. Lead pieces or pigs lie on the floor.

Newcastle, The Sandhill, 1832/3. The Guildhall stood to the right.

Newcastle Guildhall, (upper floor) and Exchange (ground floor), 1789. The Quayside lay beyond.

11 Corbridge Bridge.

12

Pack horses or Galloway ponies carrying lead ore from mines to smelting mills along North Pennines moorland tracks.

13

Clerks recording lead being weighed in a smelting mill for their accounts.

14

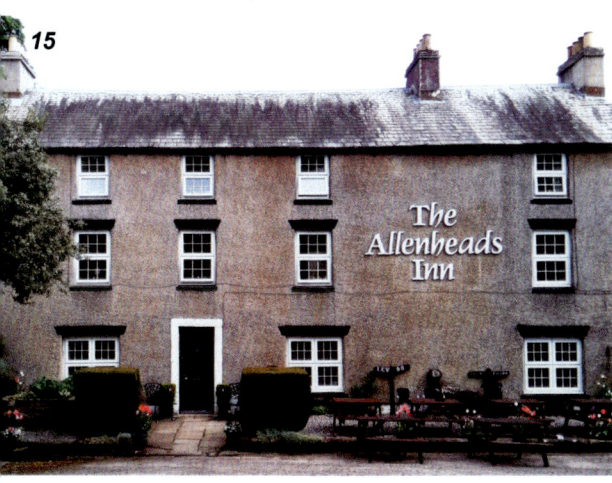

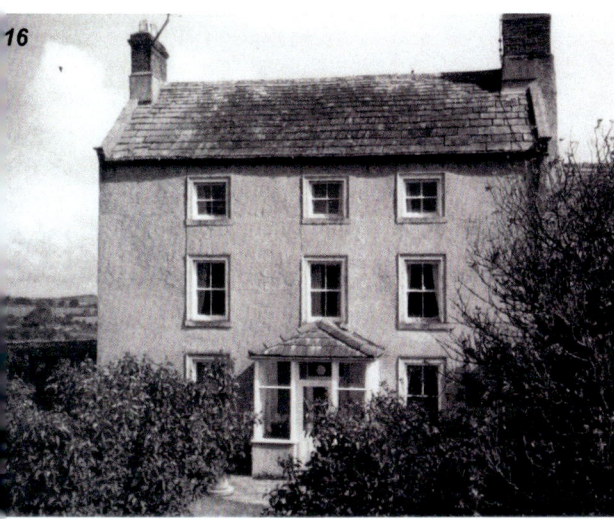

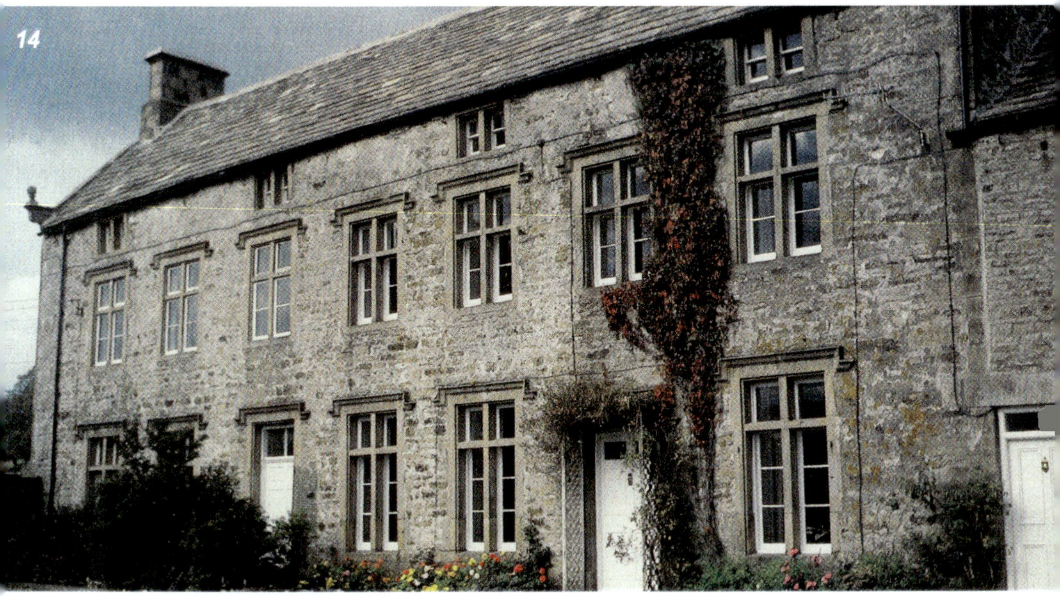

15

The legacy of lead business management under the Blacketts. Anti-clockwise from top Newhouse in Weardale, Allenheads Inn, Dukesfield Hall, Fallowfield House.

16

17

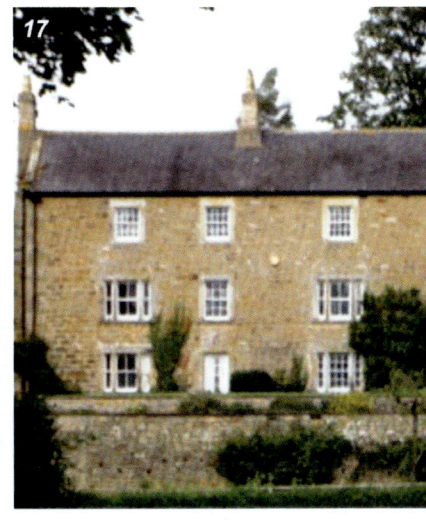

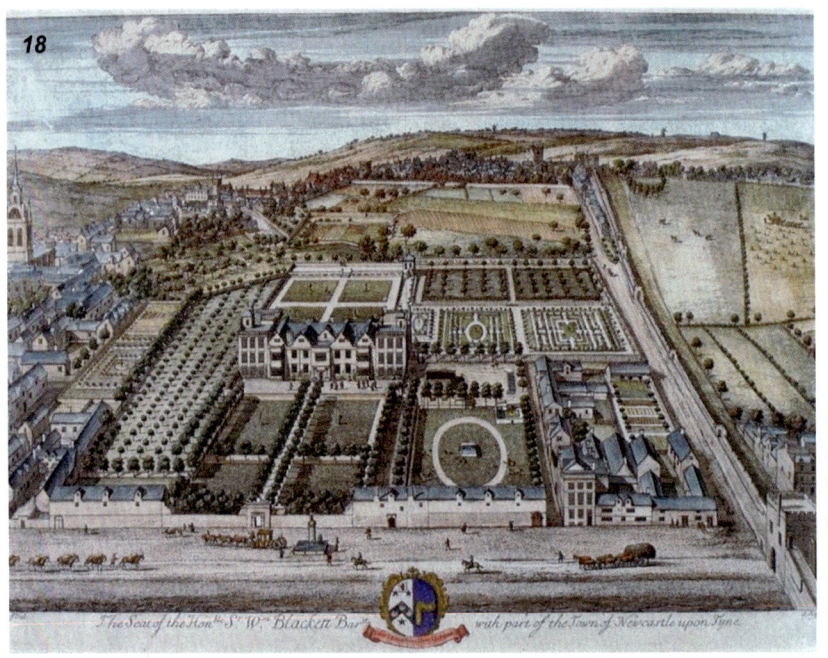

Greyfriars, Newcastle, c.1700. The grand Blackett mansion on Pilgrim Street.

Coal Waggon, Newcastle, 1773.

20 *Wallington Hall today.*

Probably William Blackett 1621-80.

Possibly Elizabeth Kirkley, 1617-74.

Possibly Margaret Rogers, 1631-1710. See Appendix 5.

Sir Edward Blackett, second baronet, 1649-1718.

Probably William Blackett, 1657-1705. *Possibly William Blackett, 1690-1728. See Appendix 5.*

Walter Calverley/ Blackett, 1707-77. *Probably Julia Conyers, Lady Blackett 1668-1722.*

the heady mid-1670s. This was probably their peak level and although the lead price seems to have been high in the 1660s, Blackett's production and income must have taken some years to reach this point. He might also have been making up to £1,500 per year from coal mining in the 1670s, though often less. He presumably still took some trading profits, an income from his tax farms and interest on his loans. His household expenditure surely rose in line with his status, but even if it reached several hundred pounds per year he could still have accumulated at a rate consistent with his wealth by 1680, with most of that coming in the 1670s.

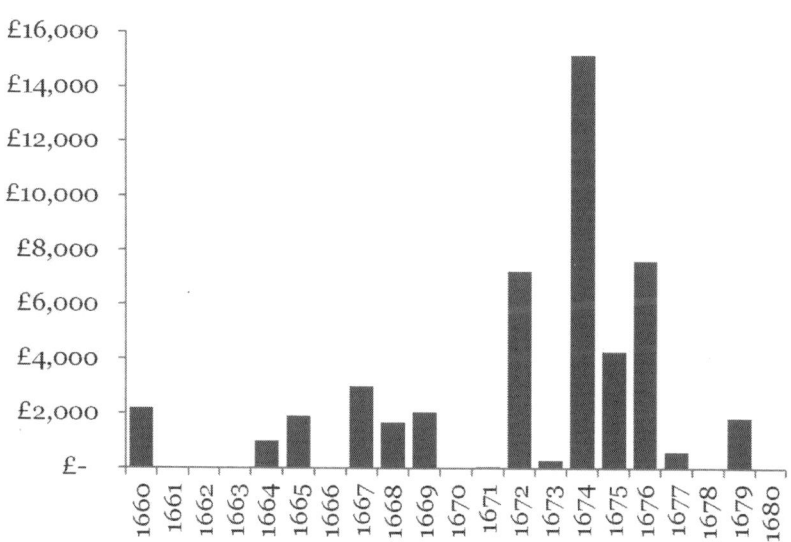

Figure 12.1. Blackett's capital outlays 1660-1680

This is reflected in the overall distribution through time of Blackett's known capital outlays between 1660 and 1680, as shown in Figure 12.1. Large amounts were expended, for example, in 1672 and 1674, on the purchase of the 'Westwater estate' in the Tyne Valley intended for settlement on Edward as his son and heir, Michael's marriage settlement, the Fenwick loan and the first instalment at Winlaton. The 15 years spent as a merchant trader following the completion of his apprenticeship and marriage into the Kirkley family had lifted Blackett to a position of material comfort, but the spectacular gains of his last two decades came mostly from Blackett's entrepreneurial and management alchemy in converting lead into gold.

His achievements hardly need recapitulation here. Had he decided to continue as an overseas trader a move to London might have been the logical next step in 1660, for he could otherwise have soon reached the limits of Newcastle's mercantile world. And perhaps then he would have been comfortably off amongst the merchants and City aldermen of the capital. Instead, branching out so boldly into lead and coal mining kept his centre of gravity firmly in the North East. He became a champion of Newcastle's interests in Parliament, and of his own, and he reached the summit of the town's society. But Blackett's truly distinctive contribution to his region's economic development was to drive the rapid growth of the North Pennines lead industry in the 1660s and 1670s. In meeting the demands for lead in the wake of London's great fire, his role was arguably of some national significance, and so too in forging another link in the complicated chains of internal and overseas trade and specialisation that drove English prosperity in the century before the industrial revolution. He was also amongst the small number of people who built enterprises on a scale that dwarfed the craft workshops and enterprises that made up most of the business landscape. A careful reading of his will shows he intended it to last.

It is possible see him torn between endowing the futures of each son and a desire to keep the mining business intact. The customary rules of land inheritance by primogeniture could have lent themselves to achieving the latter with some ease by leaving the business and the bulk of his estate to Edward as the eldest son and heir. Yet Blackett evidently did not see in the sound, meticulous, but plodding and fussy Edward the qualities needed to carry on what he had started. The same went for the hapless and occasionally erratic Michael. On the evidence of his later audacious deals, however, it seems young William II had the necessary ability and drive to seize opportunities with flair and ambition. These were surely the qualities that persuaded Blackett to entrust the business to his youngest son, not quite 23 when he drew up his last will. A certain symmetry might also have occurred to him, for he too had been the youngest of three sons and had unquestionably gone the furthest.

All three were left in material comfort. Roughly speaking, Edward was left assets worth over £29,000, some of it in land already granted, but also the important Fallowfield mine, and his wife Mary Yorke had brought him a further £4,000. Already established at Newby in North Yorkshire, magistrate and sheriff of Northumberland and about to inherit his father's baronetcy, he was the country gentleman that his father never saw as a personal priority. Michael, dear Michael, had been given a lump sum and income for life to a total equivalent value of about £11,000. He slowly wound down his trading activities from the Bridge End house in which he spent his last three years as his younger brother's tenant.[31] Had Michael lived, the later quip about Blackett having made two oldest sons could have as readily been extended to three, for they were all rich. William II was left with assets worth around £22,000. Most of the business assets were in his hands: Stella and the north of Tyne collieries, waggons and keelrooms, the management of Winlaton, lead mining rights in Allendale, Alston Moor and Killhope and the Dukesfield smelt mill. If he was good enough, the opportunity was there to earn the much higher rewards that would follow from continuing his father's empire building. 23-year-old William II was his father's executor, not 30-year-old Edward.

However, it wasn't entirely that straightforward a business inheritance. William II was entrusted with the management of Winlaton to produce an income for Dame Margaret and Michael, but after their deaths the mines and Blackett's half of the manor were to be divided between William II and Michael's families. Perhaps William I saw that Winlaton would ultimately be worked out and of dwindling importance next to the increasingly productive mines north of the Tyne. These all went to William II. Even the separation of the hitherto highly lucrative Fallowfield mine from the rest of the lead operation was not expected to fracture the dominant regional business built by William I. As shown earlier, all of Fallowfield's ore was sent to Dukesfield to be smelted and Dukesfield relied upon these supplies for half of its output. Blackett must have been confident that this interconnection would give Edward and William II every incentive to work together.

Blackett set up all three sons for life, and at the same time gave his business juggernaut the best chance to continue growing. There were compromises, some fudging of the edges. Perhaps he had seen for himself what later historians have usually concluded: that few businesses in the early modern period outlived their founder. William II was judged most closely matched to his own outlook and capabilities and evidently seen as the most likely to ensure that what he had created, fudged edges or not, would continue to flourish. As we take our leave of the first Sir William Blackett, we can move on to observe that rarity of the period, a large multi-generational business and what his offspring did with it.

Chapter 13

Brothers

William I's judgement turned out to be right. Ultimately it was his youngest son William II who drove the family business forward. Edward retained an active interest in his Northumberland land and lead interests through to the 1710s, but was very much the country gentleman at his fine new mansion of Newby Hall. Most of what follows in this and the following two chapters is therefore centred on William II, but since it is Edward's records that survive to shed light on the business and since his activities had a bearing on some of William II's decisions, he has to be considered along the way.

Superficially at least, the brothers' lives followed similar courses. They were apparently educated in the same practical fashion in Newcastle. Neither attended the Inns of Court or a university but Edward was possibly in Rotterdam at 19 and William certainly in Hamburg at the age of 17.[1] Both went on to public office at city or county level and as members of Parliament. Edward inherited his father's baronetcy; William was granted one in his own right in 1685. They 'married well' in their late 20s, proceeded to build themselves fine houses and raised large families. They also, of course, had common interests in coal and lead.

William I's division of his core lead assets between Edward and William II in 1680 leaves us a strong hint that he felt they needed mutual business dependence to keep them working closely together, given their quite different personalities. It's easy to imagine William II seeing Edward's close attention to detail and cautious deliberation as just so much plodding pedantry when there were opportunities to be seized, and likewise to see the shrewd and careful Edward worrying that his younger brother was impetuous and reckless. They nevertheless remained on good terms. Edward was godfather to William II's son and heir, William III, in 1690 and his third wife Diana did similar duty for William II's daughter of the same name in 1703. William II carried out his responsibility as his father's executor to buy Edward an 'estate of inheritance' worth £500 per year within two years.[2] Edward was nominated by his younger brother as an arbiter of any disputes that might arise from his will of 1704. These signs of filial trust and regard were not, however, enough to keep their father's business together.

As we shall see, the brothers went their separate ways as far as lead was concerned. And while William II was entrusted with managing his brother Michael's share of the Winlaton colliery, Edward ran it himself after Michael's death, when it came to him. This did not last long and in 1687 he leased his interest to Sir William Creagh. Eventually, although much later, his Fallowfield lead business went the same way.[3] Sir Edward Blackett took his share of his father's inheritance, ran it separately and later settled for the life of a gentleman rentier. As he put it in 1711: 'twas always my great desire rather to have a £200 a year without trouble than three with trouble'.[4] William II, on the other hand, sought a more adventurous path. We see this in his role as his father's executor and, particularly, in his political life, while still in his 20s.

Executor and Politician

The self-confident William II might have accepted his role as the executor of his father's estate as a great honour for such young shoulders, but it was a responsibility certain to test the young man's ability, even with the support of the trustees also named in the will, including the dependable Robert Pease and Timothy Davison's brother Benjamin. His step-mother Margaret (Rogers) had been told to take her bequest and move out of Greyfriars or challenge it through the courts. Just under £3,000 was also promised to various relations and others as single bequests and recurring payments of £1,500 per year were due to commence within six months. That implied a great deal of cash had to be found from an estate and business where much of the value was locked up in land, mines, leases, mortgages, trade debt and working stocks of coal, lead and ore. Rental income from land could not realistically cover all of the annual payments, let alone the one-off bequests. Yet William II seems to have found a way through this knot of issues briskly. Edward's additional estate was settled in 1682. There is no sign of any court challenge by step-mother Margaret to the will. The executorship was discharged smoothly and efficiently.

It might be that William II's brother-in-law Timothy Davison advanced some or all of the funds needed in the short term. Although it is now impossible to unravel the details, £9,600 was owed to the Davisons by the Blacketts in the 1710s.[5] Whether this was the fallout of practical difficulties in fulfilling the terms of William I's will or separate commitments by William II – and there were many of these, as we shall see - is not so clear, but William II and his brother-in-law Timothy certainly had a great deal to do with each other, both financially and politically.

William II was a Newcastle common councillor at the age of 22, an alderman just three years later in 1682, and mayor of the town in 1683, aged just 26. This all seems breathtakingly precocious and cannot simply have been some misty homage to his deceased father. That was not how Newcastle's calculating mercantile elite worked. Was the young man the puppet of his brother-in-law, 15 years his senior, as scathingly suggested by Alderman Henry Brabant? 'This Davison is a person of that ambition and affecting popularity that nothing less than the government of the town will serve his turn, for whoever is mayor, he is dictator'.[6] Davison and Blackett were certainly close political allies and it is entirely possible that the older man, who had been mayor in 1673 and governor of the merchants' company for 19 years from 1677, assisted William's rapid rise through the ranks of civic power.[7] But the dramatic events of the next few years showed quite clearly that Blackett was his own man and one whose confident political talent justified the backing of the town's elite in the face of a renewed threat to Newcastle's independence.

King Charles II saw off the 1679-80 Parliamentary attempt to exclude his Catholic younger brother James from the throne. With the country or Whig party in disarray and Parliament prorogued, the King set about consolidating his grip on power. A key aspect of this was to seek greater control over the troublesome independence of the borough corporations and the like-minded MPs they tended to elect. Incorporated towns and cities derived their charters from the Crown, but the changes sought by the King to allow deeper royal meddling were difficult to achieve without local consent. The Crown could, however, instigate '*quo warranto*' legal proceedings to pick holes in borough charters. Faced with just such a challenge in 1683, the City of London, not many decades on from being such a bastion of Parliamentary opposition to the King's father, called his bluff –and lost.[8] Its charter was forfeit, leaving the way open to the King to issue a new one with more intrusive powers of appointment to key civic offices. The judgement had a traumatic effect on boroughs throughout England; the mere threat of further action through the courts would be enough to persuade them to agree new charters by negotiation.

Newcastle, so important to London's fuel supply and so protective of its independence, could not hope to be overlooked. This was not just a low rumble of the distant thunder of arbitrary national power that might one day, yet again, threaten property rights and a stable business environment, but a dark cloud looming directly over the town's mercantile elite. With the storm coming, Blackett's appointment as mayor just four months after London's municipal defeat speaks of far more than a young protégé being nodded through to indulge Timothy Davison. The worldly-wise aldermen were placing great faith in the young man's ability. Blackett's task would have been challenging enough had the corporation been united behind him, but was all the harder given the presence of an internal faction intent on undermining the town's privileged elite from within.

Henry Brabant's view of Davison as a dictator was not grounded in objective observation. The son of a County Durham gentleman and near contemporary of William Blackett I, Brabant came through a merchants' company apprenticeship but was disenfranchised in 1649 for having joined the royalist cause. Following the Restoration Charles II rewarded his earlier loyalty with leadership of the Newcastle customs house and he was able to follow the path of civic life from the post of sheriff, in 1662, to the ranks of aldermen. He succeeded William I as mayor in 1667. A certain swagger can be detected from the passing comments of Michael Blackett's account given earlier of customs house vacancies, but Brabant was clearly not competent enough to prevent the bounty of his sinecure running through his fingers. He was being pursued for unpaid debts by London merchant James Burkin by 1676, if not earlier, and was to die a poor man.[9] It is easy to imagine Brabant, like Ambrose Barnes and Francis Anderson, nursing a grievance at the apparently effortless rise of turncoats like Blackett and Milbank after 1660. Already an ardent supporter of the King, Alderman Brabant probably saw opportunity for both personal salvation and revenge in the royal campaign for control of the boroughs in the 1680s. He lost no time in alleging disloyalty on the part of a self-perpetuating inner cabal running affairs in Newcastle, led by Davison.[10]

The corporation was duly asked by the Crown in March 1684 to return its charter as certain 'alterations should be made'. All customs and privileges would be upheld, so long as the right to royal confirmation of mayor and sheriff appointments was agreed. Newcastle MP Sir Nathaniel Johnson conveyed the message, adding his personal recommendation that the terms be agreed, lest *quo warranto* proceedings be launched, as with London the previous year. Playing for time, the council asked for a draft new charter to be issued rather than surrender the old one first, but was silent on the matter of having the mayoral election subject to royal approval. The list of signatures was headed boldly and firmly by Blackett as mayor. Brabant's name is also there, but he followed up a day later with his own letter to London complaining about the disloyalty of the Davison clique.[11] In the summer the Crown was back again, and lest the message not be clear, Assize Court Judge Jeffreys was present in the Guildhall to ensure the corporation's petition to the King regarding their charter was suitably humble.[12] Negotiations over the detailed terms would now take place in London, a job entrusted to Blackett and Davison, who were sent off in October with £1,000 'to be disposed of as they in their discretion thought fit' (ie. in bribes). They probably could not hope to achieve more than damage limitation, even if accompanied by the written support of Northumberland's Lord Lieutenant, the Duke of Newcastle, who described them as 'very rich and of great reputation for understanding and honesty, and, if any speaks ill of them, it is out of envy'.[13]

The new charter of January 1685 did indeed give the Crown a virtual veto over the results of municipal elections and new aldermen, but the deal done to secure the town's co-operation saw the pro-Davison/Blackett officers elected for 1684/5 remain in place and existing aldermen confirmed. It also brought Blackett his own hereditary baronetcy and, as with the uncharacteristic generosity of Charles II towards William I, the standard £1,095 fee was waived.[14] If this implies that William II was rewarded for bending to the King's will rather than standing up for the town, there is no sign of any backlash from the aldermen back in Newcastle, who perhaps accepted that Blackett had made the best of a bad job. To mollify Brabant's faction, he too was granted a knighthood by the King.

Blackett returned from London in March 1685 with more than a new town charter and a baronetcy. He was married. His wife was Julia, only daughter of Sir Christopher Conyers and she brought him a respectable £6,000 cash dowry. This was all the more impressive given that the modest Conyers estate near Easington in County Durham had already been committed to Sir Christopher's son and heir.[15] The largesse coming Blackett's way seems to have had much to do with his bride's aristocratic maternal relations – the Lumleys. Her mother's nephew was the 35 year old Viscount Richard Lumley of Lumley Castle in Durham, an army officer who helped defeat Monmouth's rebellion at the Battle of Sedgemoor later that year. The rapid timing of events within a few days in January 1685 – the baronetcy granted on the 19th, marriage settlement and £6,000 on the 20th and marriage in London on the 22nd - suggests a co-ordinated package of rewards for Blackett's co-operation over the Newcastle charter, co-ordination which might have owed something to Viscount Lumley's connections at Court.[16] Since Sir Christopher had obtained an undeniably good match for his daughter, who immediately became Lady Blackett, mistress of the finest house in Newcastle and promised a 'competent jointure' (albeit of unspecified financial value) in the event of widowhood, his agreement was presumably readily forthcoming. As usual, of course, we know nothing of the bride's view of the deal being arranged around her. How much say she had is very much open to question. Julia was 16 years old.

The granting of Blackett's baronetcy was among the last acts of King Charles, who suffered a fatal stroke within days. He was succeeded by brother James II, who before long was to prove wayward, imperious and impetuous while lacking Charles II's political understanding and guile. These were to become crucial weaknesses given widespread suspicion over the motivations of a papist monarch. James II's grant of a knighthood to Catholic Newcastle merchant William Creagh was ominous and so too the instruction to the corporation to elect the arch-royalist Brabant as MP alongside

Johnson in March 1685. However, the corporation defiantly put Blackett forward as a candidate and he defeated Brabant in one of the few contested Parliamentary campaigns in Newcastle that century.[17] Constitutional wrangles were giving way to direct political combat. Brabant was installed as mayor in October under the terms of the new charter and immediately set about purging the common council. Blackett led the aldermen out of the Guildhall saying 'they had nothing to do, since [his] Majesty took the power from them, and so departed before the Common Council could be all sworn'.[18] If Brabant thought Blackett had walked straight into a trap he was sorely mistaken. The MP set off back to Westminster to outflank the new mayor and turn the new power of royal interference in civic affairs in his own favour. He proposed an apparently magnanimous 50:50 split between his own supporters and Brabant's and persuaded fellow MP Johnson to support him in lobbying the King accordingly. He even took the cynically tactical opportunity to curry royal favour by voting for the King's highly contentious move to allow Catholic officers in the army. It all had the desired result. Blackett was able to return with his new approved list of councillors, well aware, as was Brabant, that his 50:50 split effectively gave Blackett a majority as the only aldermen resident in the town were all of his faction.[19] This was a remarkable achievement given Blackett's underwhelming enthusiasm for municipal reform (when he flounced out of the Guildhall with his supporters) compared to that of Brabant, James' slavish but now casually undermined and distraught puppet. If it also owed much to the King's unpredictable whims, this too speaks of Blackett's political understanding and bold timing in taking full advantage of them.

    A further signal of Blackett's ability to sustain belief by the King and his chief minister, the Earl of Sunderland, that he held the key to Newcastle, howsoever dubious his displays of loyalty, can be seen in Royal acceptance of the election of Blackett's faction to municipal office in 1686 and 1687. Even a typically arbitrary swing in the other direction afterwards was short-lived. In December 1687, the removal of the mayor, John Squire, and of Blackett, Davison and four other aldermen of his faction was ordered from London. In their place came a Catholic mayor, Creagh, and a mutually distrustful 'balance' of Catholics and non-conformist dissenters as aldermen, including the long-standing Presbyterian Ambrose Barnes.[20] Yet even then, under pressure to support the repeal of bans on Catholics holding high national office, Blackett was able to get away with a provocatively anodyne response in February 1688: 'I humbly beg a liberty of conscience so far that my weak opinion in so weighty a concern may be suspended till I be well informed by the learned debates of the House of Commons, if I ever happen to come there ... however, to the utmost of my conscience I shall ever be studious to facilitate his Majesty's intentions'.[21]

By the autumn, knowing that William of Orange was about to set sail for England with the Dutch army, a now desperate James II tried to shore up his position by rescinding previous changes to the municipal charters. In Newcastle, Blackett lost no time in using this to have himself and his fellow aldermen reinstated and supporters Nicholas Ridley and Matthew White elected as mayor and sheriff on November 5th. A charter from James II survives which declared Blackett lord lieutenant of Northumberland the very next day.[22] For the King, none of these hasty manoeuvres fared better than any other of his last-minute attempts to hold onto power. By the following February William and Mary had been proclaimed monarchs, and Westminster's Declaration of Rights presaged a much stronger role for Parliament in future.[23]

However, Blackett's views on this momentous transition, later to be dubbed 'the Glorious Revolution', were apparently less than enthusiastic, which is perhaps surprising in view of his previous battles with the now-vanquished Stuarts. Newcastle initially resisted William of Orange's mandate for a new Parliament in January 1689. Blackett and Sir Ralph Carr agreed to stand as MPs, but it was said 'they still persist in their obstinacy and will not pray for the Prince and Princess of Orange, but with poisoned and inveterate words declare an abhorrence of their association'.[24] Furthermore, when back in Parliament later that month Blackett apparently voted against the Commons motion to declare the throne vacant, part of the constitutional mechanism contrived in order to legitimise the new *de facto* King.[25] It might be that he shared in concerns over breaking the principle of the hereditary succession, despite the unpopularity of James II. A Dutch army was in London, inevitably putting the pressure on Parliament to bless the claim of William and Mary to the throne. It could be seen as another attempt at arbitrary rule, albeit from a different political and religious direction. No further signs of Blackett's reluctance to accept the new regime have come down to us, however, which could mean that the new King's astute acceptance of the Bill of Rights and Parliament's stronger role was enough to mollify Blackett as well as his fellow pragmatic, if suspicious, Parliamentarians and merchants. Newcastle's political priorities remained as they always were, encapsulated well in the polite but firm rebuff given during the uncertain days of December 1688 to the armed assistance 'offered' to the town by both sides. The corporation 'would take care of their own town for the King, their religion, their laws and liberties'.[26]

Is this what the young William Blackett had been exercising his undoubted political talents in London and Newcastle to achieve? It was surely for more than the thrill of the chase or to see how far his powers of oratory, persuasion, alliance-building, sense of timing and negotiating ability could take him. A stable constitutional environment was important to fostering investment, business confidence and trade, cornerstones of Newcastle's commercial life. Beyond this, though, Blackett's motivation was perhaps not far removed from the aspersions cast about by Brabant regarding the desire of the Davison clique to control the town's privileged customs and monopolies. Royal interference in civic affairs could always be resisted publicly as assaults on English liberties and customs, but they also complicated local control of the more specific liberties to which the town's leading merchants were personally accustomed.

Newcastle's inner ring of aldermen who controlled the corporation, merchants' company and hostmen had long exercised wide powers of patronage. Rising trade and prosperity in the latter part of the 17th century bolstered municipal revenues. The common council granted leases to the town's extensive property holdings, set tolls and duties on the markets and shipping and made appointments to a variety of well-paid civic offices, church and school positions. As magistrates, the mayor, sheriff and aldermen presided over the town's courts. The 1650s had seen the rebuilding of the Guildhall. Forty years later the Mansion House, the old official mayoral residence overlooking the river on The Close was replaced by a magnificent new brick structure, complete with riverside terrace. Its occupant each year enjoyed the use of a state coach, a barge and a salary consistent with projecting Newcastle's splendour through lavish entertainment.[27] Perhaps the most telling illustration of the influence exerted through these various levers of local power is that the mayor and aldermen were invariably able to control the selection of MPs in a town with over 1,000 freemen electors. The town's representatives in Parliament were paid to support its causes in London and had the opportunity to promote their own. In the spring of 1685, Sir William Blackett MP joined the committee for the rebuilding of St. Paul's Cathedral, an attractive position if you sold lead. The roof alone was going to need 1,000 tons of it.[28]

It is hardly surprising that the town's elite wished to decide who would be admitted to refresh their numbers and feared the consequences of outside impositions. But for the legal bar of his Catholicism Sir William Creagh might have joined their ranks already. He had been a boyhood friend of Blackett, was his stepbrother-in-law after marrying Mary Rogers in 1681 and continued to deal with the Blacketts well into the 1690s.[29] It was therefore the principle of James II insisting Creagh be made a merchant adventurer, hostman, alderman and then mayor in 1687 that was the problem, rather than necessarily his person. The King's intervention struck to the very heart of the town's civic and commercial inner ring, and at a time when Catholicism was widely seen as the handmaiden of arbitrary government.[30] So while there was evidently some discomfort at the unconventional means by which William and Mary ascended the throne in early 1689, the new King's acceptance of traditional municipal independence, greater Parliamentary control of his purse-strings, and the supremacy of the established church greatly eased matters in Newcastle. Recent upheavals took physical form in the great public space of Sandhill. In 1686 Brabant had been able, with royal support, to intimidate the common council into paying for an equestrian statue of James II to be placed there. In May 1689 it was unceremoniously broken down by an unruly mob of soldiers. Some parts were thrown into the Tyne and metal was recast into new bells for All Saints church.[31] Through this turbulence Blackett saw out his year in the 1689 Parliament but did not seek re-election in 1690. While he would return to Westminster at a later date, he had plenty to do at home.

Businessman

With London such an important market for lead in the decades after the great fire, Blackett's presence there must have been helpful to his business, but the scale and geographic dispersal of that business needed careful management back at home. And from the moment of his father's death William faced a number of challenges – over Fallowfield, in Weardale and on Alston Moor. The price of lead was also lower than just a few years earlier. To set this in context we need first to look at Edward's share of the business inheritance.

Edward decided to run Fallowfield independently from the outset. His accounts commenced on the very date of his father's death, 16th May 1680 and by September ore was being carried not to William's mill Dukesfield but to Plankey, his own mill in a deep ravine on the lower River Allen.[32] Edward was potentially cutting off his nose to spite his face. Plankey was not only three miles further from Fallowfield than Dukesfield by the most obvious route bridging the North and South Tyne rivers, it was in completely the wrong direction, being a good eight or nine miles further west from Newcastle than William's mill. It was a daft destination for Fallowfield ore. Edward got rid of it within a year, although not before carrying out trials to see if it made economic sense to buy in ore from Alston Moor to smelt there. It didn't. Plankey was promptly let to the Bacon family.[33] But far from carrying his ore to Dukesfield, Edward built a new smelting mill at Birkey Burn in August 1681, only a mile from Fallowfield. It was in production within a year.[34]

Reduced carriage costs to and from the new mill cut 10% from Edward's costs for each ton of lead compared to Plankey and at 1680/1 levels of production could realistically hope to recover the cost of the licence and building works in less than three years.[35] In fact it happened even faster, as mining ramped up after a subdued 1680. Between May and December 1680 only about 180 tons of ore was mined at Fallowfield at an annualised rate, less than a fifth of the amount carried to Dukesfield five or six years before. The shallow reserves at the north-east end of the vein were probably exhausted. Access to the deeper reaches to the south-west would require new shafts, drainage levels and possibly a pumping engine. The mine expenditure accounts do indeed indicate that Edward's investment in his new smelting mill in 1681/2 was followed swiftly by an increase in other investment in 1682/3.[36] Ore production was back to over 1,000 tons in 1685 and around 430 tons of lead was smelted at Birkey Burn.

Economies of scale could be enjoyed again and with the price of lead rising to over £10/ton in the mid-1680s Edward probably made £1,500-£2,000 in annual profits from lead, at a very healthy margin of well over 30% on sales. Although exaggerated or embellished with the passage of time this was probably the period he had in mind when he much later claimed to have 'gained betwixt 3 and 4 thousand pounds a year'.[37] Fallowfield continued to produce high quality lead ore at relatively low cost. Edward's neat and meticulous surviving accounts illustrate well that when his fussy attention to detail had a worthwhile object, his analytical patience informed shrewd investment decisions. It was also mostly undertaken from Newby and therefore relied greatly on his Fallowfield agent Christopher Copperthwaite, the man recruited from Swaledale by William I a few years earlier in the teeth of local opposition and for whom setting bargains with the miners was now a routine matter.

Where did this leave William II? Dukesfield was no longer supplied with the rich ore from north of the Tyne, although the volume had perhaps already fallen off significantly from the peak of the mid-1670s. And he had other problems to contend with from the outset. Very shortly after William I's death Weardale's moormaster Humphrey Wharton launched an Exchequer Court case over the recently acquired Blackett mining rights in Weardale's inclosed lands, testing the mettle of the 23 year old inheritor.[38] Wharton had clearly prepared the ground in advance, for he was able to line up ten mostly ancient witnesses to give evidence to the commissioners in Weardale in August, two months before Blackett even replied to Wharton's bill of complaint. But Blackett made a robust defence of those rights, given alongside John Mowbray, his local Weardale agent John Westgarth and the third party, Barbara Sanderson, through whom his father had acquired the lease. The case wound on, however, until the middle of the decade and probably blighted further attempts to mine the contested pastures in the meantime. Although the verdict is lost it clearly went in Wharton's favour, for Blackett sold the lease to him cheaply in 1687. He later claimed that by then 'he had tired of the contest, & owns that he had found so much difficulty in it that he gave up the cudgeals.'[39] Lest we conclude from this, however, that young William had trouble filling his father's shoes, recall that William I had also suffered reverses in his duels with Wharton - and the story was not yet over, as we shall see.

William II was also under pressure on Alston Moor in the early 1680s. Francis Radcliffe evidently felt that he was being underpaid for his duty ore under the Greengill lease held by the Blacketts since 1671. Lease holders were required to give notice to Radcliffe's agents when a batch of dressed ore was ready for inspection so that the fifth share of duty could be collected. However, to avoid the agent holding up onwards delivery, the lessees were entitled to carry away all but the duty ore if the agents 'neglect to receive it', although no time limit was set.[40] The consequences are easily guessed at. However, rather than wait for Radcliffe to launch a case against him, William II pre-empted matters by bringing a case in 1685 accusing Radcliffe of threatening a suit. Blackett sought a commission to take depositions from 'ancient witnesses' too frail to travel to London.[41] Again, the outcome is unknown. Blackett remained as leaseholder at Greengill but did not renew it in 1692.

The loss of Fallowfield ore, the question mark over the Weardale in-bye lease and apparent sniping over the Greengill duty ore meant Blackett relied heavily upon his core inheritance in Allendale to sustain the production of lead. Signs of more intensive mining are therefore unsurprising; as early as October 1680 he bought land just north of Allenheads, near the entrance to Haugh Level. Its acquisition could well help to date this ambitious drainage level, more than a mile long, and which intercepted the veins at Allenheads at a depth of over 180ft.[42] It is served by a large number of air shafts, many still visible today, suggesting that it was opened up quickly through work carried out on many lengths at once. This would be entirely consistent with a desire by William to intensify mining quickly, even at a capital cost likely to have been nearly £3,000. Over in the West Allen the Shieldridge Level can be more securely dated to 1684. Although not as long or as costly as the Haugh Level, it was still a bold undertaking as there were only six years left on the Fenwick mining rights lease by then.[43] But this was in the rising market also being exploited by Edward at Fallowfield. Michael Robinson, the Blaydon staithman, noted that William's lead carriage increased in the mid-1680s to the extent that further road repairs above Stella were needed.[44]

Newcastle shipments to home and overseas markets reached over 2,600 tons in 1686, more than double the quantity seen in 1679. Exports eastwards through the Baltic Sound also rose rapidly.[45] Radcliffe's pursuit of Blackett over his Greengill duty ore was probably given impetus by Radcliffe's decision to smelt for himself at his new mill at Woodhall during these years rather than sell the ore back to his lessees. Newcastle capital continued to flow out to the hills. John Errington developed Blagill, just across the valley from Greengill, Settlingstones was built up by Alderman William Ramsay and the lawyer John Ord was so keen to obtain the rights at Blanchland that he instructed his agent to 'break not for (the sake of) 20s, 40s or £3. Pray fail me not'.[46]

No wonder William was also buying in John Ord's ore from Hunstanworth to smelt at Dukesfield in 1687. It was not a huge amount and would yield scarcely 30 tons, but a flavour of how keen Blackett must have been to obtain it is seen in the price: at around £4.10 per ton of ore, so the lead it produced cannot have been sold for more than a 10% gross margin.[47] It is impossible to say whether this reflected weaker profitability in general as we have none of William's accounts, but unless mining costs in Allendale reduced dramatically compared to the 1670s (and they might have done if the Haugh Level opened up and drained rich lower parts of the veins) the removal of the cheap Fallowfield ore must have had a negative effect. Neither is it possible to say whether William II had made up for the loss of Fallowfield and Weardale ore with more intensive production at Allenheads. Total shipments of lead from Newcastle and Sunderland were much higher in 1686 than in 1679 (3,000 tons vs. 1,700) and Allenheads might well have contributed to this, but the intervening years had also seen a great expansion in mining by others on Alston Moor. Just eight mining leases had been issued there between 1670 and 1681 but 16 followed in the next two years alone.[48] Whether or not Allenheads held its own, by the late 1680s the market was no longer dominated by the Blacketts. Profits were probably quite respectable but the monolithic business had fractured and William II had retreated in Weardale.

Reversal was also seen in the coal business during the 1680s. The scraps of evidence available to us from the three mining estates of Stella Grand Lease, Winlaton and Whorlton Moor do not show William driving them forward. Stella remained highly productive and profitable, but Blackett's stake never rose above his father's initial 1/12 share. Winlaton's coal output continued the slow decline already evident in the 1670s. A much later revival, in the 1720s, showed that with renewed investment the mature Winlaton pits might expand again, but it was evidently not an investment William II decided to make. As mentioned earlier, Edward decided to manage Michael's share of Winlaton himself although gave up within a few years. As for the mines to the north of the Tyne, the Whorlton Moor lease was due to expire in 1686. Blackett did not renew his interest, although he spent the last few years of the old lease driving up output to new heights. Around 45-50,000 tons of coal a year had been produced at Whorlton until 1682, but it then increased rapidly to 87,000 tons in 1685. It never recovered to this level again under the new lease and was virtually worked out by 1695. In total, William I had mined nearly 70,000 tons of coal in 1680. A decade later his son was responsible for perhaps 25,000 tons.[49]

It was probably never going to have been possible for William I's sons to have maintained the rapid business expansion of the 1660s and 1670s. Mature concerns can rarely grow at the same rate as smaller ones. Both Edward and William II, operating apart, invested in their core mines in the early part of the decade but we are still left with an impression of mining stasis, if not retrenchment. This was certainly the case as far as trading was concerned, for neither brother appears in the port books for any significant quantities of coal or lead. It looks as if Edward's Fallowfield profits in the boom years of the mid-1680s were directed towards his grand building project at Newby Hall, with its innovative sash windows and flat leaded roof possibly designed by Sir Christopher Wren, in preference to new commercial ventures.[50]

William II's civic and Parliamentary engagement in the 1680s suggests that his priorities might also have lain outside further business development. Greyfriars was already the grandest house in Newcastle but it was extended further by Blackett with the addition of three-storey classical blocks to the north and south, details of which can be seen in Knyff and Kip's view of the mansion and its grounds (see Plate 18). Flat leaded rooves were surrounded by balustrades and reached by stairs emerging through cupolas from which his guests on summer evenings could enjoy the elevated views of the carefully manicured grounds, the town beyond and the distant hills. The mansion had the highly fashionable sash windows also favoured by Edward, and was surrounded by formal gardens and a neatly regular orchard to the south. Advanced 'hot beds' in the kitchen garden were imitated as far away as the Cumbrian coast. The grand staircase, sections of which were discovered in a country house attic not long ago, was at the forefront of contemporary design.[51]

The Knyff and Kip engraving probably dates from around 1700, but it seems likely that work on the extensions was underway some time earlier.[52] In 1685 the young William II was newly married, had just been created a baronet and established his reputation as a leading civic figure in his own right through his lobbying in London over the town's charter and in defeating Brabant in that year's contested Parliamentary election. His bride's £6,000 dowry was available in cash, the price of lead was rising and he was mining record amounts of coal from the last months of his lease at Whorlton Moor. It is all conjecture, but in these circumstances it is easy to see the attractions to the young man of giving highly visible material form to his social and political status with bold new architecture in the middle of the town – and keeping up with his older brother's work at Newby.* Yet despite the outward appearance that William was following Edward in taking his profits out of trade and mining, the next few years would show him taking a quite different path with a dramatic new commitment to business expansion.

---

* Newcastle's new Mansion House was built on The Close in 1691-2. It too had a classical appearance and sash windows and perhaps followed on from Blackett's introduction of the style into the town at Greyfriars: Eneas Mackenzie, *Historical Account of Newcastle-Upon-Tyne*, (1827), p.232.

Chapter 14
Resurgence

The similarities between Edward and William Blackett's lives in the 1680s were always superficial but they certainly diverged starkly in the next decade. While Edward oversaw some further important developments at Fallowfield, production slowly declined over the next 20 years and the mine was leased out to Newcastle merchants in 1710. His later letters add entertaining colour to what can already be surmised from his meticulous financial accounts of the 1680s regarding his agonised decision-making and fussy attention to detail, bearing out the aside from one of his contemporaries that he 'talks of more things than he puts into execution'.[1] In his 60s in the 1710s, ailments and hypochondria were frequent topics of correspondence. He lived on at Newby and in York until his death in 1718.*

William, on the other hand, remained at the centre of civic life in Newcastle through the 1690s and his business activities in that decade contrast sharply with the relative stasis of the 1680s. The magnificently extended Greyfriars mansion was a showcase for his industrial ambition, not an attempt to put himself above such grubby pursuits. Those flat balustraded rooves were doubtless clad with Blackett's own lead, over 200 tons of it to judge by their size, and lead statuary adorned the formal grounds.[2] This was presumably not lost on those invited to take the air and the views westwards towards the distant hills whence the lead came.

Lead

Although William gave up the lease to mine Weardale's enclosed grounds in 1687 he dramatically reinforced his commitment to the industry and increased the scale of his operations through two significant deals in the three years from 1689. Firstly, with the Allen-

---

* Sir Edward was occasionally hounded by his daughters. When Maria and Alethea wanted to move to London for a season he said it was far too expensive. How about Leeds or York? Three months later they were in London: NRO ZBL 189, 8 and 12 Dec 1709, 24 March 1710.

dale mining lease due to end in 1690, he followed his father's example in pre-empting the expiry by agreeing bold new terms with the Fenwicks. William I obtained the lucrative Fallowfield extension in 1667. William II went a stage further by buying the Fenwicks out altogether, along with their core estate centred on Wallington and the manor of Hexham.

We saw earlier how William I exploited the short-term financial needs of the entitled and extravagant Sir William Fenwick. The next head of the family, Sir John, always held in contempt by his father, was hardly more numerate or thrifty. Although an able soldier and seen by some as an amiable character, his judgement was highly suspect and discretion non-existent. Even his famed subversion and agitation for the Jacobite cause of the exiled James II and the Stuart dynasty seems to have been guided as much by a long-standing personal, and entirely mutual, grudge with King William III as by underlying principle. As one of his contemporaries put it, 'his headpiece was none of the best'.[3] As the Blacketts had doubtless always expected, the £2,000 loan advanced to Sir John's father in 1674 was not repaid. Railing against the injustice of it all when pursued by William Blackett II in Chancery in 1687, Fenwick claimed that Blackett and his father had 'got £100,000 in clear profits' from the lead mines, as if that had any legal bearing.[4] Blackett won the case, requiring Fenwick to pay him off by borrowing a further sum from elsewhere. This could only stave off the final reckoning and over the course of the summer of 1689 Fenwick was worn down. The real negotiations were between Blackett and Fenwick's various creditors, all parties to the transaction, but Fenwick was under further pressure that summer for he was imprisoned in the Tower of London under suspicion of fomenting insurrection against the newly crowned William and Mary. Blackett knew how to pick his moment. The relevant deeds were all signed between the dates of Fenwick's arrest and release.

Blackett's purchase of the Fenwick estates at Wallington, Hexham and elsewhere has generally been seen as a breath-taking bargain, consisting of an initial £4,000 payment and a £2,000 annuity for the lives of Fenwick and his wife Mary, but the initial cost was actually £15,000, clearing the debts owed by Fenwick to various creditors.[5] Given their respective ages in 1689 (Fenwick was 44 and his wife 39) it would have been reasonable for Blackett to expect to pay the annuity for another 20 years. At the then official 6% rate of interest this discounted to a present value of £22,300, taking the effective total to £37,300. Valuing the land at 17 years' purchase of the estimated gross rental – some £16,000 for Wallington and £12,000 for the manor of Hexham – leaves £9,300 as the effective cost of the mining rights in perpetuity.[6] In 1667 William I had paid £4,050 for roughly equivalent rights, but for just 23 years, and based on lead production that was probably only a third of the sum being worked in 1689-90.[7] William II's deal, if not 'breath-taking', was still an exceptionally good one.

Blackett's ambition for the lead business is seen in an even bolder move three years later. In December 1692 he finally succeeded in bringing the Blackett quest for the Weardale mines to an end. This wasn't just a reversal of the 1687 setback when he handed Wharton the mining rights to the enclosed lands, but the moormastership itself, covering the lead veins within Wolsingham and Stanhope parishes under the vast area of unenclosed land. Humphrey Wharton was 66 and possibly ill for he had just another two years to live. However, given the running battles with the two William Blacketts over the decades, it is hard to imagine him meekly handing over this rich and widespread domain because of age or infirmity. Rather, the £6,000 paid by Blackett for Wharton's lease was surely too good to refuse.[8] This was for three lives – Wharton's own and those of his son Anthony (28 in 1692) and youngest daughter Jane but further lives could be usually substituted for a one-off payment of £150, a year's rent.[9] The £6,000 purchase cost could be spread out over decades, but there were also annual charges in the form of the Bishop's rent, payment in lieu of his lott ore, the Rector of Stanhope's tithe and rent for the 21 year lease of mining rights in the enclosed lands (which Blackett had sold to Wharton in 1687 and now came back to him). These probably added up to about £875 per year.[10] This sum would need to be brought under £1 per ton of lead, preferably well under, in order for there to be any chance of Blackett making a profit, which implied producing at least 900 tons of lead annually.

It is difficult to estimate how much lead was actually being produced from the length of Weardale at the time, for any records Wharton kept have long since been lost, and the Bishop's agents and watchers always struggled to keep up with the miners. However, Wharton agreed to pay the bishop £350 in lieu of his lott ore in 1688, which, given prevailing lead prices, suggests he was already producing more, perhaps significantly more, than 1,100 tons of ore. This would smelt down to about 600 tons of lead. The output level Blackett required might not have been far off. By 1706 the Weardale mines were said to have produced 'towards 4000 bings' (1,600 tons of ore).[11] Whatever the actual level, William II was, like his father, content to accept high fixed costs as an opportunity to profit from economies of scale. The unhindered right to any new mine exploration or development at no additional cost must also have been attractive.

He had taken on a huge management challenge. The intensively worked lead mines at his small number of familiar sites, Allenheads, Coalcleugh and Greengill, occupied small areas of land within a few miles of each other, with some outliers nearby, and all within easy reach of the experienced Richard Mowbray in Allenheads. In the early 1690s these few mines probably accounted for more lead in a year than the whole of Weardale. The moormastership encompassed the parishes of Stanhope and Wolsingham. Stanhope alone, where most of the active mines and potential new reserves were located, covered 85 square miles of the sparsely populated main valley, its tributaries and high expanses of moorland. Small mines were dotted around the fastnesses of the dale. In 1684 160 were listed, under 94 separate leases, 60 of which had been granted to partnerships of miners tackling a single grove, although it is quite possible that only a small number of them were being worked at the time. Only seven were let to better-resourced partnerships working four to eight mines.[12] Geology and landform remained favourable to a domestic scale of production. Many lead veins crossed the valley and could be worked by tunnelling in from the valley sides, thereby benefiting from free drainage, or reached by shallow shafts, such as at Slitts above Westgate. It might not have changed a great deal from the work carried out in those hills by their medieval forbears.

Wharton did not trouble himself directly with mining, preferring to issue leases across his wide and windswept domain and to buy ore at a contractually low price. Weardale's geography made it hard to do otherwise. The Blacketts had always worked their own mines. They invested a lot of capital and mobilised large workforces to prospect, to drive levels, to sink shafts and to extract large quantities of ore from a few productive mines at low unit cost. The prospect of introducing this business model to tap Weardale's potential must always have been enticing and Blackett finally had his hands on the levers of control there. But given the extent of his new domain and the large number of existing leases operated by small mining partnerships, any such change was going to take time. As the leases fell in, Blackett had the option to set his own miners to work through local agents. But this would have placed a rising strain on day-to-day operations, cash-flow and development capital and require too many new supervisors of unknown reliability. At the same time production had to be maintained to lighten the load of the purchase and annual rent burden. Inevitably, therefore, we find that Blackett continued to issue new leases.

We don't know how many mining leases he issued in his early years as Weardale's moormaster, but eight survive from between early 1693 and 1696. The lease/partnership of 30 or so mines originally set up between Wharton and Charles Paulet in 1670 remained in place throughout this period, indeed until 1791, with the Blackett and Bacon families replacing the original principals.[13] Newcastle names appear amongst the Weardale lessees: Alderman William Ramsay, for example, who also had the Settlingstones mine north of the Tyne, Nicholas Ridley and Matthew White.[14] As moormaster, Blackett reserved the right to buy their ore, dressed ready for smelting and delivered to him, for £2.25-£2.50 per ton for the duration of their leases, in similar fashion to Wharton's practice. If he chose not to buy the ore, such as when the Newcastle price fell below a viable level, the lessees had to provide the duty ore (ie. just over a fifth of the produce) for free, which effectively guaranteed Blackett the backstop of a contribution towards the rent he owed the Bishop and Rector. The lessees were also required to keep the mines in production and to maintain underground works in good condition. Since Newcastle's shrewd merchants were prepared to take leases on these terms from one of their own, Weardale lead could still be worked viably using hired miners.

The lease feature of paying based on output was shared with the bargain system that was increasingly prevalent in the pay structure of miners. Far from Edward Blackett's approach of agreeing new bargains every few months with his Fallowfield miners based on the state of the groves, however, the price was fixed in the Weardale leases for 21 years. Sufficient management capacity to implement a full system of bargains was probably unavailable and was doubtless strained enough monitoring individual groves every three months throughout the dale. Nevertheless, William II made at least some effort to start mining directly, for a 1695 lease in the Rookhope valley mentions a boundary next to Blackett's own adjacent workings. But direct operation of Weardale mining lay a long way off. 21-year leases were still being granted in the 1710s.[15] Although Blackett reserved the right to buy ore at a reasonably low price from his lessees he was unable to reduce it any further as he had no direct control of their production process and there was still the burden of the lott and tithe ore rent. In a world of low lead prices, the pressure to reduce costs remained as strong as ever. The obvious places to look for economies were in smelting and transport.

The economic improvements of William I's introduction of slag hearths at Dukesfield and Plankey to improve the yield of lead from ore in the 1670s had already been obtained. As we saw earlier though, this increased the cost of smelting. How could it be reduced again? Given that good smelters were always worth holding onto there was little scope for reducing labour costs, but the 1690s did see some interesting experiments with fuel.

Wider efforts were underway across the nation to find alternatives to wood as an industrial fuel. Abraham Darby was not the only Midlands industrialist experimenting with coke, coal roasted to reduce sulphur content, to break away from dependence on charcoaled wood in smelting and casting iron in the decades either side of 1700.[16] London merchants and Bristol metallurgists, connected by a shared Quaker faith, were investing in trials to use coal in smelting lead in the 1690s, from which sprang what was later known as the 'London Lead Company' (LLC). A key innovation was said to be the reverberatory furnace which kept the coal and lead ore separate in order to reduce contamination caused by sulphur from coal in the hearth. The LLC's decision to choose the North East as a base to start smelting and refining lead with coal before 1700 was probably influenced by the availability of cheap local supplies. In locating at Ryton or Blaydon they were close to fellow Quaker Ambrose Crowley's major ironworks at Winlaton, established just a few years earlier in 1691.[17] The North East was one of those regions where industrial capital focused the spirit of patient scientific enquiry, trial, measurement and improvement on breaking practical and economic constraints to growing demand for the products of hearths and furnaces. In 1701-2 Newcastle physician and mineralogist Jabez Cay asked fellow physician Martin Lister in Surrey 'the favour of informing him of the special art of separating silver from lead ... there are many in this district who experiment with large amounts by the ordinary method ... Mr.Ridley, a rich local man ... plans to make a great profit'.[18] How many other such examples are now lost to us? We're only aware of what Edward Blackett was up to at Birkey Burn through careful examination of his financial ledgers. These show that in the early 1690s his smelting mill was switching over to the consumption of relatively cheap coal for fuel rather than chopwood, some years earlier than the claimed introduction of coal for lead smelting in the North East.[19]

It wasn't necessarily that wood was becoming scarcer or more expensive in the area. Wood appears to have been bought at much the same rate for Dukesfield Mill in the 1670s and nearby Blackhall Mill in 1691, although distance could weigh in on this and William II was fetching some of his wood fuel from Muggleswick Park in 1689, eight miles from Dukesfield.[20] It was rather that the availability of a cheaper alternative when costs were under pressure created an incentive to change. There weren't many places in the North Pennines where coal could be found, but one fuel was abundant on the fells: peat. Beyond being perhaps 40% cheaper than wood, peat fuel could also reduce transport prices. Smelting mills had hitherto located at a distance downstream from the lead veins near woodland because it was more problematic to carry bulky wood than compact sacks of ore. Mills could now be built much closer to both ore and fuel supplies, and thereby greatly reduce the carriage of the deadweight of material lost from the ore when smelted. The removal of ten miles of deadweight carriage could save about 20p per ton of lead in addition to a similar amount saved in fuel cost, thereby reducing the overall operating cost by perhaps 6-8%. This was no revolutionary transformation, but when margins were so low a 40p saving would add more than a third to William Blackett II's operating profit on each ton sold.

It was certainly compelling enough at the time to make it worth overcoming two obstacles. The first was to determine new techniques of temperature control and the mixing of fuel and ore in the hearth in view of the differences in calorific value, burning qualities and physical characteristics of peat compared to chopwood. This was presumably just a matter of time for experienced smelters if given their head and the room to practice by their employer. The second obstacle was trickier. Peat might have lain in abundant thick blankets across the open high North Pennines common wasteland but it was typically subject to the customary right of manorial tenants to take it for hedging, roofing and as domestic fuel. Rights such as these were vigorously defended by the tenants in the manor courts, where tradition and precedent held sway. They were unlikely to have taken kindly to the use by a Newcastle merchant of 'their' peat to fuel a growing industry.

This probably explains manoeuvres by William II in 1694 to establish a peat-fuelled smeltmill at Carrshield in the West Allen valley, not far from Coalcleugh. Having bought out the Fenwicks a few years earlier, Blackett was now lord of the manor, so he could grant permission for the mill – to his cousin and fellow Newcastle merchant, John Rumney.[21] Sure enough, there was local resistance, and not just muttered grumbles. The building work was disrupted and there were threats to pull down the peathouse and burn its contents. Blackett then pre-empted manor court proceedings by bringing his own disingenuous claim that 'severall copyholders & inhabitants in Allendale ... have desired & requested the Lord' to grant Rumney the right to his mill. The jurors could not be browbeaten to give more than very reluctant consent. The mill was never built, possibly because Rumney died just a few months later, but perhaps also because what Blackett really wanted was a precedent to enable the construction of upland peat-fired mills where it suited him within Allendale. By 1726, at the very latest, the Allenheads mill was in operation, not far from the entrance to the Haugh Level, but it was probably built much earlier. The purchase of the nearby tenement of Dirtpotsheeles in 1698 by Blackett's local agent George Mowbray suggests a construction date of around that time.[22] Whether or not Blackett was the pioneer of peat-fuelled upland lead smelting mills and whether or not the Carrshield affair could directly open the way to similar changes outside the manor of Hexham, the 1690s does appear to have been the point after which lead smelting mills were increasingly located up in the hills and several of the old woodland mills were discontinued.[23]

It certainly made sense for Blackett in Weardale given the location of the smelting mills used by Wharton (see Figure 14.1). Scotch Isle had been in the moormaster's hands since the 1630s, and he ran his Weardale affairs from nearby Wolsingham. By the 1680s Wharton had the Derwent and Stanhopehope mills, built in 1668 and 1677 respectively. It looks as though Blackett was obliged to buy these from Wharton in 1692 as a condition of the sale of the moormastership. Ore and peat was carried down into the deep and sinuous folds of the Derwent valley to the mill there in 1695, but 'little was done' there three years later.[24] Neither mill appears in any of the 18th-century Blackett lead accounts. Rookhope and Allenheads most certainly do.

The earliest date at which a smelting mill was definitely in operation at Rispey in the Rookhope valley is 1726, but it seems highly likely that it was built by William II as he reconfigured the business after taking the moormastership, so too the Allenheads mill.[25] Allenheads was not far from the mines at the top end of Weardale, including those bought in the late 1670s at Killhope and Welhope. Rookhope was set amongst many of the mines in that valley. Both were peat-fuelled mills on the right side of the mines for onwards carriage of the lead to Newcastle and were a good ten miles closer to the mines, on average, than Wharton's mills, saving around 30p/ton in ore carriage.

Standing back from all this, the impression left by Blackett's bold expansion of his lead business into Weardale is of a pragmatic approach to mining over such a widespread domain by continuing to issue leases to others, but active changes to the smelting operation through the creation of new mills in strategic locations and the innovative adoption of cheaper fuel. He was also pragmatic in his choice of managers. The experienced and trusted Richard Mowbray was deputed to follow up on the moormaster purchase in 1692 alongside John Featherstone, quite possibly a son of Thomas Featherstone, Dukesfield mill agent by 1690.[26] But it would surely have been impossible to run affairs over such a wide area without taking on at least some of Wharton's deputies familiar with the ter-

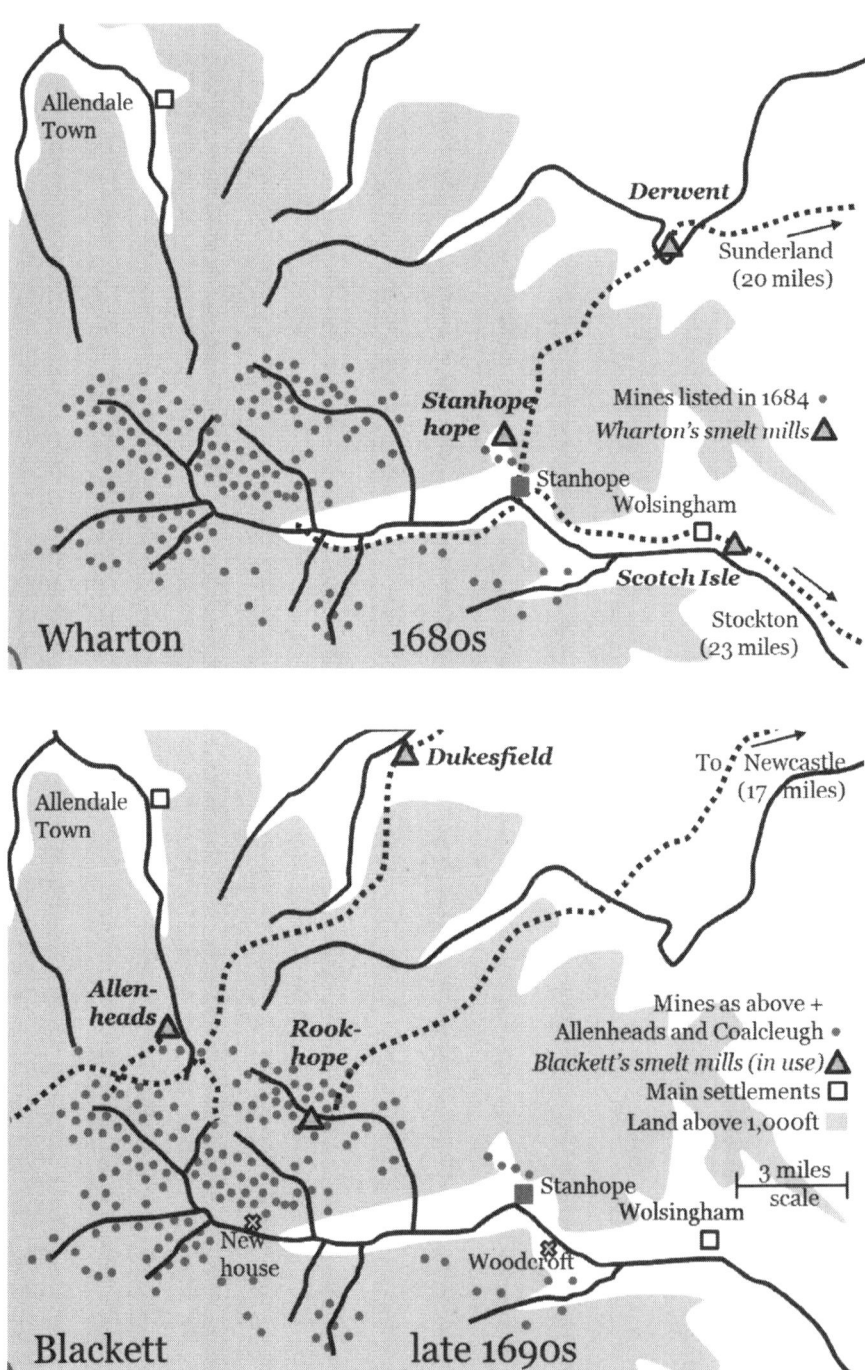

Figure 14.1 Weardale lead mines and smelting mills 1680s-90s.

222 | *The Blacketts*

ritory and people. The Robert Keys who witnessed a lease from Blackett to Ramsay in 1695 might have been one such incumbent.[27]

Pragmatic maybe, but it was nevertheless an emphatic commitment to Weardale. There are no signs of second thoughts when he renewed the moormaster agreement with the Bishop just a few years later, in 1696, despite two of the named Wharton lives still being relatively young. It probably cost Blackett £450 or more for the privilege of flushing away the Wharton link and naming himself, six-year-old son William III and eight-year-old daughter Elizabeth as the three lives.[28]

Blackett's new regime was visibly underwritten in the landscape with the construction of an imposing new residence for his chief agent in Weardale – Newhouse, at Ireshopeburn (see Plate 14). He had inherited the ancestral Blackett estate at Woodcroft, bought by his father in 1676. Basing his Weardale operation at this ancient family site might have communicated a potent symbolic message of enduring power and presence. Symbolic, but impractical. Located between Stanhope and Wolsingham it was too far to the east of the active mines, whereas Newhouse was high up the dale amongst them (See Figure 14.1). Blackett bought the Shorthorns estate on which it stands in 1693, within months of his purchase of the moormastership, and we can be fairly confident that the agent's house was built soon afterwards, surely and deliberately much grander than any other in the upper valley.[29] There it stands today with its long frontage and stone mullioned windows, Blackett's triumphal monument to the successful culmination of a three-decade family quest in Weardale.

His ambition for the lead business was not limited to Weardale in the 1690s. Blackett secured acceptance and precedent, howsoever grudging, for peat-fuelled smelting in Allendale. Dukesfield Mill's importance was reinforced through the purchase of an estate on the opposite bank of the river in 1689, securing the dam which served the mill's vital water supply.[30] At around the same time Blackett paid for a schoolteacher at Allenheads and Coalcleugh and a minister was installed to preach to the Allendale miners. The Allenheads chapel was rebuilt by Blackett in 1701, complete with the family coat of arms, and another was erected at Coalcleugh three years later. This was not simply an act of benevolence; the miners were all expected to pay half a day's wages each month to receive

Resurgence | 223

the minister's spiritual direction. If we can believe the claim some years later that 'in the time of Peace, when these Lead-Mines did flourish [the sum raised] amounted to between £70 and £80 a year' there were around 230 or more contributing miners at the turn of the century, noticeably more than the 140-180 estimated for 1677-8.[31] At the same level of productivity this translates to 1,400 tons of ore being mined at Allenheads and Coalcleugh. A similar amount might be allowed from the 'towards 4,000 bings' statement mentioned earlier for Weardale in 1705/6. These hazardous figures, plucked from circumstantial and possibly unreliable asides, are the best we can do for William II's lead business in the very early 1700s, but they potentially fit with the level of lead shipments from Newcastle in 1706. The tonnage of ore mined in Weardale and Allendale would smelt down to about 1,600 tons of lead at a time when 2,400 tons left Newcastle by sea.[32]

Blackett's lead business was possibly responsible for over twice as much annual production in 1700-5 as in the late 1680s. Since then he had bought the full rights to his existing Allendale lease, intensified activity there, and secured control of Weardale, cementing one natural geographic monopoly and securing another. His father seemed to have wanted to keep Edward and William working together but 20 years later it hardly mattered that they had quickly gone their separate ways. The Fallowfield mine was probably sending no more than 100-200 tons of lead a year down to Newcastle in the late 1690s, possibly just a mere 3-5% of his younger brother's production.[33] In a 1699 national publication Midlands metallurgist Moses Stringer named 'Sir William Blackett, who has Thousands a Year, in Lead Works in the north of England' amongst other examples of the single leading producers in each of England's main mineral producing regions.[34] Blackett's leading role within the North East evidently needed no further elaboration.

Coal

Blackett also extended his coal mining interests from 1689. In December 1688 he bought the eastern half of Kenton manor and its colliery, just to the north of Newcastle, for £6,000. This lay just beyond the Town Moor, already worked for coal under Common

Council licence (see Figure 11.1). Blackett's cousin John had been working the East Kenton mine for the previous five years but he immediately assigned his lease to William and a few months later sold him his mining workgear and stock of coal.[35] It was a decisive move worthy of William I, and appears all the more courageous when we recall that the preceding months, during which the deal must have been under negotiation, Blackett had been thrown out as an alderman during James II's erratic final year in power. When the sale was concluded in mid-December, it was still unclear who would prevail in London, and whether another descent into civil war could be avoided. Furthermore, the market had not been sending encouraging signals, judging from the Hull and London coal prices available to us. Yet Blackett clearly saw this as a strategic move, underwritten the following summer with that unambiguous symbol of 17th-century confidence in Tyneside coal – a waggonway. It was over 3 miles long and ran down to the Tyne at Scotswood.[36] Blackett's commitment to Kenton was deepened in January 1694 when he took a lease of the western half of the estate, and the level of the fixed rent he agreed to pay implies confidence that he could mine more than 10,000 tons per year there, a quantity he was perhaps already extracting from the eastern half.

He made a series of further coal investments in the early 1690s, this time downstream of the Tyne Bridge on the south bank just beyond Gateshead. In 1691 he inherited a share of his uncle Matthew Kirkley's Deckham Hall colliery, probably quite a small affair, alongside his brother and two of his sisters, and he was soon responsible for running the mine. That same summer he took a mining lease of Heworth, not far to the east, and with a river frontage. Production was ramped up quickly, reaching about 27,000 tons of coal in 1693. The summer of 1693 also saw Blackett take a lease of the Bishop of Durham's mining rights on the adjacent high open waste of Gateshead Fell, which stretched away southwards from Deckham alongside the Great North Road.[37] As with Kenton, this cluster was new yet familiar territory for Blackett for he presumably already knew something of the quality of coal in Uncle Matthew's mine and the depth at which it was found. Felling was just next door, the estate taken by William I as security for that £2,000 loan to Robert Brandling in 1676. However, Brandling's capable and industrious brother Ralph managed to retrieve his inheritance in the early 1680s and it was promptly let to others. The Gateshead mines, like those of Kenton, formed part of the general move away from the river in search of new coal reserves and they too therefore needed waggonway infrastructure. Blackett had evidently hoped to use the existing Bensham waggonway; in 1693 he agreed to lease staith rights at its Gateshead south shore terminus, not far below the Tyne Bridge, but its owners, the great coal-owning Liddells, declined to support a rival. From March 1694 Blackett's Gateshead Fell coal was being carried down his own separate waggonway to Heworth staiths instead, further downstream.

By 1700 Blackett was producing around 50,000 tons of coal per year from his various mines, perhaps double the level of a decade earlier.[38] To rebuild a strong presence in coal, there was a certain strategic logic to the Kenton and Gateshead developments. Some familiarity with local mines could have informed a reasoned judgement on prospects, underwritten by transport investment to reach down to the river. A sequence of pits was dug and levels driven into the hilly ground to assist with drainage.[39] They were substantive additions to the Blackett coal interests at Winlaton and the Stella Grand Lease, yet taken during times when the industry was not in the rudest of health.

Perhaps he'd been tempted into Kenton by record domestic shipments of more than 600,000 tons of coal from the Tyne in 1688. It was a level not to be reached again until after 1700. In the early 1690s it was rare for more than 450,000 tons to be shipped out.[40] There is no direct price data from Tyneside for the decade after 1685, but it would be unwise to assume Tyneside prices followed the apparent spike upwards in London prices from 1690, because increased bribes in the form of 'gift coals' were being offered to shipmasters as inducements to buy. These had been rare in the 1680s but in 1690 as the amount of coal sold was falling, the quantity said to have been commonly offered as gift coal was equivalent to a 20% discount and both 1691 and 1692 were little better.[41] There was no decisive increase in sales until 1697. Committing large sums of money to mine great quantities of coal in times such as these might be seen as more foolish than brave, but Blackett was not the only one on the move.

Charles Montague had arrived on Tyneside armed with London capital. He stormed in amongst the local coalowners by leasing the Gibside estate, south of Whickham, in May 1692 agreeing a fixed rent which implied annual production of around 17,000 tons of coal. It was four miles from the Tyne and he planned a new waggonway from the outset, although it was not in operation for another seven years. The region's coal barons had, of course, seen off external interlopers in the past, but Montague was no naïve adventurer. His uncle was Nathaniel Crewe, Bishop of Durham, whose patronage had already brought Montague a city of Durham seat in Parliament in 1685. His father was the Earl of Sandwich and his cousin and namesake was the founder of the Bank of England in 1694. Montague himself had funds enough to become one of its founding directors. Here was someone to be taken seriously, a man who could either upset the configuration of Tyneside coal interests or be absorbed carefully into it.[42]

Blackett cultivated Montague. It was a matter of mutual self-interest. The new man's close connections with the Bishop of Durham could doubtless be helpful to Blackett in Weardale and possibly in London. In return, Blackett's own coal estate and influence within Newcastle, not least as governor of the hostmen's company in 1691 and 1692, could smooth Montague's path into the coal oligarchy. In December 1691 Montague married Blackett's step-sister Sarah Rogers and a few years later he named Blackett amongst the local 'coal professours'.[43] They, and the other major coal owners, had a common interest in tackling the apparent divergence in London and Tyneside coal price trends in the 1690s. In coal, investment coalesced with politics, and Blackett's stake in coal took him back into that world.

Where collieries were burdened with fixed drainage and waggonway costs, profit margins could be slender even in good times. The brutally rational response in a downturn would have been to close down the more expensive pits, but few could afford to write off the large investments already sunk - literally so. A far more attractive option was for the coal barons to seek an increased share of the price at which coal sold in London, for several intermediaries stood between them and the final consumer. Under the rules of the hostmen's monopoly, all Tyneside coal owners either had to be members or to sell to the company's fitters, who in turn sold to the shipmasters. On arrival in London, coal was carried ashore by the Thames lightermen who, unlike the Tyne's keelmen, were typically dealers in their own right or working very closely with the capital's merchants who bought from the shipmasters. Control of sales to the capital's consumers by a close ring of dealers suited the City, Crown and Parliament in making it easier to levy and collect various duties and taxes on London's indispensable fuel. At the turn of the century coal cost London's householders around four times more than the price received by Newcastle's coal owners.[44] This gave ample room for suspicion and skirmishes up and down that extended chain between pit and fireplace. For the Tyneside coalowners the most obvious targets were the fitters, the London dealers and the government's taxes. Blackett was closely involved in campaigns on all three fronts in the years either side of the turn of the century.

Coal was just too tempting a commodity to avoid being taxed in the Restoration period, and the burden kept growing. By the turn of the century Newcastle's corporation and Trinity House dues and various London corporation, Royal and Parliamentary levies and taxes probably accounted for a third or more of the retail price in the capital. When the new King William III sought popularity at the start of his reign by abolishing the Hearth Tax, coal took its place. By the early 1700s the various tax revenues from coal probably matched the proceeds of the hearth tax 20 years earlier.[45] What was burned in London's fireplaces each year generated as much money for city, crown and Parliament as the hated earlier tax on the fireplace itself. In 1694 Parliament introduced a new 'temporary' tax on coal to raise funds to pay for the war with France. Blackett duly went back to Westminster for Newcastle in 1695, alongside fellow coal owner William Carr, and the new Parliament withdrew the tax in 1696. That same year, with support from the hostmen back in Newcastle, Blackett introduced a bill to control the 'extravagant rates' charged for coal carriage wayleaves and staithroom.[46] As mining moved further from the Tyne, there was ever greater scope for landowners between the pits and the river to hold coal owners to ransom over such rights and Blackett was personally vulnerable at Kenton and Gateshead. However, his lobbying skill could only take the Newcastle coal interest so far. There is no sign that his bill was successful and the war tax on coal was reintroduced in 1698.

Being mainly a local concern, neutralising the fitters offered a better prospect for success, but the institutional power of the hostmen was no trivial matter, nor was the close link between fitters and keelmen. As an unimpeachable insider and three times governor of the company, William Blackett, always a coalowner rather than the fitter of his own sales, was the obvious man to take them on. In 1697, according to Charles Montague, the formidable outsider, 'Sir W Blackett ... tolde me the merchants have A right to be free of the Hostmens Compagny at any time, & he would bring in all the merchants & confound all the fitters, by out-numbering them'.[47] Montague must have been surprised and delighted at such a blow inflicted on the hostmen from the inside. The company's minute book documents repeated attempts from 1697 to impound 'unfree coals' and warnings to members not to work with or for 'unfree tradeing fitters', showing increasing impotence rather than control. After an open breach of these rules by six company fitters in 1703 led to their suspension by the hostmen, the speed with which the Court of Queen's Bench came down in the errant fitters' favour speaks of a trap laid by well-resourced and influential sponsors like Montague and Blackett, a trap into which the hostmen's company duly fell.[48]

A charm offensive was also launched with the keelmen. They were typically employed by the fitters and were, of course, critically important in moving coal from staith to ship. When the keelmen set up a charitable mutual insurance fund in 1699 and petitioned the hostmen's company to assist with its oversight, Blackett was an early supporter and benefactor of the keelmen's hospital that was built within two years. It didn't take long for the keelmen to tire of the hostmen's direct involvement in the charity and it was 'their constant supporter and bountiful benefactor', William Blackett, whom they later claimed helped to dismiss the hostmen's stewards 'unjustly imposed upon them'. Blackett also promoted a Parliamentary bill to give their charity independent protection.[49]

Thus were the hostmen's fitters sidelined and the keelmen kept onside, enabling the coal owners to tackle the more formidable question of extracting better terms from the London dealers. The hostmen's monopoly had effectively been broken but this was not a victory for free competition. In 1701 a small but powerful group of owners around Montague, Blackett and Sir Henry Liddell of the old coal-owning family at Ravensworth in Whickham created a new cartel, the 'Coal Office'. Its six members contributed just under 1p/ton on their 1700 coal shipments and of the resulting £3,000 war-chest just under half was used to keep coal from the London market in order to drive up the price, through the good offices of a paid Thames lighterman and coal merchant.[50]

Given the traditional concerns in London at any hint of combination amongst the Tyneside coal-owners it is surprising that the new cartel apparently excited little attention in the capital. It probably helped that the London dealers had little incentive to raise the alarm lest they draw attention to their own restrictive control over the trade. Indeed, with the hostmen sidelined, the Coal Office members were able to seek an arrangement with the London dealers over the heads of the fitters and shipmasters. Newcastle's political operators were also at work in Westminster. Over the winter of 1699-1700 Blackett helped the Thames lightermen to secure their corporate charter.[51] Thereafter his political expertise was to be deployed closer to home, for he apparently declined to return to Westminster as a member in the new Parliament of January 1701. His place was taken by Liddell, equally able in matters of political judgement, persuasion and alliance building. Blackett helped manage the home front. He entertained the fitters with wine at the very public opening of the Coal Office in April. The hostmen might have been eclipsed as an effective institution, but the fitters were to be enticed by offers of employment by the coal-owners and on condition that they boycott the coal of non-cartel members.[52]

The various aspects of the scheme can thus be seen. Tyneside's major coal owners collaborated by agreeing production quotas, pressured the fitters into hindering the trade of non-members and presented themselves as the friends and supporters of the keelmen. In London they sought an accommodation with the dealers and lightermen and managed, for the time being, to keep Parliament quiet. This appears to have had the desired effect. Coastal coal shipments from Newcastle fell from around 570,000 tons in 1701 to just over 400,000 tons two years later. The London price was up to a third higher in 1702 and 1703 than in 1699 and 1700.[53]

Management

Like his father, William II was busy on a number of fronts throughout his adult life. Although there is scant evidence from the port books that he engaged in trade, he was variously an executor, alderman, mayor, governor of the hostmen, MP, cartel organiser, lead and coal miner and land owner, with many of these responsibilities overlapping in time. As the Stuart regime was replaced by William and Mary he emulated his father's earlier great bursts of business expansion. In four hectic years from December 1688 he bought Kenton and started mining and waggonway building there, acquired the Wallington estate and manor of Hexham, took on and developed the Heworth mining lease and became the moormaster of Weardale. His total capital outlay must have been in the region of £33-34,000, possibly excluding coal mine drainage works. There is no simple explanation for this manic change. It is tempting, given the timing, to see it as a vote of business confidence in the replacement of the capricious James II with greater Parliamentary influence over the reign of William and Mary, but the expensive Kenton commitment was made before this outcome was clear. Neither can it all have been a reaction to the birth of a son after two daughters, for William III wasn't born until January 1690. Perhaps it was simply that these opportunities presented themselves within a short space of time to an energetic man ready and willing to take them all on.

As a result of it all he must have employed well over 500 miners, smelters and carriers by horse and waggon in the 1690s from Weardale to Tyneside. He was now landlord for scores of additional farming and cottage tenants in Northumberland. The 'extraordinary occasions' for which he was granted leave as an MP to be absent from Westminster for six weeks from February 1697 while Parliament was sitting were probably related to the pressures of business at home.[54] He declined the King's request in 1699 that he become a Treasury commissioner because of the 'posture of [his] private affairs'. In 1702 he was away at the lead mines, continuing the inspections first undertaken for his father nearly 30 years earlier.[55] But whatever the level of his personal commitment, the sheer breadth and scale of his business and political life had to rely upon strong managers.

Unlike his father, Blackett did not recruit many merchant or hostman apprentices directly, but he did inherit them, along with other important agents and managers. Cuthbert Snow, though already a trustee of William I's will, was still an apprentice hostman until January 1682 when he was admitted to his freedom as William II's apprentice.[56] The staithman Michael Robinson continued in the Blackett service for both Edward and William II at Blaydon and Winlaton. Robinsons were still assisting with managing operations at Blaydon into the 1730s and they were not alone in providing business continuity through generations of family involvement. Brothers Richard and John Mowbray remained active in managing William II's lead business for the rest of their lives. Richard was succeeded as the chief agent at Allenheads by his nephew George in 1693 and George was still a Blackett agent in the 1720s.[57] Featherstones were at Dukesfield Mill for 30 years from the late 1680s. Joseph and then George Nixon paid the bills and accounted for coal at Heworth/Gateshead Fell. Robert Todd was engaged at Kenton from the 1690s until the late 1720s. The acquisition of the manor of Hexham in 1689 was swiftly followed by the re-appointment of the locally experienced and wily Thomas Allgood as its bailiff, commencing a long association with that family.[58]

Here, then, are some of the names of the men in place and providing continuity throughout William II's large and geographically widespread business interests in coal, lead and land. How much these family successions owed to nepotism or favours rather than merit is difficult to gauge, but far-flung operations put a premium on competence. William II surely had the same respect for management and technical skills irrespective of class shown by his father and elder brother.[59] He bore down on those who did not, dismissing Philip Leece, for 'the real diffirence he made betwixt amongst [his] work people'.[60] As far as the central co-ordination was concerned, William I managed a similar span of operations with the direct assistance of his sons. But Edward and William II had effectively gone their separate ways, Michael – whose heart seemed to have gone out of business anyway – died in 1683 and William II only started his own family in 1686. We have already seen that he was close to his brother-in-law Timothy Davison and his direct involvement in arranging uncle Matthew Kirkley's funeral in 1691 suggests a similarly close relationship.[61] The family's faithful clerk Robert Pease was certainly involved in some of his early business transactions. As time went by, however, more responsibility was taken by two key recruits – Thomas Brumell and, in particular, John Wilkinson.

In 1685 Brumell, a yeoman's son from Braithwaite in Cumberland, became a rare apprentice to Blackett in the hostmen's company. Although not admitted to his freedom until 1700 he was by then in a position of some authority on Blackett's behalf. He was overseeing the lead carriage by 1698.[62] Brumell was in London immediately after Blackett's death in December 1705, where he took charge of arranging for his body to be carried back to Newcastle in a stately winter procession from London and setting out the full funeral protocol to be followed thereafter. His correspondent back in Newcastle that December was Blackett's other leading agent, John Wilkinson.[63]

Wilkinson's connection with the Blacketts went back to at least 1676, when he was taken on as a merchant apprentice by Michael. He was possibly the boy of that name baptised in Gateshead in 1662, son of George, who described himself as a gentleman and whose home was at Byers Green near Bishop Auckland at the time of John's apprenticeship. Within months John was signing letters on Michael's behalf and engaging in exchanges with correspondents on matters that required the exercise of some business judgment rather than just administrative acknowledgement.[64] While still Michael's apprentice in 1682, he joined the extended Blackett family when he married Dorothy Simpson, the daughter of a Kirkley cousin (see Figure 4.1). This was of course wholly against merchants' company rules but we still find Wilkinson being admitted to his freedom in 1686 'out of respect to the memory of his [unnamed] grandfather', evidently once also a merchant. It was a tenuous thread of respectability for a decision that had far more to do with William II needing 'cousin' Wilkinson as a fully qualified merchant member of his central staff after Michael's death. Another cousin, Timothy Davison, was able to help see it through as governor of the company. It is equally unsurprising that Wilkinson was admitted as a hostman during Blackett's time as governor in 1691.[65]

Kirkley, Simpson, Rumney, Davison and Blackett names all

turn up amongst the godparents at baptisms of Wilkinson children in the 1680s and 1690s and John and Dorothy were honoured in return in being asked to stand for two of Blackett's daughters. Wilkinson was a member of Newcastle's common council by 1699 and in all probability had been so since Blackett's mayoralty of the previous year.[66] The rising business manager was inside the clan. Brumell might have written to Wilkinson from London in December 1705 in a tone that suggested they were equals, but Wilkinson had good reason to see it differently. Brumell was not even mentioned in Blackett's will. Wilkinson was appointed one of his executors. Already a man of high authority within the business, Wilkinson was to go on to play a crucial role in the years that followed. It would not be easy. William II had built his father's business back up to a large scale in the 1690s, but as we move on to assess his final years and his legacy some of the problems which followed from this become clear.

Chapter 15

Popular in his Country

Last Years

Blackett's civic prominence, broad country acres, trappings of industrial power and the influence he had demonstrated on the national stage underwrote his position at the apex of Newcastle's society. Greyfriars gave tangible form to Blackett's elegant civic supremacy, the grand mansion and its extensive formal grounds and fields dominating its surroundings. But the engraving showing Blackett's coach and horses parading down Pilgrim Street in the foreground was published posthumously in 1707.[1] Those first years of the new century were the last of his life.

He was just 48 when he died in December 1705. It appears to have been quite sudden. The sealing of his will in May 1704 is more the mark of prudence by a man of means with a large and still growing family than of the expectation of imminent death, not least with its reference to 'all and every my other son and sons' at a time when he had just one. Blackett was certainly still active in civic affairs, with a leading role in the local militia. In December 1703 he had been included alongside the 'Commanders-in-Chief' of Carlisle and Berwick in letters from the Earl of Nottingham, Secretary of State, in the midst of another swirl of concern over a possible 'Jacobite' rising in the Scottish highlands in support of the exiled King James II. Blackett immediately had guards placed on Newcastle's gates and those he felt were acting suspiciously were pursued zealously in the following weeks.[2] Eighteen months later, scarcely six months before his death, he 'did in an ingenious and significant speech declare ... his intention to represent [Newcastle] himself this ensueing sessions' in Parliament, an intention readily accepted by the civic elite. It was hardly the act of a dying man.[3] He was well enough to travel to London in November 1705, but appears to have been taken ill afterwards for his fellow Newcastle MP William Carr later referred to Blackett's 'continued weakness before his death.' Even then, however, Carr added that the ailing man 'had hopes of his being better'.[4] His death on 2nd December seems therefore to have taken many by surprise, prompting Brumell's hasty journey south to make the arrangements for the ostentatious and elaborate return journey and funeral described in chapter one.

Judging by the course of his career, William II certainly shared his father's energy, ambition and willingness to take decisive and bold action in business and public life. He was a leader of Newcastle's thriving mercantile community, an able and pragmatic politician trusted by the corporation's shrewd heads to promote the town's interests on the national stage. Beyond this, however, we face the same difficulties in assessing William II's character as with his father. It is hard to read much more from the Wallington portrait than a dark-eyed faint superiority (Plate 25).[5] There is little direct evidence to set alongside the conventionally polite words that followed his death. Even those few words date from decades later. He was said then to have been 'very popular in his country, of remarkable probity, and a good speaker in the House of Commons'.[6] As an active champion of Newcastle's rights, his popularity amongst the freemen, at least, seems in little doubt and was rewarded with success in the contested 1685 Parliamentary election. He was the man picked out by his fellow cartel members in 1701 to bring the fitters and keelmen onside with treats and glad-handing. Blackett's charm and popularity were evidently more important on the Tyneside front than in Westminster that year, when Liddell replaced him as one of the town's MPs. The powers of oratory claimed for him in the Commons were endorsed by Secretary of State James Vernon in 1699 and easy to imagine given his evident persuasiveness in building political alliances. Letters from London in 1699 offering him a seat on the Treasury Board might well be grounded in calculated flattery but whether the offer was made in a genuine quest to recruit his political talent and presumed financial flair or to dampen his independence in support of his city, it underwrites a respect at the heart of government for his ability. There was talk of him being made a peer.[7]

Claims of his 'remarkable probity' sound like standard obituary-fare and it is not a phrase universally associated with those accomplished in the political arts. However, a few examples survive of behaviour which hint at a steady moral compass. Although he was no puritan zealot this was possibly grounded in a strong sense of religion. He employed a chaplain, Augustine Lumley, whose modest funeral arrangements he took care of in 1696.[8] Funds were bequeathed for the vicar of Newcastle's St. Andrew's church to appoint 'some fit person' to teach 30 poor children of the parish in the church, with the intention that they be able to read English and repeat the Church catechism from memory. We might presume that he expected the same of his own children. His charitable bequests, the proceeds of £1,000, were more generous than his father's. Alongside the educational provision there was money for apprenticeships, preference to be given to the children educated in St. Andrew's and annual payments to the poor of the parish. One of his first decisions as governor of the hostmen in 1690 was to stop the expenditure of vast sums of money on its festivals and treats.[9]

His role as his father-in-law's executor is illuminating. For whatever reason, Sir Christopher Conyers and his only son and heir, John, were estranged long before William II married Julia, John's step-sister. Sir Christopher's details on the family memorial in Easington church were left incomplete, as if his son could not be bothered, and Christopher was the last of his family to be buried there. According to his will, should any of John's children die before reaching the age of 21, it was left to Blackett as executor to dispose of his bequests to them, rather than their father. Blackett was also left the residue of Conyers' personal estate and, pointedly, anyone opposing Blackett in his execution of the will would lose all benefit from it. It would have been simple for Blackett to exploit this long-standing family rift for personal gain, but by his own will of 1704 he left Conyers' estate to John for him to pass on to his own children at he saw fit. This was no mere token gesture for it amounted to more than £1,700.[10]

Blackett came to support the 'Glorious Revolution', but this did not prevent him asking a Newcastle physician, Henry Atherton, to be godparent to his daughter Mary in 1697, despite Atherton having never acknowledged William of Orange's succession to the throne and thenceforth under a cloud within the town.[11] Perhaps we should allow that Blackett's decision to vote with the minority in the Commons in 1689 that the throne was not vacant was simply a matter of conscience and not go searching for an ulterior motive. Similarly, although some accounts assumed that he voted in 1696 in support of the attainder and execution of Sir John Fenwick for treason, a more recent closer examination suggests that he abstained.¹² Given that the removal of one of his Wallington annuitants would have brought closer the day when he would save himself £2,000 per year it would perhaps not have been seemly for Blackett to be seen taking a direct part in the proceedings.

None of this means he was a saintly figure detached from the hard-edged reality of gladiatorial business and political scheming. His abstention in the Fenwick vote might have been taken fully expecting the Commons to support execution anyway. We saw earlier that he exploited Fenwick's earlier imprisonment in 1689 to agree the purchase of Wallington and the manor of Hexham and he engineered the devious precedent for peat-fuelled lead smelting in Allendale, possibly with menaces. He was sharp in the defence of his rights, such as the collection of chopwood in Muggleswick Park.¹³ Nevertheless, the courage and confidence in his various political and business battles might yet have translated into a degree of rectitude in many of his personal affairs when, given his wealth and power, it could as easily have made him a gratuitous bully on all fronts.

The Business

What can we say of the family business a quarter of a century after its founder had died? William I's turnover in the mid-1670s had been around £25,000, providing work for some 750 people. Most of this he left to William II's management, with the important exception of the lucrative Fallowfield lead mines. Estimates for 1705 are harder to come by, but revenue from lead (perhaps £13-14,000) and coal (£8-9,000) probably meant William II's business turnover was also above £20,000. Even allowing for the removal of Fallowfield and half of Winlaton, it probably represents only modest growth during his 25 years in charge. Nevertheless the replacement of Fallowfield and Greengill lead mines with Weardale and the move to peat-fuelled smelting in mills nearer the mines were important structural changes. William II's coal interests at his death were also quite different from those of his father. Whorlton Moor mine had been exploited heavily in its last years, and later replaced with the bold initiatives at Kenton and Heworth/Gateshead. It was important to move on from older reserves as they were worked out if a long-term mining business was to be sustained at scale.

The continued pursuit of economies of scale arguably remained a Blackett objective. It was implicit in the Kenton and Heworth/ Gateshead coal developments with their expensive waggonways and agreed minimum volumes for royalty payments. At Allenheads that expensive infrastructure went underground, in the form of the Haugh Level, and the mining rights were bought out completely. The Weardale moormastership also only made sense if great tonnages of lead were mined. This approach paid off for William I, especially in the lead industry, but the outcome was different for his son.

Lead mining remained a large and growing industry but much more sedately so in Newcastle's hinterland than in the heady 1660s and 1670s. The fastest increases in lead traffic were through Stockton, drawing upon mines and mills in Teesdale and Swaledale. Stockton's contribution to regional shipments rose from around a third in the mid-1670s to half two decades later. In this context, it was impressive for William II to have probably matched or surpassed his father's level of lead production by the early 1700s. Yet he almost certainly could not have emulated its profitability. We have no idea of costs in Allendale, although with the completion of the Haugh Level, an expensive capital investment, direct operating costs could well have fallen by reducing drainage expense. The Weardale mines appear to have been worked reasonably cheaply, but were burdened with the purchase and renewal of the moormastership, mills and Newhouse (albeit this last on a grander scale than was strictly necessary) and the fixed rent paid to the Bishop and the Rector of Stanhope. Spreading this load by raising production would have been a slow affair given the unavoidable continuation of mining through issuing leases and demand was often constrained during the war with France until 1697. Substituting peat for wood fuel reduced unit costs, but only at the margin. And this all took place at a time when lead sold for a fifth or a quarter less than in the heady 1670s. The market was larger for a cheaper but still vital commodity and money could still be made. However, it is likely that the return on Blackett's capital in lead was on a par with that available elsewhere instead of vastly superior. This was certainly the case for Edward at Fallowfield in the early 1690s. The plural in Stringer's 'thousands a year' earned by Sir William from lead might have been accurate, but only just.

Returns from lead might have been unremarkable but were almost certainly better than from coal. In fact Blackett was struggling by the turn of the century. Kenton production was not spectacular and as the easiest coal was worked out adjacent to the Town Moor, deeper shafts would have been needed to the north beyond the 'Ninety Fathom Dyke', where the seams were thrown downwards. It is unlikely more than 30,000 tons were won at Kenton in any one year, which must have meant that the full capacity and scale economies of his waggonway were not exploited.[14] The surviving accounts for the adjacent Heworth and Gateshead leases show initially rapid progress and 30,000 tons were led to the staiths in 1693. But even with the addition of the Gateshead Fell lease that year and the opening of a waggonway at the end of it, coal output slumped thereafter. Blackett had agreed to a rent for Gateshead Fell based upon a minimum of 10-11,000 tons of coal per year, but this was not reached until 1698 and barely surpassed thereafter.[15] He suffered from that perennial mining hazard of inadequate drainage, to tackle which it was said he spent £11-12,000 'In endeavouring to win these collyreyes but found it inpracticable.' His remedy was to take the freehold of land lower down the slope and drive an expensive level to intercept the mining shafts.[16] Even if the sums claimed here were exaggerated, it is clear that Blackett had sunk much into drainage and waggonway infrastructure and did not achieve a level of output in the 1690s and 1700s sufficient to recoup the capital outlay. The selling price of his coal is unknown, but even at 18p/ton in 1700, which feels optimistic, he probably barely broke even. He would probably have needed to double his output from Kenton and Heworth/Gateshead to make a decent use of the capacity of his rails, engines and levels.[17]

These scale economies were apparently beyond Blackett in his final years, in stark contrast to the achievements of the new man Charles Montague. Between 1697 and 1703 the opening of his Gibside waggonway enabled a three-fold increase in coal output to about 60,000 tons. Montague's contribution to the Coal Office income in 1701 was based on an astonishing 140,000 tons of coal from Gibside and Benwell. If the increase in profits claimed by Montague from 2p/ton in 1697 to 11p in 1703 can be believed, it probably owed far more to the achievement of huge economies of scale between those years and perhaps to the acknowledged high quality of his Gibside coal than it did to any underlying increase in the price of average coals because of the Coal Office cartel.[18] In fact there is little sign that the energies invested by Blackett in the Coal Office had much effect in the end.

Even if the Coal Office could control the whole Tyneside trade, despite being directly responsible for just two-thirds of output, a big if, Sunderland accounted for up to a quarter of north-eastern coal in the 1690s and it was beyond the reach of Newcastle's monopolists. The absence of complaints from London might speak more of the ineffectiveness of the cartel than of any success by Blackett and Liddell in smoothing away dissent. What became of the Coal Office is unclear. The cartel that finally did come under Parliamentary scrutiny in 1710-11 dated back no further than 1708, but it included many of the Coal Office participants. Ellis concluded that there was generally always too much coal available from Tyneside in the early 18th century for the short-lived cartels to be successful.[19] The desire to realise economies of scale from spreading high output across large fixed capital investments in mines, drainage and waggonways was forever in tension with the need for restraint and co-operation with rival owners implied by membership of a cartel. For all the frequent attempts at 'regulation' it remained at root a highly competitive 'fighting trade'.

Table 15.1 Estimated Blackett coal production 1680-1700.

	1680	1684-5	1690	1700
Production (tons)	69,000	65,000	24,400	50,500
Revenue	£11,600	£11,600	£3,700	£8,600
Profit	£1,800	£2,400	£650	£250
Profit (%)	16%	21%	18%	3%
Tyneside sales total	580,000	620,000	400,000	540,000
Blackett % of total	11.9%	10.5%	6.1%	9.4%

Source: see Appendix 2, Tables A2.2, A2.6.

William Blackett II's prowess and wealth as one of Tyneside's coal magnates has hitherto scarcely been questioned and probably dates back to contemporary impressions that it was not in his interest to dispel. The reality seems to have been quite different. As summarised in Table 15.1 he had clawed his way back up to a position amongst the larger producers at the turn of the century with the addition of Kenton and Heworth/Gateshead Fell but it is hard to see that this constituted a profitable allocation of his capital. In devoting much of his energy and political talent to constructing and managing a cartel (and a short-lived one at that), we are left wondering whether this had more to do with trying to constrain Montague's advance than with shoring up the price of coal, and with preserving his reputation, expensively, as one of Tyneside's leading 'coal professeurs'. It is hardly surprising to find that in the end he let his interest in the Stella Grand Lease to Montague, and that Montague was also renting Blackett's share of the Winlaton colliery.[20] In the family's oldest colliery the ambitious miner had retreated to taking rents as a landlord.

Montague and Liddell built longer waggonways in order to exploit high quality reserves ever further from the river and before long would also be sinking risk capital into steam engines to drain workings at greater depth. The sums needed to search out new and distant seams of coal and to ride out losses along the way went beyond Blackett's resources, divided as he was between mining both coal and lead and siphoning off funds into land. If there wasn't enough money to compete with Montague because of his lead business, neither was there enough to exploit Weardale's potential fully because of his collieries. In contrast to the large, concentrated and directly managed Allenheads works, the capital and management bandwidth was probably not available to develop many Weardale mines directly. Leases continued to be granted to independent and sometimes quite small mining partnerships up and down that long County Durham valley. This was no basis for extracting scale economies.

From today's dispassionate analytical standpoint it is easy to conclude that the logical approach for Blackett would have been to focus on one type of mining, probably lead. It may have been less obvious at the time, and would have meant giving up the security of a diversified portfolio. Furthermore, he had committed to both Kenton and Heworth before the Weardale moormastership was taken. So he kept feet in both camps. Weardale lead was not fully exploited, but there are at least signs that Blackett achieved some cost reductions from smelting innovations and changes in mill location. In coal, however, some of his energy and political ability was consumed by ultimately fruitless cartel-building in an attempt to shore up his medium-sized collieries and rein in Montague's expansion. So while his overall business turnover in 1705 might have borne some resemblance to that of his father's in 1680, we can be confident that profitability did not. Compared to the annual profits of approximately £5,000 being generated in the late 1670s it would be surprising if William II was earning more than £1,500 from coal and lead annually in the early 1700s.

Then there was his property portfolio. Over the quarter century following William I's death, known spending on Kenton, Welton, Wallington, Hexham manor and Fallowlees added up to nearly £19,000.[21] William I had, of course also invested heavily in property in the 1660s and 1670s so this did not signal a new direction. Moreover, just as links can be seen between much of William I's investment in land and secured loans and his core mining interests, similar considerations apply in William II's case. East Kenton's purchase was obviously tied to his desire to develop its coal reserves and, since the rental income covered the funding of the land purchase, he arguably obtained the mineral rights for free. Similar logic probably held for his father's Winlaton purchase 20 years earlier. The manor of Hexham was likewise clearly important for Allendale's mining rights, but the Wallington part of the same transaction does not fit this pattern. Neither did Welton, agricultural land 14 miles west of Newcastle without any obvious mineral wealth that was taken in 1694 by foreclosing on a loan advanced to Nathaniel Johnson and others in the 1680s.[22]

The sharp-eyed William II might yet, however, have seen them as decent business propositions in their own right because of the potential to push up rental income. The Wallington estate apparently grossed £950 in 1689, but this had risen to £1,100 by 1705. Hexham was probably worth nearly £1,000 per year in 1711, a striking difference to the approximate annual income of under £700 in the early 1680s.[23] It is worth noting that at these levels the combined income from both estates now covered the annual

£2,000 annuity payment to the Fenwicks. The purchase price of Kenton in 1689, £6,000, implies either a gross rental value of around £350/year or that Blackett obtained the estate very cheaply. By 1711 it was worth £530/year, a 50% increase on its imputed purchase value in two decades.[24] With Kenton located so close to the large urban market of Newcastle, local agent Robert Todd would have been remiss indeed not to have 'improved' the rents paid by tenants able to send liquid milk, butter and cheese across the Town Moor.

Nevertheless it is hard to rationalise all of William II's land purchases in the same way. In 1702, when his Heworth and Gateshead Fell mines were evidently still in trouble, he spent £2,000 buying the remote and rough pastureland of Fallowlees, seven miles further from Newcastle than even Wallington, in the hope that it might have lead veins. At the very least this seems unfocused and risky, especially since, far from having his own surplus cash to invest, he borrowed the purchase money from two of his Davison cousins.[25] Indeed, Blackett's total property outlays might easily have consumed all the surplus profits over the 25 years between his father's death and his own. Six months after William II's death his estate owed £4,500 to Newcastle lawyer John Ord in respect of earlier loans. A mortgage had been raised in 1689 to cover the £6,000 Kenton purchase and it appears that £1,000 was still owed on this in 1711.[26]

Blackett's capital outgoings outstripped his surplus income and the shortfall had evidently been borrowed. In the long term the value of the landed assets handsomely justified their acquisition. At conventional valuations, his landed estate was probably worth around £78-79,000, already capturing the benefit of increased rents and higher valuation multiples. Conversely, the depressed state of both the coal and lead businesses in 1705 means they would hardly have realised more than £17,000 if sold as going concerns. From this combined gross value of £95-96,000, £15,350 must be deducted for known debts and a further £19,500 as the approximate present value of outstanding liabilities to William II's step-mother Lady Margaret and to Lady Fenwick in respect of the Wallington/Hexham estate. William II's net estate can therefore be estimated at around £61,000 at the time of his death. As with his father's estate, no allowance is included here for personal effects. His net worth amounted to somewhere between double and triple his 1680 inheritance.[27] Although nowhere near as spectacular as his father's ascent to wealth, it remains impressive given the depressed state of lead and coal markets by 1705 and justifies the faith his father placed in his youngest son's ability. William II ended up somewhere near the borderline between the 'very rich' and 'unimaginably rich' of Grassby's categories of metropolitan wealth. The overall profitability of his business might have been unspectacular compared to his father's heyday, but it could still support a high standard of living, enough to keep Blackett comfortably within Newcastle's mercantile elite.

Legacy

The trouble is that his generous bequests exposed the limitations of his balance sheet. William II always seemed to enjoy a higher life than his generally prudent father. The Blacketts lived well and died just as lavishly. Funerals were essential public barometers of status. For £100 a respectable merchant could make 'a good exit'; Blackett spent this much on each of his three infant children's funerals alone in the 1690s, with dozens of black-clad mourners following the tiny coffins to St. Andrew's church.[28] Greyfriars' magnificence has already been described. Blackett also redeveloped Wallington Hall after he bought out the Fenwicks in 1689, although not as quickly as later claimed by Sir Charles Trevelyan, for until at least 1692 a redoubtable elderly Fenwick aunt refused to move out of the ancestral tower and stone house.[29] In August 1692 Blackett took a lease to mine coal at Ingoe, eight miles away. The only conceivable reason for this, given its distance from any navigable water, was to carry coal for domestic use at Wallington, a visibly extravagant and novel alternative to wood from the estate.[30] The simple, well-proportioned four-square building we see at Wallington today is substantively the structure built by Blackett, although its interior and façade details were apparently much simpler until the mid-18th century. It was a modest retreat compared to Greyfriars' urban magnificence, but still an indulgence that hints at the desire for the status conferred by a country house amidst broad acres that appeared never to have been a priority for his father. The houses, the ornamentation, the coach and horses, chaplains and jewels all added up to a pretty penny of annual expenditure.

As far as his will is concerned, the bequest of £1,000 to the poor of St. Andrew's parish was noted earlier but the provisions for his family were far more generous. His 'dearly beloved wife' Lady Julia was to receive a £2,000 lump sum within two years, £800 per year, his coach and horses, jewellery and the use of Greyfriars for life. It is tempting to see in the double columns either side of the central front door of Greyfriars a deliberate echo of the same arrangement at her childhood home of Horden Hall in County Durham.[31] Each of his daughters was to have a £6,000 dowry on marriage, and £200 a year until then. At the time of his will there were five of them, aged between 18 years to ten months, and they were joined by the infant Ann, born in May 1705. Further small legacies to family members, including £100 to each of his three surviving siblings, took his commitments to not far short of £40,000, albeit some of them long-term, plus a more immediate £2,000 per year under his widow's control, and an expectation that the residue would support his son and heir, William III, not yet 16 years old. His executors, John Wilkinson and nephew William Davison, were to have all their expenses covered – lawsuits were explicitly mentioned - but the mere £10 left to each of them for their pains suggests that Blackett, elsewhere very generous, did not expect their task to be difficult.[32] In reality it dogged his successors for decades.

It is easy to see why. Blackett's net assets (most of which were highly illiquid) probably did not outstrip the liabilities he left by his will (some of which were pressing) far enough to give his executors much room for manoeuvre, especially regarding the need to find £2,000 a year in fresh annuities to his widow and daughters, continue the £2,450/year to Lady Fenwick and his stepmother Margaret and still leave something for William III. Indeed, over £1,000 was incurred in the immediate aftermath of Blackett's death and lavish funeral and an absence of cash to pay for it had been foreseen by Brumell *en route* from London with Sir William's body: 'it wd do well if you knew where the money can be had after the business be over'.[33] The question is therefore whether Blackett was carelessly over-generous with his bequests considering the true state of his business and particularly its thin cashflow, or whether at the time of his will in May 1704 he might reasonably have expected to have plenty of time to ride out slow short-term markets, relying upon his entrepreneurial talents to bring home better returns.

Perhaps he was indeed cut short in his prime. But his had always been a swashbuckling style prone to bursts of bold commitments, not all of which paid off. He might have fallen prey to a certain hype arising from his lofty public status and the high praise that followed it around. Underneath it all lay a more dubious material reality. The bright golden colours in which the spectacular wealth and talents of the second William Blackett have typically hitherto been painted need a more sombre varnish. It is important to bear this in mind when judging responsibility for what happened in the fraught years that followed.

Chapter 16

Hobbled from Above

William III was just 15 years old when his father died suddenly in December 1705. He inherited the baronetcy but as a minor he was legally unable to run the business. It appears to have been out of the question that his mother would take the reins. Lady Blackett, the daughter of a Durham gentleman, came from a very different background to the likes of William I's mother-in-law and two wives, with their mercantile background. Instead it was John Wilkinson who took charge that Christmas. The transition was an important milestone in the history of the business: a change from direct personal control by the owner to professional management. It was possible because of the mature structure and system of reporting between stewards in the field and a Newcastle head office required by the long-standing scale and wide geographic spread of mines, industrial sites and estates.

The progression from personal to corporate management has been seen as a general feature in the development of large and enduring firms, albeit normally dated to a much later period.[1] Even though the Blackett business appears to offer an example of this development, the timing driven by the happenstance of mortality, there was nothing inevitable about it proceeding to an ever more orderly future, as we shall see. The business might have been managed at one remove from ownership, but the personalities and actions of those owners continued to matter greatly and the division of responsibilities was frequently undermined by William III. Before investigating the fortunes of the business under Wilkinson's management we need, therefore, to consider young William.

William Blackett III

The third Sir William Blackett has had a bad press. To a later owner of Wallington, Sir Charles Trevelyan, he was a 'nonentity ... to whom the estate, the house, and most certainly the world at large owed little or nothing.' Welford was slightly more circumspect, saying he 'possessed neither the ability nor the aptitude for business.' Apocryphal tales are told and re-told of rollicking parties at Wallington where six servants were employed to carry drunken guests up to their beds.[2] In 1727 a 'Native American', Galba, was bound to Sir William for life. William II had taken a domestic chaplain as a household adornment; his son, a slave.[3] He has been portrayed as a typical third generation wastrel, spending his way through a fortune amassed by his capable father and grandfather and leaving huge debts to his successor. As we have already seen, however, his father's will and early death accounted for at least some of those liabilities and it is important to explore this caricature of William III through the known facts of his life.

He was presumably raised in some style at Greyfriars in the 1690s. His education took a very different course to that of his father and grandfather. While the first William had been a merchant apprentice and the second schooled in the practicalities of the family business, the third went to Oxford. This was preceded by time spent at a 'high class' school in Isleworth, west of London, which focused on teaching classics to 'noblemen's sons or gentlemen of some rank'.[4] When he proceeded to University College at the tender age of 15 in 1705 he was doubtless seen as a good catch by the College given the reputation of his father's wealth.[5] It apparently suited William II to have his son away, and Lady Julia might have thought it a more fitting place for a baronet's son than a clerk's desk. Yet within months and just two weeks after the funeral of William II he was called back home by his father's executors.[6] They were acutely aware that under William II's will if no sons lived to maturity the estate would pass to Sir Edward's eldest living son and, more importantly, an additional £15,000 would need to be found for William II's daughters. At a time when Wilkinson was already scrabbling around to fund existing provisions and the lavish funeral, he could not afford the chance that young Sir William ended up in some terminal youthful scrape in Oxford. To continue his classical education William III was accompanied back to Newcastle by a tutor who remained for at least 18 months.[7]

Was William III packed off south by his parents at a tender age, possibly as a signal of their social status, only to be peremptorily hauled back when it was more of a liability to have him out of sight? Perhaps he was indulged at home but unguided, both privileged and neglected. Sir Edward Blackett had a low opinion of William's mother. Astonished at the news in 1710 that she was intending to marry 'one Thompson, who pretended to court her' he could not believe (wrongly, as it turned out) that 'even my Lady Blackett would encourage such a business', for Thompson, a jobbing London lawyer about ten years younger than the rich widow, had a very small estate. Lady Julia's only son was contemptuous, telling his uncle he was not surprised to hear of the marriage 'alwayes believeing She would dispose of herself but indifferently'.[8] Indulging her son, Julia permitted him, at the age of 19 in 1709, to take a house in one of London's newer developments between Covent Garden and Soho, Panton Square, an area later said to have had a bad reputation for gaming-houses since it was first built. He was already by then developing an expensive interest in horse racing, having just bought a thoroughbred in Yorkshire.[9]

In that same summer of 1709 rumours also started to reach Sir Edward, William's uncle and godfather, of a dangerous liaison. He quizzed his daughter Maria in June about reports that his nephew was married and by October he had a name for his 'wife' in London: Elizabeth Ord.[10] A few years older than William, Elizabeth had, according to William's lawyer at a later date, designed since 1706 (when he was 16 and she 20) to worm her way into his affections and was subsequently 'very expensive', racking up great debts and finally prevailing with him to give her an annuity.[11] They might indeed have been acquainted for several years, though not in London. The Ords' modest estate was just a few miles away from the north Northumberland home of William III's Oxford tutor, Robert Clavering, and 1706 was when Clavering moved north with his young charge. William repeatedly reassured his uncle that he was not married to her and never would be. This was probably what he thought the anxious Sir Edward needed to hear, given the implications for the future of the Blackett family business and estate of an unplanned and unsettled formal alliance with an obscure woman of 'small estate'.

Here then was an entitled teenager set free by an irresponsibly indulgent mother with a handsome allowance to enjoy the dissolute pleasures afforded by the capital and therefore also prey to those interested in befriending his renowned wealth. One of William's first actions on attaining his legal majority in early 1711, apart from treating himself to a fine coach, was to settle a £300 life annuity on Elizabeth Ord. She gave birth to a girl nine months later.[12]

It all looked very messy. Blackett was quite possibly advised to pay up and walk discreetly away, yet what followed was a touching and poignant saga in which he appears in a quite different light. Elizabeth bore him two children in the Panton Square house in London, a daughter Elizabeth in December 1711 and son William in January 1713. However, mother Elizabeth died just a month after baby William's birth aged just 27, possibly from post-natal complications.[13] There followed an unedifying struggle through the courts over the next 12 years between Elizabeth's family and William Blackett regarding custody of the children, and their inheritance, in which the children were caught in the middle. Blackett always stuck by his illegitimate offspring, wanted them in his care and was willing to devote whatever resources were necessary to obtain judgements in his favour. It is impossible to say whether the young fun-loving man about town was the best guardian for his children, and it is noticeable that their mother entrusted their care to her aunt Elizabeth and failed even to mention William III in her will. Yet when Elizabeth the daughter was asked her own opinion at the age of 14 she said she wanted to be with her father rather than her aunt. She could not even have remembered her own mother, had endured the trauma of her young brother William dying when she was just seven and had been sent to this school and that around London. Perhaps her father, for all his faults, was there to offer a single thread of continuity through an otherwise bleak childhood.[14]

There was, therefore, more to Blackett than the sometimes simplistic, if entertaining, portrayal of him as an irresponsible and spendthrift wastrel. Of course, those less salutary aspects of his character remain undeniable, but you have to wonder how much attention and wise direction he received in his formative years, especially in view of the inheritance and expectations heading his way. Perhaps he was naïve in the face of flattery, and ill-equipped to deal with those who wanted his support, his patronage, his money. All this, and the Blackett name, certainly made him useful to others. How else to explain his puzzling selection as candidate for Newcastle in the 1710 Parliamentary election when he was not yet 21 and therefore initially unable to take his seat?

The political climate was highly charged. Whig rule was crumbling nationally in the wake of popular discontent following the trial in February of a High Church Tory, Henry Sacheverell. Newcastle, long under Whig control, was not immune.[15] The coal trade was disrupted in the summer by the ship masters and then a keelmen's strike. It attracted attention in Westminster at exactly the wrong time for the small group of coal owners whose latest cartel was seeking to restrain output and drive up prices.[16] It is therefore mystifying that the young and inexperienced William III should have the support of Newcastle's aldermen but as early as September 1709 Uncle Edward had told him that all the Newcastle aldermen and magistrates were firmly in favour of his candidacy and that he would win, for the whole town was unanimous.[17]

A plausible explanation for these manoeuvres involves the outgoing Whig MPs, William Carr and Sir Henry Liddell. Unable to agree who would take precedence between them in the stage management of the 1708 election, Liddell had threatened to bring in a third candidate. His bluff was called, so there was a rare contest, in which Liddell was chastened to come in second rather than first. He decided not to stand again in 1710, but Carr remained keen.[18] Liddell was as central to the new coal cartel of 1708-9 as he had been in the 1701 Coal Office described earlier. So too were the Carrs to start with, but not by 1710.[19] Consequently there was a risk that far from helping, as an insider, to deflect scrutiny of the cartel in the new Parliament, Carr was likely, as an outsider, to give noisy support to the opposition. He had to be stopped. To prevent him becoming an MP in 1710 he would have to be defeated in a contest. If these conjectures are right it is easy to see how young William Blackett would have appeared a suitable 'stop Carr' candidate. His name had enormous brand value, whatever his youth. While entirely lacking in political experience and quite possibly also talent, his stake in the cartel – through his father's executor John Wilkinson – meant that he would at the very least not rock the boat. It is likely that the other candidate in Newcastle, William Wrightson, was seen as equally biddable, as a relative newcomer to the town who had married a merchant's widow.

Both men have been classed as Tories and so too Newcastle's body of aldermen and the freemen electors. Perhaps so, but, as ever, labelling Newcastle's leaders as anything other than 'the Newcastle party' is difficult and arguably of limited relevance. They might simply have been 'Tories' in the autumn of 1710 because that was how to win the election that year in the wake of the Sacheverall affair. Blackett easily topped the poll with 1,177 votes, Wrightson second with 886 and Carr a distant third with 609.[20]

Apart from the candidacies and the result, all the above remains speculative and is possibly too cynical an interpretation of the course of events. However, given Blackett's youth it does seem highly likely that he was championed as a useful pawn. The coal owners of the cartel surely preferred him to Carr as an MP. It may well have suited John Wilkinson to have his master away in London so that he could get on with running the business. The immunity of MPs' families, servants and stewards from being arrested for debt was doubtless also attractive.[21] As for William, it gave him another reason to be in London with Elizabeth Ord and to enjoy the other pleasures of the capital. He was to remain an MP for Newcastle for the rest of his life.

He might also have been used during the Jacobite rising five years later. The sympathy he was claimed to show for the Jacobite cause was a deadly serious matter in 1715. There had been many rumoured plots to restore James II during the reigns of William and Mary after 1689, often involving disaffected Scottish noblemen and support from the traditional French Catholic enemy state. After the accession in 1702 of the Stuart Queen Anne, James II's daughter, the plotting receded but she too produced no heirs and was succeeded by the German George I of Hanover in 1714. His protestant faith and acceptance of the principles of 1689's 'Glorious Revolution' with a central role for Parliament appeared to secure the supremacy of the Whigs, but the ending of hopes for a Stuart succession led to a serious attempt to restore James II by force a year later. 70 years after the Civil War, hostile troops were marching on English soil again. As so often in the past, Newcastle's strategic location and vital role in supplying coal to London meant it was important to both rebels and the government. A Scottish Jacobite army was expected to join up with troops raised principally by Northumberland's Catholic gentry and supported by a French expeditionary force.[22] William Blackett III's rumoured involvement in this national drama had an important bearing on perceptions of him in Newcastle and the region.

Robert Patten's account, written shortly afterwards, is the principal source of the notion that Blackett was amongst the conspirators. Patten was the Anglican curate of Allendale and joined the rebels but later saved his neck by agreeing to testify for the Crown. He was not averse to spreading gossip. However, even Patten was cautious with his allegations, often given as the views of others. 'It was reported among them that Sir William Blackett would join them. If all that was said of this Gentleman's Conduct was true, they were not wrong to have some Dependance upon his Assistance.'[23] Whether or not based on more than hearsay Blackett was apparently included in an arrest warrant in September 1715 and subsequently went to ground rather than join up with the rebels, now flushed out into the open. They gathered in Northumberland, just a few miles from Wallington, and raised the Pretender's standard early in October under the leadership of 'General' Thomas Forster. Blackett's movements between early September and October 19th are unknown, but that night he turned up at the Yorkshire home of his brother-in-law, Walter Calverley (husband of sister Julia), claiming he had just fled on horseback from Wallington to avoid Forster. He added that 'he was no ways concerned, nor under any obligation to them'. Calverley told him to go to London and explain himself to the King.[24] Blackett only surfaced again in public in the following January, having sufficiently convinced the government and royal Court of his innocence and loyalty.*

What are we to make of all this? Henry Liddell probably judged it right in early October 1715 in concluding that, although told Blackett was amongst the rebels 'I can't imagin a man off his noble fortune would run a risque more than probably of losing all'.[25] Blackett's desperate flight south ten days later appears to bear this out but, howsoever deluded the rebels had been in general, he might well have earlier given them reason to believe he was with them, miners, keelmen and all. It is all too easy to imagine the young MP joining in with wild toasts to the 'King across the water'

---

* Blackett's absolution was possibly brokered by his step-father, William Thompson, a renowned loyal Whig. Thompson later claimed that he passed on to the King's ministers what Blackett told him about the rebellion: R.R.Sedgwick, 'William Thompson', *HistParl* 1715-54.

in late night revelries in dangerous company that mistook his crowd-pleasing casual enthusiasm for serious intent. Perhaps it took home truths from the likes of John Wilkinson to bring him to his senses and send him away in haste that October. The outcome, of course, was both the suspicion of loyalists and the sullen resentment of defeated Jacobites and their sympathisers. In 1717 he was rebuffed when seeking the Newcastle mayoralty, and was only grudgingly accepted a year later when he flourished letters from the secretaries of state in London testifying to his loyalty.[26]

Blackett's influence, his interest, to use the contemporary term, surely flowed from the status, patronage and wealth inherited from his father rather than from respect for his personal abilities and trustworthiness. Although he had been unopposed in standing for Parliament in 1715, the two next elections, of 1722 and 1727, were contested and bribery allegations flew around. His was hardly a commanding presence in the House of Commons, an 'inactive member' who was twice committed to the custody of the Westminster sergeant-at-arms for missing important votes. In 1712 Nevile Ridley pressed Blackett to help secure the passage of the bill giving Newcastle control of the keelmen's charity but he was bound for the Newmarket races instead.[27] In November 1710, shortly before he reached his majority, Blackett had been asked by John Wilkinson if he would attend a London meeting related to the coal cartel or if he would leave it to the managers. In excusing himself and wishing them well, Sir William gave the answer that was presumably both expected and hoped for.[28] Here, then, was possibly the saving grace in his reputation for licentious frivolity. It left the way clear, in this new corporate era for the family business, to those entrusted with its professional management.

John Wilkinson

Wilkinson was clearly highly thought of by William II. He had been employed by the family since his apprenticeship to Michael in the 1670s and part of the wider Blackett kinship network since his marriage to Dorothy Simpson a few years later.[29] There is no sign that, unlike his fellow executor of William II's will, William Davison, he wished to absolve himself of the challenging responsibility it suddenly brought at the end of 1705.³⁰ Indeed he was determined to stay on as chief agent once William III attained his majority early in 1711. The position also appealed to Thomas Brumell, who had ingratiated himself with Sir Edward by 1708, hoping that he would lobby William III for him. Sir Edward claimed to have spoken for Brumell but also reported that his nephew had a most extraordinary opinion of Wilkinson, and that, assuming he was to be appointed, Wilkinson alone would decide who he recruited as his underlings. Uncle Edward had his own reservations about 'Cousin Wilkinson', at one point wondering aloud to one of his own stewards how long he would 'continue such a knave in my nephews business'.³¹ Once again we see the suspicion of fraud, that enduring worry for proprietors either remote from or less knowledgeable than their agents, or, as is likely in William III's case, not terribly interested. It was never far from the pen of the fussy and paranoid Edward.

In Wilkinson's case there is little real evidence either way. He was doubtless a sharp operator; it would have been impossible otherwise to stay the course with the scheming coal-owners of Tyneside. If he was adept at dissimulation he was actively schooled in it by Michael Blackett as an impressionable apprentice. Aged 17 he was sent by his master with a lead cargo for the Mediterranean and told to be 'often civilly discourseing with the merchants [yet] pry as much into their trade as you can'. In later years he was not averse to giving commissions to merchants overseas if they promised to hide certain cargoes in ships' holds, another technique in which he had been schooled as an apprentice.³² Wilkinson obtained an eighth share of the Heworth/ Gateshead coalmine in the 1690s, but this was perhaps sold on reasonable terms by William II to give the agent a personal stake in the success of the venture he was to manage.³³ Nevertheless Wilkinson must have found sufficient informal opportunities to earn a living comfortable enough to support his growing family after 1705 to make it worth re-applying for the job in 1711. This might explain Sir Edward's scepticism.³⁴ It was certainly a very demanding occupation, which can be summarised under three main headings: coal, lead and debt management.

The problems facing the Blackett coal mines in the closing years of William II's life were documented earlier. By 1705 Winlaton and Stella had been let to Montague, leaving just Kenton and

Heworth/Gateshead under active management. Production problems, low profitability, minimal returns on capital and uncertain prospects for the trade with the withering of the 1701 Coal Office cartel, pointed towards getting out of the business altogether. This was always an unlikely course of action. Leaving aside the cachet for Wilkinson of being within Newcastle's coal-owning elite, a great deal of capital was already sunk, making it hard for a mere agent to decide to write it off. In any case, after he became directly involved at Heworth/ Gateshead in 1700/1 coal production had started to rise. In 1700 only 7,000 tons of coal was mined on Gateshead Fell, less than the 10,500 tons for which rent was paid, but by 1703 and 1704 this had risen to over 16,000 tons. The Blackett quota for 'Felling' in 1701 had been about 17,300 tons of coal; in 1708 it was just over 37,000 tons. Wilkinson had almost certainly achieved by then the required doubling of production needed to exploit the heavy capital burden and make a better return on it, perhaps around 15%.[35] Perhaps it was the progress Wilkinson wrought there and the defining experience of colliery management it gave him which made him the obvious choice to run affairs after William II's death. In 1705 it the task was unfinished. Of course Wilkinson was going to double down on the bet already made and try to make it pay off.[*]

Besides the business logic of this growth strategy, it kept him among Tyneside's leading coal owners. He had been active alongside William II in setting up the 1701 Coal Office and from 1708 represented the Blackett interest in a new cartel, the 'Regulation'. Indeed by 1710 Wilkinson was one of the five members of its executive committee, alongside Sir Henry Liddell, Alderman Matthew White, James Clavering and the ubiquitous John Ord, now agent for the Montagues. This formidable team was completed by Cotesworth as secretary and, effectively, chief executive officer.[36] Cotesworth was behind most of the scheming and shifting alliances on the south bank of the Tyne over the next decade. Attempts were made to shut out various competitors such as the Bowes, Claver-

---

[1*] A draft of Wilkinson's request in c.1706 to the Durham Dean and Chapter to renew the Heworth lease stressed the sums already sunk in the enterprise and threatened that should the lease be granted to anyone else, it would be of little value, for the water must drain through the level driven in from a small Blackett freehold downhill, which would be blocked up: NRO 324/W.3/19.

ings and Ridleys using wayleaves, money, the Equity courts and occasional recourse to axes, clubs and poison. In 1712 Wilkinson was amongst the Regulation directors who decided to have a non-cartel waggonway physically broken up. One of those involved on the wrong side was Thomas Brumell, Wilkinson's one-time colleague and aspiring competitor for the job as Blackett's chief agent. Before long, Brumell was heading into bankruptcy.[37]

The Regulation's papers also make clear, however, that Wilkinson had his own difficulties as he sought to rebuild the Blackett coal business. A passing remark in the 1711 cartel minutes indicate that he, on behalf of Blackett, had taken back the operation of the Winlaton and Stella collieries by then, several years after they had been let to Montague. However, they also report him saying that he (Blackett, actually) was about £1,000 out of pocket at Stella and wanted the cartel the take the lease of it in common.[38] And while Kenton production increased from 25,000 tons in 1701 to around 34,000 tons in 1708 (assuming it kept close to its allocated quotas) this modest advance could not have been enough to exploit adequately the expensive waggonway running three miles down to the north bank of the Tyne. The colliery was said to have been flooded by 1715. Furthermore, despite the new cartel's best endeavours, there is no clear evidence that the coal price gave much encouragement in the 1710s.[39] Once again the tension between a desire to shore up the price by restricting supply and the powerful incentive of each major owner to increase production to make the most of their expensive fixed assets was always likely to be resolved in favour of the latter, particularly as Tyneside as a whole no longer possessed much monopoly power over London's energy supply. No more is heard of 'the Regulation' after 1716.[40]

With Kenton abandoned, Stella anaemic and Winlaton output probably down to under 2,000 tons per year by 1710 they could hardly have made any material contribution to the overall business. This left Heworth/Gateshead. Even if output was sustained at the levels achieved by 1708, it is difficult to believe profits were any higher than £1,500 per year, and this optimistically assumes a price of 18p/ton. Worryingly for Wilkinson, the amount of coal led from Gateshead Fell actually dropped from 29,000 tons in 1708 to 18,000 in 1710, so that profit projection is unlikely to have been realised.[41]

What of the lead business? It was the spectacular jewel in the Blackett crown in earlier decades, and probably continued to contribute more to overall income than the collieries during William II's time. However, the first two decades of the 18th century appear to have been particularly difficult for the industry as a whole to judge from what we know of actual prices and some telling anecdotal evidence. A steward in Swaledale commented in September 1705 that the previous year had seen a 'great and unexpected fall in the price of lead' and it sold for under £8 per ton.[42] The next dozen years saw little improvement. This was probably the most serious recession for the regional industry since the great expansion from the 1650s. Around 2,400 tons of lead left Newcastle by sea in 1705, a figure that could well have halved by 1712.[43] Sir Edward Blackett wrote to his son John in Rotterdam in 1709 that 'the lead mines are good for naught and I doubt will ever mend'. By the following March he had found a Newcastle consortium willing to take a chance on a lease at Fallowfield. The Reverend George Ritschel of Hexham blamed the 'great decay of the lead trade' in 1712 and 1713 for his inability to collect church rates.[44]

John Wilkinson therefore took charge in bleak times for the lead industry, with which he was almost certainly far less familiar than coal. In July 1711, inhabitants in the Allenheads area petitioned their vicar for relief from parish rates 'now the mines are ordered to be laid in.' The slender evidence of John Robinson, a candle supplier to the Allendale mines between 1706 and 1727, lends some support to this. As the source of light underground, changing levels of candle consumption is a rough proxy measure of trends in mining activity in the absence of any other information. Robinson was not the only candle supplier and the large reduction in his deliveries in 1708-12 might simply mean others were being used instead. However, none at all went to Coalcleugh in those lean years, unlike before or afterwards, so its veins might well have been abandoned for a while.[45]

Could the Blackett lead business have avoided losing money despite this apparent retrenchment in the face of low prices? Much depends on the unknowable quality of the veins already in work and the cost of mining them. Allenheads and Coalcleugh were probably well drained by their levels and the local agent, George Mowbray, might have got away with minimal maintenance costs for a few years, so that lead ore could be brought out in low quantities in a depressed market for little more than the direct cost of labour and supplies. We can expect that in such hard times pay rates will have been pressed down compared to the boom years. Ore might have been mined in Allenheads for little more than £2 per ton, the unit cost obtained at Fallowfield in the 1690s. Assuming reasonable smelting efficiency and cost, this could have delivered a ton of lead to Newcastle's quayside for around £6.60-6.70 and therefore still just profitable if sold for £8. This would at least have been better than in Weardale, where the fixed sums payable for rents, lott and tithe added about £625 to annual costs. Spreading this burden across high production was hardly feasible for there was only so much the market could take. The days of William I's dominance of the Newcastle market were long gone. Even if Wilkinson could command as much as half of the market, at a time (1712) when shipments to home and abroad from Newcastle were probably around 1,200-1,500 tons of lead, it meant shifting no more than 600-700 tons. It would be surprising if the business contributed more than £300-400 per year in total, even with investment and maintenance cut to the bare minimum.

Some of this could be masked in the short-term because of the increasing practice of delaying payment to the miners and smelters. Robinson's candle accounts show that he was paid reasonably promptly up to 1708, but gaps then started to appear in the receipts column. By 1713 he was owed £207, about a third of the sum invoiced in the previous eight years. George Mowbray later claimed that he had been granting interim subsistence payments to the Allendale miners using his own credit with local grocers and other suppliers to the miners because of the infrequency of the pays.[46] Thus did the miners, smelters and suppliers join the other creditors of the business. The hand-to-mouth management of cashflow is illustrated well by Sir Edward's observation in 1714 that Wilkinson had sold a large consignment to a London merchant very cheaply because he needed a great sum to make a pay.[47]

Taken together it would be surprising indeed if the coal and lead concerns contributed more than £1,500 per year into the central coffers in the years around and after 1710 and perhaps much less. It was a far cry from the heady days of William I, when £6,000 or more per year was earned, or even the more modest returns of

William II's better years of perhaps £2,500-3,000 annually. It was the rental income and loan collateral of land into which those earlier profits were banked which shored up the business in William III's time. Once again the direct evidence is limited, but based on Wilkinson's calculation of the estate rental in 1711, £3,000 can have been expected that year, net of a 20% allowance for management, repairs, taxes and uncollectable arrears. Returns on land were reasonably predictable and stable, in great contrast to the lead and coal mines.[48] So in total, Wilkinson could generate income of perhaps £4-4,500 per year for William III and his mother in the years around 1710, mostly from land. This seems a highly respectable figure, but as we saw in the last chapter, William II's bequests gave Wilkinson a major funding challenge from the outset.

To recap the main financial provisions, Lady Julia was left a lump sum of £2,000, to be paid within two years, and £800 per year. Each of the six daughters was given £200 per year until their marriage, when they were to have a dowry of £6,000. Over £1,000 was incurred in the immediate aftermath of the lavish funeral and the first half year's instalment of annuities was due in May 1706. Since the daughters were all minors at the time of their father's death their mother had control of £2,000 per year. We need also to remember that William I's widow, Margaret Rogers, was still alive and owed about £450 per year, and that Lady Fenwick's £2,000 annuity consumed all the income from the Wallington and Hexham estates. No wonder a further net £1,700 had to be borrowed from John Ord in 1706.[49] A measure of the struggle these ongoing commitments posed over the next few years can be seen in a paper in Wilkinson's hand summarising the 'incumbrances' in 1711. Less than two thirds of the £7,000 owed under William II's will as annuities to his widow and three younger daughters had been paid by then.[50] The dowries were also looming into view.

Even though public access to proven wills usually required cumbersome recourse to ecclesiastical registries, the nuptial value of the widow and daughters of prominent wealthy men will have become known to the avaricious before long.[51] William II's eldest daughter Julia was the first to provide a fiscal headache to his executor, when she was 19. Once Lady Blackett had approved the suitor, 36 year old Walter Calverley of Esholt Hall near Bradford in Yorkshire, in October 1706, Wilkinson took over the negotiations. They mostly revolved around cashflow: the timetable for a schedule of payments making up the £6,000 and the accrual of interest. Terms were finally agreed in January 1707 and the wedding took place in Newcastle a day later.[52] Calverley kept careful accounts of what he was owed from then on, at one point even calculating that an additional £1 interest was due because of the distant execution date on a bill of exchange Wilkinson had given him. Only £1,000 of the dowry was paid within the first four years.[53] There was at least a breathing space until 1714 before second daughter Elizabeth was married, at the advanced age of 26, but there were still four to go after that.[54]

It wasn't all bad news. Lady Fenwick died in October 1708, thereby releasing £2,000 per year. The lifting of this heavy burden might almost excuse the distastefully expectant remark of one of Sir Edward's sons to Wilkinson hoping that 'I Shall have this good News confirmed the next post ... [and] now I wish it may be true'.[55] The death of the dowager Lady Blackett, Margaret Rogers, two years later brought further such gruesome joy, worth over £400 per year. The burden of known annual annuity payments and a reasonable allowance for interest on unpaid outstanding debt had therefore fallen from over £5,700 in 1707 to around £3,300 in 1711. Despite this, new loans were taken out. John Ord lent another £1,100 in 1709. He probably also arranged the £2,500 obtained from Newcastle merchant Nicholas Fenwick secured on Winlaton at much the same time and certainly brokered the further loan of £1,500 from Dr. John Smith, a member of Durham's wealthy Dean and Chapter in 1712, secured on Dukesfield.[56]

Newcastle's emerging capital market was at work, another aspect of the town's developing commercial sophistication. We saw earlier that the likes of William Blackett I could reinvest surpluses to develop their own businesses. There were plenty of others looking for a safe home for the accumulating profits of their landed estates or municipal, state or church offices but who were detached from those seeking funds. Property lawyers could use their networks to act as middlemen in such transactions. Ord was perhaps the greatest of them all in Newcastle in his time. He not only brokered loans between others but dealt on his own account using his own profits and funds entrusted to him, effectively making him a regional investment banker. The scale emerges from the balance sheet drawn up on his death in 1721. Amongst his assets were £44,000 in loans advanced, and he owed £20,000 to various private clients and charities.[57]

As long as the loans were backed by good land security, it mattered less to the lender whether they were put to productive use or not, for failure to repay could ultimately allow the acquisition of the security. It's unclear into which category the additional money taken by Wilkinson and Blackett through Ord's good offices in 1709-12 fell, but there are grounds for concern. The pressures on the coal and lead business have already been noted. New loans were taken despite the large reduction in annuity payments in 1708-10. There must have been enormous tension between Wilkinson and the Blacketts, between executor and beneficiaries, between manager and proprietors. William II laid down no clear governance rules in his will beyond allowing his executors to deduct their expenses and pay all costs and salaries necessary to collect his rents and profits. The proceeds were to meet his bequests with the surplus going to his heir at law, William III. Wilkinson would have been justified in arguing that reinvestment to sustain the business formed part of the expenses and costs. The new draft terms of reference he drew up for himself in the summer of 1711 sought to make this clearer still. He was to have discretion to pay 'all other sumes of money as he shall from time to time find necessary or convenient to be paid for or about the working management [of the business]'.[58]

From what we know of their behaviour, Lady Blackett and her son probably saw it differently. Day to day management control was one thing; the allocation of gross profits between reinvestment and what we today call the owners' dividends quite another. Perhaps William III, with his mother's blessing, decided it was far more agreeable to use the proceeds of some lead sales or the death of Lady Fenwick in 1708 to set up his London house the following year than to see it disappear into boring waggonway extensions or drainage engines. Doubtless the 1710 election cost a pretty penny, so too entertaining and equipping Elizabeth Ord in respectable style. A 35-guinea racehorse could surely be laughed off as mere pocket money. Uncle Edward wanted to know about the fine coach William had bought soon afterwards, and what sort of company he 'diverts himself with'.[59]

No wonder Wilkinson vented his annoyance to John Ord in 1712. Amidst all the usual frustrations of keeping the show on the road he found he was also 'hobbled from above' and had to suffer the tart observation from his feckless 22 year old employer, nearly 30 years his junior, that he had 'either a fool, or a Knave concernd for him'.[60] And so it went on. Expensive Durham Assize and Chancery tussles between Blackett and Elizabeth Ord's family commenced soon after her death in 1713. Sister Elizabeth Blackett's dowry became payable from 1714. Early in 1715 Blackett bought land to extend the grounds of Greyfriars even further and later that year came the Jacobite Rising, during which Wilkinson must at some point have wondered if his wayward master was about to bring the whole business crashing into ruins.[61] He suffered it all and kept going, until Blackett finally went too far in the summer of 1717. This time it was devastatingly personal. One of Wilkinson's daughters had disappeared that May. By September he had traced her movements to Ripon and Boroughbridge in Yorkshire, and that 'it is too plain Sir William Blackett was the person that seduced and conveyed my daughter from me, tho' he denys the whole'. Wilkinson indicated it had already been openly corroborated by others, despite Blackett denying it when confronted.[62] The long-standing manager was a respected member of Newcastle's merchant community. Doubtless embarrassed and disgusted, he promptly resigned as Blackett's chief agent.[63] His name still appears in connection with later leases, bills and accounts, but only as formalities in his role as the sole remaining executor of William II. He made his true feelings known in refusing to attend William III's funeral in 1728 and returning the gloves sent to him.

Blackett seems to have shrugged off the scandal even though it was possibly among the reasons for his failure to become mayor of Newcastle in 1717. His attitude is captured in a reported exchange in the council chamber the following November when he had the nerve to seek the mayoralty again. When one of the aldermen, Henry Reay, objected that Blackett 'kept a mistress, and debauched young women', a pointed reference to Wilkinson's daughter, Blackett insouciantly did not bother to deny it and countered instead that at least 'I do not meddle with other men's wives, and in such a place as a church porch'.[64] Such behaviour was of course not unknown amongst contemporary 'gentlemen' and perhaps he thought the whole thing an outrage manufactured for political convenience. Or he might simply have been either oblivious to the fuss, protected by status, entitlement and – by now - an unassailable self-regard and was shameless enough to laugh it all away. In any event, Blackett was grudgingly accepted as mayor and doubtless enjoyed his year in the Mansion House, the coach and generous 'table allowance'. Is it William III portrayed in a blue velvet tunic with those dark Blackett eyes at Wallington looking as though butter wouldn't melt in his mouth (Plate 26)? Of the young Wilkinson girl there is no further record. We can't even be sure of her name.*

The death of William II and the minority of William III had meant a transition from direct personal control to professional management. The events of the autumn of 1717 provide a reminder that, in this case at least, it was not an irreversibly smooth or orderly progression. In fact little in William III's direct orbit was 'smooth and orderly' in the decade that followed.

---

*It was possibly 20 year old Dorothy rather than 21 year old Anne, (surely no longer a 'child'), and hopefully not 14 year old Julia.

Chapter 17

A Fool or a Knave

The abrupt departure of John Wilkinson in the autumn of 1717 was potentially disastrous for the family business. To limit the damage some management changes were needed in short order. Robert Todd, the longstanding Kenton agent, was quickly promoted to the post vacated by Wilkinson, and was in a senior position until at least 1726.[1] Brumell appears to have been taken back on by early 1719, possibly because of his knowledge of the Winlaton estate, where he had been steward for Sir Edward's quarter share of the manor between 1709 and 1714.[2] Fifty year old merchant Thomas Salkeld was a steward supervising the lead and coal mines from Newcastle by 1723, possibly much earlier, and remained there until his death four years later. Salkeld's brother-in-law Matthew Bell managed the collieries from 1724, reporting to Salkeld.[3] Lancelot Allgood, nephew of the Thomas Allgood who had been steward in Hexham until his death in 1713, played an increasingly central role in William III's affairs from possibly as early as 1717 and certainly from 1724.[4]

Aside from whether this meant bewildering change and confusion regarding accountability and direction in the Newcastle establishment, questions surely also hung over the experience of the new appointments. Todd was industrious in raising the land rents at Kenton over the years and was evidently good enough with horses for William III to entrust him with breeding his Arabian thoroughbreds.* Although familiar with the Kenton colliery, albeit flooded since 1715, this did not mean Todd had any experience of the lead industry. Unless he was a trader in lead, the same might also be said of Salkeld. Bell, however, possibly had some colliery experience for his £50/year. As for Lancelot Allgood, his description in William III's will as 'my trusty and well beloved friend' does not necessarily inspire confidence in his commercial abilities. He was often in London with his master.[5]

---

[1] The Arabian stallion Robin was kept at stud at Kenton during the 1726 season, under Robert Todd's care: *NC* 14 May 1726. Kenton was of course conveniently adjacent to the Newcastle race-course on the Town Moor, which is responsible for the name of today's Grandstand Road.

Coal, Lead and Land

The performance of the coal and lead business during the years after Wilkinson's resignation is hard to discern, although a few coal accounts were drawn up for the mid-1720s by a new cashier appointed in 1727, Joseph Richmond. They show that production was by then down to about 30,000 tons of coal per year, mined at Heworth/ Gateshead, Winlaton and Stella. Judging by the low price at which the Stella and Winlaton coal was sold, much of it was low-grade pan coal fit only for salt and glass working. If the accounts are to be believed, and Richmond was struggling to assemble the full picture in 1728, no more than £100 profit was made annually between 1725 and 1727 from coal.[6]

The lead market showed much greater promise in the 1720s. Lead sold in Newcastle for about £8 per ton in 1717, but went for £13 by early 1724.[7] Indications survive of a rapid investment response to this change in the price signal. A merchants' consortium expanded the Ramshaw mine near Hunstanworth from 1720. Proposals were made to re-open Woodhall smelting mill in 1721. In the early 1720s the London Lead Company's (LLC) extended its operations into the Blanchland area. As for the Blackett business, the construction of a silver refinery at Blaydon, apparently under Robert Todd's direction in 1722-23, offers a rare positive contrast to the beleaguered picture of the family concern elsewhere.[8]

We saw earlier that the North East was a centre of industrial experimentation and innovation in the early 18th century. Lead had been refined to extract silver since antiquity but by the 1720s the LLC was in the forefront of refining on a large scale. Trial and error had led to the design of furnaces in which lead was melted on a bed of finely ground bone ash. The molten lead would oxidise and run off or fuse into the bone ash as litharge and, as long as the furnace temperature could be kept low enough, the silver would be left behind as a 'cake' in the furnace bottom.[9] The litharge could either be sold for use in red lead manufacture for paint or crystal glass or 'reduced' back into more malleable refined lead, which usually sold at a slightly higher price than unrefined 'common lead'. For the sake of a further intricate step in the production process and associated manufacturing infrastructure, additional value could be obtained from the dull grey metal coming down from the North Pennine hills. By 1729, from which date onwards detailed accounts have survived, around half of Blackett lead was being refined at Blaydon and, even allowing for the loss of some lead in the refining process, the profit margin was higher than on the traditional business and increased overall profits by a tenth.[10]

In overall terms, however, the dramatic improvement in prices appears not to have been reflected in any decisive increase in the shipment of lead from Newcastle. Although the 2,100 tons shipped out in 1720 was noticeably higher than the approximate 1,200-1,300 tons of 1712, only 1,836 tons was carried from the port six years later. This was all well below the peak of 3,000 tons of the 1680s. Around 1,000 tons of lead was sold for William III annually in the mid-1720s, higher than the 600-700 tons ventured as a rough guess for 1712, but not dramatically so given the much greater market encouragement.[11] Perhaps years of neglect and under-investment lay behind the difficulty of increasing production in the hills, especially after the departure from Allenheads of the highly experienced George Mowbray at the end of 1723.

Mowbray later claimed he had resigned, fed up with having to deal with the local consequences of long gaps between the miners' pays, and said Blackett had implored him to stay. It might be that in the absence of clear leadership in the Blackett regime after Wilkinson's departure Mowbray had simply had enough. For his part Blackett said he dismissed Mowbray for he had 'great reason to be dissatisfied with his conduct'. It has to be said that Mowbray, despite also claiming to be fatigued and grown older, subsequently had energy enough to attend to his own leased mines in Weardale and the smelting mill he resurrected nearby.[12] The market now gave encouragement to experienced lead agents to become masters of their own destiny. In 1724 Mowbray allegedly tried to undercut Blackett by seeking the lease of the Bishop's Weardale lott ore. If so, it was a clever move, prompting Blackett to rush to the Bishop to agree to double the rent, and it loudly proclaimed Mowbray's views of his erstwhile employer.[13] In contrast to this brisk - if costly - intervention, Blackett neglected the renewal of the mining rights to Weardale's enclosed grounds in 1727, an oversight which the Bishop later exploited when granting them back a few years later at a higher price. To the further irritation of his cashier, Blackett struck a personal deal to sell lead at a 10% discount in September 1727 to a Newcastle dealer to whom, perhaps, a favour was owed.[14] Overall, the higher price of lead, increased output and the additional contribution of silver and litharge probably meant annual profits exceeded £3,000 by the mid-1720s, as the local agents quietly got on with their work. They might have been higher still without Blackett's personal interventions or lack of them when actually needed.

The family's landed estates continued to provide a regular income. The vast majority of the rent came from the estates bought by Williams I and II between the mid-1660s and 1700, either as strategic investments supporting their mining enterprises, as attractive commercial investments in their own right or, plausibly, a secure bank in the short-term absence of any obvious industrial use for retained profits. But the annual income derived from the landed estate was not wholly the legacy of much earlier decisions taken during the days of plenty. As noted in the last chapter, rental income gradually improved over time and this process continued during William III's time. Where it is possible to compare the same estates between 1711 and the mid-1720s, annual gross rental income increased by about a quarter - albeit varying greatly between properties.

While in general terms increased demand for food and industrial raw materials from agriculture in a region of growing population and commercial development must have helped this process, some of the variation seen in Table 17.1 might be explained by differing local conditions. Kenton was perhaps already yielding as much as it could, having been driven on before 1711 to exploit its proximity to Newcastle. The estate evidently benefited from good management. In 1723 it was described by Guy's Hospital's surveyor as 'one of the most improved Estates in the County set with Quicksett Hedges and trees in the Hedge Rows [and] good Tenants Houses'.[15] The advertising of vacant farms in the recently established Newcastle Courant was calculated to attract interest from the better class of literate farmers, who were directed to 'enquire of Mr Robert Todd of Kenton, who will treat about the same'.[16]

At both Welton and, strikingly, Wallington, much further from Newcastle than Kenton, there were marked rises in rent in

Table 17.1 Gross estate annual rental income.

	1711	1720s	change
Total	£3,740	£4,620	24%
Winlaton (1/4)	£214	£214	-
Dukesfield	£104	£128	23%
Woodcroft and Short Thorns	£74	£74	-
Wallington	£1,184	£1,925	63%
Hexham and Anick Grainge	£1,220	£1,250	3%
Allendale	£148	£150	-
Kenton	£530	£527	-
Welton	£265	£350	32%

Source: Appendix 4.2, 4.3.

the 1710s and 1720s. Although no details survive as to how this was achieved, it would be surprising if the period did not witness the incremental shift from arable tillage, to which the land was generally poorly suited, to the pasturing of sheep and cattle. The lecturer of Hexham complained of just such a change in similar country to the north of the Tyne in 1703 because it reduced his corn tithe income.[17] Here we glimpse the relentless march of specialisation across the land, a process that ultimately improved output and productivity, but at the disruptive short-term cost of small-scale tenants being squeezed out. Open fields were enclosed and remote hamlets disappeared from the land, leaving only shallow earthworks and redundant 'rigg-and-furrow' to cast shadows across today's quiet pastures in low evening sunshine.

Such changes might ultimately have been driven by price incentives to supply more integrated national markets, but land owners and stewards had important roles to play. They set underway the mechanism of 'improvement': farm consolidation, investment, lease covenants to foster new farming techniques and the recruitment of forward-thinking tenants. In a letter to James Mewburn at Seaton Delaval near the Northumberland coast in 1714 Sir Edward Blackett took it almost for granted that his agent would be able to 'advance Every farme' given the shame that it had been 'so under lett' and that he would very soon be able to 'manage that Lordship much beter to my advantage than formerly it has been' under previous ownership. When Albert Silvertop was appointed Sir Edward's steward at Winlaton, he immediately suggested enclosing the common there to improve rents and this was readily agreed to by Sir Edward.[18] A pattern of acquisition of land by Newcastle merchants and lawyers for its commercial potential and subsequent action to invest in improvement, enclosure, larger farms and progressive tenants prepared to pay high rents has been observed more widely across the region during this period. To merchants, lawyers, mortgage brokers and those with money to spare in the early 18th century the potential capital gains from 'unimproved' land were as keenly understood as land's attractiveness as a safe haven.[19]

Family Conduct

The landed estate and quietly diligent local agents could therefore be relied upon to provide some regular and slowly rising income to accompany the benign effects of the resurgence in lead prices, despite the hints we saw earlier of some dysfunction in the management of the lead business. Chaos is more clearly on view, however, in what is known of the family's conduct in the late 1710s and 1720s. Blackett and his mother were not in the habit of restraining expenditure and addressing the debt burden, much of which was the consequence of his father's legacies. Confusing and partial glimpses can be had of the complicated knot of old and new obligations and the juggling of loans and mortgages to cover them. A few examples will do.

They are best set in the context of the scale of the burden by the 1720s. A colossal loan of £77,000, issued in two tranches in 1723 and 1725, was obtained from Thomas Guy of London and the hospital he founded that still bears his name.[20] The negotiation of this sum, secured on Blackett's estates and the Weardale moormaster's lease was partly the work of John Ord, the Tyneside mortgage broker, but more particularly of a fellow lawyer and acquaintance in London, George Allgood, originally of Northumberland.[21] Piecing together the first tranche of £65,000 took

Ord, Allgood and the Hospital some time. It then came as a surprise to Blackett that there was so little left for his own use that he had his people seek the additional £12,000 secured in 1725. Although often exhibited as the main evidence of William III's profligacy, this loan was actually a good deal. It consolidated most of Blackett's existing debts into a single loan and the 4.5% interest rate charged would have reduced his annual interest payments by perhaps £500 or more compared to the existing rates of 5-6%. Such were the benefits of tapping the London capital market.

But even this large sum was not enough. A few months after Blackett's death in September 1728 his cashier Richmond undertook the onerous task of listing the deceased's debts, outstanding obligations and available current assets. His present and future liabilities added up to around £105,000, of which well over a half, £61,500, represented commitments made by his father and the rest, around £43,500, his own debts and bequests.[22] Thus, while it is unfair to lay the blame entirely at William III's door, he had still racked up significant commitments of his own and had either been unable or, bearing in mind the recent increase in lead prices, simply failed to manage affairs well enough to discharge his father's long-standing liabilities.

The difficulties in dealing with those inherited liabilities were arguably exacerbated by Lady Blackett's marriage to William Thompson, to the great disdain of her son William and brother-in-law Sir Edward. Lady Blackett took her daughters with her away from Newcastle and set up house with Thompson in Hampstead. For some time after the wedding, William refused to be in her company.[23] Edward and William recognised a parasitic bounty hunter when they saw one.* Great offices certainly followed Thompson's marriage to Lady Blackett, including a knighthood in 1715 and the post of Solicitor General in 1717. Evidently a prickly and defensive character, he once allegedly threatened to cut the throat of a journalist who taunted him about his small estate.[24]

---

* Lady Blackett was not the first widow he married. Perhaps Joyce Brent of London, whom he married in 1701, was also able to supplement the income provided by his Middle Temple legal practice. He obtained a life sinecure from the corporation of Ipswich in 1707 and Parliamentary election in a 'pocket borough', positions that did not come cheap.

A Fool or a Knave | 273

Thompson was behind an agreement struck in 1719 to commute his wife's £800 annuity into a one-off payment of £8,800. It was not a good deal for William. Ord and Allgood were surely familiar with the growing practice of using life tables to value annuities and Thompson must have known that they would never have agreed to this proposal, so he took care to deal directly with his step-son instead.[25] Unbeknownst to his advisers, Blackett agreed and sealed terms with Thompson in April and by June the lawyers were scrambling to raise the funds and give Thompson the security he inevitably demanded in the meantime. Allgood told Ord he was a stranger to the arrangement and declared against it when he found out. As luck would have it for Thompson, financially at least, Lady Blackett was dead within three years. She died suddenly at her Hampstead home in August 1722 while Thompson was in London. As Allgood ruefully observed to his brother Robert in sending him the news, 'Sr Wm Thomson has made a fine hand of the match'.[26]

There must also be a suspicion that Thompson arranged the marriages of his two youngest Blackett step-daughters in 1719 and 1720. Diana was three months short of her 17th birthday when she married the 38 year old Whig MP Sir William Wentworth at St. Paul's Cathedral in London in June 1720. This was seven months after the disturbing match between her younger sister Anne, aged 14, and 50 year old Whig MP and widower John Trenchard, whose first wife had allegedly committed suicide. Both men will have been Parliamentary allies of Thompson. Perhaps the price of parental consent was a commission on the £6,000 due to accompany each child.[27] Caution is always needed in viewing the 18th century marriage practices of the wealthy through modern eyes, but it is still difficult not to wonder what their mother was thinking, howsoever 'respectable' the standing of these middle-aged suitors. Her portrait at Wallington offers few clues but there is something uncomfortable about the regal cold stare from her narrow eyes (see Plate 28).

Then there were the undertakings of Blackett's own making. In June 1719, for example, when Allgood was dragged into finalising the details of the £8,800 agreement with Thompson, he was mightily annoyed to discover, in passing, and from Thompson of all people, that Ord was simultaneously busy raising another

£9,000 for Blackett. It was to be secured on the same property as used to cover Thompson's lump sum. This was the result of another freelance initiative by Blackett and now went beyond the obligations arising from his father's will. George Mowbray was evidently under a great deal of pressure from the Allendale lead miners demanding payment. It is likely that there had been no such general pay for five years, when Sir Edward had noted that Wilkinson sold lead to cover it. Whatever had happened to the proceeds of lead sold since then, not much was available to cover the liabilities incurred in mining and smelting it. The 1719 pay amounted to £12,260 according to Mowbray, of which £9,000 was borrowed.[28] Perhaps we can allow this to have been a prudent conversion of rising debts owed to restive miners into a secured loan, but it points to problems in the husbanding of business cashflow and was still a large financial commitment made behind the backs of the people Blackett paid to juggle his debts.

Furthermore, despite the existing heavy burden, he lent money himself, and incautiously. George Allgood was exasperated in 1721 when, as he put it to Ord, 'I was a stranger to Sr W B lending of any moneys (which I perceive has been of some considerable standing) till lately. And those sums advancd I am afraid more out of friendship more than upon due consideration of the title or security'.[29] Some was lent to one of his Mitford cousins, offspring of his great-aunt Christian, and was probably bound up in some way with the eventual purchase by Blackett of Mitford lands at Ryal in remote Northumberland countryside between Wallington, Hexham and Newcastle. This estate was part of land committed by Robert Mitford on his marriage to Christian Blackett in 1669 to provide her with a jointure and the subject of a loan to Mitford by William I in 1674. For William III to end up buying the estate in 1722/3, rather than redeeming it under the settlement of a long-standing debt means either that we are missing part of the story or that it was another dubiously conceived deal.[30]

Whatever the background, Blackett had a clear purpose in buying the estate. He was in search of an eligible marriage partner with an attractive dowry. The Ryal estate, specifically excluded from the security offered to Thomas Guy in 1723, was going to provide his future wife with a jointure. By 1725 he had agreed terms with the dowager Countess of Jersey to marry her daughter, the 19 year old Lady Barbara Villiers. This looked like a good match socially, linking Blackett with the aristocracy. According to newspaper reports it was celebrated with great drunken fervour in Hexham and at Blackett's beloved Wallington, courtesy of his lavish hospitality.[31] If the marriage brought into view the prospect of a legitimate heir it might well have been celebrated by the various agents and stewards of the business, but it was not to be. When Blackett wrote his last will three years later he could express only the poignant but forlorn hope that his 'dearly beloved wife' might be with child at the time of his death. Lady Barbara's views of her husband are unknown, as is so often the case, but her remarriage within six months of Blackett's decease, and the birth of a daughter four years later perhaps tells us something. It is not even clear that Blackett had the best of the financial arrangement. Against the dowry she brought of £6,000, (£4,800 of which was spent by the time of his death), her £450 life annuity from 1728 can be valued at around £6,500 given her youth.[32]

We have no details of the cause of William III's death at the age of just 38 in late September 1728 but the speed with which his grand stately funeral was arranged and carried out suggest that it cannot have been a complete surprise. At least four different surgeons were in attendance that year in London and Newcastle. A bill was later presented for drugs given Sir William when at Ferryhill on the Great North Road in County Durham, suggesting he had perhaps been taken ill *en route* between to or from the capital.[33] His will was drawn up in the middle of August.

Without a legitimate male heir, but with a strong desire to sustain the Blackett name and influence, William III bequeathed his indebted inheritance to his then only nephew Walter Calverley, subject to Calverley marrying Sir William's 17-year-old daughter Elizabeth Ord within a year and taking the name Blackett. And so it was that the 21-year-old young man from Yorkshire walked at the head of the elaborate public parade behind his uncle's coffin through the streets of Newcastle in October 1728. It looked like a neat settlement, to be overseen by four trustees; Lancelot Allgood and his brother Major, Newcastle merchant Abraham Dixon and London lawyer Charles Clark (George Allgood having died). Blackett's will covered a number of eventualities, such as Calverley declining to take Elizabeth as his wife, or dying before any such marriage, but he clearly never asked Elizabeth, the young girl with such a traumatic childhood, if she had an opinion on the subject. Awkwardly, she did. As a lawyer for the Calverleys delicately put it at some point over the winter of 1728/9, Elizabeth had 'some aversion or dislike of his person or carriage' despite Walter having with 'manifest industry striven to please her'. There were no words in the will to cover the eventuality that 'she could not fancy him'.[34] The final mess left by Willliam III was the possibility of a constitutional impasse which could paralyse the Blackett empire.

This was the uncomfortable backdrop to the spectacular funeral described earlier. In following 'the same steps that were taken at his father's' he sought to reassure Newcastle of an orderly continuation through a reminder of the glorious Blackett heyday. In death, by drawing from the well of civic obligation and through characteristically heavy expenditure, he strove for a semblance of parity with his forbears that had eluded him in life. But whatever the temporary sedative provided by this great send-off, a hard and dark reality reappeared to his trustees and managers as the bills came in through the following winter. Not least of these was the crystallising of another £6,000 dowry obligation at the marriage of William III's sister Frances the following February.

On paper, the balance sheet would have shown the family concern to be solvent. The value of the landed estate alone must have exceeded the debts and the lead business had renewed value in the market conditions of the 1720s. When existing debts and other liabilities are taken into account, William III's net assets can be valued at perhaps £74,000. Given the way the earlier annuities turned out, especially with Lady Fenwick's death in 1708, his share of his father's inheritance was probably worth around £23,000. Yet of the implied £51,000 headline increase, rising land valuation multiples probably contributed £20,000 alone and the lead market recovery another £7,000, both of which were good fortune rather than the result of hard work. The rest of the gain in wealth is more than explained by the increase in rental income from estate improvement wrung out by the land agents.[35] But this was largely theoretical compared to the hard reality of continued cashflow problems. These remained a headache despite passing a great deal of pain onto the lead miners and smelters by delaying pay days. By the time of his death in September 1728, Blackett's workers had ef-

A Fool or a Knave | 277

fectively been forced into interest-free loans adding up to over £11,000.[36]

The financial context of those pay arrears indicates the extent to which the profits generated by the lead business in the 1720s were squandered. It was estimated above that the lead and refinery business delivered profits above £3,000 per year in the mid-1720s. From 1726 alone, after a mining pay, at least £8,000 must have been generated by the time of Blackett's death to judge from production levels, prices and approximate costs. Taking into account the pay arrears and payments due from merchant buyers, the lead business should easily have carried a positive cash balance of over £12,000 by January 1729 and this is without further contributions from silver and litharge production. Instead, there was just £232. It's not as if debts had been paid down in the meantime. In the three years since the Guy's loan was taken, Blackett was already more than a year behind with the interest payments, some £3,500.[37] The 1720s cash records show what was going on. For example, proceeds from two lead sales in September 1725 adding up to £1,020 were immediately sent to Sir William in London, where he maintained two households, instead of held back in Newcastle towards a large pay due to the mines and mills a few months later.[38] Even Lancelot Allgood complained of his master in 1724 that despite high lead prices and production 'when the pay comes to be made their will be noe great sume found … the workmen have been as ill paid as ever.'[39]

The heavy obligations left by William II had persisted for almost a quarter of a century, accounting for around £61,500 of the £105,000 of debt and liabilities in 1728. Far from working them off, William III's wanton behaviour and extravagances accompanied a seeming disregard for difficult business headwinds and he squandered any recent gains coming his way from lead. He hindered his agents more than he helped them, and left them the final quandary of an inheritance dependant on poor Elizabeth Ord's view of her Yorkshire cousin. There was plenty for those sweeping up behind him to deal with.

Chapter 18

The Foundations of Redemption

Given the problems facing the business, Blackett's trustees and heir-presumptive Walter Calverley were in a difficult bind in the winter of 1728-29. The transfer of ownership after the death of the last Sir William was potentially the most disruptive yet. Even had it been clear that the 21-year-old was to inherit, his background was not best suited to the task ahead. He grew up on a Yorkshire country estate rather than a Newcastle merchant's household, was indulged with a dancing teacher in London at the age of five and later educated at Westminster School and Oxford.[1] But his path to ownership was far from clear. In the autumn of 1728 Elizabeth Ord appeared set against marrying her cousin. As the waspish Alexander Carlyle later had it, 'she was of superior understanding to him' while Calverley was 'not a man of remarkable parts, but strong in friendships, liberality and public spirit'. He appears proper, elegantly dressed but uneasy in his portrait as a young man (see Plate 27) which was perhaps commissioned to ease his path to matrimony. The well-known Reynolds portrait at Wallington shows a stout and plain country squire in later life, faithful dog at his heel. Here was an affable Georgian gentleman interested in dogs and horses rather than intellectual pursuits, but apparently unimaginative and boring in Elizabeth's view.[2] Walter might also have failed to live up to the dashing polite society she had been introduced to by her father in London in recent years, decked out in expensive new jewellery.[3]

    This might have brought the Blackett story of industry, enterprise, supremacy, indulgence and crisis to an oblivious end in little more than three generations, another business that failed thanks to the capricious family happenstance of personality and competence. But this story has a different ending. The Blackett business was not even a third of the way through its existence in 1729.[4] We don't need to take it further than the mid-1730s to examine the foundations of its redemption. Some of these have been seen already – the solid bedrock of the landed estate and the good fortune of a positive turn in the lead trade in the 1720s. This chapter focuses on management and the mining business, but first the question of the succession needs to be addressed.

Elizabeth and Walter

The failure of Blackett, chief agent Lancelot Allgood and lawyer Charles Clark to anticipate young Elizabeth's feelings for her Yorkshire cousin was a serious oversight. She must have come under enormous pressure from Allgood and Clark in the autumn and winter of 1728-29 to conform to her father's instructions in the will. Here was yet another trial for a girl whose life had been mostly been scarred by them. But conform she ultimately did. It is impossible to know whether she was just holding out for better terms, eventually securing £500 per year to her own use under the terms of her marriage settlement, or whether she was an isolated 18-year-old woman worn down by formidable older men, the erstwhile friends and advisers of her late father. Allgood and Clark were evidently confident enough by April 1729. Clark's presentation of the previous months' difficulties had it, simply, that Elizabeth 'was not willing to marry so soon after the death of the sd Sir Wm Blackett [but that she] is now willing that the sd marriage should take effect'. Yet a month later came a nervous report from Newcastle that Richmond the cashier couldn't 'yet acquaint you that a day is fix'd for the Nuptial benediction'. At the end of June Elizabeth, having earlier agreed terms, then flatly 'declared against the match' and an agitated Newcastle lawyer called on Allgood to come north from London to persuade her.[5] It was nearly the end of August before the wedding took place, perhaps pointedly so close to the year's deadline set by William III that Elizabeth could signal her eventual acquiescence under duress.

This set the platform for Walter Calverley to take his place in Newcastle's civic elite, henceforth as Walter Blackett, in fulfilment of the second and much easier condition of his uncle's will. Despite his youth, but perhaps because of his inherited status he was quickly adopted as a freeman and alderman and served as mayor in 1735 at the age of just 28. He was elected to Parliament in the contested poll in 1734, displacing William Carr in an echo of his uncle's achievement of 1710, and remained a fairly inactive MP until his death in 1777. He epitomised the early Georgian period's 'astonishing drop in the wind-speed of politics', sedate and reasonable under Sir Robert Walpole's long premiership in comparison to the highly charged drama and factional vitriol of the decades after Charles II's death.[6] With Walter Blackett's love of racing, hunting, Wallington, women and spending freely it is hard to tell whether his personal qualities actually marked him out as much more able than his uncle, William III, other than having the crucial attribute of being willing to follow good advice. However he lived long enough to secure a far more favourable reputation, not least because it gave his amiable spirit more time in which to leave a legacy of widespread benevolence to the poor and to various institutions in Newcastle and Northumberland.[7]

As for Elizabeth, having done what was expected of her by marrying Walter, we hear no more apart from the production of an only child, another Elizabeth (who, in a further tragic twist predeceased her mother), and a dutiful obituary in 1759 which spoke of her piety, pure manners and bountiful charity. Surely, however, she had an unrecognised hand in the development at Wallington, where she was chatelaine for so many years. Her silent endurance in unblocking the constitutional impasse created by her father's will has hitherto also been unrecognised as one of the foundations of redeeming the business.[8]

Management

In 1705, potential disruption to the Blackett business in the wake of the apparently unexpected death of William II was avoided by the continuity of competent management in the hands of John Wilkinson. Likewise in 1728-29, the clumsy transition from William III to his inexperienced young nephew from Yorkshire was greatly mitigated by the continued presence of key managers and agents, from various land and mine stewards spread out between Wallington to Weardale to his chief agent and trustee Lancelot Allgood. The survival of an abundance of ledgers, accounts and letters from this date onwards also means the Blackett management structure and system, the calibre of people who ran it and the results they achieved are easier to see.

17th and early 18th-century business structures and systems are rarely this visible, and infrequently considered.[9] For the vast majority of enterprises they were unnecessary, for farmers, craftsmen and manufacturers worked on a small scale and could see what was going on within their fields and workshops. The effective operation and control of a large business, on the other hand, needed the rules of day-to-day processes, quality control, accounting and reporting to be understood and followed, especially where many of those operations could not be seen deep underground or were spread widely across the countryside. It was tedious stuff, and usually still is. Internal procedures or the counting of pay, supplies, transport, deliveries and sales lack the drama and colour of character, personality clashes, decision-making, success and failure which swirl around the reconstruction of real people's lives. But it is worth noting those mundane webs of rules, reports and organisational relationships where they existed, for they can indicate an institutional maturity sometimes more enduring than the careers of those who worked within them.

Noting their presence is often all we can do, but even then some powerful observations can be made. For the main line of the Blackett business, there is little left between Michael's letters to his father in the 1670s and those written in the 1730s. Yet some interesting similarities emerge regarding the structure of management responsibilities and reporting relationships across those 60 years as far as the lead business is concerned (see Figure 18.1). As we saw earlier, responsibility for the lead smelting mills was separate from the mines by 1675, and the same distinction was made in the 1730s. This means the mills agent, for example, had a primarily functional responsibility for smelting and arranging the ore and lead carriage, irrespective of location. In 1675 John Mowbray was responsible for the mills. In 1730 Isaac Hunter was the resident at Dukesfield Hall overseeing the mill down the lane and also for Rookhope and Allenheads, even though the last-named was just two miles away from John Armstrong, who was in charge of Allenheads mine. The respective agents were therefore focused on particular stages of the lead production line, with their very different processes, skills, and economics. Where land was let in the immediate surroundings, however, the agents were typically expected to account for the rents. In the 1730s Armstrong covered the Allenheads properties, many of which were let to his miners, Hunter the Dukesfield farms and Joseph Peart the Weardale mines and lands.[10] They all reported to the chief agent in Newcastle. In 1675 this role was shared between Michael and William Blackett II. By the late 1720s it was in Lancelot Allgood's hands.

Figure 18.1   Management structure: Blackett lead, 1675, 1730.

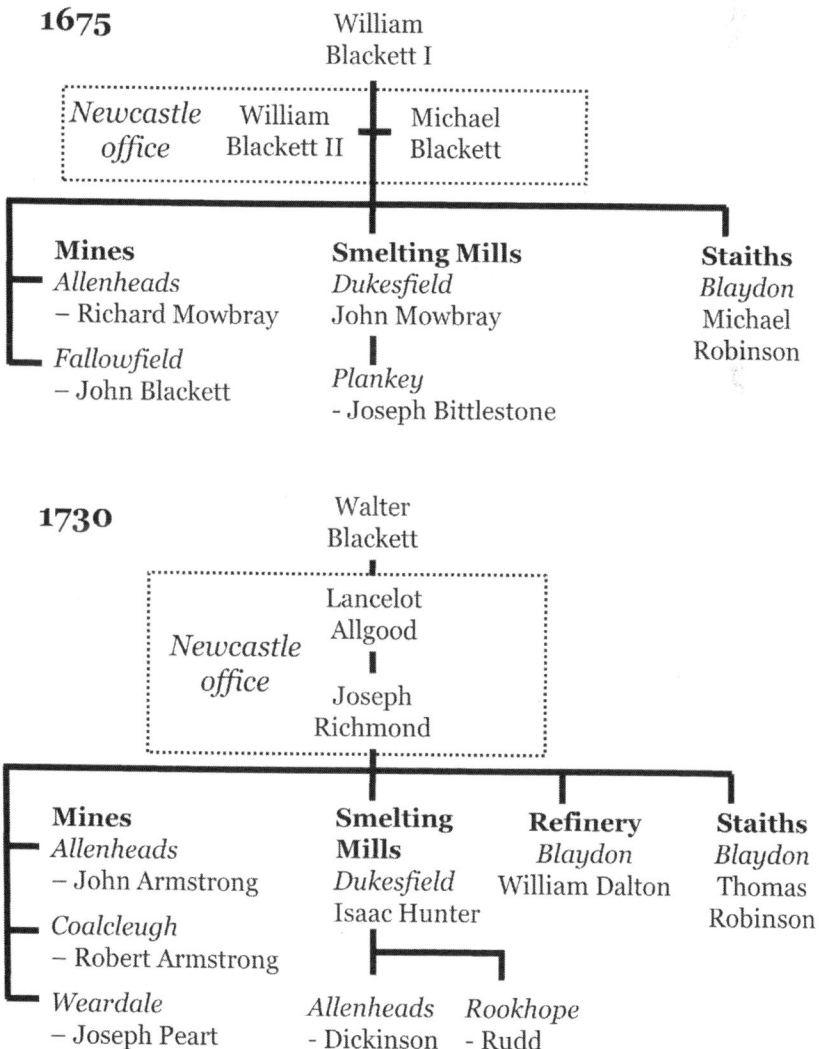

There also appears to have been continuity in the nature of accounting information and reports flowing from the field to the centre. Michael's reports to his father in the 1670s followed a standard pattern from which the status and cost of key indicators of performance of the lead business could be adduced. In his 1711 self-penned draft terms of reference Wilkinson had William III emphasise the need to 'cause & take care that all the accts touching & concerneing my sd Leadmines & Collyeryes shall be kept & entered with such p.son as att the same place & in such manner as the sd accts were Kept in the life of my late father Sr Wm Blackett'. George Mowbray recited the quarterly submission of accounts by his sub-agents and reckoning-papers between those agents, workmen and creditors in the 1727 Chancery bill.[11] An expectation of precision in the returns to Sir Edward Blackett from his agents might just reflect his constant pedantry but is also likely to have been ground into him since childhood.* It probably helped that there was also longevity of service in many positions and often the succession into posts of younger family members, as with the Robinsons at Blaydon shown in Figure 18.1. A stable organisational structure, an expectation of accurate and timely production and financial reporting and long continuity of service must have fostered a corporate culture suited to operating a large and widespread business.

Continuity was one thing, but of limited value without competence. Doubts might linger over how impeccably honest the likes of John Mowbray and John Wilkinson had been in their time, but their ability seems clear. When it comes to chief agent Lancelot Allgood, however, William III's 'trusty and well beloved friend', there are questions on both counts. His probity must be questioned over the lease he took of the defunct Stanhopehope smelting mill, which William II had been obliged to take from Humphrey Wharton in 1692 as part of the moormastership purchase and was long out of use. The lease from Blackett to Allgood was dated 22nd August 1728, eight days after the date of Blackett's will, the drafting of which must have involved Allgood and in which the property was not mentioned. The lease paperwork was evidently then promptly mis-

---

*The meticulous detail of his accounts in 1680 was still expected when he criticized James Mewburn and Joseph Peart in 1710 for quoting different numbers of lead pieces smelted that winter at Birkey Burn adding up a variance of only 0.5%: NRO ZBL 273/15, EB to JM 26 Jan 1710: ZBL 189.

laid, and Blackett died a few weeks later. It disappeared from the Blackett property register until later agents were alerted to it by chance in the 1760s.[12] The rent was unaccounted for during the intervening decades. Not so trusty after all.

Allgood apparently had some legal training for he was also referred to as Blackett's solicitor in the 1720s, but it is questionable whether he applied it with any diligence to protect his master's interests. The oversight in failing to renew the Weardale enclosed grounds mining lease in 1727 must be laid at his door. There is also little excuse for not anticipating in Blackett's will the possibility that Elizabeth Ord might refuse to marry her Calverley cousin. Allgood of all people might have been alert to this. His distant relative, the London lawyer George Allgood, had apparently sought just a few years earlier to marry off his niece (also his adopted daughter) to Lancelot, and upon her utter refusal to do so, she eloped.[13] The office correspondence of the early 1730s gives an impression of laziness, leaving us to wonder whether his appointment in the first place was a personal favour –at a generous £320 per year- from an old friend allowing them to spend more time together in London. Thomas Salkeld and then Richmond in 1727 were quite possibly recruited by Allgood to do most of the work, so that he could enjoy his sinecure without undue effort.[14]

On this reading it is a small further step to see the attractiveness to Allgood of his master being succeeded by the uncertain young Walter Calverley. The ailing William III directed through his will that Allgood be continued in his present employment and 'under the same yearly salary.' On its own this did not bode well given the difficult position of the business in 1728. However, the saving grace and, in the longer term, possibly the most valuable instruction contained in that will was the further stipulation that Joseph Richmond also be continued as book-keeper and cashier.

Joseph Richmond

Richmond's ability and effectiveness as a manager was arguably the single most important foundation of the recovery of the Blackett business in the 1730s. It might well have been different without the cushion of income from the landed estate, without the management structure and system and indeed without Elizabeth Ord breaking the logjam of ownership, but he turned out to be the catalyst which converted those other advantages to positive use. It was Richmond who supervised the military-grade logistics of William III's funeral and dealt with the niggling complaints from the grandees who attended. The copious and systematic business records and letters that survive from his time allow much finer judgements of his record than of his predecessors and, while caution is needed, because nearly everything we know of him is from his own pen, the business consequences are clear.

Joseph Richmond was born in about 1693 and a boy of that name was baptised in Aspatria in Cumberland in that year. He was therefore about 34 years old when he started working as Blackett's cashier early in 1727.[15] He married Elizabeth Brickell at Poole in Dorset in 1718 and was at Deal in Kent two years later where son Henry was baptised. Taken with the observation that he was a Customs House clerk in Newcastle in January 1726 when his daughter Elizabeth was baptised, it is reasonable to conclude that he had entered a Customs career as a young man and was subject to the policy of long distance staff moves between coastal postings in order to try to reduce corruption. It was perhaps the elderly Blackett cashier and merchant Thomas Salkeld, presumably familiar with the Customs House and its staff, who was impressed by what he saw of Richmond and persuaded him of the benefits of being able to remain in Newcastle at a salary of £140 per year. Richmond was soon installed in Lambert's House, adjacent to Greyfriars' grounds, from where he took an increasingly firm and orderly grip of Blackett affairs and into which flowed regular and detailed reports from the agents in the field.*

---

*It is one of the houses shown around three sides of a quadrangle at the bottom left hand corner of Plate 18, roughly where Shakespeare Street joins Pilgrim Street today. Richmond lived there rent-free: 1737 Blackett estate survey, NRO 11603/Box 8.

The Dukesfield accounts were initially in disarray and he was annoyed to find gaps in the Allenheads accounts for the chaotic years after 1719. 'Mr Allgood remembers not he ever had them, & they are not in the Office'. Richmond occasionally sought information from the aging John Wilkinson and eventually managed to obtain a 'large bundle of his papers relating to Sr Wm's Trust'. The trunk carried from Wilkinson's house further down Pilgrim Street included rentals, coal stocks, colliery and staith bills, receipts, lead mine accounts and tack notes, the very listing of which implies work undertaken by office clerks to set them in order. It all meant that, later on, Richmond was able to lay his hands quickly on the papers which protected the Blacketts' many and varied rights. In 1755, for example, in the face of a claim over coal mining rights on a disputed boundary at Stublick Fell west of Hexham, Richmond was quickly able to produce vital evidence from more than half a century earlier.[16]

He also immediately set about giving directions to all the under agents on the exact and consistent form in which he demanded they submit their quarterly reports of production, stocks and costs so that he could track business performance. Richmond used the word 'exact' often, normally in combination with persuasion or threats. John Armstrong, the Allenheads agent who had replaced Mowbray in 1724, was encouraged to use Richmond's new reporting form 'which after trial you will find easier & better.' When the Allenheads smelting agent failed to send in any returns for 1728, his direct line manager, Isaac Hunter at Dukesfield, was instructed to obtain 'his Reasons for the Omission & let him know I expect he won't neglect it for the future'.[17] Thus was the reporting system tightened up and strengthened, the long-standing management culture renewed. The flow of information it produced, particularly for the intricate web of operations which made up the lead business, was neatly summarised into elegant tables in consistent form for a further century, cross-referenced to the underlying accounting ledgers and journals.[18]

They were subject to rigorous analysis in Lambert's House. Although Richmond's background was in the Customs service, his letters display a good grasp of husbandry and of farming leases. Richmond's understanding of the lead industry is particularly impressive. Vigilance over cost control, output and production quality led to a series of questions and instructions back to the mines, mills, staiths and estates. The higher unit cost of mining lead in Weardale compared to Allendale was a concern in 1731, for even after improvements in recent years 'they are by much the most chargeable groves all the oar got there standing to about 35s a Bing [£4.37/ton], besides the Rents, which when added this brings the charge to 43s a bing [£5.38/ton] before its lifted from the groves.' Unit costs might have been lower at Allenheads but Richmond still quizzed Armstrong about a high ratio of candle to labour costs.[19] He also keenly tracked smelting yield, that key performance indicator evidently recognised decades earlier by William I as a crucial determinant of the overall cost of lead. Hunter was chastised in the 1750s for 'extream bad Management' on his watch, especially in Rookhope where 'very near 5 bings have been smelted for every fodder of lead [a poor 52.5% yield]', and later examples show it being calculated to two decimal places.[20] He was equally vigorous in pursuing the consequences of shoddy work. Hunter was instructed in 1730 to reprimand his Dukesfield smelters for poor quality lead, which would give it 'an ill character at all markets' and saying of one smelter that 'hanging is too good for him'.[21] The cost of refining lead at Blaydon to extract the silver was broken down between labour, fuel, waste in the process and the opportunity cost of the lead diverted from immediate sale as raw material. This permitted fine judgements to be made on what to refine based on small scale trials of the silver content of lead smelted at the mills, and the price of silver, litharge and refined lead, with the obvious intention of optimising profits.[22]

Joseph Richmond clearly ran a tight ship from his office at the gates of Greyfriars. He managed cashflow within the close constraints of sales, rent, outgoings, interest payments to Guy's Hospital and various annuitants and Blackett's drawings for his 'personal occasions'. A deep professional attachment to the Blackett business is revealed by his comment to Allgood in 1731 that he was personally 'ashamed to hear it said we are forc'd to pay Intrest to so many persons'.[23] Given the high standards he set for his underlings and the constant pressure on cash reserves it is not surprising that he became increasingly irritated with the behaviour of Allgood, his boss. In late 1730 Richmond 'had Numbers of the Weardale people abt me' clamouring for a pay, and reminded Allgood to make sure money was retained from lead sale proceeds in London for that purpose lest they give up their bargains.[24] Certain in 1733 that Allgood had some important deeds that Allgood claimed not to be able to find, Richmond 'desired him to examine narrowly for them'. By that year he was confident enough of his direct relationship with Walter Blackett to pointedly remark that he could 'only guess at Mr Allgood's Arrears etc because I have rece[ive]d no Acco[un]ts thereof for the last year' in respect of the Hexham rents for which Allgood was directly responsible. None had been received since 1730. Richmond saw fit to remind Blackett in the same letter that Allgood was paid £320 per year, more than double his own salary.[25]

Richmond was also far more than a forensically analytical accountant and hard-driving manager. He showed confidence, nerve, guile and dexterity in the renegotiation of the Weardale lott ore rent due to Bishop Chandler of Durham in 1732, leading to grumbles from Chandler about sharp practice.[26] And with Walter Blackett away in London a great deal, Richmond provided regular updates on Newcastle's civic political scheming. He gave much shrewd advice on how to advance Blackett's interests, particularly in dealing with his rivals in the Ridley family in the 1730s and in charting a path to being elected mayor in 1735. He even attempted, though with less success, to rein in Blackett's personal spending. A delicate letter of 1733 articulated the need to build up reserves to put lead pays on a regular footing and that, in consequence, 'it's my humble opinion you can't now exceed 3 or £4000 a year at most, without Lengthening your payments to the mines which will be certainly to your own Loss, I hope you won't take amiss my telling you what I take to be the reall truth, & conducive to your sole Intrest'.[27] That year the Blacketts worked their way through £6,300 for their personal, household and related expenditure, right up to the bells installed on the new Wallington stable block. If the relentless discipline of the annual interest charges on the Guy's loan didn't force the need for a coherent and successful business strategy, Walter Blackett's extravagance certainly did.

A Business Strategy

William Blackett I had the rare ability to combine a meticulous attention to detail with a sweeping strategic view and the judgement and decisiveness to carry out a programme of action. Richmond displayed similar qualities. Since he was merely a manager, however, he also needed skills of persuasion to have his recommendations adopted. Because some of his arguments are set out in his letters we are on surer ground in assessing his overall strategy than was the case with William I, whose planning has to be inferred, speculatively, from the evidence of his actions alone. Context was also different by Richmond's time. In contrast to William I in 1660, who depended upon trading profits, the land now provided a stable foundation of regular income. It is worth briefly summarising this here before moving on to the mining concerns.

Elizabeth's marriage to Walter Blackett brought to the estate her own landed inheritance west of Berwick-upon-Tweed, and another £500 of annual rental income.[28] By then the whole of the estate inherited by Walter Blackett (including his wife's lands) was worth around £178,000 gross.[29] For this he could be grateful to his grandfather and great-grandfather and to increasing land values. However, he was also the beneficiary of the active part played by his agents in encouraging better use of that land and capturing its returns. The noticeable increase in rents discussed in previous chapters, part of a general trend observed in the region, probably means that nearly one half of the rental income contributed to the business by the late 1730s came from improvements made since acquisition. Where estates can be compared 'like for like' between 1690 and 1737 it appears that rents were around 75% higher at the later date compared to 1690. Nevertheless, the overall net rental income from all property in the 1730s, a little over £5,000, did not leave much surplus cash after covering the £3,465 annual interest charge on the Thomas Guy loan and various other annuities of a further £1,200. A great deal more would be needed to support the Blackett lifestyle. Richmond concluded that lead must be the focus of increasing overall business performance, supplementing property rents that provided a vital cushion but which could not be expected to keep growing rapidly. It was therefore time to end the decades-long coal adventure.

With the survival, on Richmond's watch, of the accounts of the coal mines at Stella, Winlaton and Heworth/Gateshead in the late 1720s, we can see that they were hardly breaking even. He drew up a summary showing a profit of £933 on revenue of £24,320 in the five years 1725-9, a margin of just 4%. The Blackett business was by then mining 35,000 tons of coal per year, less than 5% of Tyneside output, and even basic maintenance must have been an unaffordable and unrewarding drain on capital.[30] An opportunity to force the issue arose in late 1730, when the West Kenton estate came up for sale, the land adjacent to the Blackett East Kenton grounds, and where William II had taken a coal mining lease in the 1690s. To Richmond's dismay Walter Blackett was interested in buying it, supported by Allgood, and in the superficial attraction of reopening the flooded mines in a united estate. Asked by Allgood to report on the practicalities and cost of this, Richmond quickly took further local advice and replied with a detailed report in February 1731. It was a brilliant piece of analysis. He set out the likely remaining workable coal reserves, draining and pumping costs, wayleave rights for the waggonway that ran down to the river at Scotswood, the general outlook for the coal market and the interests and potential tactics of local competitors and neighbours.[31]

Richmond concluded that there was certainly value in combining the two halves of Kenton but that it was in Blackett's best interest to sell East Kenton instead or, if that was not possible on good terms, to lease out his colliery there instead of working it directly. He determined what rent could be achieved by putting himself in the shoes of potential lessees, estimating their unit costs of working and transport and comparing their potential profit with the alternative of investing in safe securities allowing for the 'hazard' or risk of mining. Even the coal enthusiast John Wilkinson, from whom Richmond had sought an opinion, allegedly felt West Kenton would be a costly purchase for Blackett. Richmond also told Allgood that Wilkinson had 'given Mr Blackett such a hate of the Colliery that when [he] considers it he won't be so eager about the purchase'. He had his way. By 1737 all of the Blackett coal mining interests, including East Kenton, had been sub-let, the risk transferred to a new generation of colliery optimists elsewhere. Between £700-900 of rental income per year was earned from the mines thereafter, certainly more than in many of the years of direct operation, and for no capital outlay.³² More than 70 years after William I's first foray into coal mining at Stella, followed by the great expansions between the 1660s and 1690s that took him and his son into the front rank of Tyneside's coal barons, the family's painful lingering direct involvement was brought briskly to a conclusion by the company cashier in the early 1730s.

A new and dispassionate manager was able to draw this conclusion, make a persuasive case for action (to an owner and chief agent who also lacked emotional attachments to coal's black heroism) and then drive the change. It is hard to imagine John Wilkinson or Robert Todd conceiving or seeing through such a painful shift, let alone the first two Williams. Walter Blackett had the sense to follow Richmond's advice.

Expanding the lead business was now the priority. Here there was a clear focus on more intensive exploitation of the existing assets, rather than grand acquisitions in the manner of William II, and selling to merchants in Newcastle rather than engaging directly in trade. The substantial increase in the lead price in the early 1720s was sustained throughout the decade and reached over £15 by 1729, higher than the peak of £12.40 seen in the 1670s. However, those earlier days under William I when ore could be mined in Allendale and Fallowfield for around £2/ton were long gone. In 1728 the average mining cost for the Blackett business in Allendale and Weardale was £4.50 per ton of lead ore.³³ Much of this increase was inevitable with the exhaustion of the more easily reached parts of the veins, but it might also reflect, once again, the higher burden of fixed costs spread across low production. Richmond was well aware of how heavily the £815 annual cost of the various rents in Weardale bore down on low output. The day after William III's funeral in October 1728 he signalled his determination to secure economies of scale when he wrote to John Armstrong at Allenheads having 'considered that it will be expedient to have the groves revived with the utmost expedition'.³⁴ In that year 1,800 tons of ore were mined. By 1736 the total had more than doubled to 3,800 tons. Just over 1,000 tons of lead was smelted in 1729, and 2,000 tons six years later, a remarkable increase of more than 9% each year. It was achieved in impressively short order and mostly from existing mining areas and mills. The level of lead production under William I was finally surpassed.

The summary accounts left to us do not allow capital expenditure and operating costs to be prised apart but some of the investment required to drive this great expansion is mentioned in the correspondence. In March 1729 work on a drainage engine at Coalcleugh was completed and the mine was expected to flourish. A new hearth had been installed at Dukesfield 'at no small charge' and the new agent there, Isaac Hunter, was trying to get reluctant workmen there to make changes to take full advantage of it. Blaydon quay was extended in 1731 to cope with the additional volume of lead being carried down from the hills. A stamp mill to break up slags for resmelting at Rookhope mill was installed in 1735. High hopes were attached in 1732 to opening up a mine at Mohope on a tributary of the West Allen, three miles from Coalcleugh, hopes that were realised when its annual production exceeded 300 tons of ore the following year, and 600 tons in 1736.[35] In addition to capital investment this also relied heavily upon retaining experienced miners and smelters and adding to their number. Richmond constantly reminded Allgood and Blackett of the need to ensure funds were available to make timely pays to the miners and pressed the agents in Allendale and Weardale to keep on top of agreeing bargains.

He felt that the Bishop of Durham had driven a hard bargain in 1732 when agreement was reached on the Weardale lott ore, renewing the lapsed inclosed grounds mining lease and updating the moormaster's terms. Yet this was handled with far more assurance and nerve than in William III's day. At one point during the negotiations, concerned that a silver trial of some Weardale lead had mistakenly shown such spectacularly good results that word of it would get back to the Bishop, Richmond ordered that it be run again by mixing in some common ore in order to 'deceive the country'. The Bishop's agents felt that they had been outwitted in their games of bluff with Blackett's man and the miners he employed, grumbling about the 'artifices of these underground people'.[36] The Bishop effectively obtained a £900 'windfall' in that year, much to Richmond's annoyance, but it amounted to no more than 7% of total lead business costs that year and secured rights in Weardale during a period of growth and high prices.

Although production rose rapidly, returns varied from year to year, mostly as a consequence of fluctuations in the volume of sales. Richmond's correspondence shows that he was alive to the tactics of when and when not to bring lead to the market, but also well aware of the limited influence any one producer could have. Even William I was probably unable to exert any meaningful influence on lead prices in the 1670s and this was certainly the case 60 years later, in a much larger national market. What we see instead is a steady concentration of sales into the hands of a small number of Newcastle dealers. The top four buyers of Blackett lead in Newcastle accounted for 56% of sales in 1727-8, but 83% by 1735, led in each year by the merchant Peter Bernardeau, on The Close.[*] This was a manageable number of merchants with whom long-term relationships and large contracts could be developed, but still numerous enough to avoid being trapped at the mercy of a single buyer.

Fluctuations in lead, litharge and silver sales compared to production –with lead still accounting for around 90% of all revenue –makes it difficult to draw a clear picture of profitability from a single year's accounts. Table 18.1 therefore averages the data available for 1728-9 and 1734-6, each of which periods include years of strong and weaker sales. With the high price of lead in the late 1720s it should be no surprise that profits averaged nearly £4,000, which was probably better than at any time since the 1680s, but they increased still further in the next decade, both absolutely and as a share of sales revenue. As before, it is difficult to say what this represented as a return on capital, but a reasonable estimate for the mid-1730s would be a highly respectable 25% to 30%.[37]

In such a buoyant market it ought perhaps to have been straightforward to make such large returns. However, the price of lead in Newcastle actually declined from a peak in 1729 of £15.60/ton to just under £12 in 1734, a drop of a quarter, making the higher profits of the mid-1730s even more impressive. Much of it is explained by an even larger reduction in the unit cost of mining. Each ton of lead cost £4.50/ton to mine in 1728, but the cor-

---

[1] Bernardeau was also an insurance company agent, a natural extension of his trading business and a reflection of the increasing maturity of the commercial services that grew up around trade: *NC*, 2 Dec 1721. Since there is no sign that Bernardeau was ever a merchant adventurer, his ability to buy and sell in Newcastle on a grand scale speaks of the merchants' company's waning influence. Sales ledgers 1728-35: NRO 672/E/1B/1-2.

responding figure between 1734-6 was just under £3. It is likely that a higher proportion of the expenditure in 1728-9 was capital investment compared to the mid-1730s, paving the way for increased production, but it also allowed economies of scale to be enjoyed as the output of ore doubled. Part of the attraction of the new Mohope mine from 1732 was its very low cost, for each ton cost under £2 until 1737, and it contributed nearly a fifth of all the Blackett ore in 1736. Richmond's detailed command of the cost structure is illustrated well in his instruction to Joseph Peart in Weardale in 1734 to stop mining in locations where it cost more than £2.75-2.87/ton because the price of lead had just fallen below £12/ton in Newcastle.[38]

Table 18.1 Blackett lead business profits 1728-1736.

	Lead price	Revenue	Net income	Margin %
1728-9	15.0	£15,150	£3,970	26%
1734-6	12.1	£20,600	£6,300	31%

Source: NRO 672/E/1B/1-2; Appendix 3.5.3.

As far as 'downstream operations' are concerned, although smelting and carriage costs were held down, by the late 1720s smelting yields appear to have deteriorated slightly from the 60% level probably obtained in the 1670s. There is no sign of any marked improvement until much later in the 1730s, when it reached 65%. Static or falling smelting yield, and Richmond's complaints about poor quality lead suggests that the rapid increase in production exposed a problem in recruiting and training additional smelters. Richmond analysed in detail which lead to refine with a view to optimising the additional returns from litharge and silver. In overall terms, expansion, mining economies of scale and strong cost control enabled profits to rise despite the falling lead price and concerns over smelting quality.

Furthermore, the Blackett lead business stands favourable comparison with their principal competitor, the Quaker London Lead Company (LLC). Between the 1720s and 1750s the LLC greatly expanded their North Pennines operations, in particular by taking on many of the Alston Moor mines. Their revenue and profitability has been estimated from surviving accounts for the sample years of 1738 and 1750.[39] The Blacketts' underlying profitability was probably around 30% in each of these years. However, in 1738 the LLC operated at a loss of nearly 10% and matters were not much improved 12 years later. Their output had, astonishingly, more than quadrupled in that time but the company was probably still trading at a loss. It is hard to be sure of this at the later date for the quality of their accounting had deteriorated and was greatly inferior to the standards Richmond maintained for Walter Blackett.

Given the equivalence in prices at which each company sold its output, relative costs largely explain the variation in profitability. It cost the LLC much more to mine the ore, they carried it over longer distances to where they located their mills and smelted it at higher cost.[40] They typically refined more of their lead for silver, the ore containing decent silver levels by regional standards, but apparently could still not make a profit. None of this necessarily means the LLC wilfully disregarded making money. The North Pennines formed only part of their business nationally and they were intent on rapid expansion. By 1750 the company was producing at least as much lead in the region as the Blacketts and was certainly refining more silver. The two companies went on to dominate regional lead mining into the next century.

The LLC's prioritisation of growth over cost control and profitability during the 1730s and 1740s was the opposite of Richmond's strategy. High profits lightened the Blackett debt burden and, in a market where prices had long been set nationally or internationally, ceding regional market share was not a significant business threat. Richmond's approach is illustrated well by what did *not* happen during these years. The Earl of Derwentwater's estates, including Nentdale and Alston Moor, were confiscated by the Crown after his doomed leadership of the 1715 Jacobite Rising and given to the Greenwich Hospital in 1735. When the mining rights were let in the following year Walter Blackett was not even mentioned as a bidder. It is hard to imagine William II, for example, passing up the opportunity to secure such a dominant position by adding these extensive mines to his control of Allendale and Weardale, but in 1736 they went to Colonel George Liddell, one of Henry Liddell's sons, and his partners. Liddell achieved little beyond building the Nenthead smelting mill and he retreated after a few years of heavy losses in which little ore was raised. The LLC stepped in and committed the investment needed to revive mining in the district, but it weighed heavily on their profitability.[41]

This all bears out Richmond's strategic judgement of focusing on more intensive exploitation of the existing Blackett lead mines rather than embarking on large-scale expansion. Given the choice between these two paths, heady enthusiasm and prestige would usually have won out over caution in the past. Walter Blackett certainly showed an appetite for prestige worthy of his antecedents but in business he usually took his agent's advice. The capable Richmond was given his head. Unlike Wilkinson he was not 'hobbled from above'.

He delivered results. Walter Blackett's spending on himself, his wife, houses (especially Wallington), horses, dogs, charities and political influence rose steadily through the 1730s before levelling off at around £8,000 per year, a sum that even William III might not have reached. Walter could now afford it. Richmond told him with some satisfaction in December 1732 that the lead pays were up to date for the first time in 20 years. The arrears of interest payments to Guy's Hospital had been cleared by the end of 1734 and so too the last known personal debts incurred by William III.* Ongoing payments on the Guy's loan and to the various family annuitants were covered by income from the land. By the end of the 1730s, outstanding debt and the present value of annuities had been reduced by £10,000 since William III died.[42] Even after all these outgoings, over the 1730s as a whole it is likely that there was a slight surplus of income over expenditure. The business was back on a secure footing, a firm stage provided for later generations of colourful characters. Joseph Richmond was arguably its most accomplished custodian since the first Sir William.

---

* Richmond had been aware of £2,300 of William III's debts when he took the inventory in January 1729, but the final amount cleared was at least £5,600. He must have winced each time the post brought claims from previously unknown irate creditors enclosing bonds or promissory notes bearing Sir William's undeniable signature and seal.

The Foundations of Redemption | 297

The mid-1730s, a tumultuous century after William Blackett I's entry into plague-ridden Newcastle as a young apprentice, do not mark a natural break in the history of the family and their business. Walter Blackett lived on until 1777. Joseph Richmond remained in Lambert's House at the gate of Greyfriars until his death in 1763, when he was succeeded by his son Henry, another example of management apprenticeship and continuity. However, there are a number of suitable excuses for ending the story here. The framework of landed assets, a focused and profitable lead business, practical and sophisticated management system and highly competent agents had established a successful pattern by the mid-1730s. Furthermore, Joseph Richmond received his just rewards early in 1735. The death of Lancelot Allgood, just 44 years old, removed a potential problem and tension within Blackett's management hierarchy and the cashier was, sensibly, promoted to the position of chief agent.

It is also worth noting the death of that earlier agent of the Blacketts, John Wilkinson, in January 1734. He was the last man to have known them all at close quarters. As a young apprentice to Michael Blackett down on the quayside in the 1670s he might not even have dared to speak to the formidable first Sir William, but following his own master's death in 1683 he had evidently impressed the second William. Married into the family via one of the Kirkley descendants he rose to prominence alongside the expansive and expensive acquisitions at Kenton, Heworth, Wallington and in Weardale. For more than a dozen years he then navigated the much more turbulent waters stirred up under the third Sir William before his abrupt resignation in 1717. Wilkinson pursued his own coal interests thereafter, but remained close enough to witness the further depths and then recovery of his erstwhile employers' concern in his last years.

Did Richmond walk down Pilgrim St from time to time to sit with the older man and learn about the heritage of the business as well as seek specific information that might help resolve issues of the day? Although they followed different early paths from Durham and Cumberland, they were nevertheless both men of Newcastle who found in it the opportunity to make successful careers from their talents, as had the first William Blackett many years earlier. They were a generation apart and had very different opinions on the coal industry but still had much in common. In particular, despite being virtually invisible in Newcastle's story compared to the Blackett dynasty, they played key roles in sustaining one of the town's most important businesses decades after its creation. It's highly unlikely that Blackett's creation owed its origins to the fabled shipload of flax but rather to opportunity, judgement, confidence, flair, accumulation - and luck - over the crucial quarter century between 1650 and 1675. That, the corporate structure he put in place and the culture he fostered that could recruit and make the most of able men like Wilkinson and Richmond, was the real ship that came home.

Chapter 19

Blacketts, Newcastle and History

The rise to prominence of the Blacketts in Newcastle in the century from the 1630s was of great contemporary significance to the town. Given the transformational impact of William I on the North Pennines lead industry and the scale and geographic reach of their business, they were of wider relevance to the region as a whole. This concluding chapter briefly summarises the family saga, its personalities and considers the key features behind their emergence and sustained importance. It is a case study of one family. General conclusions cannot be drawn from a single example regarding the role of business in this century of great turmoil and change in England's economic development. The Blacketts' story does, however, prompt some wider possibilities to leave as questions for others to pursue. And, finally, what traces of the 17th-century Blacketts are left today?

Personalities

William Blackett I's merchant apprenticeship spanned nine traumatic years of plague, blockade, the death of his master, military invasions, a siege and eventual Parliamentary ascendance between 1636 and 1645. From what can be said of his father's background as a clerk or agent working in several places around the region as his young sons grew up, William I had to bear these formative years in Newcastle without the cushion of generous family financial support. His talent was spotted by Elizabeth Kirkley, who recruited him, via marriage to her daughter, to help rebuild the family trading business and thus launch his mercantile and civic career during the Commonwealth years. In 1659-60 a decisive move and investment in coal and - especially - lead mining was the real turning point. Numerate, analytical and bold, Blackett surely recognised the potential of mining to generate much higher returns on his capital than was possible from mercantile trade as long as production could be driven up to a large scale and thereby make intensive use of fixed assets.

His risky gambles on Allendale's lead veins and a buoyant market paid off handsomely. The huge expansion in his business earned him great wealth and transformed the North Pennines industry as a whole. From perhaps 400-500 tons in the late 1650s, Newcastle's lead shipments reached nearly 2,000 tons by the mid-1670s and Blackett was responsible for the majority of it. In strengthening a connection over great distance between demand and supply Blackett was one of the many in this period who responded to incentives in the market to deepen economic integration. He was worth perhaps £5,000 in 1660 and over £80,000 by his death 20 years later.

Figure 19.1 is a somewhat simplistic view of the net assets held by each generation and shows the critical importance of the 1660s and 1670s, two decades that set the foundation for the fortunes of his family over several subsequent generations. The desire to support family members meant that each William, and Walter, started from a lower base than their predecessor, although still very well off. Each managed to grow their share again. Most of the other shares at each death were set aside in small amounts to widows and children and recycled into other gentlemen's estates, office purchases or frittered way. By far the biggest exception to this pattern was the £29,000 bequeathed by William I to his son and heir Edward between 1674 and 1680. Edward's landed property value increased in line with the market, but the Fallowfield lead mine, so important in 1680, was of minor consequence by the time of Edward's death in 1718. In overall terms then, Edward's inheritance from his father was quite possibly worth little or no more after nearly 40 years than when he obtained it, which left a great headache for Edward's much put-upon second son and executor, John. The Newby estate was mortgaged by 1723.[1]

William II made much more of his share than did his elder brother and remained far more involved in mining. He and Edward went their separate ways after their father's death, although both were much less active in trade. In swashbuckling style William II greatly extended his mining commitments in just a few years from 1689 and raised himself into the front rank of Tyneside's 'lords of coal'. This cannot, with the benefit of hindsight, be judged a finan-

Figure 19.1 The Blackett inheritance.

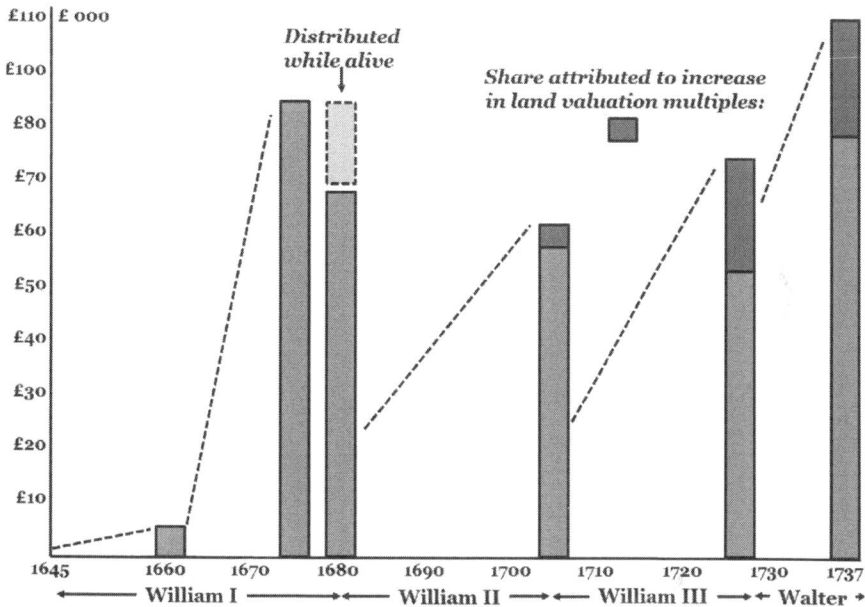

Source: Appendix 4.6.

cial success. But what might appear now an unhelpful diffusion of capital and management focus between lead and coal by both William I and II could well have seemed a rational diversification of risk between commodities at the time. In William I's case, he might only have made that substantial commitment to coal at Winlaton in 1668 because he had just lost any realistic chance of taking the Weardale lead moormastership. The Blackett coal mines cannot be judged a long-term success, but the lead market had its own troubles between the 1690s and 1720.

Far greater security in the longer run was provided by land. As a share of estimated gross assets it rose dramatically from about a quarter at the death of William I to four-fifths 25 years later when William II died. This reflects the acquisition of Wallington, the manor of Hexham, Kenton, Welton and Fallowlees and the increase in land values. The share of gross assets accounted for by land remained at around four fifths at the death of William III and in 1737. Gross rental income by the 1730s was over £7,700, the vast majority of it in Northumberland, placing Walter Blackett in the front rank of the county's landowners.[2] It is tempting to see in this the archetypal retreat from business success to country estate, accompanied by the traditional markers of rising social status. Both William I and II were granted baronetcies by King Charles II. The family assumed an almost hereditary position of power and influence in Newcastle from their grand mansion of Greyfriars and represented the town in Parliament whenever they wanted. Note that the three daughters of William I married men useful to the Blackett business in the 1660s and 1670s: a Newcastle merchant, a Northumberland coal-owner and a London lawyer. Forty years later, however, the six daughters of William II took their generous dowries into the families of landed gentlemen under his widow's 'guidance'. Not a merchant's training for William III, but a place at Oxford University.

This appeared to set the scene for the next traditional stage on the road from clogs to clogs: the third generation's dissolute free-spending waster who took on a huge and highly visible burden of debt. A very young William III was ill-equipped to manage the problematic legacy of his father's apparently sudden death in1705, and both the lead and coal businesses were troubled in the next two decades. His able chief agent John Wilkinson was an important presence but a chaotic decade followed Wilkinson's abrupt departure in 1717, his patience finally snapping in the wake of Blackett's seduction of one of his daughters. William III was only 38 when he died in 1728, leading to the uncertain succession of his nephew Walter Calverley/Blackett. But the stereotyped arc of rise and decline in three generations is too simplistic. Walter's interest in spending freely in London, Newcastle and at his beloved Wallington almost certainly eclipsed his late uncle's but he represented a successful fourth generation and others were to follow. Although Walter's early years in charge were dogged by the usual cashflow problems he did at least benefit, unlike previous generations, from inheriting the majority of William III's net assets. Within ten years his net wealth surpassed the total amassed by his great-grandfather William I over 50 years earlier, thanks in no small degree to continued rises in land values.

The enduring foundation of the land was therefore one of the key features underpinning the survival of the family business.

Although legacies had to be found at each generational transition, the landed estate and industrial assets were largely kept intact, apart from the bequest of Westwater, Fallowfield and half of Winlaton to Edward. The pay-offs were made either in cash extracted from business profits or loans raised against land, especially the rational £77,000 Thomas Guy loan of 1723-5. This reflected one of the attractions of land to a family business enterprise – it could bank surpluses earned elsewhere and fund new investment at later dates by supporting cheap mortgage borrowing. Land was often also an attractive commercial proposition in its own right rather than simply somewhere to retire to. Many Newcastle merchants bought land around the turn of the 17th century and proceeded to enlarge farms, enclose fields, change farming practices and raise rents. Wallington and Hexham manor produced far more income in the 1730s than the 1690s. At Winlaton and Kenton, where the land accompanied coal mining ventures, the rental income, especially when subsequently increased through commercial improvement, effectively paid for the mining rights. Income from land supported the Blacketts' mining business instead of replacing it.

The other key pillar of business survival was the corporate management structure, system and culture created by William I and the continuity of able people, sometimes over many decades. It was arguably an important counterbalance to the caprice of inheritance. John Wilkinson greatly eased what would otherwise have surely been an abrupt transition between William II and III in 1705 and marked a shift from direct owner control to professional management. Even after his departure in 1717 the network of agents, accounting reports and structure provided some resilience in very difficult years. The recruitment of the exact, exacting and highly talented Joseph Richmond shortly before William III's death was especially important. Under Richmond's strategic guidance and attention to the detail of delivery, the recovery in the lead market in the 1720s was translated into renewed profitability, assisted by the withdrawal from coal mining.

The system later presided over by Wilkinson and Richmond emerged in the 1660s and 1670s to support a competitive business enterprise of rare scale, geographic range and complexity for its times. While William I's lead business did not have to manage huge numbers of people on a single construction site, unlike in a great naval shipyard, it still had to direct the work of hundreds of miners in different places and co-ordinate the varying seasonal logistics of ore and fuel delivery over the fells to the smelting mills. Smelting yield, quality and cost had to be closely overseen, the lead delivered to Newcastle along miles of trackway and by river from Blaydon, then sold and despatched to home and overseas markets. This was all alongside the coal mines at Stella, Winlaton and north of the Tyne, which probably employed as many people again as in lead – 400 or more - and Blackett's continued direct involvement in maritime trade. These various concerns were managed separately, but cashflow, credit arrangements, capital allocation, customs and shipping must have needed tight central discipline. The Blackett management system sustained this scale between generations. It must also have created the temptations of monopoly where market conditions permitted. We see this most clearly in the actions of William II in the last decade or so of his life.

Surveying the breadth of William II's business at the time shows a striking difference in approach between his coal and lead concerns. In lead, where there was no realistic prospect of influencing prices, he sought to remain competitive by reducing costs through adapting smelting to the innovative use of peat fuel and by relocating mills to reduce ore transport distance. Such incremental change, which possibly also included business process improvements, made their own contribution to business success and, more widely, to economic growth. At the very same time in the coal business, by contrast, William II's energy and political ability went into the Coal Office cartel, because the goal of restricting supplies from the vast Tyneside coalfield to drive up prices appeared within reach. It proved ineffective in the end, but his intent was clear.

There was an important political dimension to this. Then, as now, cartels and large organisations were prone to lobby the state for protection and favours. It would be naïve to believe that the successive Blacketts sought civic, guild and Parliamentary positions simply from a sense of duty and service. Time and expense dedicated to skilful manoeuvring for favours, special rights and privileges might be undertaken on behalf of Newcastle, the merchants' company or hostmen but there was usually also the prospect of personal advantage. Amongst the possibilities of the age revealed by this case study of the Blackett business are not just that impressively large, sophisticated and enduring competitive enterprises could be created at great speed in the 17th century, or that new patterns of regional economic activity could be established in short order to the mutual benefit of local producers and distant consumers, but also that where commercial heft presented the chance of monopolistic control, attention was often diverted towards its pursuit. It is probably idle to speculate what might have been achieved had William II inherited all his father's assets but there are hints enough in the Coal Office episode to suggest that the region might have seen the emergence of a lead monopoly on a colossal scale for the times, and an even larger Blackett presence in Tyneside's coal industry.

William II and William III started instead from a lower point of material wealth, which arguably makes it easier to run the rule over their abilities and achievements. William II was clearly an energetic and able businessman in his own right, so too his chief agent John Wilkinson. But the first century of the Blackett business surely owed most to its founder and then to Joseph Richmond. Possibly the most important of William III's bequests was to ask his trustees to keep Richmond in his post in the engine room of the business in Newcastle, much to the later benefit of Walter Blackett. Long-term themes and emerging patterns might be seen from the vantage point of history, but it is the unique combination and sequence of events, personalities, relationships and decisions that ultimately weave the fabric of a family story such as this – and provide much of its fascination.

This study of the Blacketts might push further back in time the date at which a large and sustainable industrial/mining company trading in competitive markets came into being in Britain and at striking speed. However I do not claim that William I and his business was the first of this or the largest of that. He's just the one studied. Firm general conclusions cannot be drawn. Nevertheless an immersive study of a single business, its people and its times still prompts questions that could be of wider relevance. Several have already emerged in the course of this book, but here are four other possibilities to conjure with. They all relate to Newcastle's central role in the Blackett story.

Possibilities

Firstly, was there something special about the personality of William Blackett I or was he a product of his environment and times? Was he born or made? The youngest son of a modest clerk or agent from County Durham, he had to survive all manner of upheavals and trials in the course of his Newcastle merchant apprenticeship. Here, apparently, was a triumph of willpower and exceptional talent, a heroic navigation of the traumas of his formative years in order to break into exclusive civic institutions, open up a new dimension in regional economic power and establish a lasting business and dynasty. It was a remarkable achievement against the odds. Perhaps so, and it makes for a dramatic tale of endeavour, but careful consideration of the wider context suggests a different possibility.

Newcastle was, by early 17th-century standards, a highly sophisticated centre of maritime trade in which economic expansion was assisted by the great rise of coal mining alongside the Tyne from the 1570s. Its civic and guild institutions fiercely defended their ancient monopolistic privileges but they were not closed to able newcomers. Long exposure to international trade and its commercial fruits fostered an open, numerate and largely tolerant business culture in which additional talent was needed as trade grew. The merchants' company twice relaxed its rules on the number of apprentices allowed to each freeman. Apprenticeship to a good master could provide the equivalent of today's business school MBA qualification. The foundational skills were bookkeeping, product, legal, commercial and geographic knowledge, often including foreign travel and language proficiency. Beyond this, bright apprentices would observe and develop productive relationships with buyers, sellers, shipmasters, officials and acquire a sense of market trends, the confidence to engage in long-distance risky ventures and a certain resilience to setbacks.[3] In expansive times, masters had a vested interest in seeking out talented apprentices far and wide, young men who could be recruited and trained to sustain or extend their business and help put their capital to productive use.

In many societies a great deal of talent never had - or has - the opportunity to fulfil its potential, and pre-industrial England was no exception to this. Nevertheless, encouraging signs can be seen amongst Tyneside's 17th-century merchants. Without downplaying Blackett's clear talent and determination, he was perhaps as much a product of his environment as the shaper of his own destiny. He was fortunate to grow up near a booming international trading port, with parents who could see the possibilities and whose means were modest but still sufficient to launch two of their sons into that commercial hothouse. It might be too deterministic to say that a Blackett was bound to emerge from such a fertile environment, but he was not the only young man from the 'middling sort of society' to flourish there. Between the 1620s and 1660s a higher proportion of Newcastle merchant apprentices with craftsmen or yeomen fathers went on to become merchants able to take on apprentices of their own than did the sons of professionals, gentlemen and even other merchants. Mark Milbank was one such and William Cotesworth another.[4] Nicholas Ridley's father was a gentleman according to his apprenticeship indenture in 1661 but, despite an illustrious past, family circumstances in the Northumberland countryside appear to have been quite modest after the civil war. As a freeman in the 1670s Ridley started trading in cloth and moved on, as had Blackett before him, into lead and coal mining in a substantial way.[5] The careers of others would be worth exploring. As for Blackett, he certainly made the most of his abilities, but was it a particularly benign and fertile environment in Newcastle that gave him the chance?

Secondly, was Newcastle uniquely able to foster a business management culture in this period because of its port and mines? Management of large geographically widespread concerns was not new. Landlords had long relied upon distant estate stewards to maintain and let property, collect rents and account for it all. However, this was arguably a simpler and more sedate responsibility than managing the various planning, investment, labour recruitment, supervision, operations and transport logistics of mining and related activity, especially in an era of rapid development. For now, the Blackett business provides one of the earliest known examples of advanced large-scale company management and astute recruitment in north-eastern England, but it was not alone. Philip Wharton set out an elaborate system of management controls to enable him to run his Swaledale lead mining concern from a distance in the 1670s, assisted by another highly able manager in Robert Swale. The astute managerial and entrepreneurial ability of William Gilpin developed the Cumberland business interests of Sir John Lowther in the late 17th century.[6] Ambrose Crowley, the owner of the great works at Winlaton Mill from the 1690s, was a 'giant in an age of pygmies' according to Michael Flinn, and was instanced by Pollard in his seminal history of business management.[7]

A more recent study of 18th-century accounting and estate management in the North East found other, later, examples of sound management of mining concerns and the essential role of accounting as an adaptable tool promoting efficient operations. Many managers had backgrounds as colliery viewers, men who often worked with each other and on contracts for a variety of mine proprietors. Their ability to appraise and monitor colliery ventures using practical knowledge of geology, draining, engineering, mining and cost accounting skills gave them a firm analytical basis for investment decision making and advice. William Leaton, chief steward to the Bowes family in County Durham for over 35 years started out as a coal viewer, as did Nicholas Walton and Hugh Boag, agents to the Greenwich Hospital estate from the 1730s.[8] Blackett's experience of the expansion of the Stella Grand Lease colliery surely informed the system he built to support the huge growth of his lead business from the late 1660s. His first exposure to how accounting, reporting and management differed between collieries and trade probably came in his early days apprenticed to William Sherwood, who had coal mining interests at Whickham.

Management capability was arguably one of the northeast's key contributions to Britain's economic progress from the 17th century. The development and diffusion of management talent, accounting and culture, allowing larger workplaces and organisations to be controlled and run efficiently, is unspectacular and largely unseen. Unlike pioneering voyages, heroic discoveries and breakthrough inventions, it does not catch the eye of history, yet must be counted among the innovative mechanisms that ultimately enabled the special to become the normal, the chaotic and noisy bridgeheads of progress to become boring and regular reality. The increasing number of large collieries requiring deeper shafts and drainage and waggonways reaching from the staiths ever further inland demanded advanced management control as well as engineering skill alongside an open recruitment approach to attract and train practical and numerate talent. The importance of these skills can be seen in early examples of the export of regional management talent. William I's nephew and erstwhile apprentice William Blackett was opening up lead mines for James Standsfield in Scotland from the 1670s and William Wilson of Allendale was there as a mine agent from 1680. Sir John Clerk recruited a manager from Newcastle in the 1730s to take care of his Scottish colliery and Nicholas Emerson of Weardale was an agent helping develop lead mines in Montgomeryshire in Wales by the 1740s at the latest.[9] Pollard felt that the northern counties contributed a disproportionate share of British management talent by the later 18th century, and saw the link with mining.[10]

William Blackett's creation of a large and enduring business illustrates what it was possible to achieve in 17th-century northeastern England when there were opportunities to seize at scale and at speed. He was probably able to tap into an existing culture of managing growth and complexity, a relatively literate and numerate educated local population and then make his own contribution to deepening this distinctive regional capability that was soon being deployed elsewhere. The timing of the emergence in Britain of more elaborate forms of business organisation than the purely personal might need to be pushed back in recognition of the existence of precociously large enterprises in the North East before 1700.[11] Was this possible principally because of the early development of large-scale coal mining, itself stimulated by a constant flow of capital from the able, bold and calculating merchants who thrived in Newcastle?

Thirdly, another question arises from thinking about the nature of Newcastle's trade. How important was the town's business culture to accelerating economic integration in the 17th century? At the risk of grossly simplifying the work of economic historians in recent years, from the mid-17th century there was much greater regional specialisation in English farming.[12] Land use gravitated towards the type of farming best suited to prevailing soil and weather conditions. At an individual level it must often have meant wrenching disruption and great hardship, the result of unseen distant and baffling changes. Fewer people engaged in farming were largely able, however, to produce enough food, industrial raw materials and transport power – wool, hides, tallow, timber, and horses - to support more people working in other jobs in industry and services. We saw earlier, for example, how a new supply of lead from the North Pennines to meet overseas and London demand in the 1660s brought secondary changes in its train, adding many jobs in relatively highly paid mining work there in short order. Poor hill land was increasingly used for pasturing carrier horses and food was brought in from elsewhere to feed the miners.

It exemplifies the increased specialisation in land use and the allocation of labour to more productive occupations that were arguably the main drivers of the quickening pace of English economic growth in the later 17th century. Output per head of population rose by about 50% between 1650 and 1700. This was a remarkable increase in productivity before the era of widespread application of advanced technology to production.[13] Adam Smith identified the key principle with his famous example of workers in a pin factory becoming more productive by specialising in one process step each.[14] The division of labour he described within a single building was increasing across the country as a whole. Flourishing and highly specialised mining villages like Whickham and those fostered by Blackett at Allenheads and Coalcleugh illustrate this process, concentrations of non-agricultural activity seen in different locations around the country, sometimes described as 'proto-industrial'.

Greater specialisation implies increased trade and heavier demands on transport. Land carrier capacity to London from the provinces more than doubled between 1637 and 1715 and coastal shipping tonnage increased by two thirds between 1660 and 1702.[15] Many new jobs must have been in transport: leading packhorse trains, cattle droving, providing and servicing the carrier network, crewing cargo vessels on hazardous journeys around Britain's long coastline and the hard labour of lugging loads from horse to warehouse, from ship to shore. They played a vital part by moving more goods over longer distances from where they were more productively grown or made to where they were consumed, and then *vice versa* on the way back.

But this in turn relied upon millions of buying and selling

decisions by farmers, landowners, miners, merchants, shippers and shopkeepers. Merchants and traders were no more 'producers' than transport workers, but their gathering of price information, appraisal of shipping and sale risk and decisions to buy and sell were also critical to the sorting of production into increasingly advantageous locations. As Bristol merchant John Cary put it in 1695, 'let us begin with the shopkeeper or buyer or seller, who is the wheel whereon the inland trade turns'.[16] But exchange on any significant scale or over long distances was not for the faint of heart or shallow of pocket. Most of the small-scale traders, chapmen, packmen and carriers, earning a basic living in familiar country between markets a day's travel apart could not take risks with their meagre capital in extending their dealings beyond face-to-face contact with known counterparties. However, the greater distances implied by nationwide changes in farming and the evidence of a national English market for wheat by 1690, must have made longer distance transactions far more efficient and worthwhile than a long chain of local steps in which each middleman took a cut.[17] Risks doubtless increased alongside rising volumes of domestic and international trade, but clearly they were taken, presumably because of the opportunity for great profit and wealth.

Here is where the business culture of Newcastle mattered. Its merchants had long been used to building up the trust, long distance connections and the associated correspondence infrastructure necessary for successful international trade. Whether engaging in triangular trade between multiple locations, settling foreign currency accounts through Amsterdam and Hamburg or developing new markets, they were sophisticated entrepreneurs comfortable with risk and alert to calculating and exploiting new opportunities. They were also armed with the capital to do so, as shown by the rapid expansion of coal mining to supply London. These were the very cultural attributes needed to stretch and deepen the network of English internal trade and stimulate the specialisation of production and exchange that drove economic growth before the age of steam. According to Defoe, the domestic wholesalers and dealers who were at the centre of this work in the early 18th century were quite separate from the overseas merchants.[18] In Newcastle at least, however, we know that several overseas merchants were also engaged in domestic trade, principally to London, and in building networks deep into the north of England to bring goods to the quayside for onward despatch.

Fourthly, if this conjecture about Newcastle's mercantile culture is right, what about the other major English seaports? It seems unlikely that Newcastle was unique. The other great ports must have shared the attributes that fostered increased specialisation and trade over long distances. Exeter merchants played a key role in developing the cloth industry in 17th-century Devon, and Bristol had a similar relationship with lead mining on the Mendip hills from Tudor times. It was certainly at the centre of exchange networks along the western seaboard by 1700. Hull merchants, long familiar with northern European trade, were well placed to stimulate the West Riding cloth industry.[19] Above all there was London. They were all established ports, buttressed by restrictive mercantile guilds as in Newcastle, but their institutions surely had the same commercial incentives to be as open to talented apprentices and pragmatic adaptation as the Company of Merchant Adventurers on Tyneside.

By the same token, their civic leaders presumably shared the general desire of Newcastle's merchants for peace and open sea-lanes. Political stability and constraints on arbitrary state power were important to fostering confidence that their investments would not be confiscated during the years of profitable production needed to make them pay. Whether the Parliamentary ascendancy after 1645, the Restoration of Charles II or the political settlement of William and Mary after 1688/9's 'Glorious Revolution', Newcastle's pragmatic mercantile elite and its Parliamentary representatives were generally supportive. Stability was more important than ideology. Party badges were as likely to be the result of tactical prudence as of philosophical conviction, the choice of rational actors adjusting to prevailing circumstances. William Blackett I was only one of several men who remained active members of Newcastle's civic establishment under both Parliamentary and Royal rule. Members of the corporate bodies running the other major ports were surely similarly motivated. Through their Parliamentary representatives they must, together, have created a powerful national lobby for an environment conducive to business. Did the commercial outlook, encouragement of fresh talent, civic-mindedness, spirit and discipline of rational enquiry and favourable institutional environment seen by Mokyr as crucial to Britain's industrialisation a century later have England's expansive 17th-century seaports prominent amongst its cultural roots?[20]

There is surely plenty here to consider regarding Newcastle and the other great ports around England's coast. However, compared to its prominent role at the heart of a great industrial region by Victorian times, Newcastle's strategic and economic importance two centuries earlier has not received quite the same attention. The passage of time and limited survival of the fabric of the old town compared to the soaring engineering achievements of later days and the elegance of 'Grainger town' perhaps have something to do with this. So what survives of the Blacketts' domination of the town 300 years ago? What of their posterity?

Posterity

Sir Walter Blackett, as he became after inheriting his father Walter Calverley's baronetcy in 1749, was succeeded in 1777 by another Yorkshireman, his cousin Sir Thomas Wentworth. He too took the name Blackett, but not the Wallington estate, which went to Walter's favoured nephew Sir John Trevelyan. Thomas Wentworth/Blackett was in turn followed by his formidable daughter Diana Beaumont, whose shrewd custody of the family business between the 1790s and 1830s would probably have been admired by her great-great-grandfather William I.

Under the Blacketts and then the Beaumonts the lead business dominated the regional industry alongside the London Lead Company. After Joseph Richmond's son Henry died in 1776, the long-established management system was presided over by Sir Edward Blackett's grandson John Erasmus Blackett, four times mayor of Newcastle. Another distant relation, Christopher, descended from William I's eldest brother of the same name, was agent to Diana Beaumont in the early 19th century and he went on to support George Stephenson's work on steam locomotion at the Blackett estate and colliery at Wylam. In a distant echo of the days of William III, Diana's wayward son and heir Thomas Wentworth Beaumont, TWB, was greatly assisted in preserving the business in the early Victorian period by a mature corporate structure and competent managers. Although the lead market never again reached the heights scaled in the 1820s, the Beaumont concern, still centred in Allendale and Weardale, survived for another century. When TWB's son, Wentworth Blackett Beaumont (note that middle name) was elevated to the peerage in 1906 for long service to politics as a Whig/Liberal MP, he took the name Lord Allendale, thereby recognising the mainspring of the family's wealth over more than two centuries. The lead business was finally wound up in the 1920s, but land acquired by Williams I and II is still owned by Allendale Estates and run by the Fourth Viscount Allendale and his son the Hon. Wentworth Beaumont. This includes the site of the Dukesfield smelting mill, the first known land purchase by William I in 1665.[21]

Sir Edward Blackett's descendants returned from Yorkshire to the Tyne Valley in the mid-18th century. Through the marriage in 1751 of John Erasmus Blackett's eldest brother William to the granddaughter of John Douglas, Newcastle's busy Restoration period lawyer, the Blacketts acquired land in the Matfen area.[22] It was another of the estates developed as a successful enterprise by an energetic and able product of the town's nursery of commercial talent in the late 17th century. The baronetcy given to William I by King Charles II in 1673 is still in place today, held by Sir Hugh Blackett, twelfth baronet, who runs Matfen Estates.

So the families are still nearby, but there are few material remains today of the 17th-century Blacketts. The lead agents' houses at Dukesfield, Fallowfield, Allenheads and Newhouse in Weardale are still there, silent monuments to the family's elaborate management structure. The bridge over the Tyne at Corbridge stands in mute and subtle tribute to William I's skills of political manipulation. Wallington Hall is a popular visitor destination but more generally associated today with the Trevelyan family. The identification of many of its Blackett portraits is uncertain.

Fewer still are the traces of the family in Newcastle. Greyfriars and its grounds were swept away in a new era of energetic civic confidence in the early 19th century by the 'Grainger town' development that graces the town to this day. Blackett Street still runs nearby, on the line of the old town wall past the Monument, though it is named after John Erasmus Blackett rather than his great-grandfather William I. The memorial tablet marking the place of interment of the three Sir Williams in St. Nicholas' church is no longer present.* William I's old house at Bridge End has long since disappeared. Its site is occupied by the toll house built with the hydraulic Swing Bridge by the great engineer William Armstrong in the 1870s, a much better-known historical figure, and understandably so.

Although there is no hint that this site was once the nerve centre of William I's business, it is a good place to contemplate his life and what his times and the town enabled him to achieve. Above the quayside pathway runs the Swing Bridge where the old town bridge once stood, connecting Newcastle to Gateshead and the south by road. Just downstream beyond the arch are the large first-floor windows of the Guildhall, where the Common Council, merchants' company and hostmen gathered, now overshadowed by the soaring 20th century Tyne Bridge, alive with the wheeling and squealing of kittiwakes. The offices and bar below the Guildhall were once the town's Exchange, epicentre of the information flow, gossip, haggling, buying and selling of the great trading network that spread out across northern Europe. For all the trauma and upheaval of the 17th century, the town's merchants who met there operated in an environment that was more open and stimulating than repressed by vested interests and ancient convention. Turning to look out at the river, strong incoming tides can hold up its flow and sometimes even appear to reverse it. But then, like its historic commerce, the Tyne surges on again to the east, out to the open sea and the world.

---

* It was still there in the early 1890s, but refurbishment of the cathedral in 2020 allowed the careful examination of the surviving memorial stones, which confirmed its absence: Welford, *Men of Mark*, Vol 1, (1895), p.319; Pat Halcro, *pers comm.*

Appendices and Bibliography

Frequent references in the text to various appendices indicate the dependence of the arguments and findings on a broad foundation of primary research, consideration and analysis. The full set of six appendices can be downloaded from dukesfield.org.uk/appendices. They contain discussion of the usefulness and reliability of the source material, methodologies and assumptions, the extended numerical tables and other conclusions derived from that material and the balance of judgement regarding their likely accuracy and bias. The rest of this section provides a very short guide to the content of the appendices by way of a brief overview of the principal sources used and an introduction for those who wish to investigate further.

Appendix 1: Trade

This appendix focuses on estimating the overall level of Newcastle's overseas and domestic trade from the 1630s to the 1660s, the years covering William Blackett I's apprenticeship and the subsequent period in which trading was his main business activity. The principal surviving sources available from which the changing volume – if not the content - of maritime trade is assessed are described, reviewed and the principal interpretative problems identified: Exchequer customs port books, Newcastle Corporation's Chamberlain accounts, Trinity House records and the Danish Sound Toll records. Various sources are compared in order to assess the reliability of the customs port books. They are also used as the basis for estimating the value of Blackett's import and export trade in 1661.

Appendix 2: Coal

For coal, the seventeenth century context is reasonably clear given the amount of research conducted on Tyneside mining over many years, and I have drawn on a number of key works from which regional data on coal weights and measures, production and prices have been extracted and considered. As far as the output from the Blackett family's own mines is concerned, a patchy variety of primary sources have survived, mainly in Northumberland, Tyne and Wear, Durham and Newcastle university libraries, and the Duke of Northumberland's Alnwick Castle archives. Summary estimates and interpolations have been constructed from these sources for their principal known mines: at Stella, Winlaton, Whorlton Moor, Kenton, Heworth and Gateshead Fell. These direct accounts and those from other contemporary mines in the region have also been used to estimate key capital and operating cost factors – sinking shafts, drainage, waggonways, hewing, land and river transport, along with an attempt to assess how they varied based on mine location and geology. Views and assumptions, caveats and cautions on price and cost are then brought together to assess profitability and the return on investment through time.

Appendix 3: Lead

This is organised in the same way as Appendix 2, including discussion of contemporary weights: bings and fothers in lead's case. Determining overall production of lead is difficult because the industry has attracted only a fraction of the attention bestowed upon coal by economic historians. Little more than occasional snapshots are available, complemented by estimates of the Baltic trade through the Danish Sound between the 1630s and 1720s, and the reasoning behind likely demand for lead to rebuild London after the Great Fire of 1666. North Pennines production is assessed using the infrequent overseas and coastal Exchequer customs port books for Newcastle, Sunderland and Stockton. The Blackett share of exports can be counted in some of the years covered, complemented in the mid-1670s by the evidence of Michael Blackett's reports. A price series for lead at Newcastle and Stockton between 1666 and 1735 has been constructed from a range of primary and secondary sources of varying reliability. Capital and operating cost estimates, including an allowance for fixed asset depreciation, are assembled from various cost account records in the same way as for coal, covering mining, carriage, smelting, refining and working capital tied up in ore, lead and unpaid sales. Detailed assumptions are set out and assessed from which William I's profitability and return on investment is estimated for the mid-1670s with a high level of caution. The greater detail extracted from later company accounts and sales ledgers permits more confident conclusions on turnover and profitability from the mid-1720s, and a measure of comparison with the performance of the London lead Company in 1738 and 1750. A new list of known North Pennines smelting mills in the seventeenth and early eighteenth centuries is also included.

Appendix 4: Estate Valuations

These are estimated for the key milestones of the deaths of the three Sir Williams in 1680, 1705 and 1728, together with an assessment of Walter Blackett's net worth in the 1730s. Though reliant on limited contemporary valuations in estate papers and rentals from various dates they still provide some quantitative perspective alongside the largely narrative account of their careers and the development of the family business. They are estimated based on likely market valuations, but a final section on asset allocation compares these with estimates of historic cost.

Appendix 5: The Wallington Portraits

Despite the inscriptions added to the portraits of many members of the Blackett family at Wallington Hall, now owned by the National Trust, their true identification remains highly problematic for the inscriptions were in all likelihood added at a much later date. This illustrated appendix nevertheless seeks to identify the central family characters with reference to artistic styles and the context in which they are found alongside other portraits.

Appendix 6: Family Trees

Fuller details of family members, dates and relationships are shown in versions of the three family trees included above as Figures 2.2, 4.1 and 10.1.

Bibliography

All manuscript, printed primary and secondary sources cited in the course of this book are indicated in the footnotes. They are also drawn together in a full bibliography which can be found alongside the appendices described above.

Guide to abbreviations used in notes

AA *Archaeologia Aeliana* followed by series and volume number
BL British Library
CSPD *Calendar of State Papers Domestic* transcribed volumes:
Charles I, 1638-9, ed. J.Bruce & W.D.Hamilton, (1871)
Charles II, 1660-1, ed. M.A.E.Green, (1860)
Charles II, 1665-6, ed. M.A.E.Green, (1864)
Charles II, 1666-7, ed. M.A.E.Green, (1864)
Charles II, 1673-5, ed. F.H.B. Daniel, (1904)
Charles II, 1683-4, ed. F.H.B. Daniel and F.Bickley, (1938)
Charles II, 1684-5, ed. F.H.B. Daniel and F.Bickley, (1938)
Charles II, Addenda, 1660-85, ed. F.H.B. Daniel and F.Bickley, (1938)
Contents available at British History Online (british-history.ac.uk)
CTB *Calendar of Treasury Books* transcribed volumes as follows:
1672-5, Vol 4, ed W.A.Shaw, (1909)
1676-9, Vol 5, ed W.A.Shaw, (1911)
1685-9, Vol 8, ed W.A.Shaw, (1923)
Contents available at British History Online (british-history.ac.uk)
DCRO Durham County Record Office
DD Dukesfield documents, a free online archive of transcripts of many documents centred on the Blackett family and northern lead industry: www.dukesfield.org.uk/documents. Transcripts of many of the original manuscripts referred to in this book are available in DD, including the letters of Michael and Edward Blackett, Joseph Richmond and Ralph Grey and the wills of William Blackett I-III.
DN Archives of the Duke of Northumberland at Alnwick Castle
DPR1 Durham Probate Registry original wills and associated documents held by DULASC. Many of the wills can be viewed online via the North East Inheritance database: http://familyrecords.dur.ac.uk/nei/data/intro.php
DULASC Durham University Library, Archives and Specials Collections

EconHR *The Economic History Review*
Fighting Trade G.Bennett, E.Clavering, and A.Rounding, *A Fighting Trade. Rail Transport in Tyne Coal 1600-1800*, (1989)
Hatcher J.Hatcher, *The History of the British Coal Industry*, Vol 1 (1993)
HH Hexham Historian
HistParl *History of Parliament: the House of Commons* volumes as follows:
    1604-1629 ed. A.Thrush and J.P. Ferris (2010)
    1660-1690 ed. B.D.Henning (1983)
    1690-1715 ed. D. Hayton, E. Cruickshanks and S. Handley (2002)
    1715-1754 ed. R.Sedgwick (1970)
Contents available at www.historyofparliamentonline.org
HN *A History of Northumberland* volumes as follows:
    3, A.B.Hinds, *Hexhamshire Part 1*, (1896)
    4, J.C.Hodgson, *Hexhamshire Part 2*, (1897)
    6, J.C.Hodgson, *Bywell St.Peter, Bywell St.Andrew, Slaley*, (1902)
    9, H.H.E.Craster, *Earsdon and Horton*, (1909)
    10, H.H.E.Craster, *Corbridge*, (1914)
    12, M.H.Dodds, *Ovingham, Stamfordham and Ponteland*, (1926)
    13, M.H.Dodds, *Heddon on the Wall, Newburn, Long Benton and Wallsend*, (1930)
    15, M.H.Dodds, *Simonburn, Rothbury, Alwinton*, (1940)
Hostmen F.W.Dendy (ed), *Extracts from the records of the Company of Hostmen of Newcastle-upon-Tyne*, SS 105, (1901)
Howell R.Howell, *Newcastle-upon-Tyne and the Puritan Revolution*, (1967)
LMA London Metropolitan Archives
MA Records-1 J.R.Boyle and F.W.Dendy (eds), *Extracts from the Records of the Merchant Adventurers of Newcastle-upon-Tyne*, SS 93, (1895)
MA Records-2 F.W.Dendy (ed), *Extracts From the Records of the Merchant Adventurers of Newcastle-Upon-Tyne*, SS 101, (1899)
MB/ MBL Michael Blackett and his letters, two volumes of manuscript copy out-letters in Cambridge University Library Special Collections: MS.Add .91 (9 Sep 1675 - 13 Feb 1677), Dd 7/26 (16 Feb 1677 – 15 Jun 1683). Transcripts available in DD. Letter dates given in the text indicate the volume in which the original is found. His own letters are indicated by use of his initials; those by others by MBL.
NC *Newcastle Courant*
NEIMME North of England Institute of Mining and Mechanical Engineers
NRO Northumberland Record Office, now Northumberland Archives at Woodhorn
NRS National Records Scotland
ODNB H.C.G.Matthew and B.Harrison, (eds), *Oxford Dictionary of National Biography*, (2004)
PSAN *Proceedings of the Society of Antiquaries of Newcastle-upon-Tyne*
SS Surtees Society
TNA The National Archives
TWA Tyne and Wear Archives

Notes and References

Chapter One: Newcastle

[1] After London, Norwich and Bristol: P.J.Corfield, 'Norwich on the cusp -from second city to regional capital', in C.Rawcliffe and R.Wilson (eds), *Norwich since 1550*, (2004), Table 3. Even today, over 130 years since it was formally elevated to city status, Newcastle is still generally referred to as 'the town'.

[2] BL Add Ms 27,420.

[3] 60 volleys at half minute intervals: Executorship accounts: NRO 11603/Box 16.

[4] *NC*, 12 Oct 1728. A detailed manuscript account now available as BL Add MS 27,421 was summarised in M.A.Richardson 'Obsequies of Certain of the family of Blackett of Newcastle' in *Reprints of Rare Tracts,* Vol 1, (1847).

[5] The executors accounts include £2 6s spent on 'carpentry work to the state room' in readiness for the funeral: Executorship accounts.

[6] Today's map of this part of Newcastle is quite different because of the 19th-century development of 'Grainger town', which fills out the space previously occupied by Greyfriars and its grounds. The Theatre Royal overlies the site of the mansion. Blackett Street –a later mark of the family's legacy- follows the line of the old town wall between Pilgrim Street and Percy Street. The likeliest processional route led up Pilgrim Street and through the town gate into the straggling suburb already developing along Northumberland Street and then back down the present Percy Street, through the walls again, tracking the Greyfriars boundary to the left into Newgate Street and so to Fleshmarket and the church.

[7] H.Bourne, *History of Newcastle* (1736), p.72. The memorial slabs were moved when the church was restored in 1783-4.

[8] Richardson, 'Obsequies', *op cit*, pp.21-30.

[9] Accounts for 1729, NRO 672/E/1B/2.

[10] Joseph Richmond to William Wentworth, 15 October 1728, NRO 673/2.

[11] Hatcher, Table 14.1(a), pp.487-9.

[12] Riddell: J.C.Hodgson (ed), *Wills and Inventories from the Registry at Durham Vol III*, SS 112, (1906) p.167; Kirkley: DPR1/1/1620/K2.

[13] L.Muller, 'Britain and Sweden: the changing pattern of commodity exchange 1650-1680' in P Salmon and T Barrow (eds), *Britain and the Baltic*, (2003), p.69. For Sound Toll records, see Appendix 1.5.

[14] A.Burn, 'Work and Society in Newcastle upon Tyne, c. 1600-1710', University of Durham, Ph.D thesis, (2014), pp.42-3.

[15] The importance of Newcastle's cloth market is exemplified by the consignment of Yorkshire cloth to Christopher Lowther in Dublin in 1632 that had been bought in Newcastle, carried overland to Whitehaven and thence across the Irish Sea: D.R.Hainsworth (ed), *Commercial papers of Sir Christopher Lowther 1611-1644*, SS 189, (1977), p.6.

[16] The huge tonnages of coal command attention but it rarely sold in Newcastle outside the range of 3s to 4s per ton, so 300,000 tons in 1616 was worth perhaps £60,000 as it moved from keel to ship: Hatcher, p.488. The cloth export trade alone was valued at £37,800 in 1616: quoted in Howell's indispensable study of Newcastle before and during the English Civil War: Howell, p.20.

[17] Calculated from the apprentice registers given in MA Records-2.

[18] Mann and Briggs: MA Records-2, pp.235, 253,266. Archer: DPR1/1/1647 /A5.

[19] The intricate deal of which this change was part perfectly illustrates the relation-

ships of the Newcastle Corporation, the Crown, the Bishopric of Durham and the shrewd and ruthless Newcastle 'lords of coal' in the later Tudor period: D.Levine and K.Wrightson, *The Making of an Industrial Society, Whickham 1560-1765*, (1991), pp.18-24.

[20] MA Records-1, p. 135.

[21] *Hostmen*, pp.266-7. Most of the rest were probably also merchant company members, the real seat of power in Newcastle.

[22] From a 1630s account of a Catholic lady, published in the 19th century: William Palmes, *Life of Mrs. Dorothy Lawson, of St. Anthony's, near Newcastle-upon-Tyne*, (1851) p.52.

[23] Eneas Mackenzie, *Historical Account of Newcastle-Upon-Tyne Including the Borough of Gateshead* (1827) p.612. Although written two centuries later Mackenzie's account still reflected 17th-century procedure and, therefore, institutional endurance.

[24] Howell, p.46.

[25] *Ibid*, p.125. In the 22 general elections held during the 17th century it appears there were contests in Newcastle on just three occasions: in 1640, 1661, and 1685: C.H.Hunter-Blair, 'Members of Parliament for Northumberland and Newcastle-upon-Tyne, 1559-1831', *AA*, 4th ser., 23, (1945); *HistParl*, Constituencies, Newcastle: 1604-29 (S.Healy), 1660-90 (G.Hampson), 1690-1715, (E.Cruikshanks, R.Harrison). 'Inner Ring': Howell, pp.39-41.

[26] Derived from data in Burn, thesis, *op cit*, table 4.2, p.106.

[27] See J.M.Fewster, *The Keelmen of Tyneside. Labour Organisation and Conflict in the North-East Coal Industry, 1600-1830*, (2011), and A.Burn, 'Seasonal work and welfare in an early industrial town: Newcastle upon Tyne, 1600–1700', *Continuity and Change* 32 (2), 2017.

[28] K. Wrightson, *Ralph Tailor's Summer: A Scrivener, His City and the Plague*, (2011), p.11. See also Simon Healy, 'The Tyneside Lobby on the Thames: Politics and Economic Issues, c.1580-1630' in D.Newton and A.Pollard (eds), *Newcastle and Gateshead before 1700*, (2009), pp.219-40.

[29] *ibid*, p.174.

[30] W.Gray, *Chorographia, or A Survey of Newcastle upon Tyne 1649*, (6th edition 1883), p.90.

[31] Calculated from the tables compiled in MA Records-2.

[32] Bewick: MA Records-2, p.xiii; R.Welford, *Men of Mark 'Twixt Tyne and Tweed*, Vol 1, (1895), p.280; Bonner: DPR1/1/1660/B3.

[33] C.Brooks, 'Apprenticeship, Social Mobility and the Middling Sort, 1550-1800' in J.Barry and C.Brooks (eds), *The Middling Sort of People: Culture, Society and Politics in England, 1550-1800* (1994), pp. 52-83.

[34] MA Records-1, pp.11-2.

[35] *Fighting Trade*, Vol 1, pp.20-1.

[36] Succinct biographical summaries are provided by M.Blackett-Ord, *ODNB*, and A.W.Purdue, *The Ship That Came Home*, (2004), pp.19-32. Allan Kirtley, Patricia Longbottom and Martin Blackett, *A History of the Blacketts*, (2013), gives a genealogical account of the Blackett family over the centuries.

[37] C. Trevelyan, *Wallington, Its History and Treasures*, (1930), pp.10.

[38] J.Straker, *Memoirs of the Public Life of Sir Walter Blackett of Wallington*, (1819), pp27-8.

[39] Welford passed on the anecdote uncritically as a mark of the 'shrewdness of William Blackett at the beginning of his career' (*Men of Mark, op cit*, 1, p.298) but both Blackett-Ord and Purdue, *Ship That Came Home*, p.21 are more circumspect. See also Ap-

pendix 1.6.
[40] Plates 21-23, 25-6, 28, and Appendix 5.
[41] R.Burt, 'Lead Production in England and Wales, 1700-1770', *EconHR*, 22, (1969), p. 267.
[42] J.M.Ellis, 'A Bold Adventurer: The Business Fortunes of William Cotesworth, c.1668-1726', *Northern History*, (1981); M.W.Flinn, *Men of Iron* (1962).

Chapter Two: Hamsterley to Gateshead

[1] The early genealogy of the Blacketts confused local historian H. Conyers Surtees in the early 20th century whose laborious notes are now in Durham Cathedral Library (GB-034-SUR/3,5,22) but has more recently been unravelled by Kirtley *et al*, *op cit*, and their informative website www.theblacketts.com. The basic genealogy of the family covered in this chapter is taken from chapter 3 of their book, pp.41-51, unless otherwise stated.
[2] Inquisition Post Mortem of George Blackett 30 Aug 1628 TNA DURH 3/186 f14
[3] J.Foster (ed), *Pedigrees recorded at the Visitations of the county palatine of Durham,* (1887): Blackett of Woodcrofte pp.16-7, 1575.
[4] NRO ZBK/B/1/2; Durham Cathedral Library Surtees MS SUR 5, f.34.
[5] DPR1/1/1628/B5, and published in H.M.Wood, (ed), *Wills and Inventories from the Registry at Durham, Part IV*, SS 142, (1929, reprinted 1968), p 213-215
[6] A.T.Brown, *Rural Society and Economic Change in County Durham, Recession and Recovery, c.1400-16140*, (2015), esp pp.227-47. Edward was called upon to appraise and value the goods of his fellow comfortable farmers, such as those of near neighbour John Lisle, gentleman of Bedburn Park in 1623: Atkinson, J.A., Flynn, B. and others (eds) *Darlington Wills and Inventories 1600-1625* SS 201, (1993), pp.191-5.
[7] C.Fraser (ed), *Durham Quarter Session Rolls 1471-1625,* SS 199, (1991), p.195; Foster, *Pedigrees, op cit*:, Lilburne of Thickley pp.214-5.
[8] Attributed to David Jenkins, Welsh royalist judge imprisoned with Lilburne: *Notes and Queries*, 4, (1852), p.134. For biographies of Robert and John see B.Coward, 'Lilburne, Robert (*bap.* 1614, *d.* 1665)', and A.Sharp, 'Lilburne, John (1615?–1657)', *ODNB*.
[10] M.Meikle, 'The Scottish Covenanters and the Borough of Sunderland 1639-1647. A Hidden Axis of the British Civil Wars', *Northern History*, 54:2, (2017), pp.172.
[11] NRO ZBK/B/1/10 Bargain and sale of Hoppyland, 1678-9.
[12] Fraser, *op cit*, p.186.
[13] DPR1/1/1611/C12 William CROOKE, yeoman, of Wolsingham in the countie of Durham dated 25 August 1611 probate 7 December 1611
[14] Gateshead Churchwardens Accounts 1626-40, DCRO, EP/Ga.SM 4/1 f24; TWA GU.MA 3 1 f114.
[15] DULASC TUR (1958) 25 Sale deed 28 Jan 1631 of Red House at Middleton St. George
[16] MA Records-2, p.255 TWA GU.MA/3/1 f122v
[17] DPR1/1/1640/T2, (14th April 1640) William Thomson, Sunderland Pans. Blackett's signature closely resembles that given on the Hoppyland purchase deed of 1618: NRO ZBK/B/1/2. In September 1640 the Scottish army occupied Sunderland and remained for a year: Meikle, *op cit*, pp.170-1. It was almost certainly William Snr who signed the Protestation return in Hamsterley in February 1641: H. M. Wood, (ed.), *Durham Protestations*, SS 135, (1922).

[18] The Durham Chapter collected £7 6s from *'tenants for salt rent'* at Cowpen near Billingham in the 1620s, DULASC: DCD/E/Ba Miscellaneous surveys

[19] J.M.Ellis, 'The Decline and Fall of the Tyneside Salt Industry, 1660-1790. A Re-examination', *EconHR*, 33.1, (1980) pp.45-58.

[20] DULASC DCD/E/Ba, Miscellaneous surveys; Harle - DPR1/1/1636/H4.

[21] M.Meikle andC.Newman, *Sunderland and its origins, monks to mariners*, (2007), pp.115-6; Briggs et al, *Sunderland Wills and Inventories*, SS 214,(2010).

[22] *Englands Grievance Discovered in relation to the Coal Trade*, (1655).

[23] Howell, pp.34,58; TWA Newcastle Chamberlains Accounts MD.NC/FN/11-13; P.D.Wright, 'The Ballast Trade: An Economic Driver In Seventeenth And Eighteenth century Newcastle Upon Tyne', *Northern History*, (2020). Inevitably some ballast was dumped in the river itself to avoid charges, increasing navigation hazards.

[24] TWA MD.CC/2/1 ff 294. The common council minutes of the 1640s record frequent complaints about ballast management and claims for overdue payment from shore keepers.

[25] C.S.Terry, 'The Visit of Charles I to Newcastle in 1633, 1639, 1641, 1646-7, with some notes on contemporary Local history', *AA*, 2nd ser., 21, 1899, pp.87-8. Chapman's will: DPR1/1/1633/C4.

[26] *HN*, 12, pp.373-5; DPR1/1/1631/F3. Henry and Hugh were the Blackett appraisers of Fenwick's will, neither of whom could sign their names.

[27] DULASC DDR/EJ/PRC/2/1637/1; MA Records-2, p.271. A 19th-century descendant claimed Christopher was an officer in the royalist army during the Civil War, but there is no mention of him in any of the known lists of Royalist officers: Purdue, *Ship That Came Home*, pp.10,20; P.R.Newman, *Royalist Officers in England and Wales, 1642-1660: A Biographical Dictionary*, (1981).

[28] *HN*, 12, p.230.

[1] Deposition of George Myers of Rookhope: TNA E 134/36Chas2/Mich 47. In the years in which William Snr was back in Hamsterley in Weardale, after 1641, the moor-mastership was held by a Richard Hutton of nearby Hunwick, in trust for Humphrey Wharton, a minor. Hutton appears to have known George Lilburne: Thomas Wharton's will 1641: TNA PROB 11/196/80.

[29] MA Records-1, p.11. If not otherwise stated, all references to the company's rules are taken from this volume.

[30] MA Records-2. John Crooke retained his links to his Wolsingham home, taking on John Snow from there as apprentice in 1626; pp.219, 245. However, he took on neither of his Blackett great-nephews, possibly because he had fallen on hard times. In 1641 his widow obtained some relief from the merchant company for her 'great poverty' and funeral debt: MA Records-1, p.130. William Crooke's will: DPR1/1/1611/C12.

[31] Based on an annual food budget for a keelman, wife and 3 children in the 1620s, around £7/year can be allowed for William and Isabel Blackett once the children had left. Doubling this allows a generous measure for accommodation, fuel and clothing. A.Burn, 'Seasonal work' *op cit*, Table 1, p.163.

[32] R.Grassby, *The business community of seventeenth-century England*, (1995), pp.261-2.

Chapter Three: Troublesome Tymes

[1] W.H.D.Longstaffe (ed), *Memoirs of the life of Ambrose Barnes*, SS 50, (1867), p.37.

[2] MA Records-1, p.22.
[3] *ibid*, p.162.
[4] Quoted and analysed in P.D.Wright, *Life on the Tyne: Water Trades on the Lower River Tyne in the Seventeenth and Eighteenth Centuries, a Reappraisal*, (2014), chapter 7.
[5] Newcastle Common Council order book, TWA MD/NC/1/3 ff.227-8. Ord was born in 1657; B.Mains and A.Tuck, (eds), *Royal Grammar School, Newcastle upon Tyne: a history of the school in its community*, (1985), pp.31-7.
[6] Sunderland school quoted in Howell, p.329; J.Taylor, *Journey to Edenborough*, ed. Wm Cowan, (1903), p.86, which from internal evidence can be dated to 1706. All Saints: Bourne, *op cit*, pp. 102, 106.
[7] W.Banson, *The Merchant's Penman*, (1702), and *An Arithmetical Exercise*, (1709). The latter included weights, measures, exchange rates and techniques to carry out calculations of interest rates, discount, allocation of profit shares in trade ventures, ships and collieries and rates of return based on time invested; J.Hunter, (ed) *The Diary of Ralph Thoresby*, (1830), Vol 1, pp.428-9.
[8] W.London, *A Catalogue of the most vendible Books in England*, (1658), https://corbettsbookshop.omeka.net/, S.Carter and K.Gibson, 'Printed Music in the Provinces', *The Library*, (2017).
[9] Blackett of Wylam papers, NRO ZBK/B/1/5
[10] Available from Google Books. Its existence was signalled down the years to Jennifer Britton of the Dukesfield Documents team in one of Michael Blackett's letters. He asked for a copy to be sent up to him from London: MB to Humphrey Willett, 27 Aug 1678.
[11] *ibid*, p.134. Vernon's book followed the style of an earlier work of 1636 by Richard Dafforne, *The Merchant's Mirror*, popular for being methodical, orderly and systematic. Was this new work at William I's elbow in his master's house? All such books, and there were many, followed the 1494 work of Italian mathematician Luca Pacioli: J. Gleeson-White, *Double Entry. How the Merchants of Venice created modern Finance* (2011), p.121.
[12] MA Records-1, p.127-8.
[13] *ibid*, p.145. Edward's term was over at Christmas 1640, and the next few years were indeed 'troublesome times' in Newcastle, as we shall see. Edward eventually obtained his freedom in 1647.
[14] Edward Blackett married Christiana Hering in Amsterdam in 1643. Their offspring are given in Appendix 6, Table A6.2. Stadsarchief Amsterdam, DTB 137, pp.70-88; archive 5001, DTB 459, p.295: https://www.openarch.nl/.
[15] Wm Blackett to Jacob Momma-Reenstierna, Sweden, July-Sept 1670: Sweden Riksarchivet, Momma-Reenstierna MSS, E2499
[16] Carr: MA Records-1, p.137; John Lancaster's will: DPR1/1/1660/L2.
[17] Wrightson, *Ralph Tailor, op cit*. Tailor was a professional legal writer, and therefore much in demand during that dreadful summer. In August he had climbed onto the town wall to lean against the upper window of a plague victim to take the verbal declaration of his hurried last will and testament through the sealed casement. Hundreds of victims were buried each week.
[18] Longstaffe, *op cit*, p.38. Based on the dates of his apprenticeship under Rawling this must have been during the plague outbreak of 1651. The house was on Sandhill across the road from the Exchange.
[19] Wrightson, *op cit*, p.52. Weekly mortality fell sharply from October onwards, though the infection remained present until into December, and apparently still claimed vic-

tims into 1637: p.31.
[20] *CSPD, 1638-9*, p.260. See also J.U.Nef, *The Rise of the British Coal Industry* (1932), Vol II, p.115.
[21] S.Schama, *A History of Britain, The British Wars 1603-1776*, (2001), pp. 86-97.
[22] A.W.Purdue, *Newcastle The Biography*, (2011), pp.81-3; Howell, chapters III and IV.
[23] *Ibid*, pp.118-22.
[24] *Ibid*, pp.133-7. The Common Council under Bewick agreed in September 1640 to pay £200 per day to the Scots, so that the army could 'buy' its provisions.
[25] The Scots left in August 1641 after being granted £80,000 of 'brotherly assistance' from an English Parliament eager to avoid another winter of interrupted coal supplies: M.R.Greenhall, 'The Evolution of the British Economy: Anglo-Scottish Trade and Political Union, an Inter-Regional Perspective, 1580-1750', Durham Ph.D thesis, (2011), pp.111-14.
[26] Howell, pp.154-6. Municipal receipts, largely derived from tolls on trade and which in normal times might reach £7,500, plummeted to £243 in 1643-4. New apprenticeships also fell sharply in many of the town's guilds.
[27] R.Serdiville and J.Sadler, *The Great Siege of Newcastle 1644*, (2011), chapter 7.
[28] Levine and Wrightson, *op cit*, pp. 38, 109-10. Much of the detailed knowledge we have today on Whickham coal derives from the stream of litigation between the many coal owners at work here in the 17th century.
[29] *Hostmen*, pp. 66, 69, 73. The quota was almost certainly expressed in 'vending tenns' of 26.5 tons (see Appendix 2.1) making Sherwood's quota of 240 tenns in 1617 equal to 6,360 tons. Estimated productivity of 150-200 tons/employee/year, implies a total of around 40 miners: Hatcher, pp.344-6.
[30] R.Welford, *History of Newcastle and Gateshead*, Vol 3, (1887), p.237-8.
[31] TNA E 179/158/104, Newgate Ward. An undated manuscript quoted by Brand in his *History and Antiquities of Newcastle* (1789) as being amongst the archives of the corporation, shows this to have been a very small ward, consisting of little more than the east side of Fleshmarket, given under its earlier name of Clothmarket; pp. 7, 13.
[32] Gray, *Chorographia, op cit*, p.68.
[33] St. Nicholas' burial registers, NRO EP 86/1.
[34] TWA GU.MA.3/3; MA Records-1, pp.16-7, 130.
[35] DPR1/1/1635/C2.
[36] MA Records-1, pp.131,149-151; will TNA PROB 11/211. Joan wished to be buried with her late husband Ralph at St. Nicholas' church. Her daughter Jane was married to Samuel Rawling, master of Ambrose Barnes, who lived just around the corner in Sandhill.
[37] TWA GU.MA/3/3

Chapter Four: Kirkleys and Commonwealth

[1] Grassby, *op cit,* p.236; Sweden Riksarchivet 756/1/B 11/3 Court papers 1660-4.
[2] H.Roseveare (ed), *Markets and Merchants of the Late Seventeenth Century*, (1991), pp.66, 84, 92, 105. The firmest conclusion to be drawn is of wide fluctuations from year to year, port to port, commodity to commodity.
[3] Drawing on Pete Lee's tabulation of Newcastle Overseas Exchequer Port Book, 1676: TNA E 190/196/6.
[4] Calculated as follows: £250 spent on cloth six months earlier, £150 on various ship-

ping, customs, port dues and overseas agents fees and commissions three months earlier. The cost of borrowing £400 for a weighted average loan period of five months, using the prevailing rate of interest of 6%, is £10.

[5] Grassby, *op cit*, p.83.
[6] R.Grey to G.Potts 24 Jan 1674, NRO 753/J.
[7] D.Defoe, *The Compleat Tradesman*, (1726), Vol 1, p.77.
[8] King quoted in Grassby, *op cit*, p.256; Marescoe: Roseveare, *op cit*, pp.17-8; P.Earle, *The Making of the English Middle Class*, (1989), p.112.
[9] J.M.Ellis, 'A Study of the Business Fortunes of William Cotesworth, c.1668-1726', unpublished Oxford D.Phil thesis, 1975, p.179.
[10] By the 1660s, such bequests might have supported six young merchants at any one time with sums from £25 up to £100, perhaps just one in seven of new freemen. Calculated using E.M.Halcrow, B.Harbottle, J.Slipper, 'Merchant Charities of Newcastle-upon-Tyne', *AA* 4th ser., 30, (1952), and MA Records-1, pp.264-5.
[11] J.M.Ellis, Bold Adventurer, *op cit*, p.120.
[12] DPR1/1/1620/K2. His gross estate was valued at around £2,100 in 1621, but this excludes debts owed, which must be expected on any active merchant's balance sheet.
[13] Welford, *Men of Mark*, *op cit*, 1, pp.517-9.
[14] Richard Warren and Edward Jermyn *vs* Elizabeth Kirkley, widow: TNA E 134/11Chas1/Mich16 & E 134/12Chas1/East1, C 8/55/189; Welford, *Hist Newcastle, op cit*, 3, pp.237-8.
[15] MA Records-1, p.135.
[16] In his will of 7 July 1636 Timothy Cooke commended his 'poor fainting soule' to God's mercy. Two infant children had been buried on the 8th and 12th May. DPR1/1/1636/C9. Ann Cooke's probate bond 9 Dec 1638: DPR1/3/1638/B295.
[17] Howell, p.320.
[18] TNA PROB 11/215/681. It was dated three days before she died.
[19] MA Records-2, p.265, TNA PROB 11/215/681. Glover was left £1 by Elizabeth.
[20] Blackett had taken on the Presbyterian Ambrose Barnes in August 1646. Barnes was set over to Rawling in July 1647 and Rawling's apprentice George Carter was set over to Blackett on the same day: MA Records-2, p.263.
[21] Howell, pp. 169-75; Purdue, *Newcastle, op cit*, p.85.
[22] Haselrig to Wm Lenthall, speaker of the House of Commons, 13 Sep 1649: Bodleian Library Oxford, MS Tanner 56 fol. 103.
[23] Howell, pp. 227-32.
[24] C. Pamela Graves, 'Building a New Jerusalem: The Meaning of a Group of Merchant Houses in Seventeenth-Century Newcastle upon Tyne, England', *International Journal of Historical Archaeology*, Vol. 13, No. 4 (2009), pp. 385-408.
[25] Howell, pp.232-4.
[26] MA Records-2, p.69; William Bonner's will: DPR1/1/1665/B9.
[27] M.Dodds, *Extracts from the Newcastle-upon-Tyne Council Minute Book 1639-56*, (1920) pp. 50, 128. His previous salary was unstated.
[28] TNA PROB 11/216/426 Edward Wood 1651. See Wrightson, *op cit*, pp.82-4 on clues to puritan leanings contained in wills.
[29] John Rawlet, 1642-86, '*conformist minister, a devout and laborious lecturer at St. Nicholas*': Longstaffe, *op cit*, p.54.
[30] Longstaffe, *op cit*, p.110.
[31] Purdue, *Newcastle, op cit*, p.84.
[32] T. Sopwith, *A historical and descriptive account of All Saints' Church in Newcastle upon Tyne*, (1826), p.121.

[33] Common Council calendar 1645-50, TWA MD/NC/2/1 f285.
[34] Dodds, *op cit*, pp.102-4.
[35] TWA MD.NC/1/1 ff 289, 321.

Chapter Five: Merchant and Trader

[1] Howell, pp.200-8.
[2] Quoted in P.Kennedy, *The Rise and Fall of British Sea Mastery*, (1976), p.48.
[3] See Appendix 1.4 for the basis for these estimates.
[4] 139 tons of coal/vessel arriving in London in 1639 (Hatcher, p.474); 178 tons/vessels calculated from Newcastle in 1661 – TNA E 190/193/1.
[5] Howell, pp.296-300. The frontage seen today from Sandhill was added in the 1790s.
[6] T. Oliver, *Actual Survey of Newcastle upon Tyne*, (1830); TNA E 179/158/101: Hearth Tax assessment for Newcastle, Lady Day 1664-5. Michael Blackett's will and inventory DPR1/1/1683/B7. The site is now partly occupied by the Swing Bridge's old toll house.
[7] R.Fraser, C. Jamfrey and J.Vaughan, 'Excavation on the Site of the Mansion House, Newcastle, 1990', *AA*, 5th ser., 23, (1995), p. 147; Will of Thomas Bonner: DPR1/I/1660/B3; enumerated with 4 hearths in Closegate Ward in 1664: TNA E 179/158/101. The site is now part of the Copthorne Hotel.
[8] R. Welford, 'Local Muniments', *AA*, 2nd ser., 23, (1902), p.252.
[9] MA Records-2, pp.55-6.
[10] MA Records-2, p.269.
[11] MA Records-1, pp.12-3, 162; MA Records-2, p.271.
[12] MA Records-1, p.152. Emerson took his own third apprentice five months later, a year earlier than normally allowed. Blackett was not the only person Emerson swore at. On a separate occasion he told the town beadle that he was 'a lying, stinking, base knave': Anon, 'Eve of revolution' in *Rare Tracts*, Volume IV, *op cit*, p.18. None of this stopped Blackett being sheriff alongside Emerson's mayoralty in 1660, or renting warehouse space from him in the 1670s: Emerson will DPR1/1/1673/E2.
[13] This was part of a tedious long-running dispute between the Newcastle and London Merchant Adventurers regarding their respective rights. Glover was twice sent to Hamburg to test the London company's adherence to an agreement claimed by the Newcastle company, which was found wanting on each occasion: MA Records-1, p.186; MA Records-2, p.70.
[14] MA Records-1, p.182.
[15] S. E. Åström, *From Cloth to Iron*, (1963), p.138.
[16] Muller, *op cit*, p.69; Sound Toll; *CSPD, Addenda 1660-85*, pp. 282-3. Blackett was exchanging cloth for iron again in 1660: Sweden Riksarchivet, 756/1/B 11/3 Court papers 1660-4.
[17] Åström, *op cit*, p.139. Boij: Scotland, Scandinavia and Northern European Biographical Database (SSNE): www.st-andrews.ac.uk/history/ssne. 1669: Roseveare, *op cit*, p.277.
[18] Muller, *op cit*, p.70; Åström, *op cit*, p.146.
[19] J.Rund to T.Western, MBL 3 Feb 1677.
[20] Sunderland imports and exports are also included for 1661, but none are recorded in Blackett's name.
[21] Roseveare, *op cit*, pp.19-23.
[22] Gardiner, *England's Grievance, op cit*, eg. pp. 102, 119.

23 TWA CCB 1650-9, f.406, March 1656.
24 Howell, pp.180-2. George Dawson was, once again, the mayor.
25 Common Council calendar, 1650-59, TWA MD.NC/2/2, f.467; Longstaffe, *op cit*, p.99.
26 Merchants' company Order Book 1639-75: TWA GU.MA/3/3; Order Book, TWA MD.NC/1/3.
27 The Common Council calendar shows this to have been in September 1659, but a much more confused, chronologically creative and ultimately self-serving account appears in Barnes' memoirs: Longstaffe, *op cit*, p.173.
28 R. Surtees, *The History and Antiquities of the County Palatine of Durham*, Vol 1, (1816), p. 274.
29 Howell, p.212.
30 *CSPD, 1660-1*, 2 Oct 1660, p.315; R. Welford, *Men of Mark, op cit, 1*, (1895), p.299.
31 In October 1661: *CSPD, Addenda 1660-85*, p. 282-3. The Danish King's debt to Blackett was still being pursued a century later.

Chapter Six: Underground Ventures

1 NRO 324/W.3/18/3/7.
2 TWA MD.NC/2/2, ff.522, 530; G.Jackson, *The British Whaling Trade*, (2005), pp. xi, 18-20.
3 Derbyshire RO D7676/ Bag C/3295.
4 See p. 74 above. The cloth was valued by the Danes at 7,142 riksdollars, which Blackett claimed was well below its true value. In forlornly pursuing the unpaid debt a century later, his descendant's agent converted it to £1,600 using the exchange rate said to have applied in the 1650s: Henry Richmond to Walter Blackett 24 June 1760: NRO 672/E/1E/1.
5 To eldest son Edward in 1676. This letter was a chance find in one of Edward's later account books and evidently copied out by Edward from his father's original: NRO ZBL 273/12.
6 Quoted in R.Grassby, 'The personal wealth of the business community of Seventeenth-century England', *EconHR*, 23, (1970), p.228. This would produce around £1,200 per year at 6% interest.
7 Bird quoted by Hatcher, p. 265. Hechstetter: J.R.Edwards, G.Hammersley and E.Newell, 'Cost Accounting At Keswick, England, c. 1598-1615: The German Connection', *The Accounting Historian's Journal*, (1990). Hechstetter had dealings with the Butler family, into which Edward Blackett was apprenticed in 1630.
8 Mann: R.Howell, *Monopoly on the Tyne*, (1978), pp.55-7; Winlaton: Jeremy Tolhurst and partners - R.Welford (ed), *Records of the Committees for compounding, with delinquent royalists in Durham and Northumberland during the civil war, 1643-1660*, SS 111, (1905), p. 287.
9 Hatcher, pp.264-9; Newcastle UL Misc. MSS. 85 Montague, C, 21 June 1697. Gibside lay four miles south of Whickham in County Durham.
10 W.B.Stephens, *Seventeenth-century Exeter, A Study of Industrial and Commercial Development, 1625-1688*, (1958), pp.131-44.
11 1661: TNA E 190/193/1; 1676: E 190/196/6. For prices see Table A1.5.
12 J.T.Millington and S.D.Chapman (eds), *Four Centuries of Machine Knitting: Commemorating William Lee's Invention of the Stocking Frame in 1589*, (1989); Kendal: J.Thirsk, 'Industries in the Countryside' in F. J. Fisher (ed.), *Essays in the Economic*

and Social History of Tudor and Stuart England (1961), p.70. Grey to Robert Thorogood, 18 Jan 1676: NRO 753/J.

[13] Mentioned in a French traveller's account: A. de Rochefort, *Le voyageur d'Europe...* Vol III, (1672).

[14] A.Burn, 'Work before Play: The Occupational Structure of Newcastle-upon-Tyne, 1600-1710', p.126, and L.Houpt-Varner, 'Maintaining Moral Integrity: The Cultural and Economic Relationships of Quakers in North-East England, 1653-1700', pp.148-9, in A.Green and B.Crosbie (eds), *Economy and Culture in North-East England 1500-1800*, (2018).

[15] Burn, thesis, pp.99-100.

[16] Flinn, *Men of Iron, op cit*, p.253.

[17] *Ibid*, pp. 34-9, 174-6. In 1728, Crowley's business made gross profits of around £3,000, which overstates the true position because the depreciation charge on his factory and other fixed assets is unknown. But even at this level it was less than a 2% return on the £153,000 capital assets of the business. Most of this huge capital sum was more a burden than a mark of success. Unsold goods and unpaid debts earn nothing. The Navy was a major customer of Crowley's works but notoriously slow to pay its suppliers.

[18] NRO 753/J, 20 November 1675.

[19] Longstaffe, *op cit*, p.48.

[20] As quoted in Grassby, *Business Community*, p.240.

[21] Roseveare, *op cit*, pp.112-5, Tables 13, 14, but excluding Marescoe's holdings of East India stock, ship shares, loans and mortgages, which are more akin to surpluses re-invested elsewhere than current trading business capital.

[22] Newcastle Overseas Port Books. 1661: TNA E 190/193/1; 1666: E 190/193/9. He did continue importing wine, as shown in later port books and occasional court cases: TNA C 10/477/47 Clark vs Blackett, 1668; C 7/520/10 Chesman vs Blackett, 1669.

[23] Hatcher, pp. 330-1, 337-8.

[24] In 1684-5 the Winlaton mine produced a profit of 18% on 7,000 tons per year: NRO ZBL 273/18, and in 5 years at Stella between 1674 and 1683 Sir George Vane achieved 31%: NRO ZCO IV.47/1-17. See Appendix 2.5.

[25] Gray, *Chorographia, op cit*, pp.84-5.

[26] *Ibid*, p.86.

[27] NRO ZCO VIII.1. Carr had also recently taken a mining lease on the Gibside estate in Whickham parish, in 1657: Levine and Wrightson, *op cit*, p.60.

[28] See Appendix 2.2.

[29] For a useful geological map see R.I.Hodgson, Coalmining, Population And Enclosure In The Seasale Colliery Districts Of Durham (Northern Durham), 1551-1810, A Study In Historical Geography, unpublished thesis, Durham University, (1989), Vol 2, p.34.

[30] *Fighting Trade*, Vol 1, pp.8-9.

[31] Levine and Wrightson, *op cit*, pp. 50-1. Some of this was surely double-tracked. Single track waggonways of more than a mile or two must have have been impractical to operate at the volume of up and down traffic required to recover the cost of construction and maintenance.

[32] See Appendix 2.2.2.

[33] Stella Grand Lease partners minutes: NRO ZCO VIII.1, Blackett deeds: NRO 2762/E/DEEDS/C61, NRO 324/W.3/18/3. Blackett was nobody's fool. In 1662 he was careful not to commit himself in writing to the quality of about 500 tons of coals he sold to the wily fitter Thomas Fawdon: TNA C 10/67/53.

34 *Hostmen*, p.263.
35 The economics of a mining enterprise loosely based on Stella and its waggonway is modelled in Appendix 2.5. Bennett *et al* believed that around 14,000 tons of output per year was the minimum needed for a waggonway to be viable, although without specifying distance: *Fighting Trade,* Vol 1, p.14.
36 NRO ZCO IV.47/2. This difference more than compensated for the slightly higher cost of keel transport to Newcastle from Stella: 0.85p/ton compared to 0.5p/ton from Whickham, 2 ½ miles closer to the town.
37 L.Müller, *The Merchant Houses of Stockholm, c.1640-1800,* (1998), p.31
38 TWA Newcastle Common Council Order Book, 1656-1723 MD.NC/1/3, ff 65, 84. As a common councillor and governor of the hostmen's company at the time Blackett could surely have taken one of the shares had he wished to.
39 DPR1/1/1660/C1. Blackett was amongst the witnesses to Carr's will.
40 NRO ZCO IV. 47/1-2, VIII.1
41 Assuming 30,000 tons from Stella Grand Lease, and 470,000 tons shipped from the Tyne in 1659-60: Hatcher, Table 14.1 (a), p.489

Chapter Seven: The Plastic of its Age

1 I.Forbes, B.Young, C.Crossley and L.Hehir, *Lead Mining Landscape of the North Pennines Area of Outstanding Natural Beauty,* (2003), provides a well-illustrated summary of the North Pennines geology.
2 S.Primatt, *The City and Country Purchaser and Builder,* (c.1667), quoted in J.Thirsk and S.Cooper, *Seventeenth Century Economic Documents,* (1972), p.288.
3 I.Forbes, *Images of Industry,* (2015). Plates 6 and 12 are from this collection.
4 Coal: Hatcher, p.346; lead: Appendix 3.4.1.
5 A.Raistrick and B.Jennings, *A History of Lead Mining in the Pennines,* (1965), p.99.
6 D.Kiernan, *The Derbyshire Lead Industry in the Sixteenth Century,* (1989), pp.169, 189-91.
7 Appendix 3.2.1; Hatcher, Table 4.1, p.68 and Table 14.2. p.497.
8 Coal: Hatcher, Table B.5, p.584; Lead: W.Beveridge, *Prices and wages in England from the Twelfth to the Nineteenth Century,* 2nd edition, (1965), p.487.
9 Kiernan, *op cit,* pp.38-9.
10 R.Burt, 'The transformation of the nonferrous metals industries in the seventeenth and eighteenth centuries', *EconHR,* 48, (1995), p.33.
11 *ibid,* p.32.
12 To Sir Thomas Bludworth in London, 10 March 1674: NRO 753/J. Newcastle shipments of lead into the Baltic through the Sound had scarcely ever amounted to more than 40 tons per year, but they had reached 100 tons in 1673 and would nearly double to 198 tons in 1674.
13 Burt, 'transformation', *op cit,* p.34. Export duty of £1 was levied on each ton of lead in the 1670s, therefore 8% when the price was £12: TNA E 190/196/6.
14 W.Bray (ed), *The diary of John Evelyn, Volume 2, 1665-1706* (1901), p.21.
15 Stephen Porter, 'The great fire of London', *Oxford Dictionary of National Biography,* (2014), http://www.oxforddnb.com/view/theme/95647.
16 'An Act for the Rebuilding of the City of London (18-19 Chas II, 8)', *Statutes of the Realm: volume 5: 1628-80* (1819), pp. 603-12.
17 The calculation of rough estimates is given in Appendix 3.2.3.
18 W.Skinner to C.Marescoe 23 Dec 1668: Roseveare, *op cit,* p.260.

[19] Earle, *op cit*, p.22. St Pauls' alone might have required between 800 and 1,000 tons of lead: see Appendix 3.2.3.
[20] Kiernan, *op cit*, p.228. See Appendix 3.2.1.
[21] A.Wood, *The Politics of Social Conflict, The Peak Country, 1520-1770*, (1999), pp.84-7.
[22] D.Crossley and D.Kiernan, 'The Lead smelting-mills of Derbyshire', *Derbyshire Archaeological Journal*, Vol 112, (1992), pp.10-11.
[23] J.Freyhoff to C.Marescoe: Roseveare, *op cit*, p.88.
[24] Burt, 'Lead production', *op cit*, p.267.
[25] Kiernan, *op cit*, p.96; R.Welford, *History of Newcastle and Gateshead Vol 2 Sixteenth Century*, (1885), pp.104-5.
[26] Gray, *Chorographia, op cit*, pp.80-90.
[27] Burt, 'Lead production', p.267.
[28] Raistrick and Jennings, *op cit*, pp.9-11.
[29] TNA E 134/17&18Chas2/Hil6, 11 Jan 1666.
[30] At Eggleston in Teesdale by 1614, Blackhall in Hexhamshire c.1629/30 and at Wolsingham in Weardale, probably soon after 1632: see Appendix 3.7. Derbyshire mills: Crossley and Kiernan, *op cit*, p.10.
[31] G.Finch, 'The North Pennines lead industry in the seventeenth century', *Proceedings of the National Association of Mine Historical Organisations conference 2015*, (2020), section D, p.6.
[32] DULASC, Cosin's Survey, 1662, Add.MS 1930, f.59.
[33] Kirby, *op cit*, p.152; Cosin's Survey, f.59.
[34] NRO SANT/DEE/1/35; NRO ZMD 147/7; TNA E 134/17&18Chas2/Hil6.
[35] Newcastle Overseas port book 1638-9: TNA E 190/192/4.
[36] Welford *Cttee compounding, op cit*, p.314.
[37] W.F.Heyes, 'A History of Mining in Teesdale in the 16th and 17th Centuries', *British Mining*, 90, (2010), p.45.
[38] W.F.Heyes, *pers comm*; G.Ritschel, *An account of certain Charities...in Tynedale*, (1713), p.64; G.Dickinson, *Allendale and Whitfield; Historical Notices of the two parishes*, 2nd edition (1903), p.54; NRO 753 Box 1, Bundle J: accounts of Grey and Briggs 1672-7.
[39] Three barrels of red lead were enumerated amongst the possessions of Gervis Gascoyne of nearby Gingleshaugh when his probate inventory was taken in early 1660: DPR1/1/1660/G2/3 7 March 1659/60. Red lead is a derivative of litharge, produced, alongside silver, when refining lead. The riverbank at Red Lead Mill is called Silverhaugh.
[40] For example 'leade was on the riseinge hand beyond seas' according to Thomas Wright, of Stokesley, near Stockton, in December 1668: Roseveare, *op cit*, pp.259-60.
[41] See discussion of Derbyshire ore and lead costs in Appendix 3.3.
[42] Wright to Marescoe, 17 Dec 1668: Roseveare, *op cit*, pp.259-60.
[43] The Allendale parish register records the marriage in February 1665 of 'Hercules Hill, a smelter, and Elizabeth Blande, ye daughter of Thomas Blande, who all of them came out of Darbyshire.'

Chapter Eight: A Great Many Men

[1] Newcastle Customs Coastal outwards port book: TNA E 190/192/11. In the absence

of Newcastle port book records for most of the Interregnum the full extent of his trade in lead cannot be known. Letters from Mr Blackett to the Earl of Northumberland's agent re Hawdonfield: DN Sy: Q.VI.128 1655. Duty ore receipts: DN Sy: C.X.3.a.

[2] NRO SANT/DEE/1/35/26.

[3] NRO 324/W.3/18/3. This is one of a series of summary entries in a dry abstract listing the Allenheads mining leases. The bare facts and dates of the subsequent transactions between Pearson, Blackett and the landowner Fenwick are drawn from the same document.

[4] R.A.Fairbairn, *Allendale, Tynedale and Derwent Lead Mines*, British Mining Monographs, Vol 65, (2000), p.37.

[5] N.Baxter, 'The Missing Family Portrait', *Journal of the Northumberland and Durham Family History Society*, Vol 10, (1985), p.13. With Blackett's money Pearson was able to move up in the world: by 1663 he was at the Spital, a gentleman's residence just west of Hexham: *HN*, 3, p.313.

[6] From a private collection. The Great Limestone, so productive elsewhere in the North Pennines, rises to the surface on the line of the western end of the vein.

[7] See assumptions and calculation in Appendix 3.2.6, Table A3.7.

[8] TNA C 7/520/10 Chesman *et al* vs Blackett, 1669; chapter 11, p.195.

[9] Haggatt and Ward's survey of the manor of Hexham, 1608, in *HN*, 3, pp.95-7.

[10] NRO ZPA/18.

[11] As often documented in the lead agents' letters, eg. Henry Richmond to Caleb Hunter, 11 Dec 1772: NRO 672/E/1E/3.

[12] Blackburn, 'Mining without laws', *op cit*, pp.70-1.

[13] MB to WB 9 Oct 1675 & 19 Oct 1675.

[14] W.H.D.Longstaffe, 'Francis Radcliffe, First Earl of Derwentwater', *AA*, 2nd ser.. 1, (1857), p.99.

[15] G,Finch, 'William Blackett, Dukesfield, and the 17th century lead industry', *HH*, 25, (2015), pp.7-8.

[16] P.Hopkins, 'Sir John Fenwick c.1644-97', *ODNB*.

[17] NRO 324/W.3/18/3.

[18] F.Brook, 'Fallowfield', *Industrial Archaeology*, (1967).

[19] J.Richardson, *The Gentleman's Steward*, (1730), p.xxv.

[20] NRO 2762/E/X16.

[21] DN Sy: R.IV.1.b.

[22] A small smelting mill had been at work at Fallowfield in the 1650s, but Blackett's interest lay in using Dukesfield's capacity: TNA C 5/31/41.

[23] *HN*, 10, pp.229-30.

[24] MBL, *passim*. Unless otherwise stated, all data in this section is taken from these letters. This next generation of Blacketts will be properly introduced later.

[25] See Appendix 3.2.5.

[26] MB to WB 9 Oct 1675.

[27] TNA ADM 75/68, Sir Francis Radcliffe to Wm Blackett, 23 Sept 1671.

[28] Longstaffe, 'Radcliffe', *op cit*, pp.99-100. Ralph Grey claimed that Blackett had bought Radcliffe's duty ore at the rate of £4.50/ton in early 1674, outbidding a rumoured earlier price of £3.75: Grey 20 Feb 1673/4: NRO 753/J.

[29] MB to WB 9 Oct 1675, 26 Feb 1676, 24 Feb 1677.

[30] Finch, 'Dukesfield', *op cit*, p.10. R.Carlton, 'A Third Season of Fieldwork on the site of Dukesfield Smeltmills, Hexhamshire', unpublished report, (2015): https://www.dukesfield.org.uk/ research/ archaeological-reports/, pp.18-9.

[31] It was not present in 1671. Blackett bought the land in March 1672 and the mill was

mentioned in his eldest son Edward's marriage settlement of April 1674: NRO ZBL 273/16, ZBL 1/58 a-b, ZBL 261/1.

[32] NRO 753 Box 1, Bundle J: accounts of Grey and Briggs 1672-7.

[33] Raistrick and Jennings, *op cit*, pp. 185-6. Newcastle port books from 1696 onwards show outwards shipments of litharge, indicating lead being refined by then: TNA E 190/205/3.

[34] MB to WB 18 May 1678. See Appendix 3.4 for workforce estimates.

[35] WB (nephew) to WB 18 July and 7 Nov 1676: NRO ZBL 193.

[36] DULASC, Cosin's survey, f.59;

[37] TNA E 126/9 Exchequer Court orders and decrees 1667.

[38] Cosin's survey: DULASC, Add.MS 1930, f.59, assuming £4.25 per ton of ore.

[39] TNA E 134/2Jas2/Mich42. The 1661 deed is dated 5th March 1661, only three months after Cosin had journeyed north on his return from exile.

[40] See for example, his letter to Archbishop of Canterbury Sheldon, 27 Aug 1666: G.Ornsby (ed), *The Correspondence of John Cosin, Vol 2*, SS 55, (1872), p.153.

[41] *Journal of the House of Commons*, 1660-1667, (1802), 26 Nov 1666, pp. 653-654. Wharton's sons Humphrey and Robert were named as the other lives.

[42] DCRO D/X 1361/1. Wharton built another just to the north of Stanhope in 1677: NRO ZWN A/1 f336.

[43] TNA E 126/9; Hutton Wood, *Collection of Decrees in Tithe Causes...* (1798), Vol 1, Pp 83-4.

[44] Ornsby, *op cit*, pp.162-3.

[45] Spreading the increase over even as little as 600 tons of ore, it probably added no more than 7-8% to his unit costs and Wharton might have forced some of this onto his miners by increasing the discount at which he bought from them.

[46] Moormaster accounts for August 1666 to March 1667 presented in the course of Basire's case admitted production of 563 tons, an annual rate of 965 tons: TNA E 126/9. This probably understated the true figure, and came from just 12 mines. If Blackett managed to collect three quarters of his dues and paid £20 to local agents it would cost him £4.40/ton, which was not cheap but manageable in such a buoyant market.

[47] *CSPD, 1673-5*, p.55.

[48] TNA E 190/196/1,3,5,8, 196/6. Lambton carrier: deposition of William Steward of Stanhope in 1686: TNA E 134/2Jas2/Mich42.

[49] NRO ZWN A/1 315 f317.

[50] Blackett's 'stalking horse' for the lease was Barbara Sanderson. She was granted the 21-year lease in September and assigned it to Blackett within a month: NRO ZWN/A/1/315 f118. Copyholds: NRO 324/W.3/18/3, MB to WB 5 Apr 1679.

[51] *Journal of the House of Commons*, 1667-1687 (1802), 22 May 1679.

[52] TNA E 134/32/Chas2/Mich18, 1680.

Chapter Nine: A New Industrial Giant

[1] See Appendix 3.5.1.

[2] R.Grey 30 Oct 1674: NRO 753/J; TNA E90/196/2,6.

[3] 58% of Blackett's overseas shipments exports went to Amsterdam and Rotterdam in 1676, destinations for just 16% of the lead of other Newcastle exporters: TNA E 190/ 196/6.

[4] O.Gelderblom, J.Jonker, and C.Kool, 'Direct finance in the Dutch Golden Age',

EconHR, 69, (2016), pp. 1178–1198.
[5] MB to W.Chaytor, 9 Sep 1676. He also wrote to Humphrey Willett on Dec. 15th saying that he had buyers for his lead 'who can dispose of itt for ready money'.
[6] R.Grey to J.Pannell, 5 May 1676: NRO 753/J.
[7] Nephew William to WB, 7 Nov 1676: NRO ZBL 193.
[8] R.Grey to W.Peacock, 29 Nov 1673: NRO 753/J.
[9] In 1676 over 80% of Stockton's lead exports were in the hands of Robert Jackson, who had links with the Blacketts, John Wells and William Atkinson: TNA E 190/196/6.
[10] Accounts and other papers showing mining at Grassgroves and Haydon Fell, smelting at Red Lead Mill and revenue between 1672 and 1677 allow approximate production figures to be calculated: NRO 753 Box 1/ Bundle J. In 1675 and 1676, Grey exported 19 tons from Newcastle in each year.
[11] The ore mined under Wharton's control in Weardale was almost certainly far higher than the 630 tons stated between November 1674 and February 1676. Reprised in a Durham Chancery Court ruling in 1685: DCRO D/Bo/F/138.
[12] I. Forbes, 'Charles Paulet, Weardale's forgotten mining entrepreneur and the origin of Weardale's partnership mines', *Friends of Killhope Newsletter,* 90, (2017); NRO 2762/E/Deeds/C61; North Yorks RO ZBO V LR7.
[13] Tim Gates, *pers comm.*
[14] Wolsingham Parish Registers; NRO 324/W.3/18/3; NRO ZBL 2/9.
[15] Richard was steward at Allenheads in early 1669, but 'of Slaley' a year earlier, suggesting a recent move from the Dukesfield area: Allendale Parish Registers.
[16] WB I's original will: NRO 2762/Box C74. Subsequent references to WB's will are to this document unless otherwise stated. Robinson's substantial house was still owned by Blackett's descendants in the 1810s: DULASC GBV/76. Its site is now occupied by the roundabout outside Blaydon railway station.
[17] MB to WB 9 Oct 1675 and 19 Oct 1675. Michael also had to explain why some chopwood fuel cost 1/2d per sack more than the rest: MB to WB 15 Jun 1678.
[18] MBL, 1676-8; Report by J.Armstrong, 1734: NRO ZBL 84/10. Blackett might have experimented with using gunpowder to speed underground progress. Michael mentioned powder barrels in a letter to overseas merchant Hubert Aylwyn 6 Jun 1679. T.Crawhall, 'An account of Instruments formerly used for the Purpose of Blasting', *AA,* 1st ser., 1, (1822), p.184 gives evidence for the use of gunpowder at Allenheads prior to 1716, but closer dating is impossible.
[19] MBL, *passim.* See Appendix 3.4. Fallowfield was particularly lucrative, with ore costing under £2 per ton to mine.
[20] NRO ZBL 273/15. They ranged between the equivalent of £1.31 and £1.75/ton during this short period. A staggering 30 different rates were used over the course of 1681 at five named shafts.
[21] A baptism of that name was recorded at Grinton in Swaledale in 1644.
[22] MB to WB 18 and 27 May 1677; 1680s: NRO ZBL 273/15. John Blackett was at Wylam between 1679 and 1685: *HN, 12,* p.230.
[23] J.C.Hodgson, 'Some forgotten epitaphs and monumental inscriptions in Hexham Priory church', *PSAN,* 2nd ser., 8, (1897), pp. 145-50.
[24] 1706 Moormaster lease renewal: NRO ZWN A/1 f.118-9 Abstract of title.
[25] *Hostmen,* p. 287.
[26] MB to WB 26 Feb 1677. Stoute was to stay and tend the Allenheads engine, a decision which cost him his life for he died in the mine within four months.
[27] John Bittlestone, possibly Joseph's father, was mentioned in the will of George Fair-

lamb of Dukesfield in 1652: DPR1/1/1663/F1; ZBL 261/2; J.Fenwick (ed), 'Extracts from the Accounts of the Steward of Sir Francis Radclyffe, Bart', *AA*, 2nd ser., 2, (1858), p.163.

[28] NRO ZBL 273/13-15.; Raistrick and Jennings, *op cit*, p.120. See Appendix 3.4.3.

[29] MB to WB, 18 May 1678.

[30] NRO ZBL 273/14; N.Walton and H.Boag to Thos Corbett Esq 23 Dec 1735, TNA ADM 66/105 p.13

[31] R.A.Fairbairn, 'Plankey Mill – 17th century lead Smelting Mill', *British Mining*, Vol 59, (1997), p.90

[32] NRO ZBL 273/13, f4. In small-scale trials at Plankey Mill in 1680-1 the reworking of slags added 23% to the lead produced at first smelting: ZBL 273/15.

[33] see Appendix 3.4.3

[34] S.Pollard, *The Genesis of Modern Management*, (1965), p.71 noted Crowley's impressive ironworks developed at Winlaton from the 1690s. D.Oldroyd, *Estates, Enterprise and Investment at the Dawn of the Industrial Revolution: Estate Management and Accounting in the North-East of England, c.1700-1780*, (2007).

[35] The source data and calculation methodology are explained further in Appendix 3.4. These estimates include conservative provisions for fixed asset depreciation.

[36] See Chapter six, p.88

[37] Michael Blackett's letters indicate that the family also had some form of business relationship with Robert Jackson, Stockton's principal trader, who accounted for just under half of Stockton's 900 tons of lead exports, easily more than any other single merchant.

[38] To Thomas Lemon, London merchant, 1 May 1675: NRO 753/J.

[39] Hearth Tax assessments TNA E 179/254/18, E 179/158/110 r.29, 33-4. G. Finch, 'Allenheads Transformed', *HH*, 29, (2019)

[41] NRO ZBL 261/1; M.Y.Ashcroft, (ed), *Documents Relating to the Swaledale estates of Lord Wharton in the 16th and 17th centuries*, (1984), pp.81-3; Levine and Wrightson, *op cit*, p.189.

[41] A very rough estimate based on 1660s hearth tax assessments for the Hexhamshire, Allendale and St. John Lee: E 179/254/18, household totals for townships in the parishes of Stanhope, Wolsingham, Muggleswick, Edmondbyers and Hunstanworth given in A.Green, E.Parkinson, M. Spufford (eds), *Durham Hearth Tax Lady Day 1666*, (2006), pp. cvi-cxxiii, and providing for Alston Moor at a similar population density.

[42] James Standsfield to WB (the nephew), 5 March 1680: NRS, RH15/102/6/2.

[43] For example on the Allendale/Hexhamshire common at Harwood Shield and on Slaley fell above Dukesfield between the 1650s and 1680s: TNA C 10/346/10; *HN*, 6, p.383.

[44] MB to Edward Allen, 31 Dec 1675.

[45] Edward Willett 20 Nov 1674: NRO 753/J. Lead mining in Derbyshire encouraged an exchange network with deeper farming specialisation to the south: Wood, *op cit*, p.93. Newcastle's trading infrastructure extended the northeast's exchange network far into Europe.

Chapter Ten: The Newcastle Grandee

[1] TWA MD.NC/1/3 f29v, and NC.2/2 f75v.

[2] MA Records-2, pp.140-144; M.Sellers, *The Acts and Ordinances of the Eastland*

Company, (1906), pp. xi, xlviii-ix.

3 MA Records-2, pp.108-25.

4 R.Welford, 'Newcastle householders in 1665. Assesssment of Hearth or Chimney Tax', *AA*, 3rd ser., 7, (1911), p.55, quoting *CSPD*, December 1666.

5 Fewster, (2011), *op cit*, pp.17-18; J.A.Bennett (ed), *The Manuscripts of S.H.Le Fleming Esq. of Rydal Hall*, RCHMC 12th report, Appendix, Part VII, (1890), p.79.

6 Henry Cavendish, Earl of Ogle to WB, 9 and 19 June 1671: NRO ZBL 193. Ogle was also a privy councillor and close to the King.

7 *CSPD, 1673-5,* 1 Dec 1673, p.41.

8 *CTB 1672-5*, 24 Dec 1673, p. 448.

9 B.Coward, *The Stuart Age, England 1603-1714*, (1994), pp.309-13; G.Hampson, 'Blackett, William (c.1620-80)', *HistParl* 1660-90.

10 NRO ZBL 264/1. This was for the 'seventeen month tax' to fund the building of 30 warships.

11 J. Raithby (ed), *Statutes of the Realm: Volume 5, 1628-80*, (1819), pp. 802-836.

12 MBL, 11 and 19 May 1677.

13 NRO ZBL 194; 'Exhibition of Silver Plate of Newcastle Manufacture', *AA*, 2nd ser., 21, (1899), pp.34-5.

14 J.Rushworth to WB, 26 April 1676, NRO ZBL 193.

15 R. Harris, 'Government and the economy, 1688-1850' in R.Floud and P.Johnson (eds), *The Cambridge Economic History of Modern Britain* (Cambridge, 2004), p.216.

16 John Basire, *CTB, 1676-1679*, 31 May 1677, p.447.

17 *CTB, 1672-1675*, p.267.

18 Nef, *op cit*, Vol 2, p.307; *CTB, 1676-9*, 24 Dec 1677, p. 497; *CTB, 1685-9*, 22, Jun 1685, p.231.

19 Hatcher, pp.490-1, 494-5, 506-7. Assuming an average of 65,000 tons exported per year, taxed at the equivalent of £7.54/100 tons, the overall yield would come to £4,900/year. Deducting collection costs of, say, £500, to would pay for 15 clerks/collectors in the major ports this leaves £1,200/year after the rent paid to Townsend.

20 E.R.Edwards and J.P.Ferris, 'O'Brien, Henry, Lord Ibrackan (c.1642-78)', *HistParl*, 1660-1690.

21 MB to WB 23 April and 3 May 1678. A year later Anthony Isaacson was Newcastle's customs controller.

22 Åström, *op cit*, p.160.

23 NRO 324/W.3/19; R.Welford, 'Local Muniments', *AA*, 3rd ser., 5, (1909), pp. 115-6; *HN*, 9, p.66. Christian had even more children than her sister Elizabeth, 17 in total, in the space of 21 years. She outlived her husband by three years, dying in 1716.

24 MB to WB 22 Feb 1676; MA Records-2, p.307.

25 Mains and Tuck, *op cit*, pp. 18-19.

26 NRO ZBL 189-91, Edward Blackett copy letters, 1709-15; ZBL 273/14-17.

27 NRO ZBL 1/58-91; 261/1 indenture dated 28 April 1674; cases brought by Edward Blackett against Mary's father and family between 1677 and 1680: TNA C 6/228/10, C 5/451/105.

28 NRO ZBL 273/12, WB to EB, 18 Jan 1676. The letter was copied out in Edward's hand into one of his ledgers, endorsing the value of turning each tedious page of largely irrelevant accounts for the chance of such finds.

29 Thomas Norton to WB 11 and 18 May, EB to WB 22 June, Martin Lister to WB, 19 May 1676: NRO ZBL 193. Poor Mary died a month later. Edward was soon pursuing her father's family for her estate.

30 As reported by Michael to Edward, 15 August 1676.
31 MB to Humphrey Willett, 10 March 1677; Ashcroft, *op cit*, p.146. The Yorke lead business was based near Pateley Bridge in Nidderdale.
32 NRO ZBL 261/2; Lady Mary Yorke to WB 21 & 30 Nov, 19 Dec 1676: ZBL 193.
33 To WB, 19 Dec 1676: NRO ZBL 193; MB to EB 21 Oct 1676.
34 Surtees, *History of Durham,* Vol 3, (1823), pp.355-7.
35 Per William I's will.
36 MB to Charles Banks 22 Jan 1678.
37 MB to John Strother 20 Mar 1677; to Michael Clipsham 7 July 1676.
38 MB to WB 23 Feb 1676.
39 MB to WB 16 Nov 1675, 5 Apr 1679.
40 See Appendix 5.
41 EB to John Wilkinson, 29 March 1711: NRO ZBL 189.
42 NRO ZBL 1/80.
43 W.W.Thomlinson, *Denton Hall and its associations,* (1894), pp.36-8.
44 A marriage settlement between them was dated 22 March 1675: NRO 324/W.3/19. There is little reason to doubt the assertion that Blackett bought Greyfriars in 1675 or 1676, although no primary evidence documenting the purchase survives today. The property was purchased from his fellow Newcastle MP, the financially stretched Sir Francis Anderson, whose mayoralty commenced in October 1675. See R.Pears and B.Atherton, 'Anderson Place, Newcastle upon Tyne', *AA*, 5th ser., 44, (2015), pp. 175-224.
45 NRO ZBL 1/58-94, 324/W.3/19. The £7,500 mentioned earlier was augmented with the Fallowfield estate, excluding the lead mines, conservatively worth £1,600 based on the rental income of around £100/year in the mid-1680s: NRO ZBL 273/10.
46 TNA E 190/196/2,6; MB to Robert Jackson, 7 Sep 1675.
47 TNA PROB 11/518.

Chapter Eleven: Strange Histories of their Coal Works

1 Thomlinson, *op cit,* pp.36-8. Blaby, Rogers' home, is not far from Noseley Hall, the Leicestershire seat of Haselrig's family. The Newbiggin Hall and Brunton mines were owned by Haselrig and his descendants: *HN*, 13, pp.149, 211-2, 373; NRO ZCK 14/1. Rogers also had a part share in the Hunstanworth lead mines by the late 1660s, possibly taking on the late Edward Blackett's interest after his death in 1667: NRO SANT/DEE/1/35/26.
2 Will of John Rogers, 30 May 1671: DPR1/1/1673/R9.
3 Lease to Christopher Blackett, January 1665: DN Sy: M.VI.13.d; coal accounts: DN Sy: C.X.2.a(1), summarised in Figure A2.1 in Appendix 2.3. Christopher was of Newburn in 1649 and 1652 and his wife was buried there in 1663.
4 NRO ZWN A/1 f338 and NRO 324/W.3/18/3: Winlaton deeds schedule and abstract, pp. 1-2. The Winlaton transactions discussed in this chapter are all drawn from this abstract unless otherwise indicated. The remaining eighth of the manor was owned by Sir Francis Anderson, who evidently decided to stand in the way of Blackett gaining full control of Winlaton. R.Anderson *et al, A History of Blaydon*, (1975), p.26.
5 See Appendix 2.2.2.
6 *Fighting Trade,* Vol 1, pp.47-8.
7 See Appendix 2.2.
8 He signed the declaration of 27 April 1665 alongside the other principal hostmen,

all of whom expressed similar sentiments. Quoted by T.J.Taylor, *The Archaeology of the Coal Trade*, (1852, repr 1971), p.69.

[9] Roger North, *The life of the Rt Hon Francis North*, (1746), p. 136.

[10] NRO 324/W.3/18/3: Winlaton deeds schedule, pp.3-4. The same approach was taken with the Hodgson lease.

[11] NRO ZBL 273/18. For coal prices, see Appendix 2. 'Mine' does not mean a single shaft. Most larger Tyneside mines had numerous shafts sunk, exploited and either abandoned or used as air shafts as the coal seams were worked out.

[12] Gross rental income for the year from November 1682 was just under £380: NRO ZBL 273/1. Allowing for repairs, maintenance, land taxes, county rates and uncollectable arrears, net rent could be a fifth or more lower than the gross figure, so £300 is estimated here.

[13] *Fighting Trade*, Vol I, pp.57-69.

[14] R. Welford, 'Local Muniments', (1909) *op cit*, p.137. For the role of overmen see Hatcher, pp.297-9; Levine and Wrightson, pp.183-4.

[15] John Blackett to WB, 24 June 1676: NRO ZBL 193.

[16] See Appendix 2.5, Table A2.12. In the early 18th century, a 20% return on capital in coal mining was seen as reasonable given the '*hazard of money*': E.Hughes, *North Country Life in the Eighteenth Century*, (1952), pp.156-7.

[17] Mitford loan: NRO 324/W.3/19. Brandling: NRO 324/ M1/1-2. Brandling had intended this to be a short-term loan, to be repaid in February 1678, but the Blacketts were still pursuing repayment in 1681.

[18] Quoted in M.Turner, J.Beckett, B.Afton, *Agricultural rent in England, 1690-1914*, (1997), p.217. The prospect of capital gains on 'improveable' land was a further attraction.

[19] Ellis, thesis, *op cit*, pp.193-4.

[20] *CSPD, 1665-6*, 17 Jul 1666, p.547; *ibid, 1666-7*, 7 Sep 1666, p.105.

[21] 'Miscellanea. extracts from Newcastle Custom House books', *PSAN*, 3rd ser., 3, (1909), p.168; MB to WB, 10 and 20 Feb 1677.

[22] Appendix 4.5.

[23] It is clear from Michael Blackett's letters that John Mowbray was expected to use such receipts to help defray the mill paybills.

[24] W.W.Gibson, 'The Manor of Winlaton', *AA*, 4th ser., 23, (1945), p.21. Bennett *et al* suggest that the Selbys of Winlaton were one of those families whose estates were 'fast slipping into the outstretched hands of new men', including Blackett: *Fighting Trade*, Vol 1, p.23.

Chapter Twelve: Taking Stock of William Blackett

[1] The lead business probably employed around 430 workers in the mid-1670s (see Appendix 3.4) and he would have needed around 300 coal miners given the level of output.

[2] Nef, *op cit*, Vol 1, p.140.

[3] NRO ZCO IV/47/8-9. See chapter 6.

[4] Hampson, 'Blackett 1620-80' *op cit*; MB to James Ward, 15 Aug 1676.

[5] TNA E 190/196/6.

[6] MB to Robert Jackson 19 Oct 1675.

[7] 30 Sept 1676: NRO ZBL 193.

[8] Pease: MA Records-2, p.256. Rushworth wrote frequently to Blackett on the pro-

gress of legal cases in 1676: NRO ZBL 193.
[9] MB to WB 9 and 16 Nov 1675.
[10] Hatcher, p.294.
[11] Flinn, *Men of Iron, op cit*, pp.98-9, 194-200.
[12] NRO ZBL 273/14-15; Henry Richmond to Walter Blackett, 19 Feb 1765: NRO 672/E/1E/3. Such documentary riches now lost to us!
[13] NRO ZBL 273/15 (Plankey analysis), 13 (overheads).
[14] J.R.Edwards, *A History of Financial Accounting*, (2014), pp.89-90.
[15] Dr George Neale to WB, 1 Aug 1679, NRO ZBL 193. Neale started a book on the Knaresborough spa wells: D.H.Atkinson, *Ralph Thoresby, the topographer; his town and times*, (1885). Healthy diets: Earle, *op cit*, pp.273-5.
[16] The dates of Michael's letters to his father in London coincide with Parliamentary sessions. Common Council, June 1679: TWA MD.NC/1/3.
[17] Coward, *Stuart Age, op cit,* pp.329-32.
[18] G.Hampson, 'Carr, Sir Ralph (1634-1710)' and M.Helms and G.Hampson, 'Anderson, Sir Francis (1614-79)' in *HistParl*, 1660-90.
[19] TWA, MD.NC/1/13.
[20] 29 Dec 1679, Birkhall Close, Thorngrafton: NRO ZBL 1/96.
[21] NRO 324/M.2/1-2. Blackett's lengthy deposition was taken on 19th April. Documents in the Chancery case appear in TNA C 6/385/95 Brownell vs. Gray.
[22] Earle, *op cit*, pp.311-2.
[23] H.Bourne, *op cit*, p.72; plan of memorials within the church drawn up by Charles Hutton in 1769. The ever self-confident young Blackett had reserved a double-sized burial place amongst the town's great and good in the Choir 30 years earlier: St. Nicholas' register, NRO EP 86/1.
[24] Straker, *Memoirs, op cit*, p. 30.
[25] TNA C 10/67/53, Fawdon vs Blackett, 1662; C 10/477/47 Clark vs Blackett 1668; C 10/133/84 Milburne vs Blackett and Rogers 1677.
[26] Longstaffe, Barnes, *op cit*, pp. 44, 194. For Milbank, see chapter 5.
[27] Pears and Atherton, *op cit*, (2015), p.191; Helms and Hampson, *op cit*.
[28] Wm Rollinson to WB, 9 and 18 March, 6 April 1676: NRO ZBL 193.
[29] Mary Rogers to WB, 26 May, 20 June, 1 and 22 July 1676: NRO ZBL 193. Despite her childish tone and handwriting Mary was about 20 years old.
[30] Grassby, *Business Community, op cit,* pp. 247-9.
[31] Michael willed almost all of whatever estate he had left in 1683 to his widow Dorothy: DPR1/1/1683/B7.

Chapter Thirteen: Brothers

[1] 6 Dec 1668, Amsterdam notarial records. Amsterdam City Archives 5075/ 3607/ 113247; MB to Charles Banks, 19 June 1676.
[2] At Sockburn and Girsby, in the lower Tees valley: NRO ZBL 273/1, W.Page (ed), *A History of the County of York North Riding, Volume 1*, (1914), pp. 198-9.
[3] NRO ZBL 273/5 Estate ledger, f12. Fallowfield mine was leased in 1710: EB to Jacob Peart, 28 Nov 1709, NRO ZBL 189.
[4] 15 Feb 1711: NRO ZBL 189
[5] Davison and his wife Elizabeth were beneficiaries under William I's will to the tune of a recurring £160 per year and one-off current and committed future bequests of £2,600.

⁶ Brabant to Secretary of State Sir Leoline Jenkins, 8 March 1684, during William II's mayoralty: *CSPD, 1683-4*, pp.314-5.
⁷ M.Ridley, *A History of the Merchant Adventurers of Newcastle-upon Tyne*, (1998), p.44.
⁸ J.Miller, 'The Crown and the Borough Charters in the Reign of Charles II', *English Historical Review*, 100, (1985), p.75.
⁹ Welford, *Men of Mark, op cit*, 1, pp.360-1.
¹⁰ M.S.Child, 'Prelude to Revolution: The Structure of Politics in County Durham, 1678-88', unpublished Durham University Ph.D thesis, (1972), pp. 138-41.
¹¹ TWA MD.NC/1/3 f.166-166v; Brabant to Jenkins, *CSPD, 1683- 4*, pp.314-5.
¹² MD.NC/1/3 f.169. Jeffreys became notorious a year later for the savage punishment of rebels supporting the Earl of Monmouth against King James II after the Battle of Sedgemoor.
¹³ *CSPD, 1684-5*, 9 Nov 1684, p.207.
¹⁴ *CTB, 1685-9*, 16 Feb 1685, p.3.
¹⁵ It had been worth £500 per year when Sir Christopher's royalist father was penalised by the Commonwealth: Welford, *Cttee Compounding, op cit*, pp.176-7.
¹⁶ NRO 324/W.3/18. J.Foster (ed) *London marriage licences, 1521-1869*, (1887), p.135. Baronetcy: *CSPD, 1684-5*, p.295; Each of Julia's parents was later to be a godparent to Blackett offspring, as was Viscountess Lumley: Newcastle St. Andrew's parish registers.
¹⁷ G.Hampson, 'Newcastle-upon-Tyne' in *HistParl*, 1660-90.
¹⁸ According to Brabant, as given in Richardson, 'Eve of Revolution', p.8, in *Rare Tracts*, Vol 4, *op cit*.
¹⁹ Child, *op cit*, pp.161-3; Welford, *Men of Mark, op cit*, 1, pp.358-9.
²⁰ 'Diary of Mark Browell for 1688' pp.12-3 in Richardson, *Rare Tracts*, Vol 1.
²¹ Hampson, 'Blackett, Sir William (1657-1705)', *HistParl*, 1660-90.
²² F.Bradshaw, 'Sir William Blackett', *PSAN*, 3rd ser., 3, (1907), pp.327-9.
²³ J.Hoppitt, *A Land of Liberty? England 1689-1727*, (2000), pp.20-6.
²⁴ Newsletter to Sir Daniel Fleming, 19 Jan 1689: *Le Fleming, op cit*, pp.233-4.
²⁵ Hampson, 'Blackett 1657-1705', *op cit*. Edward Blackett was also elected to the 1689 Parliament, as MP for Ripon (his first time at Westminster), and he too voted that the throne was not vacant.
²⁶ Reported by Sir Christopher Musgrave to Daniel Fleming on 13th December: *Le Fleming, op cit*, p.228.
²⁷ Mackenzie, *op cit*, pp.232-3.
²⁸ Hampson, Blackett 1657-1705, *op cit*; see Appendix 3 for St. Paul's cathedral.
²⁹ Creagh and the 19 year old William II had gone to Hamburg together in 1676: MBL 19 June 1676. Creagh leased Edward Blackett's half of Winlaton Colliery between 1687-99: NRO ZBL 273/5, f12; NRO 11603/Box 16.
³⁰ Hoppitt, *op cit*, p.20.
³¹ Richardson, *Rare Tracts*, Vol 4, *op cit*, p.11.
³² NRO ZBL 273/15. All references to Fallowfield in this chapter are taken from this neatly kept ledger unless otherwise stated.
³³ NRO ZBL 273/17.
³⁴ The mill lay on Acomb common, so permission was obtained from Sir John Fenwick, as manorial lord: NRO 2762/E/DEEDS/C61
³⁵ Assuming £250 outlay for the mill and site and £25 for each of three hearths.
³⁶ See also Appendix 3.4.1.
³⁷ Sir Edward Blackett to Newcastle merchant Matthew Featherstone, 22 Sept 1709,

NRO ZBL 189. Revenue probably was above £3,000/year, but not profits.

[38] Chapter 8, p.131; TNA E 134/32Chas2/Mich18, E 112/395/120/32Chas2.

[39] This was in a letter of 1704, now lost, but evidently still easily found in the Blackett office files in 1761: Henry Richmond to William Darwin 24 Feb 1761, NRO 672/E/1E/1.

[40] Lease of Greengill to Blackett, 1671: TNA ADM 75/68.

[41] Blackett vs Radcliffe: TNA C 10/411/17.

[42] At Peasmeadow: NRO 2762 /E/Deeds/C61. There is no mention of it in any of Michael's reports, which ran up to December 1678.

[43] Westgarth Forster, *A Treatise on a Section of the Strata*, (1821), p.272. It probably ran south for some 500 yards.

[44] Given in a case brought by Blackett against Thomas Tempest for levying new tolls on lead traffic: TNA E 134/2W&M/Trin15, April 1690.

[45] See Appendix 3.2.

[46] Woodhall: Longstaffe, 'Radcliffe', *op cit*, pp.95-130; Fenwick, 'Radclyffe Accounts', *op cit*, pp. 159-164; Blagill: TNA ADM 75/68; Settlingstones: TWA DF.HUG/43/1-12; Blanchland, 1687: NRO ZPA/7/3.

[47] Hunstanworth mining accounts, 1686-7: NRO ZPA/18. Margin calculation based on assumptions documented in Appendix 3.4.

[48] TNA ADM 75/68-9.

[49] DN Sy: C.X.2.a.(1); Appendix 2, Figure A2.1; Table A2.2.

[50] P.Smith, 'A house by Sir Christopher Wren? The second Newby Hall and its gardens', *The Georgian Group Journal*, (2008). Wren must have known of the Blacketts given their importance to the supply of building lead to London.

[51] Pears and Atherton, *op cit*. Hotbeds: D.R.Hainsworth (ed), *The Correspondence of Sir John Lowther of Whitehaven, 1693-98,* (1983), pp.473-4; M.Roberts, 'The staircase from Anderson Place, Newcastle-upon-Tyne', *English Heritage Historical Review*, vol 1, (2006), pp.46-61.

[52] Although published in *Britannia Illustrata* in 1707, commissions were taken from 1697. Both Edward and William signed up, and the plates of Newby and Greyfriars were numbered sequentially, 53 and 54, so were possibly part of the first batch completed by 1701: A.Jones, 'Johannes Kip (1652-1721) and the Gloucestershire engravings', *The Local Historian*, 50, (2020), p.311.

Chapter Fourteen: Resurgence

[1] E.Cruikshank and R.Harrison, 'Blackett, Sir Edward', in *HistParl, 1690-1715*. Three volumes of copy letters survive dated between 1709 and 1715: NRO ZBL 189-191.

[2] The statues were later moved to Wallington, where they now line the terrace of the walled garden.

[3] W.Buckley (ed), *Memoirs of Thomas, Earl of Ailesbury*, (1890), Vol 1, p.273; Hopkins, *op cit, ODNB* provides an excellent summary of Fenwick's colourful life and the final 'trial' for his life.

[4] Lord Chancellor's summary and judgement of the case: NRO 2762/E/X16.

[5] NRO ZWN/A/1/315 f123-6; N.Luttrell, *A brief historical relation of state affairs, from Sept. 1678 to Apr. 1714*, (1857), Vol 1, pp.526, 532, 595-6; Trevelyan, *op cit*, p.10.

[6] Wallington's gross rental in 1689 was later recorded as £950 and a 1682 Hexham rental, with a reasonable additional allowance for Anick Grange, was about £700: Miscellaneous Hexham manor documents (NRO 11603/Box 16). Each estate brought

with it a decent house – the old stone pele tower at Wallington and Hexham Abbey house adjacent to the parish church.

[7] See Appendix 3.3, Table A3.10. The Fallowfield mines were of course in Edward's hands in 1689 but the records are silent on any contribution he might have made. The right to any *future* mines was left with Fenwick but Blackett bought out this residual claim for £150 in October 1695: NRO 2762/ E/ X16.

[8] NRO ZWN/A/1/315 f118.

[9] G.Harrison, *History of Yorkshire*, Vol 1, (1885), p.94; 1737 Blackett estate survey, NRO 11603/Box 8.

[10] NRO ZWN/A/1/315, f118. The right of each new bishop to renegotiate his dues brought created some uncertainty but as it turned out Bishop Crewe lived for a further 30 years.

[11] Joseph Richmond to Walter Blackett, 17 Feb 1730: NRO 673/2.

[12] Blackburn, 'Mining without laws', *op cit*, p.71.

[13] NRO 11603/Box 8 Estate survey, 1737; Forbes, Paulet, *op cit*, (2017).

[14] TWA DF.COT/CA/19/36, DF.COT/CK/1/27 (Ramsay), NRO ZRI/21/11 (White and Ridley).

[15] Lease of Stotfoldburn near Rookhope - Blackett to Ramsay, 6 May 1695: TWA DF.COT/CA/19/36; NRO 2762/E/DEEDS/C61.

[16] P.King, 'The production and consumption of bar iron in early modern England and Wales', *EconHR*, 58.1, (2005), p.3; G.Hammersley, 'The Charcoal Iron Industry and its Fuel', *EconHR*, 26, (1973), pp.610-11.

[17] A.Raistrick, *Quakers in Science and Industry*, (1950), pp. 164-170; Flinn, *Men of Iron*, p.42.

[18] Cay to Lister, 19 Sept 1701, 18 April 1702, Bodl. Lib MS Lister 37: 41-2, 53-4, summarised in Early Modern Letters Online, www.culturesofknowledge.org. Ridley was Nicholas Ridley, one of the Newcastle merchants increasingly engaged in lead mining, and who had a Weardale lease from Blackett.

[19] See Appendix 3.4.3. The mill was adjacent to the Oakwood coal pits, so there were no transport costs to speak of.

[20] Dukesfield: MBL *passim*; Blackhall: smelting accounts 1691 TWA CM/1/90; Muggleswick: W.Blackett to Dean of Durham, 10 Sept 1689; Surtees, *History of Durham*, Vol 2, (1820), pp.391-2.

[21] G.Finch, 'The Carrshield lead mill dispute of 1694', *AA*, 5th ser., 44, (2014), pp.249-56 has full details of this affair.

[22] NRO 2762 /E/Deeds/C61.

[23] See Appendix 3.7, Table A3.28.

[24] Blackett's men were fined at the Muggleswick manor court in 1695 for taking peat and breaking the park wall 'with their lodes': DULASC DCD/MAN/5/29; T.Featherstone, Dukesfield to T. Brumell, 29 April 1698: DULASC Add.MS 1623/3.

[25] Sales ledger, 1723-7: NRO 672/E/1C/1.

[26] ZWN/A/1/315 f118 as before. Thomas Featherstone of Dukesfield Hall took part in the Hexhamshire Common boundary riding in July 1690: NRO 11603 Box 5. John Featherstone succeeded him: J.Richmond 1 Oct 1728: NRO 673/2.

[27] TWA/3415/CA/19/36.

[28] April 1696: NRO ZWN/A/1/315 f.119.

[29] N.Pevsner, *The Buildings of England, County Durham*, (1953), p. 204.

[30] The Steel, purchased from John Mowbray's heirs in August 1689: NRO 2762/E/Deeds/C61

[31] *HN*, 4, p.100; Ritschel, *op cit*, pp.16-7, and assuming 30p per week as average earn-

ings. For 1677-8 see Appendix 3.4, Table A3.13.
[32] Burt, 'lead production', *op cit*, p.267. See Appendix 3.2, Table A3.5. Given his control of both Allendale and Weardale, a two-thirds share for Blackett seems reasonable.
[33] See Appendix 3.2, Table A3.9.
[34] M.Stringer, *English and Welsh mines and minerals discovered*, (1699), p.5.
[35] Welford, 'Local Muniments', (1909) *op cit*, pp.108-9; *HN*, 13, pp.364-5.
[36] Blackett was granted permission to run it along the town moor towards Scotswood by his fellow Newcastle common councillors in July 1689: TWA MD.NC/1/3 f.190v.
[37] Deckham: DPR1/1/1691/K5; Heworth: DULASC DCD/K/LP5/6-21; Gateshead Fell: NRO 2762 /E/Deeds/C61.
[38] Hughes, *op cit*, p.155; *Fighting Trade*, Vol 1, p.79; DULASC DCD/K/LP5/6; Appendix 2, Table A2.2.
[39] This much is clear from correspondence related to the Heworth lease from the Durham Dean and Chapter in 1705-7, and the Chapter's accounts of coals wrought and led there: NRO 324/W.3/19, DULASC DCD/K/LP5/21-95.
[40] Hatcher, Table 14.1(a), pp.491-2.
[41] *ibid*, pp.538-9.
[42] Levine and Wrightson, *op cit*, pp. 61-2.
[43] *Hostmen*, p.263; Montague to George Baker, 17 August 1697: Newcastle Univ SC, Misc. MSS. 85, Montague.
[44] Hatcher, p.534.
[45] M.Dunn, *An Historical, Geological, and Descriptive View of the Coal Trade of England*, (1844), p.20; Nef, *op cit*, Vol 1, pp.310-12.
[46] *Hostmen*, pp.151-2.
[47] Montague to Baker, 14 Aug 1697, Newcastle Univ SC, Misc. MSS. 85 Montague, C, f.275.
[48] *Hostmen*, pp. 153-63.
[49] *ibid*, pp. 153-4, 173; Fewster, (2011), *op cit*, pp.22-4.
[50] NRO ZCO IV/47/19. The Coal Office was literally that. Around £30 was spent on rent, desk, tables, chairs, 'upholstery and sundry other petty charges' and office supplies in the first year.
[51] Hughes, *op cit*, pp.182-3.
[52] NRO ZCO IV/47/19; *Fighting Trade*, Vol 1, pp. 91-5; E.Cruikshanks, 'Henry Liddell' in *HistParl*, 1690-1715. Liddell was later one of the bearers at Sir William's funeral: Richardson, 'Obsequies', *op cit*, p.27.
[53] *Fighting Trade*, Vol 1, pp.96-7; Shipments: TWA DF.COT CK/3/47; Prices: see Appendix 2, Figure A2.2.
[54] *Journal of the House of Commons, 1693-7*, (1803), 20 Feb 1697, p.715. Within weeks Blackett was paying his restless miners with Scottish coin which he had arranged to be minted in place of widely discredited English currency in the wake of the 1696 recoinage: Hainsworth, *Lowther correspondence, op cit*, p.391.
[55] Charles Montague to WB, 11 and 27 May 1699: Wallington Hall MSS; G.Iley to L.Vane, 29 May 1702: NRO ZCO VIII.1.
[56] *Hostmen*, p.273.
[57] Richmond letters 1728-34: NRO 673/2, *passim*.
[58] G.Finch, (ed), *A Pack of Idle Sparks*, (2013), pp.53-4.
[59] On 26th Jan 1710 Edward reminded one of his agents of the importance of the advice of able workmen in assessing the potential of lead veins: NRO ZBL 189.
[60] According to brother Edward in a later letter to Jacob Peart, 15 Feb 1711, NRO ZBL 189. Leece had been an apprentice of Michael Blackett in the 1670s.

61 Richardson, 'Obsequies', *op cit*, p.13.
62 *Hostmen,* pp.274, 288; Featherston to Brummel, 29 April 1698, DULASC Add.MS 1623/3.
63 The letters which survived long enough for Richardson to publish them in the 1840s: 'Obsequies', pp. 21-31.
64 eg. JW to Henry Maister, MBL 15 Dec 1677; MA Records-2, p.305.
65 *ibid*, p.317, and *Hostmen*, p.273.
66 Corporation calendar 1699-1718: TWA MD.NC/2/3 f21a.

Chapter Fifteen: Popular in his Country

1 *Britannia Illustrata, op cit.*
2 H.Horwitz, *Revolution Politicks, The career of Daniel Finch, Second Earl of Nottingham, 1647-1730*, (1968), pp.191-4; TNA SP 44/104, pp.385, 395-7, 404-5, and SP 34/3/67, 88-89b,95.
3 *Hostmen,* pp.247-8.
4 11 Dec 1705, quoted in J. Fewster, (ed), *The Keelmen of Newcastle-upon-Tyne 1638-1852,* SS 225, (2021), p.8.
5 See Appendix 5, Figures 12 and 16
6 E.Kimber and R. Johnson, *The Baronetage of England*, vol 2, (1771), p.371, although Welford attributed this line to Wotton's edition of 1741, which could place it within living memory, albeit still over 30 years after his death: *Men of Mark, op cit*, 1, p.305.
7 Vernon to Shrewsbury, 19 Jan 1699: G.James (ed), *Letters Illustrative of the Reign of William III*, Vol 2, (1841), p.253; Cruikshanks and Harrison, 'Blackett, Sir William', *HistParl*, 1690-1715.
8 Richardson, 'Obsequies', *op cit*, pp.40-1; St. Andrew's registers, 1696. Given his name, possibly a relation of Lady Blackett.
9 *Hostmen,* p.145; *HN* 4, p.100.
10 Surtees, *History of Durham*, Vol3, *op cit*, p. 18; Conyer's will of March 1692: TNA PROB 11/487/231; Blackett's will: TNA PROB 11/486; NRO 324/W.3/19.
11 St. Andrew's registers, Welford, *Men of Mark, op cit,* 1, pp. 127-30.
12 Hampson's account of Blackett in the 1660-90 *HistParl* volume claimed he had voted for Fenwick's execution but Cruikshanks and Harrison's entry in the 1690-1715 volume cites a contemporary account of his abstention.
13 W.Blackett to Dean of Durham, 10 Sept 1689; Surtees, *History of Durham*, Vol 2, *op cit*, pp.391-2.
14 See Appendix 2.2.2.4.
15 DULASC: DCD/K/LP5/6-95; TWA DF.COT/CK/2/325-420.
16 John Wilkinson, draft notes c.1706: NRO 324/W.3/19.
17 See Appendix 2. 5.
18 *Fighting Trade*, Vol 1, p.97; Levine and Wrightson, *op cit*, pp.73, 82; NRO ZCO IV/47/19.
19 Hughes, *op cit*, pp.166-7; J.M.Ellis, 'Cartels in the coal industry on Tyneside, 1699-1750', *Northern History*, 34, (1998), pp.134-48.
20 Winlaton was still in William's hands in June 1699 but Montague was there by 1705. The transfer might have occurred at much the same time as he took on Blackett's share of the Stella Grand Lease, c. 1703: NRO 2762/E/Deeds/C61; Creagh to Edward Blackett: NRO 11603 Box 16; Montague in account with Wilkinson, 5 Oct 1708: 324/W.3/19; *Fighting Trade*, Vol 1, p.93.

21 I simplistically assume that his wife's £6,000 dowry paid for the Greyfriars improvements and extensions, so it is excluded.
22 NRO 324/W3/18/3, 2762/E/X15.
23 Wallington: NRO 11603/Box 16. In a summary 1711 rental Wilkinson gave Hexham and Anick Grainge as worth £1,220 year but an out-rent of £233 to the Crown probably needs to be deducted from this figure: found with the 1737 estate survey: NRO 11603/Box 8.
24 Using a valuation rate of 16-18 years rent: C.Clay, 'Landlords and Estate Management in England' in J.Thirsk (ed), *The Agrarian History of England and Wales, Vol V.II, 1640-1715*, (1985), p.250.
25 J.Hodgson, *History of Northumberland, Pt 2, Vol 1*, (1827), p.259; NRO ZWN A/1 f22. No lead is known to have been extracted there.
26 Wilkinson to Ord, 20 June 1706: NRO 324/W.3/18/1. Kenton: NRO 2762 /E/Deeds/C61; 1711 rental, *op cit*.
27 See Appendix 4.2.
28 Earle, *op cit*, pp.311-14; Richardson, 'Obsequies', *op cit*, pp.15-20.
29 Trevelyan, *op cit*, p.10; Fenwick annuity case, 1692: NRO 2762, Box C74.
30 NRO 2762/Deeds/C61.
31 Pears and Atherton, *op cit*, pp.201-3. In the Knyff and Kip engraving of Greyfriars he had the Blackett arms halved with his wife's Conyers arms.
32 TNA PROB 11/486.
33 Brumell to Wilkinson 23 Dec 1705: Richardson, 'Obsequies', *op cit*, p.30.

Chapter Sixteen: Hobbled from Above

1 J.F.Wilson, *British business history, 1720-1994*, (1995), pp.12-13
2 Trevelyan, *op cit*, p.14; Welford, *Men of Mark, op cit*, 1, p.306; Purdue, *Ship That Came Home*, p.44. The third Sir William, our 'William III' was actually the second baronet, having inherited the title first bestowed on his father.
3 Galba's 'bond for life' of 17 Aug 1727: NRO ZBL 35/3.
4 I.Green, *Humanism and Protestantism in Early Modern English Education*, (2009), p.70.
5 Admissions Register, University College; C.E.Doble, (ed), *Remarks and Collections of Thomas Hearne*, Vol I 1705-1707, Oxford Historical Society, (1885), p.7. Although undergraduates typically were young by modern standards, being admitted at 15 was still rare.
6 College Register, 10 Jan 1705/6: UC:AR2/MS1/11, p.216.
7 *ibid*; the tutor was Robert Clavering, originally from Northumberland; C. Jackson (ed), *Yorkshire Diaries and Autobiographies of the Seventeenth and Eighteenth Centuries*, SS 77, (1886), p.116.
8 EB to daughter Maria, 24 March 1710, to son Christopher, Nov 1710: NRO ZBL 189.
9 EB to WB III, 13 Sep 1709: NRO ZBL 189; C.Hibbert and B.Weinreb, *The London Encyclopedia*, (2010), p.215; the horse: Calverley's diary, 27 May 1709, BL Add.MS 47218, f.218.
10 EB to Maria, 20 June, 16 Oct 1709: NRO ZBL 189. Elizabeth's family was unrelated to John Ord, the Newcastle lawyer and fixer.
11 Papers relating to an Ord vs Blackett Chancery case: NRO ZWN C1/1/4 f14-5.
12 *ibid*; EB to Maria, 15 May 1711.
13 NRO ZWN C1/1/4, 6.

14 I.Forbes, 'Elizabeth Ord: a woman of the 18th century', *HH*, 28 (2018) gives the whole messy and tragic tale.
15 Hoppitt, *op cit*, pp.233-4.
16 Fewster, (2011), *op cit*, pp.61-5, Hughes, *op cit*, pp.166-8.
17 EB to WB 13 Sep 1709, 3 Sep 1710, to Thos Brumell 5 Jan 1710: NRO ZBL 189.
18 E.Cruikshanks, 'Newcastle' in *HistParl*, 1690-1715.
19 Hughes, *op cit*, pp.167-8. Carr's uncle, Sir Ralph, was listed amongst the cartel members in 1708.
20 Cruikshanks, 'Newcastle', *op cit*.
21 D.Hainsworth, *Stewards, Lords and people. The estate steward and his world in later Stuart England*, (1992), p.41.
22 L.Gooch, *The Desperate Faction?* (2001).
23 R.Patten, *The History of the Rebellion in the year 1715* (1746 edn), p.23. This third edition was arguably the most candid, given the passage of time.
24 Calverley's journal, in Jackson, *Yorkshire Diaries, op cit*, pp.140-2; *NC*, 7-9 January 1715/6.
25 Liddell from London, 10 Oct 1715, to William Cotesworth, who was active with surveillance in Newcastle's defence from the Jacobites: J.M.Ellis, (ed), *The Letters of Henry Liddell to William Cotesworth*, SS 197, (1987), pp.183-4.
26 E.Cruikshanks, 'Blackett, Sir Wm (1690-1728)' in *HistParl*, 1690-1715, 1715-54.
27 *ibid*; Fewster, *op cit*, (2021), pp.54-5 . Ridley soon gave up on Blackett's help.
28 Hughes, *op cit*, p.175.
29 Dorothy was a Kirkley, a second cousin of William III. See Figure 4.1.
30 NRO 324/W.3/19, DULASC SHA/Deeds/488 Beamish estate.
31 EB to Brumell, 15 Dec 1709, 13 Nov, 22 Dec 1710: NRO ZBL 189; to James Mewburn, 21 July 1715: ZBL 191. Sir Edward subsequently took Brumell on as a steward at Winlaton, but sacked him in 1714 when suspected fraud compounded concerns regarding his ability: EB to Mewburn, 27 May 1714, ZBL 190.
32 MB to JW 29 and 31 Oct 1679; John Blackett to Thomas Brumell, 5 Feb 1709: NRO ZBL 192.
33 NRO 2762/E/Deeds/C61.
34 Wilkinson drafted his own terms of reference in 1711: NRO 324/W.3/19.
35 Appendix 2.1.5, 2.5; TWA DF.COT/CK/2/325-420.
36 Hughes, *op cit*, pp.166-70, p.196.
37 *ibid*, pp. 161, 196. See Hughes' chapter 5 and *Fighting Trade,* Vol 1, chapter 6, for the whole dismal account of the waggonway and cartel wars of the 1710s, albeit an absorbing one for those interested in the battlefield tactics and politics.
38 *ibid*, p.190-2.
39 *HN*, 13, p.37; Kenton colliery survey, 1732: NRO 3410/For/1/5/56 pp.63-4 (NEIMME). Prices: see Appendix 2.3, Figure A2.3.
40 Hughes, *op cit*, p.197.
41 Winlaton: *ibid,* p.192. Gateshead Fell: TWA DF.COT/CK/2/450-460. No data survive for the Heworth side of the colliery.
42 Marriott's accounts for Grinton in Swaledale, 1698-1705: TNA LLRO 3/85. Price trends are shown in Table A3.10 in Appendix 3.3.
43 Appendix 3.2.4. The volume of Newcastle lead shipped through the Baltic Sound also dropped noticeably between 1700-4 and 1705-9 (Table A3.2).
44 EB to John Blackett 13 Sep 1709, to Jacob Peart, 30 March 1710: NRO ZBL 189. Hexham: 24 July 1712 and 13 April 1713: *Idle Sparks, op cit*, pp. 135, 141.
45 Appended to a Chancery submission by Robinson, of Appleby, in the Blackett vs

Robinson case of 1727: TNA C 11/1466/10. 1711: *HN*, 3, p.11 quoting NRO QSB/34.
[46] TNA C 11/1466/10; *Idle Sparks, op cit*, p.135.
[47] EB to Nicholas Fenwick: 22 July 1714, NRO ZBL 190.
[48] 1711 rental, *op cit.*
[49] JW in account with JO, 20 June 1706: NRO 324/W.3/18/1.
[50] 1711 rental, *op cit.*
[51] T.Arkell, 'The probate process' in T.Arkell, N.Evans, N. Goose, (eds), *When Death do us part: Understanding and Interpreting the Probate Records of Early Modern England*, (2000), pp.7-13.
[52] Jackson, *Yorkshire diaries, op cit*, pp.113-5.
[53] BL Add.MS 47218, f242; 1711 rental, *op cit.*
[54] Elizabeth's husband was William Marshall of a landed Essex family. £4,000 of her dowry was still outstanding ten years later: Thomas Guy accounts, London Met Archives, H09/GY/A/8/1.
[55] J.Blackett in Rotterdam to JW, 23 Nov 1708: NRO ZBL 192.
[56] NRO ZWN A/1; Smith loan followed Ord's 'proposal for mortgage' regarding the Dukesfield estate: NRO324/W.3/18/1. The Fenwick loan was rolled over to Smith in 1715.
[57] Hughes, *op cit*, pp.79-81; Ord's accounts: NRO 324/O.1/45. Having obtained safe outlets for their capital and a regular interest income, lenders were sometime reluctant to have their loans repaid, as was the case with Smith's widow: John Ord to Robert Todd, 17 Nov 1719, NRO 324/W.3/18/1.
[58] NRO 324/W.3/19.
[59] EB to Maria, 5 Jan and 15 May 1711: NRO ZBL 189.
[60] JW to John Ord, 19 December 1712: NRO 324/W.3/18/1.
[61] Forbes, 'Elizabeth Ord', *op cit*, p.7; NRO 2762/E/Deeds/C61.
[62] JW to Edward Ridsdale, Sir Edward Blackett's son-in-law, 23 Sep 1717: NRO ZBL 260/2.
[63] He signed orders for Allenheads supplies until around this time, but the candles delivered in mid-December had been ordered in Robert Todd's name: TNA C 11/1466/10. In the callous terms of the day Blackett had, of course, also hugely reduced the value of Wilkinson's daughter as a marriageable asset.
[64] Rev'd Thomlinson's diary, in J.C.Hodgson (ed), *Six North Country Diaries*, SS 118, (1910), pp.146-7.

Chapter Seventeen: A Fool or a Knave

[1] Todd must have been in post by November. He continued to authorise candle orders for Allenheads until 1726: TNA C 11/1466/10.
[2] EB letters: 5 Nov 1709: NRO ZBL 189, 29 Apr 1714: NRO ZBL 190; Ord to TB, 11 Apr 1719: NRO 324/W.34/18/1.
[3] George Allgood, March 1724: NRO ZAL 57/12; TNA C 11/1466/10; Jos Richmond to A.Featherston, 26 May 1732: NRO 672/E/1B/1, 673/2; Salkeld will: DPR1/1/1727/S2. Bell: NRO 672/E/1A/1, f.32. His son was apprenticed to Salkeld in 1724: MA Records-2, p.347.
[4] Allgood was named as a trustee on a March 1717 deed alongside Wilkinson (DULASC BRA/1041/3) and appears in the cash accounts from August 1724, if not earlier: NRO 672/E/1A/1. He was an 'estate receiver' by the following March: NRO ZWN A/1 f10.
[5] Bell: Hughes, *op cit*, p.11. Allgood: WB's will - NRO 324/W1/16; London accounts:

NRO 672/E/1B/2, p.26.
[6] NRO 672/E/1B/1 f.32
[7] See Appendix 3, Table A3.11.
[8] Woodhall: Charles Busby to Anna Radcliffe, 17 April 1721, *PSAN* 3rd ser, Vol 7, (1915-6), p.124; Ramshaw: NRO ZPA/18. The LLC took a lease of Shildon lead mines and Acton Mill in 1722: DCRO D/Bo/B/124. The Blaydon refinery site on the banks of the Tyne immediately east of the lead wharves was claimed by Raistrick, without supporting evidence, to have been the old LLC 'Ryton' works, allegedly let to the Blacketts in 1706. However, Blackett cash accounts from the early 1720s document a new construction: *Lead Mining, op cit*, p.121; cash accounts: NRO 672/E/1A/1, 11603/Box 16.
[9] A.Raistrick, *Quakers, op cit*, pp. 179-80.
[10] See Appendix 3.6.1. As early as 1724 the Blaydon 'extracting house' was said to be providing great advantages: Lancelot Allgood, NRO ZAL 38/130/13.
[11] See p.289 above, Appendix 3.2.6. One hint of further exploration underway is seen in the £11 paid for boring rods sent to Coalcleugh in May 1725: 672/E/1A/1.
[12] TNA C 11/1466/10, bill, answer and candle accounts; DULASC CCB D/1981/ 54328. I.Forbes, 'George Mowbray and Burtreeford Smelt Mill', *Friends of Killhope newsletter*, (2020); Wilkinson to Mowbray lease 1714: NRO 2762/E/Deeds/C61.
[13] Richmond to Walter Calverley, 31 Dec 1731: NRO 673/2.
[14] 1737 Estate survey; Sales ledger 1727: NRO 672/E/1B/1.
[15] LMA H09/GY/A/8/1.
[16] For example, *NC* 12 Jan 1723, 31 Oct 1724, 24 Sep 1726, 9 Dec 1727.
[17] *Idle Sparks, op cit*, pp.84-5.
[18] EB to Mewburn, 7 Dec 1714, NRO ZBL 191. EB to Silvertop 21 Apr 1714, ZBL 190
[19] P.Brassley, 'Northumberland and Durham', in J.Thirsk (ed), *The Agrarian History of England and Wales, Vol V.I, 1640-1715 Regional Farming Systems,* (1984), pp.43-6; Hughes, *op cit*, pp.79-81. Clay observed that compared with a yield of just 4-5% when buying land, investment in 'improvement' of land already owned typically gave a far higher return of perhaps 10-12% during this period: Clay, *op cit*, p.250.
[20] A bookseller by trade, Guy owned South Sea company stock and sold it before that notorious bubble burst in 1720 and thereby left a large fortune. Blackett loan papers: LMA H09/GY/A/008/001, and in NRO ZWN A/1 ff10-28.
[21] George Allgood was a distant cousin of Lancelot Allgood, mentioned earlier.
[22] Joseph Richmond, 1 Jan 1729: NRO 672 E/1B/2 pp.1-6.
[23] Jackson, *Yorkshire Diaries, op cit*, p.128.
[24] D.W.Hayton, 'William Thompson, c.1676-1739)' in *HistParl*, 1690-1715.
[25] NRO ZWN/1/A; various letters 11 April-18 June 1719: NRO 324/W.3/18/1. Very roughly, based on contemporary views on longevity, Julia's age in 1718 and a 5% interest rate, her annuity was probably worth no more than £7,500. Derived using D.R.Bellhouse, 'A new look at Halley's life table', *Journal Royal Statistical Society*, (2011), p.830.
[26] NRO ZAL 38/122.
[27] Foster, *marriage licences, op cit*; E.Cruikshanks, 'John Trenchard', *HistParl*, 1715-54. In his will of 1739, Thompson left legacies to his step-daughters, including, to Anne, £200 and a heart-shaped brooch that had come down from his mother, perhaps a gesture of affection, or of guilt: K.M.Rowland, 'Sir William Thompson', *William and Mary Quarterly*, Vol 3, (1894), p.222. As for Anne, Trenchard was dead within a few years, she outlived her second husband and reached the age of 78 in comfortable circumstances.

[28] TNA C 11/1466/10; NRO 324/W.3/18/1 as above. Blackett originally thought £8,000 would do for the pays but on second thoughts raised this to £9,000.
[29] Allgood to Ord, 11 April 1721: NRO 324/W.3/18/1.
[30] Ryal, Ingoe and Kearsley: R.Welford, 'Local Muniments', (1909) *op cit*, pp. 115-6; NRO 324/W.3/18/1 and 19.
[31] *NC,* 9 Oct 1725, p.3. Greyfriars remained the more important house, however. The art, plate and furnishings there were valued in 1728 at seven times more (£1,800) than those in Wallington: NRO 672/E/1B/2, f21.
[32] Marriage settlement of 18 Sep 1725: NRO ZBL 261/10. Shortly afterwards Blackett took delivery of six racehorses, ten coach-horses and four others and was spending more money for a London coachmaker's services: NRO 672/E/1B/2. Barbara's second husband was the 30-year-old Baron Mansell.
[33] They included the much-respected Dr Adam Askew of Newcastle, and William Hanby of Gateshead: Executorship accounts; Ferryhill: NRO 672/E/1B/2.
[34] Undated anonymous legal opinion found amongst Calverley papers and clearly prepared in the aftermath of William III's death: West Yorks Archives DB16/C7/9L.
[35] Estimated in Appendix 4.3.
[36] January 1729 inventory: NRO 672/E/1B/2.
[37] Guy's Hospital accounts: LMA H09 GY/D/88.
[38] In Panton Square and at Hampstead: Executorship accounts, cash book: NRO 672/E/1A/1, f12.
[39] To George Allgood, 4 May 1724: NRO ZAL 38/130/13.

Chapter Eighteen: The Foundations of Redemption

[1] Jackson, *Yorkshire Diaries, op cit,* p.134; he entered Balliol Collage in 1724: J.Foster, (ed), *Alumni Oxoniensis, 1715-1886,* (1888), p.210. Walter did not take a degree at Oxford.
[2] J. Burton (ed), *Autobiography of the Rev Dr Alexander Carlyle,* 2nd edition, (1860), pp.415-6. When away from the north Walter constantly asked about his dogs and horses: NRO 673/2, *passim.*
[3] According to her father, by 1726 Elizabeth, not quite 15, was 'very much pressing … to have some necessary jewels and ornaments': NRO ZWN/C1/1/16.
[4] The lead business was wound up in the 1920s.
[5] April 1729: Petition to the Lord Chancellor. Elizabeth, an orphan and minor, was his ward: NRO ZWN C1/1/19. Richmond to Clark 24 May 1729: NRO 673/2. 1 July: George Grey to Allgood, ZWN C1/5/4. In the marriage settlement of 26 August 1729, Allgood and Clark 'acted for' Elizabeth Ord *als* Blackett and Grey was a witness: ZWN/1/A, ff 57-60.
[6] Schama, *op cit,* p.350.
[7] Much has been written elsewhere of Walter Blackett's life —Sir Walter after the death of his father in 1749 - including Straker's *Memoirs,* Welford's *Men of Mark,* Purdue's *Ship That Came Home.* See also Namier's biography in *HistParl,* 1754-90.
[8] Forbes, 'Elizabeth Ord', *op cit.*
[9] Flinn's study of Ambrose Crowley's Winlaton factory and his system of control is an illuminating exception: *Men of Iron, op cit,* and *The Law Book of the Crowley Ironworks,* SS 167, (1957).
[10] 1675: MBL *passim*; 1730s accounting journals: NRO 672 1/E/1B/2; Dukesfield

Documents/ Background and Support/ Business Structure... Coal mines responsibility cannot be compared in the same way but Robert Todd was responsible for both the mines and the land at Kenton under William II and III. By the late 1720s Matthew Bell reported on the Felling, Winlaton and Stella mines, while Thomas Robinson accounted for the Winlaton rents: further functional specialisation of tasks.

[11] NRO 324/W.3/19; TNA C 11/1466/10.

[12] H.Richmond to C.Johnson 8 Dec 1764: NRO 672/E/1E/3.

[13] Notes to the 'Allgood of Nunwick' pedigree: *HN*, 15, facing page 200.

[14] NRO 673/2, *passim*. Allgood was the nephew of Thomas, William II's Hexham steward, and so possibly knew his near contemporary William III from childhood.

[15] He was 'about 50 years of age' in a 1743 lawsuit: Allendale Estate uncatalogued documents. The Joseph baptised in Aspatria in 1693 was son of a Henry Richmond, later the name of our Joseph Richmond's eldest son.

[16] Richmond (JR) to John Armstrong (JA) at Allenheads, 2 Sep 1729: NRO 673/2; deed abstracts, NRO 2762 /E/Deeds/C61, JR to Walter Blackett (WB), 24 Jan 1755: NRO 672/E/1E/1.

[17] JR to JA, 22 Jan 1729, JR to Hunter, 1 Jan 1729: NRO 673/2.

[18] NRO 672/E/1B/2-8.

[19] JR to Allgood, 27 Mar 1731, JR to JA, 2 Sep 1729: NRO 673/2.

[20] JR to IH, 8 Apr 1755: NRO 672/E/1E/1; HR to IH, 30 Jun 1767: 672/E/1E/3.

[21] JR to IH, 10 Jun 1730: NRO 673/2.

[22] For example, journal entry format in 672/E/1E/2 f 31, JR to John Bacon, 15 May 1730: NRO 673/2. Between a fifth and a half of the lead was refined.

[23] JR to LA, 24 Apr 1731: NRO 673/2.

[24] JR to LA, 19 Dec 1730. At the start of 1729 the lead miners, smelters and suppliers had been owed £11,000: NRO 672/E/1B/2.

[25] JR to Christopher Denton, 19 Jun 1733, JR to WB, 13 Feb 1733: NRO 673/2.

[26] Chandler to WB, 9 Jul 1732: DULASC CCB/B/182/121.

[27] JR to WB, 2 March 1733: NRO 673/2.

[28] 1737 estate survey; JR to Walter Blackett, 13 Feb 1733: NRO 673/2.

[29] See Appendix 4.4.

[30] NRO 672/E/1B/2, pp.53-4; *Hostmen,* p.261.

[31] JR to LA, 2 Feb 1731: NRO 673/2.

[32] *ibid*, and 8 Dec 1730, 2 Jan 1731; 1737 estate survey. East Kenton colliery was let at Mayday 1731, just three months after Richmond made his case. Getting out of the coal business probably freed up £1,500 of working capital, based on 1720s production levels, and avoided the need to invest in mines and drainage. West Kenton was not bought by Blackett and East Kenton was sold at a later date.

[33] NRO 672 E/1B/1-2. Instead of the Weardale mines being leased they were increasingly worked directly by the late 1720s.

[34] JR to JA, 8 Oct 1728, NRO 673/2.

[35] JR to JA, 24 Mar 1729, 26 Sep 1732, JR to IH, 4 Nov 1728: NRO 673/2; accounts 672/E/1B/2. The Mohope vein lay near the Hexham and Whitfield manor boundary. Its discovery led to a boundary line dispute, resolved only in the 1750s: NRO 324/W1/28.

[36] JR to Peart, 1 Feb 1732, NRO 673/2; J.Butler to Bishop Chandler, 11 Aug 1732: DULASC CCB/B/182/121.

[37] See Appendix 3.5.2.

[38] JR to JP, 18 Jun 1734: NRO 673/2. Note that this cost threshold for closure was far lower than the £4.37/ton Weardale average Richmond had complained about just

three years earlier (see p.318), perhaps indicating that some higher cost mines had already been closed in favour of higher production from the lowest cost mines. Unfortunately we have no direct evidence for what this observed cost reduction meant for miners' pay. Since labour accounted for much of the cost of mining a direct link between the falling cost per ton of ore and pay per miner seems likely. However, although Richmond and his agents might well have tried driving hard bargains as the lead price fell, this would have been tempered by the need to recruit more miners as the business grew. Furthermore, actual earnings depended upon how easy it was to raise ore. With productive veins such as at Mohope being opened up, it is possible than earnings could have held up better than the piece rates paid for each bing of ore.

[39] Appendix 3.6.2. Raistrick and Jennings, *op cit*, pp.142-8 summarises the LLC's development in Alston Moor in the 18th century.

[40] Table A3.27, Appendix 3.6.

[41] Raistrick and Jennings, *op cit*, pp.144-6; Liddell's notebook: TNA ADM 79/35, N.Walton and H.Boag, Greenwich Hospital receivers 24 Aug 1736 *et seq*: TNA ADM 66/105.

[42] JR to WB, 11 Dec 1732: NRO 673/2. LMA H09 GY/D/88, Blackett accounts: NRO 672 E/1B/1-2. See also Appendix 4.4.

Chapter Nineteen: Newcastle, Blacketts and History

[1] John Blackett's executor accounts NRO ZBL 195; extrapolation from estate valuations in M.Hughes, 'Lead, Land and Coal as sources of Landlord Income in Northumberland between 1700 and 1850', unpublished Durham D.Phil thesis, (1963), Vol 2, pp. 100-102.

[2] See Appendix 4.6. The Duke of Northumberland's estates produced about £6,000 in 1719 and the Earl of Carlisle's around £4,500 in the mid-1730s: P.Brassley, *Agricultural Economy in Northumberland and Durham 1640-1750*, (1985), pp. 78-9, 84. The Radcliffe/Derwentwater estates in Northumberland grossed £4,400 in 1717: TNA FEC 1/501/D2.

[3] Dutch letters from William I to Jacob Momma-Reenstierna, 1669, 1670: Sweden Riksarchivet E2499. In 1680 William's nephew Timothy Wright went to France to learn '*la langue*': MB to Edwd Willett 3 Apr 1680.

[4] See Table 4.1 above. See chapter 5 for Milbank, and Ellis, Bold Adventurer, *op cit*, for Cotesworth in Gateshead.

[5] MA Records-2, p. 287; Welford, *Men of Mark, op cit*, 3, p. 317; MB letters, 2 and 14 June 1679; NRO ZRI/21/11; *Fighting Trade*, Vol 1, p.110. Ridley was also active in Newcastle's civic elite until his death in 1711.

[6] Ashcroft, *op cit*, pp.120-4; Hainsworth, *Lowther Correspondence, op cit*.

[7] Pollard, *op cit*, p.71; M.W.Flinn, *Men of Iron*, (2019 edition), p.252. Also see chapter 12 above.

[8] Oldroyd, *op cit, passim*.

[9] NRS, RH15/102/6/2/8,17; Hatcher, p.293; T.W.Hancock, 'Pennant Melangell: its parochial history and antiquities', *Collections Historical & Archaeological relating to Montgomeryshire and its borders*, XII, (1879), p.68.

[10] Pollard, *op cit*, pp.78-9, 129-30.

[11] Wilson's *British business history, op cit*, places the development of business organisational forms beyond direct personal control to later in the 18th century: pp.12,21-3.

[12] A.Kussmaul, *A general view of the rural economy of England, 1538-1840*, (1990), pp.98-102, 114-25.
[13] S.Broadberry, B.Campbell, A.Klein, M. Overton and B. van Leeuwen, *British Economic Growth 1270-1870*, (2015), calculated GDP/head as £8.85 in 1650 and £12.68 in 1700: pp. 204-8, 259-62.
[14] A.Smith, *An Inquiry into the Nature and Causes of the Wealth of Nations*, (1776), Book 1, chapter 1.
[15] J.A.Chartres, 'The Marketing of Agricultural Produce', in Thirsk, *Agrarian History, op cit*, (1985), pp.465-8.
[16] J.Cary, 'An essay on the State of England in relation to its trade..', 1695, quoted in Thirsk and Cooper, *op cit*, p.323.
[17] Kussmaul, *op cit*; Chartres, *op cit*, pp.460-5.
[18] Defoe, *op cit*, p.6. In 1989 Peter Earle noted the important role played by wholesalers, but his call for more research on them seems not to have been heeded much since: *op cit*, p.51.
[19] Stephens, *Exeter, op cit*, chapter 7; D.Hussey, *Coastal and River Trade in pre-Industrial England, Bristol and its region, 1680-1730*, (2000), chapters 1 and 2; R.Davis, *The Trade and Shipping of Hull 1500-1700*, (1964), p.27.
[20] J.Mokyr, *The Enlightened Economy*, (2009), pp.368-9, and *A Culture of Growth: The Origins of the Modern Economy*, (2018), pp.6-13.
[21] See Dukesfield Documents/ Background and Support/ Business Structure and Biographies for further information and sources.
[22] Purdue, *Ship That Came Home*, chapter 2. John Douglas had worked for William Blackett II in his purchase of Wallington from the Fenwicks.

Index

References to figures are shown in **bold**.

accounting 84, 184, 310, 326, 331, Plate 13
   present value analysis 122, 274
   unit cost calculations 184-5, 288, 292, 295
   see also Blacketts, business, merchants
agriculture 24, 148, 270-2, 311-2
   see also land
Allendale 80, 99-100, 109, 116-18, 220, 213, 271, 292 see also Allenheads, Coalcleugh, lead
Allenheads 136, 146, 209, 223-4, 232, 312, Plate 15
   lead mine 116, 119, 124, 138-9, 208, 236, 287
   smelting mill 220 see also Mowbray
Allensford, iron forge 148
Allgood
   George 272-4, 276, 285
   Lancelot 267, 276, 280-5, 291, 298
   Major 276
   Thomas 232, 266
Alston Moor 100, 110, 209-10, 296-7 see also lead, London Lead Company, Radcliffes
Alvey, Anne 31-2
Amsterdam 6-7, 40, 68, 74, 76, 103, 133 4 see also lead trade, merchants
Anderson, Sir Francis 153, 163, 186, 188, 339
Anglo-Dutch Wars
   First 18, 67-8, 74, 87, 92
   Second 118, 121, 152, 170, 176
   Third 53
Anne, Queen 254
annuities 165, 192, 214-5, 238, 244, 246, 251-2, 262-4, 274, 276-7, 290, 297, 350
apprenticeship 8-9, 15-6, 33-42, 55-7 see also Merchant Adventurers, business
Archer, Edward 20

Armstrong
   John 2, 282-3, 287-8
   William, Lord 317
Atherton, Henry 237
Atkinson, William 336

Bacon family 207, 217
   George 111, 113, 120
ballast shores 31-3
Baltic Sea trade 6-7, 18, 74 see also Copenhagen, Danzig, Elbing, Konigsberg, Riga, the Sound Toll, Stockholm
Banson, William 39, 326
Barbon, Nicholas 176
Barnes, Ambrose 37, 41-2, 65, 71, 77- 9, 188-9, 204, 326, 328, 330
Basire, Isaac 128-30
Bawtry 106
Beaumont
   Diana 315
   family 315-6
   Huntingdon 91
Bedale, Yorks 160
Bell
   Matthew 267-8, 352
   Peter 174
Bernardeau, Peter 294
Berwick-on-Tweed 43, 154-5, 290
Bewick, Robert 15, 44
Billing, Weardale 131
Birkey Burn smelting mill 140, 207-8, 219, 284
Bishopfield 115, 119
Bittlestone, Joseph 139, 336-7
Blaby, Leics 163, 339
Black Dean, Weardale 131
Blackett
   business 261-4, 270, 275-8, 282, 290, 296-7; coal 19, 162-3, 167-175, 257-9, 268, 289-92, 303; lead 260-2, 268-9, 292-7; management 282-4, 287-8, 305-7, 310-1, Plates 14-17; trade 19
   family 16-21, **25**, 28, 155, 158-63, **303**, 316, 319-20
   heraldic arms 24, 155, 190

Index | 355

landed estate 261, 270-2, 290, 303-4
Blackett, Alethea 213
Blackett, Anne 274, 350
Blackett, Lady Barbara nee Villiers 2, 5, 275-6
Blackett, Christian (1651-1716, m Robert Mitford) 158, 164, 275, 338
Blackett, Christopher (1613-75) 23, 28-9, 32-3, 167-8, 325
Blackett, Christopher of Wylam 315
Blackett, Christopher (1659-78) 160
Blackett, Diana 4, 274
Blackett, Edward (d.1628) 22-7, 324
Blackett, Edward (c.1615-67) 23, 28, 30, 32, 40-1, 72, 74, 76, 86, 114, 120-1, 326
Blackett, Edward (1649-1718), 2nd baronet 18, 83, 160-1, 163-4, 172, 181, 190, 192-8, 207-8, 211-3, 219, 251, 253, 260, 264, 271-3, 302, 316, 343, 344, Plate 24; business 184-5, 198, 207-8, 257, 284; marriages 160-1; politics 342
Blackett, Lady Elizabeth nee Kirkley 51, 57, 59, 163, Plate 22
Blackett, Elizabeth (1646-94) 158
Blackett, Isabel nee Crooke 27-9, 34
Blackett, Isabella (1648-87) 158
Blackett, John (1635-1707) son of Christopher 39, 136-7, 167-8, 173-4, 225
Blackett, John (1683-1750) son of Edward 260, 302
Blackett, John Erasmus 315
Blackett, Lady Julia nee Conyers 202, 212, 246, 248, 250, 273-4, Plate 28
Blackett, Julia (1686-1736) 262-3
Blackett, Lady Margaret: see Rogers
Blackett, Maria 213
Blackett, Michael 18, 70, 124, 134, 136, 149, 157, 160-4, 181-2, 195; civic roles 161, 186; marriage 161
Blackett, Walter, previously Calverley 5, 276, 279-81, 291, 297-8, 315, 351, Plate 27; and Joseph Richmond 297; alderman, mayor & MP 280-1; lifestyle & extravagance 289, 297; marriage to Elizabeth Ord 280
Blackett, William (1587-1648) 23-35, 115, 155, 325
Blackett, William (1621-80), 1st baronet Plate 21; background and apprenticeship 4-5, 34-5, 45-50; character and outlook 62, 78-9, 155-6, 187-91, 301-2; family life in Newcastle 51, 59-60, 70, 77, 163-5, 191-2, 341; later life 185-7
business 60-1, 71-3, 122-3, 155-6, 173-5, 177-8, 181, 184, 189-90, 299; coal 82, 91-2, 165, 168-75; expansion and scale 179-80; investment & capital 81-9, 175-7; land 172, 176; lead 81-2, 115-32, 164; management 146, 173, 179-85; as trader 17-8, 69, 73-7, 80, 82-3, 87-9, 118, 180
public office: merchants' company and hostmen 75, 93-4, 151-2; as MP 153, 180-1, 186; and Newcastle corporation 62, 65-6, 77-80, 151-3
impact & legacy: achievements 145, 149, 187-8, 194; assets and wealth 70, 83, 143-4, 177, 188, 191-4; baronetcy 153, 155-6; political ability 123, 154-5; will & bequests 164-5, 186, 191-7
Blackett, William (c.1633-95) son of Christopher 71-2, 74, 127, 311
Blackett, William (1657-1705) 1st baronet of the 2nd creation 16, 18, 124, 162, 174, Plate 25; character 231, 236-7; family 202, 245-6; later life 4, 235-6, 245-6; lifestyle 211-3, 245-7
business 231-2, 238-9, 242-5, 345; coal 211, 224-30, 240-2; expansion and scale 216, 231, 238-9, 243, 246; land 214-5, 243-4; lead 207-11, 213-25, **222**, 239-40; monopoly 306-7
public office: guilds 239; as MP 202-6, 228-30, 235-6; Newcastle corporation 186, 199, 203, 235; political ability 200, 202-5, 229-31, 236, 306-7
impact & legacy: achievements 198-9, 201-2, 237-8; business scale 231, 239; wealth 244-5; will & bequests 223, 235, 237, 245-7, 262
Blackett, William (1690-1728), 2nd

baronet of the 2nd creation 16, 197, 249-51, Plate 26; character 249-52, 257, 265-6; family with Elizabeth Ord 251-2; later life and funeral 1-5, 276-7, 351; lifestyle 251, 264, 272-5, 277; marriage 275-6
   business: debts 264, 272-5, 277-8, 297 *see also* Blackett, business
   public office: mayor of Newcastle 265-6; as MP 253-6 *see also* Jacobites
   wealth and legacies 275-7
Blackhall, Hexhamshire, lead smelting mill 111, 115, 119-20, 139-40, 219
Blagill, Alston Moor 210
Blakiston
   George 78-9
   John 63, 66
Blanchland, lead mine 210, 268
Blaydon, 111, 136-7, 169;
   coal 91;
   silver refinery 268-9, 278, 288, 350;
   staiths 127, 169;
   see also Robinson, Winlaton
Blyth 91
Boag, Hugh 310
Bonner, Thomas 15, 63-6, 77-80, 151
   William 70
Bordeaux, France 76, 106, 181
Boroughbridge, Yorks 265
Bowes family 110, 310
Brabant, Henry 157, 199-206
Bradford, Yorks, 8, 262
Brandling
   Ralph 225-6
   Robert 175, 177-8, 225, 340
Bridges, Shem 158
Briggs, James 8, 111, 120, 135
Bristol 106, 218, 313-4, 322
Brumell, Thomas 233-4, 246, 257, 259, 267, 348
Burkin, James 200
business
   analysis and decision making 84, 141-3, 184, 287-9
   apprenticeship and education 38-41
   culture and open-ness 13-6, 311-5
   finance and cashflow 129-30, 183-4
   history 19-20, 249, 307, 310-1
   management 96-7, 133-7, 231, 249, 281-3, 310-1; development 309-11; governance arrangements 264; land agents 270-2; operations and process control 281-9
   monopoly & restrictive practices 145-6, 178, 306-7
   operations 124-7, 133-45
   profitability 141-5
   strategy 81-91, 129-30, 133-5, 178, 242-3, 257-8, 290-302
   structure 109, 124, 211; large organisations 179, 307-11; longevity 195-6, 304-5
   see also accounting, Blackett, capital, economic growth, innovation, merchants, ports, trade
Butler family 118
   Gregory 111
   John 40, 110-1, 115, 120-1, 135
Byers Green, Co. Durham 233

Calverley, Sir Walter (1669-1749) 255, 262-3
Calverley, Walter (1707-77)
   see Blackett, Walter
capital
   requirements for, in mining 88-9, 311; fixed assets 84, 144; working capital 51-5, 88
   returns on 88, 144-5, 175
   sources of: credit 52, 55-6; mortgages 82, 172, 198, 244, 263, 272, 302, 304-5, 349; Newcastle market 263-4; re-invested profits 82-3, 86-7, 264
   see also business, land, merchants
Carr family 172
   Joan 48-50, 60, 66, 327
   Leonard 62, 78-9
   Ralph (d.1635) 48-9
   Sir Ralph (1634-1710) 186, 204
   William (d.1660) 41, 82, 91, 96
   William, MP (1664-1720) 228, 235, 253
   William, MP (d.1742) 280
Carrshield, lead mill dispute 220
Carter, George 36, 65, 71-3, 328
Cary John 313
Catholics 16, 43, 91, 124, 153, 186, 199, 202-4, 206, 215, 254
Cavendish, Henry, Earl of Ogle 153

Index | 357

Cay, Jabez 219
Chandler, Edward, Bishop of Durham 289
Chapman family 31
    Henry 31-2, 59
    Matthew 59
Charles I, King 26, 43
Charles II, King 16, 79-80, 153, 157, 187, 199-202
    borough independence 199
    Restoration of 78-81, 156
Chatham Naval Dockyard 178
Chaytor, William 134, 336
Chester, Cheshire 106
Chesterfield 111, 113
Chester-le-Street 130
Civil war 43-5
    see also Newcastle, Parliament
Clark, Charles 276, 280
Clavering family 171, 258-9
    James 258
    Robert, Oxford tutor 251, 347
Clerk Sir John 311
cloth-making 85-6, 148
cloth trade 8-9, 74, 89
    see also Newcastle, merchants
Company of Merchant Adventurers see Merchant Adventurers
coal 8, 45-6, 89, 318, 322, 327
    demand for and growth 89-90
    owners 16, 172
    seams 92, 167-70
    transport costs 92, 332
    waggonways 84, 92-4, 96, 169-70, 225-7, 231, 240-2, 259, 291, 310-1, 332, Plate 19
    see also collieries, Newcastle, Tyneside
coal mining 45-6, 91, 167-75
    and capital 89-90
    drainage 89, 92, 170-1
    economies of scale 89-91, 94-5, 170
    fixed assets 94-5
    High Main seam 167-9
    management of 172-5, 310-1
    miners 172
    production 46, 166-75, 226-7, 230
coal trade 6, 44-6, 228, 268, 338
    cartels and competition 45, 228-9, 230, 241, 252, 259; Coal Office 230-1, 240
    embargoes 42-3, 152, 170
    fitters 75, 175, 227-9
    gift coals 226
    London market 89, 228
    and politics 228
    prices 231, 259
    taxes and duties 154, 156-7, 228
    see also Hostmen, keelmen, London, merchants
Coalcleugh 124-5
    lead mine 118-9, 260; drainage 209-10, 293
    village 146, 223, 312
Cocke
    Henry 163
    Ralph 79
    Samuel 151
collieries 167-73, 179
    Benwell 182, 240
    Deckham Hall 225
    Gibside 84, 227, 240-1
    Ingoe 245
    Newbiggin Hall 167
    Oakwood, Acomb 344
    see also Heworth/Gateshead Fell, Kenton, Stella Grand Lease, Whickham, Whorlton Moor, Winlaton
Conyers
    Sir Christopher 202, 237
    Sir John 237
    Julia: see Blackett, Lady Julia
Cooke, Timothy 59, 328
Copperthwaite, Christopher 131, 138, 208
Corbridge bridge 123, 316, Plate 11
Cosin, John, Bishop of Durham 110, 127-30, 178
Cotesworth, William 20, 57, 176, 258, 309, 348
Country party 154, 186
    see also Whigs
Court party 186
    see also Tories
Creagh, Sir William 198, 202-3, 206
Crewe, Nathaniel, Bishop of Durham 226, 344
Cromwell
    Oliver 64, 66-7, 80
    Richard 80

Crooke,
  Isabel *see* Blackett, Isabel
  John 34, 325
  William 27
Crowley, Ambrose 20, 87, 183, 219, 310, 331, 337
Cumberland 6, 14, 122, 310
customs *see* taxation

Danzig (Gdansk) 6-7, 43, 103-4, 106
  see also Newcastle, trade
Darby, Abraham 218
Davison
  Benjamin 158, 198
  Family 158, 244
  Thomas 158, 161
  Timothy 158, 173, 198-200, 205, 232-3, 341
  William 258, 268
Dawson
  Cuthbert 109
  Henry 63-5, 78-9
  Michael 48, 64
Defoe, Daniel 54-5, 313
Delaval, Diana nee Booth, later Lady Blackett 197
Derbyshire 102,106-7, 109, 111-3, 146
  see also lead, Peak District
Derwent
  lead smelting mill 129-30, 135, 221
  valley, ironmaking 148
Dixon, Abraham 276
Douglas, John 316
Draycott, Francis 181, 191
Dublin 322
Dukesfield, Hexhamshire
  estate and land 120, 177, 263, 271, 283, 316
  Hall 136, 282, Plate 16
  smelting mill 120, 123, 125-7, 136, 139-44, 180, 195, 207, 210, 219, 221, 223, 232, 287-8, 193
  see also lead smelting
Durham, Bishop of: *see* Cosin, John; Chandler, Edward; Crewe, Nathaniel
Durham, Bishopric of
  coal leases 11, 91-3
  lead leases, Weardale 78, 108-9, 269, 289

Easington, Co Durham 202
Eastland Company 151
economic growth
  and integration 19, 86-7, 148-9, 194, 311-5
  productivity and specialisation 19, 138-9, 148, 194, 271, 311-2
  see also business, innovation, merchants, trade
education 38-40, 223
  see also apprenticeship
Elbing (Eblag) 6
Ellison, Robert 63, 71, 79-80, 151
Emerson
  John 49, 72, 79, 151, 329
  Nicholas 311
entrepreneurship, *see* business
Errington
  family 121
  George, merchant 39
  John, Blagill 210
Esholt Hall, Bradford, Yorks 5, 262
Europe, northern 7
Exclusion crisis of 1679 186, 199
Exeter, Devon 85, 314

Fallowfield
  House 136, Plate 17
  lead mine 110-1, 121-4, 137-41, 146, 160, 195, 198, 207-10, 213, 224, 239, 260, 334, 336, 339, 344
  miners 146, 218
  purchase by Blackett 214
  see also Blackett, Edward; lead mining
Fallowlees estate 243-4, 303
Featherstone
  family, Dukesfield 221, 232
  John 221
  Thomas 221, 344
Felling estate, Gateshead 178, 225-6
Fenwick
  Alice 23, 32
  annuity from Blackett 242, 262-3
  Sir John (c.1570-1658) 110, 116
  Sir John (c.1644-97) 121, 214-5, 237-8
  Lady Mary *nee* Howard 121, 262-3
  Nicholas, merchant 263
  Thomas 32-3

Index | 359

Sir William 117, 121-3, 214
  See also Wallington
flax 7, 14, 17-8, 49, 57, 85
Foster, Robert 140
Forster, 'General' Thomas 255

Gardiner, Ralph, *England's Grievance* 31, 78
Gateshead 28, 34, 55, 57, 86, 92
Gateshead Fell colliery: see Heworth
Gdansk: *see* Danzig
George I, King 254-5
Gibside *see* collieries
Gillery, John 173, 182
Gilpin, William 310
Gingleshaugh, Hexhamshire 333
Glass making 86, 102, 111, 127, 269
'Glorious Revolution' of 1689 204, 254
Glover, Thomas 58, 71-4, 328, 329
Government
  local: *see* Newcastle Corporation, Northumberland
  national: *see* Parliament
Gray, William, *Chorographia* 14-5, 46, 90, 106
Greengill lead mine 124-5, 208, 216
Greenwich Hospital 296, 310
  see also Alston Moor, Radcliffe
Grey, Ralph 53, 86, 88, 104, 111, 115, 133-4, 144-5, 149, 334, 336
Greyfriars: *see* Newcastle
Guild system 8-9, 12-4, 37, 56
  See also Hostmen, Newcastle, Merchant adventurers
Guy's Hospital 270, 272, 297

Hamburg 6-7, 40, 42, 53, 69, 72, 103, 151, 197, 329, 342
  see also Newcastle, trade
Hamsterley, Co. Durham 23, 25, 27-9, 32-3, 59, 167, 324, 325 *see also* Hoppyland
Hargrave, Henry 71-3
Hartlepool 28
Haselrig, Sir Arthur 63, 66, 78, 93, 110, 167, 339
Headlam, George 174
Hechstetter, Daniel 184, 330
hemp 7
Heworth staiths 226

Heworth/Gateshead Fell colliery 225-6, 232, 238-40, 257-9, 268, 291
Hexham 123, 139, 260, 271, 276
  manor of 110, 123, 214-5, 232, 243-4, 262, 267, 271, 287, 289
Hexhamshire 109, 126
  lead industry 111, **117**, 119, 148
  see also Blackhall, Dukesfield, Red Lead Mill
Hodgson, William 169, 178
Hoppyland, Co. Durham 24, 27, 29, 33
Horden Hall, Co Durham 246
Hostmen's company, Newcastle 9, 12-3, 38, 41, 46, 59, 63, 75, 93, 151-2, 180, 227-30, 237
  apprentices 174, 230
  coal tax 121
  see also coal trade, Newcastle
Howard, Mary: *see* Fenwick, Lady Mary
Hull 6, 103-7, 113, 152, 314
  see also merchants, trade
Hunstanworth, Co. Durham 111, 115, 118, 124, 210, 268, 339
  see also lead mining
Hunter Isaac, Dukesfield 282-3, 287-8, 293
Hutton, Richard, moormaster 325
Hutton Roof, Westmorland 8

industries 85-7
innovation 140-2, 218-20, 306
interest rates 122, 134, 176, 213-4, 273, 326, 328, 350
investment 143-4
  see also Blackett, business, capital, merchants
iron 7, 74, 87, 171
iron-making 87, 148, 183, 218-9,
  see also Crowley, Winlaton
Isaacson, Anthony 338
Isleworth, Middx, school 250

Jackson
  Ralph, Newcastle 38
  Robert, Stockton 336, 337
Jacobites 214, 235, 254-6, 296
James II, King 186, 202-4, 206, 214, 225, 231, 235, 254
Jarrow 28-30, 46, 166
Jeffreys, Judge George 201, 342

360 | *The Blacketts*

Jenison
    Ralph 66, 79, 82, 91, 93
    Robert 13, 43-4
Johnson, William 64

Kaliningrad: *see* Konigsberg
keelmen 12-3, 152-3, 229-30, 236, 255
    see also coal trade
Kendal 8, 75, 85, 86
Kenton 224-5
    colliery 225-6, 240-2, 257-9, 291
    estate 243-4, 267, 270-1, 291, 352
Keswick copper mines 84
Keys, Robert, Weardale 223
Killhope lead mine 131, 162, 177, 185
Killhope Law 99
King, Gregory, 55
Kip, Jan, *Britannia Illustrata* 1, 212
Kirby Lonsdale, Westmorland 8
Kirkley family 56, **58**, 62, 65, 233
    Elizabeth *nee* Chapman 48, 59-61, 65
    Elizabeth: *see* Blackett, Elizabeth
    Matthew 60, 66, 71, 173, 225, 232
    Michael 6, 57
Knaresborough spa, Yorks 185
Konigsberg (Kaliningrad), Prussia 7
    see also Newcastle, trade

La Rochelle, France 106
    see also Newcastle, trade
Lambton staiths 73, 130,
land
    as capital 'bank' 176, 272, 305
    estate improvement 270-2, 350
    rental valuation 176, 244
    see also agriculture
lead 19, 99, 204-10, 213-24, 192-7, 319
    demand and uses 102-5; litharge 102, 126, 268; red lead 268; refined lead 268; silver 268
    economics 137, 139-43, 148
    geology and veins 99-101, 216-7
    industrial structure, operations and integration 109, 124-7, 133-45, 148-9
    innovation 141-3, 219-20, 306
    landowner leases 109-11, 215-7
    prices 102, 111-**112**, 137, 148, 268, 292, 294-5
    production 102, 128, 135, 137, 148, 269, 302, 335; 1680s expansion 210; 1700s recession 260-1; revival from 1720s 268-9; work force 118, 146
    profitability 143-4, 260-1
    refining 126, 268-70
    supply chain 148
    transport and carriage 102, 119, 126-7, 130, 135-6, 142, 148, 211, 219, Plate 12
    see also Blacketts, business, London Lead Company, North Pennines, Weardale
lead mines
    Bates Hill, West Allen 124
    Dufton, Eden Valley 124-5
    Glen Lyon, Scotland 127
    Grassgroves, Teesdale 111, 336
    Lunehead, Teesdale 125, 182
    Mohope, West Allen 293, 295, 352
    Ramshaw 268
    Redgroves, Alston Moor 124
    Rookhope 125, 218
    Settlingstones 210, 217
    Wellhope, Weardale 131
    Wellhope, West Allen 125
    see also Allenheads, Alston Moor, Coalcleugh, Fallowfield, Green-gill, Killhope, Weardale
lead mining 99-101, Plate 6
    miners 135
    pays and pay policy 137-9, 275, 277-78, 352-3
    productivity 101
    tacks 110
lead smelting 101-2, Plate 8
    bail hills 109
    efficiency, lead yields 139-41, 295
    fuel 101; peat 219-21; wood 127
    geography and location **147**, 218-9
    innovation 218-21
    ore hearths 102, 126
    slag hearths 125, 140-1
    smelters 102, 125-6, 139-40; Derbyshire migrants in Allendale 113, 333
lead smelting mills
    Burtreeford 350
    Rookhope 221, 282, 288, 293
    Ryton 140, 218, 350
    Whitfield 140

Wolsingham 136-7, 221
  see also Birkey Burn, Blackhall, Derwent, Dukesfield, Plankey, Red Lead Mill, Stanhopehope , Woodhall
lead trade 19
  London 103-5
  Newcastle 103-4, 107-8, 294
  Overseas 103-4, 133-4
  Stockton 135
  Sunderland 130
Leaton, William 310
Leece, Philip 232, 345
Liddell
  family, coalowners 45-7, 172, 191, 226
  George, and Alston Moor 297
  Sir Henry 229-30, 243, 253, 255; 258, see also coal trade, cartels
  Sir Thomas 46
Lilburne family **25**-6
  Ann 24, 26, 27
  George 26, 30-1, 65, 325
  John ('freeborn') 26
  Richard 26
  Robert 26, 65
linen 14, 30, 85
Lister, Martin 219
Little, William 110
London
  and Newcastle 13
  City charter battle with Charles II 199-200
  College of Arms 155
  Great Fire of 1666 and rebuilding 104-5, 112, 121, 152; St. Paul's Cathedral 105, 206
  Lightermen 227-8, 230
  Panton Square and Wm Blackett (b.1690) 251
  see also coal trade, lead, Parliament
London Lead Company 218, 268, 350
  and Alston Moor mines 297
  growth and profitability 295-7
  see also Blackett business
Lowther
  Sir Christopher 322
  Sir John 310
Lumley
  Augustine, domestic chaplain to Wm Blackett (b.1657) 237
  family 202
  Richard, Viscount 202

Maddison family of Newcastle 91, 187
  Peter 27
management 133-7, 231-4, 309-11
  clerks and agents 270-2
  fraud 136, 182-3, 257
  process, reporting and structure 967, 136-7, 281-4
  see also Blacketts, business
Mann, Edward 8, 84
manufacturing industry 12, 85-7, 95, 148, 268
Marescoe, Charles 52, 55, 77, 88, 105-6, 112-3
Marley, John 43-5, 155
Matfen, Northumberland, Blackett family 316
Mendip Hills 102
Merchant Adventurers company 8-9, 14-6, 32-3, 48-50, 62-3, 72-3, 151-2, 181, 199, 294, 314
  see also apprenticeship, business, Newcastle
merchants 48-9, 158, Plate 5
  as agents of economic development 96, 149, 313-4
  apprenticeship 308-9
  capital and investment 95, 178
  and politics 9-12, 306-7, 314-5
  shipping 176-7
  see also apprenticeship, business, capital
Mewburn, James 271, 284
Middleton-in-Teesdale 100
Milbank, Mark 71, 79, 188, 200, 309
Mitford
  family 158-9, 275
  Robert 154, 158, 164, 179, 275
Monck, General George 67, 80-1
monopolies: see business
Montague, Charles 84, 182, 226-7, 229, 240, 257-8; and Gibside 240-2
  see also coal trade
moormastership, Weardale 33, 110, 119, 127-32, 215
  see also Hutton, Richard; lead; Weardale; Wharton, Humphrey
Morpeth, Northumberland 154-5

mortgages 272-3
see also capital sources
Mowbray
　family 136
　George, Allenheads 139, 220, 261, 269, 275, 284
　John, Dukesfield 131, 136, 139-40, 182, 208, 232, 282, 340, 344
　Richard, Allenheads 136-9, 216, 221, 232
Muggleswick Park 219, 238
Myers, George of Rookhope 325

Narva 6-7
　see also Newcastle, trade
Naval shipyards 179, 306
Navigation Act of 1652 14
Neale, Dr George 185
Newburn, North'd 44, 84, 167
Newby Hall, Yorks 16, 190, 195, 197, 208, 211, 213, 302, 343
Newcastle-upon-Tyne 1-16, 315-7
　social structure 3, 12-3; strategic importance 6, 43, 62-3, 254
　Anderson Place: *see* Greyfriars
　Blackett Street 316
　business culture 8, 13-4, 20, 263-4, 308-9; management 309-11
　churches 43-4, 63-4; All Saints 7, 39, 49, 59, 66, 70, 206; St Andrew's 2, 237, 245-6; St John's 38; St Nicholas' 2, 4, 10, 46-7, 70, 158, 164, 187, 316-7
　Close, The 10, 69-70, 205, 212, 294; Tyne Bridge End house 70, 162-3, 191, 193, 317, Plate 3
　Corporation, civic government and offices 3, 10-2, 62-6, 77-80, 151-2, 199, 201-3, 205-6, 253-4, 265; *see also* political culture
　education 38-9, 160; *see also* apprenticeship
　Fleshmarket 10, 46-7, 322, 327, Plate 1
　Greyfriars 1-4, 65, 163-4, 188, 190, 211-3, 245-6, 265, 286, 316, 322, 339, 343, 351, Plate 18
　Guildhall 10, 63, 69, 201, 203, Plate 10
Haddrick's Mill, Gosforth 165
Heaton 158

Jesmond 178
merchants 6-7, 95, 178, 294, 316; apprenticeship 309; investment 110-3, 178; land purchase and improvement 305
Nuns Moor 178
Ouseburn 81-2, 86, 111
and Parliament 12, 153-5, 201-2, 256, 323
Pilgrim Street 10, 235, 286, 322
plague outbreaks 42, 59, 67
political culture, rivalry and strife 44-5, 62-80, 203-5, 253-4, 289; witch trials of 1649 63
population 12
quayside 7, 10, 13, 31, 69-70, 72, 317, Plate 4
Sandgate 13, 42, 59, 152
Sandhill 10, 40, 46, 49, 63, 66, 158, 206, 326, Plate 9
Side, The 10, 49, 57, 70, 158, Plate 2
trade 7, 63-4, 67; customs 6, 141, 157, 286; lead trade 145
war and siege 43-5, 61-2, 65
see also Blacketts, business, coal, Hostmen, Kenton, Merchant Adventurers, merchants, trade
Newcastle Courant 2-3, 270
Newcastle, Duke of 201
Newhouse, Weardale 223, 239, 316, Plate 14
Nicholson, Christopher 71
Nixon
　George 232
　Joseph 232
North Pennines **100**
　agriculture 148-9, 312
　lead mining and smelting 107-13, 135, 145-9
　population 146-8
　see also Allendale, Alston Moor, lead, Teesdale, Weardale
North, Francis 170-1
North Shields 31
Northumberland 154-5
　see also Allendale, Berwick-upon-Tweed, Fallowfield, Hexham, Morpeth
Norton
　Mary m. Edward Blackett 160-1

Index | 363

Thomas 160-1
Noseley Hall, Leics 339

O'Brien Lord Henry 157
Ord
    Elizabeth (1686-1713) 251-2
    Elizabeth (1711-59) m Walter Blackett 252, 276-7, 279-81
    estate, Northumberland 290
    family 265
    John, of Fenham 38, 210, 244, 258, 262-5, 272, 274-5
Oxford, University College 250

Parliament 154, 280-1, 186, 254, 280
    Bill of Rights 1689 205-6
    and coal 121, 154, 156-7, 170, 228, 241, 253
    under the commonwealth 43-5, 63-5, 81
    Exclusion crisis 186, 199
    mercantile constituency 204-5, 314
    political parties 154
    see also Newcastle, taxation
patronage and office purchase 157
Patten, Revd Robert, *History of the late Rebellion*, 255, 348
Paulet, Charles, Marquess of Winchester 135, 217
Pauston, Henry 47
Peak District 101, 106-7, 109
    see also Derbyshire, lead
Pearson, William 81, 116-8
Peart, Joseph 283-4, 295
Pease, Robert 181, 198, 233
peat: see lead smelting
pewter 102
Plankey smelting mill 126-7, 139-42, 162, 184, 207, 218
    see also lead smelting
Pollard, Sidney, *Genesis of Modern Management* 151, 311
ports and business culture 309, 313-5
    see also Newcastle, trade
Presbyterians 41, 43, 62-4, 66-8, 77, 91, 204
productivity 312-3
    see also economic growth
Protestants 186, 254
Puritans 13, 16, 30, 38, 43-5, 63-6, 77-8, 91
Quakers 218-9, 295, 331

Radcliffes of Dilston 110-1, 124
    estate confiscation 296
    Sir Francis 120, 139, 209-10
Ramsay, William 210, 217, 223
Rawlet, Revd John 187, 328
Rawling, Samuel 41, 60, 326, 327
Reay, Henry 265
red lead: see lead demand and uses
Red Lead Mill, Hexhamshire 111, 119-20, 126, 139-40, 333, 336
Regulation, The, coal cartel 259
    see also coal trade
religion and business co-operation 16, 91-2, 124, 206
religious antagonism 30, 153, 186, 254
Richmond
    Henry 315
    Joseph 268, 285-9, 297, 307
        business and management ability 286-9, 293-5, 298
        lead industry 292-7
        political understanding 289
Richmond, Yorks 161
Riddell, Henry 6
Ridley family 259, 289, 309
    Nevile 256, 348
    Nicholas 204, 217, 219, 309, 344, 353
Ridsdale, Edward 349
Riga 7
    see also Newcastle, trade
Ripon, Yorks 265
Ritschel, Revd George 260, 271
Robinson family, Blaydon 284
    Michael 136, 173, 210, 232
    Thomas 352
Robinson, John, Appleby 260-1, 348-9
Rogers
    John (1631-71) 163, 167-8, 339
    John (1656-1709) 167, 173
    Margaret nee Cocke, later Lady Blackett 163-8, 198, 262, Plate 23
    Mary 191, 206, 341
    Sarah 227
Rollinson, William, London 190-1, 341
Rotterdam 49, 133-4, 197, 260
    see also Newcastle, trade

Rumney, John 220
Rushworth, John 155-6, 182
Ryal 275
rye 7, 27, 49, 57, 68, 75
Ryton 93, 140, 218, 350
    see also Stella Grand lease

Sacheverell, Revd Henry 253-4
Salkeld, Thomas 267, 285-6
salt making 29-31, 34, 85-6, 268
Sanderson, Barbara 208, 335
Scandinavia 6
    see also Newcastle, trade
scientific enquiry 218-9
Scotland 6, 13, 43-4, 74, 134, 148, 235, 254, 311
Scottish sieges of Newcastle: *see* Newcastle
Seghill, Northumberland 158
Selby family 169, 171-2
    Sir George 169
Shaftesbury, Earl of 186
Shafto, Robert 62, 79
Sherwood, William 45-8, 64
Shildon, Co. Durham 26
shipbuilding 85, 87
silver 102
    see also Blaydon, lead
Silvertop, Albert 272
Simpson, Dorothy 233, 256
Smith
    Adam, *The Wealth of Nations* 312
    Dr John 263
Snow
    Cuthbert 139, 174, 232
    John 139
social mobility 139-40
Sound Toll 6-7, 69, 103, 318
    see also trade
South Shields 10, 29-31
specialisation: *see* economic growth
Standsfield, Sir James 311
Stanhope
    parish 24, 127-31, 215-6
    Rector of 110, 128-32, 239
    see also lead, Weardale
Stanhopehope smelting mill 135, 221, 284
Startforth, Barnard Castle 73
Stella Grand Lease colliery and lease 82, 89, 91-7, 170, 172, 179, 195, 211, 242, 257, 259, 268, 291, 310
    see also coal mining, collieries
Stockholm 7, 52, 73-4, 96
    see also trade, Newcastle
stocking knitting 86
Stockton 19, 107, 113, 135, 141, 148, 239, 319, 336, 337 *see also* lead trade
Stoute, Edward, miner 139
Straker, John, *Memoirs of Walter Blackett* 17-8
Strother, John 73-4
Sunderland, Earl of 203
Sunderland 26, 29-30, 38-9, 45, 87, 130, 145, 148, 210, 241, 319, 324
    see also lead trade, Wharton
Swale, Robert 310
Swaledale, Yorks 107, 110, 127, 138, 148, 239, 260, 309-10
    see also lead mining
Sweden 7, 74, 181
Swinburne family 139

taxation and duties 154-6
    coal taxes 9, 121, 156, 228
    customs 6, 107, 157, 319
    farmers of taxes 156
    hearth tax 146, 152, 228
    see also Sound Toll, coal trade
Tees, River 99
Teesdale 107, 109-11, 333
    see also lead mining
Teesside 28
Tempest family 91-2
    Richard 82, 93
Thompson, William 251, 255, 273-5, 350
    see also Blackett, Lady Julia
Thursby, George 72
timber 7, 85, 170, 176, 180
Todd, Robert, of Kenton 232, 244, 267-8, 270, 349, 352
Tory party 186, 253-4
    see also court party, Parliament
trade 318
    bills of exchange 76, 134
    foreign exchange 7, 313
    internal 19, 106, 194, 312-4
    overseas 6-7, 52-3, 66-7, 313-5
    profitability 88-9
    see also capital, economic growth,

merchants, Newcastle
Trenchard, John 274
Trevelyan
   Charles 16, 245, 249
   Sir John 315
   see also Wallington
Triplet, Thomas 30
Tyne, River 10, 99, 123, 317
Tynemouth 53, 67
Tyneside 218-9
   coal mining 6, 226-7, 230
   coal trade 256, 258-9
   see also Newcastle

Vane, Sir George 94, 96, 172, 331
Vernon
   James 236
   John, *The Compleat Counting-house* 39-40
Villiers *see* Blackett, Lady Barbara

waggonways 84, 92-4, 96, 170, 226-7, 240, 259, Plate 19
   Gibside 84, 240
   Kenton 225, 259, 291
   see also coal, Heworth/Gateshead Fell, Stella Grand Lease
Wales and lead 106, 311
Wallington 2, 16, 18, 164, 250, 276, 279
   estate 214-5, 243, 262, 270-1, 315, 343-4
   Hall 18, 110, 164, 245, 281, 289, 297, 316, 319, 343, 351, Plate 20
   see also Blacketts, Fenwick, Trevelyan
Walpole, Sir Robert 281
Walton, Nicholas 310
Wanlockhead lead mine and mill 148, 311
Warmouth, Henry 63
Weardale 99, 110, 129-30, 271
   lead mining 216-7, 269, 288, 292, 295
   lead production and management 130, **222**, 224, 261, 335
   leases and rights 78, 110, 208-9, 215, 217, 269-70, 289, 293
   see also Bishop of Durham, Blackett, Killhope, lead, Newhouse, Stanhope, Wharton, Wolsingham, Woodcroft

Welton, Northumberland 243, 270-1
Wellhope: *see* lead mines
Wells, John 336
Wensleydale 86
Wentworth
   Sir Thomas 315
   Sir William 5, 274
Westgarth, John 208
Westgate. Weardale 131, 216
Westmorland 8, 14
   see also Kendal
Westwater estate, Northumberland 193
whale oil processing 81-2
Wharton
   Humphrey 127-31, 135, 145, 156, 178, 208-9, 215
   Philip, Swaledale 309
   Robert 135
   Thomas 110
Whickham, Co.Durham 11, 45-6, 79, 94, 96-7, 146, 170, 230, 312
   see also coal mining
Whigs 186, 254
   see also country party, Parliament
White
   Matthew 204, 217, 258
   Robert 49
Whorlton Moor 167-8, 174, 211
   see also coal mining
Wilkinson, John 5, 186, 287, 291
   background and apprenticeship 233-4, 257
   coal interests and cartel 253-4, 256-9, 291, 298
   as manager for Blacketts 246, 249-50, 257-65, 275, 284, 286, 307
   rupture with Sir Wm Blackett (b.1690) 4, 265
   death 298
   see also Blacketts, business, coal trade, Heworth/Gateshead Fell
William III, King 204, 214, 231
   see also Fenwick, Sir John
Wilson, William of Allendale 311
Winlaton 177-8, 188
   coal mining 169-71, 211, 268, 291
   colliery 84, 169-70, 198, 242, 259, 342, 346, 352
   estate 271, 339, 348
   ironworks 183

see also Blacketts, Blaydon, coal, Crowley, Selby family

Wolsingham, Weardale 24, 27, 100-1
see also lead smelting, Wharton

Wood, Edward 59, 64-5

Woodcroft, Weardale 24, 131, 177, 223

Woodhall smelting mill 139, 141, 210, 268

Wrightson, William 253-4

Yorke
    Lady Mary (1635-96) 161
    Mary, later Lady Blackett (by 1657-96) 161

Yorkshire 5, 8, 14, 28, 106-7, 138, 160-1, 195, 255, 262, 265, 316

NEW RELEASES FROM TYNE BRIDGE PUBLISHING

The Brasilia of the North - Sixty Years of Regeneration
Paperback | £7.99 | ISBN 9781838280949

Experienced City Guide Tony Flynn has produced this indispensable companion to his tour around Newcastle upon Tyne and the Quayside. Asking the question, did the city become the 'Brasilia of the North' after it embarked on a series of major regeneration projects from the 1960s onwards. The reader is allowed to make their own mind up, using this book as a helpful guide around the significant landmarks in the history of the city's regeneration. From the Civic Centre to the Sage Gateshead, the book complements an enjoyable walk through some of the major features of what has become one of the UK's top tourist destinations.

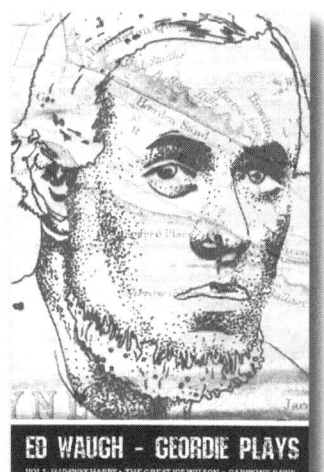

Ed Waugh - Geordie Plays | Paperback | £8.99 | ISBN 9781838280932

Harry Clasper, Joe Wilson and Glenn McCrory; three Tyneside heroes, each with a magnificent tale to tell.
It's important we are still talking about these icons who have added so much to our culture. And in his Geordie Plays, Ed Waugh brings to the stage the essence of what it means to battle against all odds to make an impact, in what is often a brutal and unforgiving world.

Geordie Newcastle - How we used to live | Hardback
£12.99 | ISBN 9781838280925

'Geordie Newcastle' is a unique collection of evocative photographs from a golden age in Newcastle's past. This book is the result of hours of research in Newcastle City Library's archive to restore photographs from the original glass plates, which hadn't been touched for decades. From the end of the 19th century to the 1950s, the pictures chosen offer us a glimpse into a world that many of us will remember with fondness and that helped shape what it means to be a Geordie today.

Historic Tales from Newcastle | Paperback | £8.99
ISBN 9780950317892

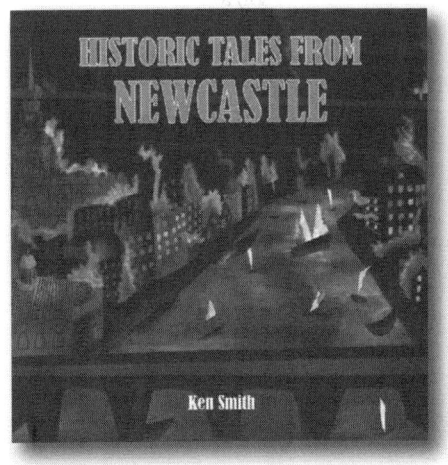

Newcastle's colourful and sometimes dramatic history is brought to life in this series of tales spanning several hundred years. Including some of the most fascinating accounts of true stories from the city's stirring past. From the Great Fire of 1854 to explosions on the Town Moor, this book covers the major events that helped shape the city. Featuring some of it most influential figures like Lord Armstrong and George Stephenson, as well some much-loved landmarks like the Newcastle Keep and City Walls, Historical Tales from Newcastle is a must-read for those wanting a starting point into the history of the city.